The last decade has seen a fundamental rethinking of the concept of context. Rather than functioning solely as a constraint on linguistic performance, context is now also analyzed as a product of language use. In this new perspective, language and context are seen as interactively achieved phenomena, rather than predefined sets of forms and contents. The essays in this collection, written by many of the leading figures in the social sciences, critically reexamine the concept of context from a variety of different angles and propose new ways of thinking about it with reference to specific human activities such as face-to-face interaction, radio talk, medical diagnosis, political encounters, and socialization practices. Each essay is prefaced by an introduction by the editors which provides relevant theoretical and methodological background and demonstrates its relation to other essays in the volume. The editors' general introduction provides a lucid overview of the issues currently debated.

Rethinking context will be required reading for everyone working within the fields of linguistic anthropology, sociolinguistics, discourse analysis, pragmatics, conversation analysis, and the sociology of language.

Studies in the Social and
Cultural Foundations of Language No. 11

Rethinking context

Studies in the Social and Cultural Foundations of Language

The aim of this series is to develop theoretical perspectives on the essential social and cultural character of language by methodological and empirical emphasis on the occurrence of language in its communicative and interactional settings, on socioculturally grounded "meanings" and "functions" of linguistic forms, and on the social scientific study of language use across cultures. It will thus explicate the essentially ethnographic nature of linguistic data, whether spontaneously occurring or experimentally induced, whether normative or variational, whether synchronic or diachronic. Works appearing in the series will make substantive and theoretical contributions to the debate over the sociocultural-function and structural-formal nature of language, and will represent the concerns of scholars in the sociology and anthropology of language, anthropological linguistics, sociolinguistics, and socio-culturally informed psycholinguistics.

Editorial Board

1. Charles L. Briggs: *Learning how to ask: a sociolinguistic appraisal of the role in the interview in social science research*
2. Tamar Katriel: *Talking straight: Dugri speech in Israeli Sabra culture*
3. Bambi B. Schieffelin and Elinor Ochs (eds.): *Language socialization across cultures*
4. Susan U. Philips, Susan Steele, and Christine Tanz (eds.): *Language, gender, and sex in comparative perspective*
5. Jeff Siegel: *Language contact in a plantation environment: a sociolinguistic history of Fiji*
6. Elinor Ochs: *Culture and language development. Language acquisition and language socialization in a Samoan village*
7. Nancy D. Dorian (ed.): *Investigating obsolescence: studies in language contraction and death*
8. Richard Bauman and Joel Sherzer (eds.): *Explorations in the ethnography of speaking*
9. Bambi B. Schieffelin: *The give and take of everyday life: language socialization of Kaluli children*
10. Francesca Merlan and Alan Rumsey: *Ku Waru: language and segmentary politics in the Western Nebilyer valley, Papua New Guinea*
11. Alessandro Duranti and Charles Goodwin (eds.): *Rethinking context: language as an interactive phenomenon*

Rethinking context

Language as an interactive phenomenon

Edited by

Alessandro Duranti

Department of Anthropology, University of California at Los Angeles

and

Charles Goodwin

Department of Anthropology, University of South Carolina

CAMBRIDGE
UNIVERSITY PRESS

Published by the Press Syndicate of the University of Cambridge
The Pitt Building, Trumpington Street, Cambridge CB2 1RP
40 West 20th Street, New York, NY 10011–4211, USA
10 Stamford Road, Oakleigh, Melbourne 3166, Australia

First published 1992
Reprinted 1993, 1997

Printed in Great Britain at the University Press, Cambridge

British Library cataloguing in publication data

Rethinking context: language as an interactive phenomenon.
– (Studies in the social and cultural foundations of
language)
1. Spoken language
I. Duranti, Alessandro   II. Goodwin, Charles
400

Library of Congress cataloguing in publication data

Rethinking context: language as an interactive phenomenon/edited by
Alessandro Duranti and Charles Goodwin.
    p.   cm. – (Studies in the social and cultural foundation of
language: 11)
Includes bibliographical references and index.
ISBN 0 521 38169 X (hardback). – ISBN 0 521 42288 4 (paperback)
1. Language and culture.   2. Context (Linguistics)   3. Oral
communication. I. Duranti, Alessandro.   II. Goodwin, Charles.
III. Series: Studies in the social and cultural foundation of
language: no. 11.
P35.R46   1991
302.2′24–dc20   90-26850   CIP

ISBN 0 521 38169 X hardback
ISBN 0 521 42288 4 paperback

Transferred to digital reprinting 2000
Printed in the United States of America

TS

Contents

Contributors

Charles Goodwin
Professor of Anthropology, University of South Carolina

Alessandro Duranti
Associate Professor of Anthropology, University of California at Los Angeles

William F. Hanks
Associate Professor of Anthropology, University of Chicago

Lamont Lindstrom
Associate Professor of Anthroplogy, University of Tulsa

Richard Bauman
Professor of Folklore and Anthropology, Indiana University

Marjorie Harness Goodwin
Professor of Anthropology, University of South Carolina

Emanual A. Schegloff
Professor of Sociology, University of California at Los Angeles

John J. Gumperz
Professor of Anthropology, University of California at Berkeley

Ellen B. Basso
Professor of Anthropology, University of Arizona at Tucson

Frank Gaik
Assistant Professor of English, Cerritos College, California

Aaron V. Cicourel
Professor of Cognitive Science and Sociology, University of California at San Diego

Susan U. Philips
Professor of Anthropology, University of Arizona

Adam Kendon

Elinor Ochs
Professor of Applied Linguistics, University of California at Los Angeles

1 Rethinking context: an introduction

CHARLES GOODWIN and ALESSANDRO DURANTI

Context has long been a key concept both in the field of pragmatics[1] and in ethnographically oriented studies of language use[2] as well as quantitative ones.[3] When we look at the work done within the last twenty years on the relation between language and context in these various fields, we can see a trend toward increasingly more interactive and dialogically conceived notions of contextually situated talk.

In the mid 1960s Gumperz and Hymes appealed for studies that would analyze in detail how language is deployed as a constitutive feature of the indigenous settings and events that constitute the social life of the societies of the world. Anthropological linguistics could no longer be content with analyzing language as an encapsulated formal system that could be isolated from the rest of a society's culture and social organization. Their call to arms was met by a host of detailed studies in societies all over the world. Initially it might appear that the appeal of such research would be primarily to linguists and other students of language, i.e. it would contribute to the empirical analysis of the social life of language (and it certainly has). However, this research has also had surprising and far-reaching consequences for the analysis of human social organization. Traditionally both social anthropologists and sociologists have focused their attention on the larger institutions that coordinate the behavior of members of a society, for example kinship and political organization. However, one of the most pervasive social activities that human beings engage in is talk. Indeed, Schegloff has identified it as "the primordial locus for sociality" (Schegloff 1987). Moreover, work by conversation analysts and other students of human interaction has richly demonstrated that the types of social organization required to accomplish mundane talk are both intricate and dynamic, and permit analysts to look in detail at how social organization is performed as an interactively sustained, time-bound process. Similarly Ochs and Schieffelin (Ochs 1983, 1986, 1988; Ochs and Schieffelin 1984; Schieffelin and Ochs 1986) have demonstrated that the process through which a child learns to speak cannot be analyzed simply as **language acquisition** (i.e. an encapsulated process of interest only to students of language), but instead constitutes a profound process of **language socialization** through which the child by learning how to speak in a community becomes a competent socialized member of his or her society. Such research has made it clear that it would be blatantly absurd to propose that one could provide a comprehensive analysis of human social organization without paying close attention to the details of how human beings employ language to build the social and cultural worlds that they inhabit.

Since the mid 1970s, however, the research encompassed by the synthesizing collections of Gumperz and Hymes has become fragmented into quite separate fields. Thus, it is now not uncommon to find collections devoted exclusively to the ethnography of speaking (Bauman and Sherzer 1974), conversation analysis (for example Schenkein 1978 and Atkinson and Heritage 1984), or research inspired by Gumperz' study of contextualization cues and conversational inference (Gumperz 1982b). While the presence of such diverse collections demonstrates the independent achievements of each of these fields, it is our belief that each of them would be strengthened by direct communication with one another. Moreover, students being introduced to any particular perspective on language use could only benefit from being exposed to more than one perspective. Although by no means exhausting the great variety of studies employing (whether explicitly or implicitly) the concept of **context**, the present volume brings together research from different analytic traditions, all of which share a strong commitment to the study of situated discourse. By juxtaposing a variety of perspectives on context we hope to provide both researchers and students with an opportunity to compare and synthesize these traditions. In order to facilitate such comparison, and to place each chapter within the tradition from which it emerged, each one is preceded by an introductory commentary.

1   The notion of "context"

Providing a formal – or simply explicit – definition of a concept can lead to important analytic insights. Thus, as Gazdar (1979) notes, with such a definition we are often able to see inconsistencies or contradictions that were not visible before. However, it does not seem possible at the present time to give a single, precise, technical definition of **context**, and eventually we might have to accept that such a definition may not be possible. At the moment the term means quite different things within alternative research paradigms, and indeed even within particular traditions seems to be defined more by situated practice, by **use** of the concept to work with particular analytic problems, than by formal definition.[4] From our perspective, lack of a single formal definition, or even general agreement about what is meant by context, is not a situation that necessarily requires a remedy. Instead the fact that so many investigators recognize the importance of context and are actively involved in trying to unravel how it works is precisely why this concept provides such a productive focus for study at the present time. As Vološinov (1973: 45) notes:

at the outset of an investigation, it is not so much the intellectual faculty for making formulas and definitions that leads the way, but rather it is the eyes and hands attempting to get the feel of the actual presence of the subject matter.

In order to explore differences in approach to context it is useful to begin with a tentative description of the phenomenon, even if this will ultimately be found inadequate. Consider first the behavior that context is being invoked to interpret. Typically this will consist of talk of some type. However, simply referring to an event being examined as talk is inadequate. Thus, talk can be seen as hierarchically organized, and different notions of context may be appropriate to different levels of organization (see Kendon 1982; Gumperz, this volume). For example in the present volume Bauman analyzes both how prose-narration frames verse within a story, and how talk between teller and recipient frames the story as a whole as an event of a particular kind. Talk **within** the story (the prose frame) creates context for other talk (the verse), while yet other speech creates an appropriate context for the story itself. The **prose narration** in this story is thus at the same time, but from different analytical perspectives, **context** for something embedded within it, and talk that is itself **contextualized** by other talk. Use of the word "talk" to identify one element in this process can thus lead to confusion. From a slightly different perspective behavior that is interpreted by reference to a context is by no means restricted to talk. Indeed just as nonvocal behavior can create context for talk (Kendon and the Goodwins, this volume) so talk can create context for the appropriate interpretation of nonverbal behavior (C. Goodwin 1987, Goodwin and Goodwin 1989). We will therefore use the term **focal event**[5] to identify the phenomenon being contextualized. More generally an analyst can start with the observation, as Kendon does in this volume, that participants treat each other's stream of activity (talk, movement, etc.) in a selective way. The question then becomes **what** in each other's behavior do they treat as "focal" and what as "background". The job of the analyst is to delineate this.

When the issue of **context** is raised it is typically argued that the focal event cannot be properly understood, interpreted appropriately, or described in a relevant fashion, unless one looks beyond the event itself to other phenomena (for example cultural setting, speech situation, shared background assumptions) within which the event is embedded, or alternatively that features of the talk itself invoke particular background assumptions relevant to the organization of subsequent interaction (Gumperz, this volume). The context is thus a frame (Goffman 1974) that surrounds the event being examined and provides resources for its appropriate interpretation:

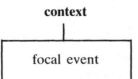

context

focal event

The notion of context thus involves a fundamental juxtaposition of two entities: (1) a focal event; and (2) a field of action within which that event is embedded.

2   Issues posed in the analysis of context

A relationship between two orders of phenomena that mutually inform each other to comprise a larger whole is absolutely central to the notion of context (indeed the term comes from the latin *contextus*, which means "a joining together"). From this perspective the relationship between focal event and context is much like that between "organism" and "environment" in cybernetic theory (Ashby 1956, 1960; Bateson 1972; Buckley 1968).

When context is viewed in this light a number of questions can be posed. For example what precisely is to be included within the system being examined (i.e. the conjunction of focal event and relevant context), and where is the boundary to be drawn between context and the behavior that it is context to. In attempting to formulate a cybernetic definition of "mind" and "self," Bateson (1972: 459) poses these issues with particular vividness:

But what about "me"? Suppose I am a blind man, and I use a stick. I go tap, tap, tap. Where do *I* start? Is my mental system bounded at the handle of the stick? Is it bounded by my skin? Does it start halfway up the stick? Does it start at the tip of the stick? But these are nonsense questions. The stick is a pathway along which transforms of difference are being transmitted. The way to delineate the system is to draw the limiting line in such a way that you do not cut any of these pathways in ways which leave things inexplicable. If what you are trying to explain is a given piece of behavior, such as the locomotion of the blind man, then, for this purpose, you will need the street, the stick, the man; the street, the stick, and so on, round and round.

But when the blind man sits down to eat his lunch, his stick and its messages will no longer be relevant – if it is his eating that you want to understand.

Bateson's metaphor poses with particular clarity a number of issues that are central to the analysis of context. First, it demonstrates the crucial importance of **taking as a point of departure for the analysis of context the perspective of the participant(s) whose behavior is being analyzed**. What analysts seek to describe is not what they consider context, for example their map of the city in which the blind man finds himself, but rather how the subject himself attends to and organizes his perception of the events and situations that he is navigating through.

Second, the metaphor vividly illustrates how what a participant treats as relevant context is shaped by the specific activities being performed at that moment. The task of walking, but not the activity of eating a sandwich, makes relevant and salient the physical environment provided by the city, with its corridors for movement, its constraints, and its obstacles becoming especially prominent. Moreover that city is not simply a physical environment, but also a social one, built by other human beings through an historical process, which requires knowledge about its social dimensions (for example division of space into areas for pedestrians and areas for vehicles, historical solutions to the problem of how one navigates when these areas overlap [traffic lights and traffic regulations], a distinction between "public" and "private" space that constrains movement through the physical space, etc.) if one is to move through it successfully. One of the great difficulties posed in the analysis of context is describing the socio-historical knowledge that a participant employs to act within the environment of the moment.

Even if an analyst were able to provide a satisfactory description of how participants organize their experience of, and interaction with, such an environment, that would not provide anything like an adequate account of context. In so far as participants' articulation of their environment is shaped by the activities of the moment, the context that is relevant to what they are doing changes radically when they move from one activity to another, for example stop walking and begin to eat. The dynamic mutability of context is complicated further by the ability of participants to rapidly invoke within the talk of the moment alternative contextual frames. Indeed this is one of the key insights provided by Gumperz' notion of **contextualization cues** (1982a, this volume).

Such phenomena demonstrate the importance of, first, approaching context from the perspective of an actor actively operating on the world within which he or she finds him- or herself embedded; second, tying the analysis of context to study of the indigeneous activities that participants use to constitute the culturally and historically organized social worlds that they inhabit; and third, recognizing that participants are situated within multiple contexts which are capable of rapid and dynamic change as the events they are engaged in unfold.

While Bateson's metaphor of the blind man and his stick provides a useful point of departure for thinking about some of the issues involved in the study of context, the work in this volume goes beyond it in a number of significant ways. Most importantly, in Bateson's metaphor the blind man is navigating through a world that is solid, fixed and immutable, at least from the perspective of his walking. He does not rebuild the city as part of the activity of conducting his walk. However, within social situations a key constituent of the environment that participants attend to is other human beings, who are active agents in their own right, with their own plans and agendas. As Ray McDermott (1976) has remarked, "people become environments for each other." Such possibilities for dynamic interaction increase the complexity of the events being analyzed immeasurably. Of particular relevance to the themes being addressed in this volume is the capacity of human beings to dynamically reshape the context that provides organization for their actions within the interaction itself. Indeed, the dynamic, socially constitutive properties of context are inescapable since each additional move within the interaction modifies the existing context while creating a new arena for subsequent interaction (see Hanks' discussion in this volume of how the indexical ground changes over the course of speech, and Heritage 1984: 106–10). Moreover, as strategic actors, individual participants can actively attempt to shape context in ways that further their own interests. This does not mean that context is created from scratch within the interaction so that larger cultural and social patterns in a society are ignored. Instead, as the chapters of Duranti and Lindstrom illustrate, even those participants who are strategically rearranging context to further their own goals invoke organizational patterns that have an existence that extends far beyond the local encounter. Moreover, in so far as the processes to which context is relevant are social and interactive, one party's proposals as to what should constitute operative context might fail to achieve ratification by others (see for example Kendon's chapter on how frame changes are accomplished through a collaborative process of interaction). Indeed, one of the key lessons of research on contextualization cues by Gumperz and those who follow him is that miscommunication and active challenges to a proposed redefinition of the situation are very real possibilities (see for example Gaik's chapter). In brief the chapters in this volume explore the ways in which context is a socially constituted, interactively sustained, time-bound phenomenon.

3   Dimensions of context

In an important attempt to specify some of the basic parameters of context, Ochs (1979: 1) notes that the analyst must use as a point of departure "the social and psychological world in which the language user operates at any given time." This is especially difficult since even an observer who has access to a setting and the talk that occurs within it may nonetheless not have access to all of the phenomena that participants are utilizing as context for their talk (Ochs 1979: 2). Briefly reviewing the contextual attributes noted by Ochs (1979: 2–6) provides an opportunity to both get a firmer empirical grasp on the range of phenomena that the notion of context must cover, and acquaint the reader with some of the themes explored by chapters in the present volume.

   (1) **Setting**, i.e. the social and spatial framework within which encounters are situated. In Chapter 2, Hanks provides extensive analysis of how **deictic systems** provide participants with systematic, interactively based resources for organizing their mutual access to the environment they share and attend to in their talk. In his analysis he demonstrates how the figure/ ground contrast provides powerful conceptual tools for the study of context, and uses it as a point of departure for investigation of the **indexical ground** of deixis. Duranti explores the reciprocal relationship between social attributes of participants (for example the status of someone as chief), the talk through which those attributes are invoked, and how constituting, i.e. establishing and renegotiating, the social personae of those present, is relevant to the larger activities they are

engaged in. As each of these chapters makes clear, neither the physical nor the social setting for talk is something that is fixed, immutable and simply "out there." Instead these phenomena, and the very real constraints they provide, are dynamically and socially constituted by activities (talk included) of the participants which stand in a reflexive relationship to the context thus constituted.

(2) **Behavioral environment**, i.e. the way that participants use their bodies and behavior as a resource for framing and organizing their talk. Kendon's chapter describes how participants socially organize the space in which they meet. Through spatial orientation and posture, participants both display their continuing access to the actions of others present and frame the talk they are producing. Of particular importance is the way in which postural framing establishes the preconditions for coordinated social action by enabling participants to both project and negotiate what is about to happen. Kendon also provides extensive discussion of how **attention** is organized as an interactive phenomenon. A class of events that are treated as officially irrelevant to the activity in progress can be used to interactively negotiate changes in the frame that provides context for the activity of the moment. Kendon's analysis of the "disattend track" complements Hanks' discussion of how the figure/ground contrast is relevant to the organization of context. The Goodwins provide detailed analysis of how participants use each other's nonvocal displays to both frame the talk of the moment and project future events within it. Consistent with Kendon's analysis, they demonstrate how by attending to such phenomena participants are able to synchronize their individual actions so as to achieve precise coordinated action. Rather than constituting a separate "nonverbal" level of organization, the context provided by the behavioral environment of talk is intricately and reflexively linked to it within larger patterns of social activity.

(3) **Language as context**. The way in which talk itself both invokes context and provides context for other talk is given extensive analysis by the chapters in this volume. The seminal notion of **contextualization cues** and the theoretical motivation for such a concept is described in some detail by Gumperz himself, who then applies the concept to the analysis of specific data. Contextualization cues figure prominently (sometimes implicitly) in other chapters as well. Basso investigates how contextualization is cued within narrative and in fact constitutes the culturally relevant meaning of the narrative text as a biographical and historical performance. Gaik examines how different forms of therapeutic interaction – different frames for the conduct and interpretation of what is happening between the participants at a particular moment – are cued by alternative speech styles.

Duranti demonstrates how choices between alternative lexical forms (namely common words vs. respectful words) in Samoan can be used by speakers to shape context or, more specifically, the mutual alignment of those present and the obligations they have toward each other. His work integrates recognition of the power that standing patterns of social organization have as context for the activities in a society with analysis of how participants who accept the constraints of such structures are nonetheless able to deploy them strategically and thus reshape context in ways that further particular interests. While all of these chapters describe what can be glossed as contextualization cues, they also reveal how much of the structure of contextualization cues, and precisely how they work to frame interaction, remains to be discovered. In proposing the notion of contextualization cue Gumperz has given us not a static category but instead a point of departure for a rich field of further research.

The way in which genres contextualize talk is also given considerable attention in this volume, especially in the chapters by Bauman and Basso. Bauman, drawing on the work of Bakhtin, uses the notion of contextualization to rethink what is meant by both genres and traditionalization, analytical categories that are central to the field of folklore. One product of such questioning scrutiny is a greatly expanded view of the range of genres available for future folklore research; observing that one genre can be embedded within another, Bauman calls for further analysis of such "dialogic genres." Hanks explores how basic co-participation structures are coded in language forms, and describes how the production of new talk continuously changes the context of the moment. The Goodwins investigate how participants' close attention to structure in an emerging stream of speech provides them with resources for the organization of subsequent action. In addition they describe how larger social process can on the one hand be invoked within individual utterances, and on the other provide organization for the very talk that is invoking them (for example the organization of a story both invokes and is shaped by the larger social processes within which it is embedded). In sum, unlike some earlier views of context which conceptualized it as a frame that surrounds talk, all of the chapters in the volume emphasize the way in which talk itself constitutes a main resource for the organization of context.

(4) **Extrasituational context**. Cicourel provides an extended demonstration of how the appropriate understanding of a conversational exchange requires background knowledge that extends far beyond the local talk and its immediate setting. Indeed he argues strongly against work which proposes to analyze a sequence of talk without providing a rich ethnographic description of the background knowledge and frames of relevance within which that talk is embedded. Philips describes how phenomena that have typically been taken to be locally organized (slight hesitations and other forms of repair in talk) can in fact be seen as systematic features of much larger processes when the ethnographer collects repetitive examples of comparable events within a particular setting. Lindstrom, taking as a point of departure the work of Foucault, analyzes discursive rules and conditions that give different people unequal rights and opportunities to contribute to a debate, and to control the public meaning of what gets said there. He also identifies the "policing" effects of several domains of cultural knowledge on what counts locally as true talk, and what counts as false, i.e. culturally inappropriate, talk. At the same time, however, he demonstrates how individuals are able to "move around" within their culture's discursive order. Maneuvering to win the debate, disputants

strive to control the public meaning of what is said, and to make their statements sound true while those of their opponents sound false, by shifting context and evoking particular local discourses that are more favorable to their positions.

The work in this volume differs in significant ways from other approaches to the study of context. For example there is a long linguistic and philosophic tradition in pragmatics[6] which invokes context to help account for aspects of meaning in language that go beyond the scope of semantics. Workers in this tradition typically use as data isolated sentences and descriptions of contextual features that have been constructed by the analysts themselves to illustrate the theoretical argument being developed. Within this tradition, processes of interaction between participants are rarely, if ever, examined. By way of contrast all of the chapters in the present volume are based on recordings of actual events, ethnographic fieldwork, or a combination of the two. Rather than restricting analysis to the resources used by an ideal, passive observer to make sense out of a sentence of a particular type, the research reported here focuses on how participants attend to, construct, and manipulate aspects of context as a constitutive feature of the activities they are engaged in. Context is thus analyzed as an interactively constituted mode of praxis.

4   Figure and ground

Some of the analysis developed in the present volume offers insight into why many very successful approaches to the analysis of language and speech genres have been able to effectively ignore context. One key way in which context and focal event differ is in their perceptual salience. Generally the focal event is regarded as the official focus of the participants' attention, while features of the context are not highlighted in this way, but instead treated as background phenomena. The focal event is placed on center stage, while context constitutes the stage itself. In line with this, the boundaries, outlines, and structure of the focal event are characteristically delimited with far more explicitness and clarity than are contextual phenomena. Focal event and context thus seem to stand in a fundamental **figure–ground** relationship to each other, a point developed in considerable detail by Hanks in this volume. These themes constitute the main focus for Kendon's chapter as well, in which he provides quite detailed analysis of how the **main attentional track** in an encounter is sustained, and indeed shaped, by ongoing interactive work in a **disattend track**, "a stream of signs which is itself excluded from the content of the activity but which serves as a means of regulating it, bounding, articulating and qualifying its various components and phases." Viewing the relationship between focal event and context in this fashion demonstrates its central relevance to one of the key issues that has emerged in contemporary studies of language and interaction: the use of **background information** to produce and understand action, and the question of how such background information is organized, recognized, invoked, and understood.[7] We want to use the perspective advocated by Hanks as a point of departure for discussing some of the reasons why the analysis of context has proved so difficult and intransigent.

4.1   Focusing on the figure and ignoring the ground

In our view the fundamental asymmetry of the **figure–ground** relationship of focal event and its context has had enormous consequences on how these phenomena have been studied. First, differences in salience are accompanied by corresponding differences in structural clarity. The effect of this is that the focal event, with its far more clearly articulated structure, receives the lion's share of analytic attention while methods for analyzing, or even describing, the more amorphous background of context are not given anywhere near the same amount of emphasis. Thus linguists have taken the segmental structure of language as the key focal phenomenon that is relevant to the production and organization of talk. One result of this is a vast disparity between the incredible amount of work that has been done within formal linguistics on language structure, and the very small amount of research that has focused explicitly on the organization of context. With the exception of artificial intelligence researchers interested in simulation of discourse-based inferential processes (Dyer 1983, Schank and Abelson 1977, Schank and Riesbeck 1981), formal linguists have been skeptical of psychologically oriented studies of mental units of behavior such as scripts, plans, and other such notions (cf. Mandler 1979; Nelson 1978, 1981; Parisi and Castelfranchi 1976). Indeed this disparity is found not only in formal analysis but also in the methodology available for simply describing the phenomena being examined. For thousands of years human beings have put great ingenuity and effort into the development of methods for accurately describing and writing down[8] relevant distinctions within the stream of speech. Comparable attention to precise description of the context of a speech situation has been almost nonexistent, and indeed a major task facing contemporary students of context is uncovering what are its constitutive features and how they are to be described. In our opinion this mixture of sharp, sustained focus on the details of language structure combined with a complementary neglect of its context is not accidental, but rather strong support for the arguments made by Hanks and Kendon about the intrinsic figure–ground relationship of focal event and context.[9]

4.2   Extracting the focal event from its context for analysis

The structural articulation of the focal event is matched by an apparent clarity in its shape, outline, and boundaries. The effect of this is that it becomes easy for analysts to view the focal event as a self-contained entity that can be cut out from its surrounding context and analyzed in isolation, a process that effectively treats the context as irrelevant to the organization of the focal event. Stories provide a classic example. In much research in anthropology, folklore, and sociolinguistics, stories have been analyzed as self-contained packages, entities that can be nicely "collected" in an exotic setting and then safely transported back to the laboratory of the researcher. It is tacitly assumed that the process of removing the story from the setting in which it actually emerged and placing it in a new and often radically different context, the analytic collection of the investigator, does little if any damage to its intrinsic structure. Indeed a number of features of narrative readily lead to such a view. Thus a story told in one setting can be performed in another (as speakers demonstrate when they retell stories). Moreover, participants themselves often delimit the boundaries of a story (Jefferson 1978) so that it stands out from other talk as a coherent entity. Many analysts have therefore found it both fruitful and unproblematic to devote their energies to description and analysis of the internal structure of stories while ignoring the interaction through which they were in fact told in the first place. The work of Levi-Strauss (1963) on myth provides a classic example, although the chapters by Bauman and Basso in this volume suggest that much of what is important in a story or myth is not the "content" but its inter-textuality (see also Halliday and Hasan 1976, Kristeva 1981, Silverstein 1985a). In brief it is very convenient to be able to extract speech forms from local contexts of production, a process that is facilitated by the clarity with which an event such as a story can be perceived as a discrete, self-contained unit.

There is however a range of work focusing on both the contributions made by the audience to a telling (see for example the special issue of *Text* on "The Audience as Co-Author" [Volume 6.3, 1986] edited by Duranti and Brenneis, C. Goodwin 1984, Sacks 1974, and Schieffelin 1986) and on how the internal structure of stories reflects their embeddedness within larger interactive processes (M. H. Goodwin 1982a, 1982b; Ochs, Smith, and Taylor 1988) that calls into question whether it is indeed appropriate to analyze stories in isolation from the local indigenous circumstances of their production. In the present volume Bauman demonstrates the major analytic gains that can be made by going beyond traditional assumptions about the ease with which stories can be extracted from their local context. By including within the scope of his analysis not only the story, but also the process of how it was told to the researcher, he is able to reexamine and reconceptualize a range of concepts that lie at the very heart of folklore, including **contextualization** (here approached as an active process), **tradition**, and **genre**, placing them within a dialogic, interactive framework.

4.3   Restricting analysis to the sentence.

The effort to limit the scope of analysis by finding easily extractable units is by no means restricted to elaborate speech genres such as narrative, but instead constitutes a core component of most contemporary approaches to the study of language. For example as both conversation analysts and the Bakhtin Circle (see especially Vološinov 1973) have amply demonstrated, a crucial context for talk is the surrounding speech within which the talk being treated as focal emerges. This is also one of the main points of Silverstein's (1985a, 1985b) recent work on metapragmatic verbs, namely verbs of saying, and their relation to the "culture" of a text. The author's and character's attitudes and stances toward a certain transaction or event are often revealed by the inter-textual play of the particular verbs which frame what is being said and thus reveal or suggest what to make of it (and of its author) – namely the difference between *said, objected, interjected, shouted, complained, remarked,* etc. However, Bloomfield's (1946: 170) definition of the sentence as "an independent linguistic form, not included by virtue of any grammatical construction in any larger linguistic form" and Chomsky's more recent methodological practices have provided a warrant for formal linguistics to restrict the scope of its inquiry to the individual sentence and its subcomponents. Not only is language analyzed in isolation from the interactive participation frameworks that align speakers to hearers and actualize a state of discourse (for analysis of how such participation frameworks are relevant to the organization of the talk that occurs within them see for example C. Goodwin 1981, Heath 1984, Kendon 1982, and the chapters by Kendon and the Goodwins in this volume), but in addition the individual sentence or utterance is treated as though it had no ties to the talk that surrounds it (with the exception of those indexical signs such as pronouns, demonstratives, spatial and temporal adverbs which evoke or require knowledge of the textual or spatio-temporal context for an interpretation of the referential–propositional meaning of the speech act within which they occur). The sentence is thus divorced from any relevant context and becomes a self-sufficient, self-contained world.

As the development of linguistics as a science in this century amply demonstrates, limiting the scope of analysis in this fashion has proven to be enormously successful. Note that what is accomplished by delimiting boundaries in this manner is not simply a quantitative restriction on the range of data that a theory has to deal with it, but more importantly a qualitative distinction in the types of phenomena to be examined. Structure within the sentence is well outlined, sharply defined, and well articulated, while the phenomena to be included within its context, as ground rather than figure, can appear far more amorphous, problematic, and less stable. The frame of relevance established by the focal event, in combination with the analytic interests of the researcher, act as kind of a moving searchlight on the ground of context, now picking out from the surrounding darkness certain features of the terrain but a moment later shifting focus to something else. Not only the internal structure of context, but the prior question of what is to count as context at a particular moment, is capable of dynamic reformulation as local frames of relevance change. Simply getting one's hands on the shape of context is a major analytic problem. By way of contrast the individual sentence provides a clear, highly structured, well-ordered world, one that lends itself well to systematic description and analysis of the organization it displays so prominently. However, that analytic clarity may be purchased at the cost of ignoring fundamental aspects of the ways in which human beings construct, interpret, and use language as a constitutive feature of the activities they engage in.

5   Traditions in the social analysis of context

One of the strengths of the present volume is that it brings together research on the social and interactive organization of context from a variety of different perspectives. A reader well versed in one of these traditions might be unfamiliar with others. It is therefore useful to note briefly several of the research frameworks that the chapters in this collection use as their point of departure. Such an overview helps provide context for the chapters themselves by situating current interest in the social and interactive dimensions of context within broader theoretical trends. In addition we hope that awareness of alternative perspectives will help foster dialogue between different traditions. The following will be briefly examined: (1) ethnographic and (2) philosophical precursors to the notion of language as action; (3) Soviet dialogical approaches to language and cognition; (4) work in human interaction, with particular emphasis on the cybernetic and dramaturgic metaphors; (5) the ethnography of speaking tradition; (6) ethnomethodology, including Cicourel's cognitive sociology; (7) conversation analysis; and (8) Foucault.

This overview is designed to highlight those approaches to the study of context that are most relevant to the perspectives treated in the present volume, in essence those that focus on language as a socially constituted, interactive phenomenon. As such it provides a very selective history rather than a comprehensive review of all of the ways in which context has been argued to be relevant to the analysis of human language and cognition (such a review would require a volume of its own). Thus no attempt is made to cover work in **pragmatics** by formal linguists and philosophers in which context is invoked to account for aspects of meaning that fall outside the scope of semantics (cf. Levinson 1983). Relevant to such research is a logical semantic tradition which includes work by Stalnaker (1979) and others on presuppositions and possible worlds (Lewis 1973, 1986) and continues with more recent proposals such as Heim's (1981) notion of "file change semantics" (see also Kamp 1981), which try to reconcile traditional formal accounts of natural language expressions with discourse phenomena (e.g. definiteness) not easily accountable for in terms of truth-functional semantics (e.g. via quantification). The basic intuition in these works, which lean toward possible artificial intelligence applications, is the idea of a continuously evolving set of presuppositions which draws from and at the same time affects the "actual" world as well as other "possible" worlds. There is also an important ordinary language tradition, possibly deriving from the later Wittgenstein but with a strong life of its own, that encompasses not only speech act theorists but also work from Ryle and Strawson through to Baker and Hacker (1984). Within sociolinguistics, social attributes of participants (class, ethnicity, gender, etc.) have been used to account for language variation (see for example Labov 1970, 1972a). Such work provides new insights into such central topics of linguistic theory as language change, and demonstrates how linguistic phenomena are relevant to the organization of social inequality in a society. It must also be argued that Geertzian and Beckerian ideas about rich interpretation, or work in hermeneutics or the new literary criticism, including work on reader-response theory (Tompkins 1980), provide yet other perspectives on context. Despite their intrinsic value, we have made the decision not to discuss these traditions since we believe that such a discussion would take us far afield. Instead, we will focus on how the relationship between language and context has been analyzed from ethnographic and interactive perspectives.

5.1   An ethnographic precursor

In a seminal essay on "The Problem of Meaning in Primitive Languages" Bronislaw Malinowski (1923) elaborated two important themes that were to figure prominently in subsequent work on context:

(1) Language is embedded within a **context of situation**. After noting how words only become comprehensible when one takes into account the larger sociocultural frameworks within which they are embedded. Malinowski argues that the utterance itself

becomes only intelligible when it is placed within its context of situation, if I may be allowed to coin an expression which indicates on the one hand that the conception of *context* has to be broadened and on the other that the situation in which words are uttered can never be passed over as irrelevant to the linguistic expression. We see how the conception of context must be substantially widened, if it is to furnish us with its full utility. In fact it must burst the bonds of mere linguistics and be carried over into the analysis of the general conditions under which a language is spoken.

(Malinowski 1923: 306)

Malinowski thus proposes that linguistic analysis must be supplemented by ethnographic analysis of situations within which speech occurs. Indeed he argues that "linguistic analysis inevitably leads us into the study of all the subjects covered by Ethnographic field-work" (Malinowski 1923: 302). The sentiments expressed here have motivated generations of anthropologists in their attempts to tie language to the ethnographic context within which it emerges.

(2) Language must be conceptualized as a mode of **practical action**, rather than a mere reflection of internal, abstract thought. Malinowski was led to this pragmatic view of language by observing how it functioned within the task activities, such as fishing, of the people he studied:

The study of any form of speech used in connection with vital work would reveal . . . the dependence of the meaning of each word upon practical experience, and of the structure of each utterance upon the momentary situation in which it is spoken. Thus the consideration of linguistic uses associated with any practical pursuit, leads us to the conclusion that language . . . ought to be regarded and studied against the background of human activities and as a mode of human behavior in practical matters . . . In its primitive uses, language functions as a link in concerted human activity, as a piece of human behavior. It is a mode of action and not an instrument of reflection.

(Malinowski 1923: 312)

While Malinowski initially phrased such ideas with reference to "primitive" uses of language, this notion was later dropped (Malinowski 1935), and issues such as these were framed as general properties of language.

Such a perspective on language as "an indispensable element of concerted human action" (Malinowski 1923: 316) led him at a very early date to articulate a view of meaning as something embedded within trajectories of action:

A word is used when it can produce an action and not to describe one, still less to translate thoughts. The word therefore has a power of its own, it is a means of bringing things about, it is a handle to acts and objects and not a definition of them.

(Malinowski 1923: 321)

Meaning . . . does not come . . . from contemplation of things, or analysis of occurrences, but in practical and active acquaintance with relevant situations. The real knowledge of a word comes through the practice of appropriately using it within a certain situation.

(Malinowski 1923: 325)

In brief, Malinowski not only introduced the notion of a "context of situation," but also anticipated much later work in pragmatics by drawing attention to the importance of studying language, and the process through which it is interpreted and becomes meaningful, within indigenous systems of action (see also Malinowski 1935). In addition to his influence on ethnographic approaches to the study of context, Malinowski's work constituted the point of departure for an approach to the analysis of language that extends from Firth (1957) to Halliday (1973), one of the grammarians most committed to the instrumental view of language.

5.2   Philosophic approaches to context, intentionality and action

Philosophers who have turned their attention to natural language have typically adopted one of two basic stances. Most frequently language is viewed as a flawed and defective mechanism for logical thinking. Effort is therefore invested in programs for developing a formal calculus that will overcome its limitations and provide a framework for rigorous analytical work. Research that originated within or was inspired by the Vienna Circle in the 1920s belongs to this tradition. However, other philosophers have rejected the assumptions that underlie such an approach. They argue that analysis must begin by treating language as something embedded within contexts of human action. By attending to its intrinsically context-bound nature, human beings are able to make definite sense out of talk despite the indefinite resources provided by language as a formal system. Instead of seeking to specify the properties of a single, ideal, formal system, analysis must focus on the variety of ways in which language is deployed to accomplish understanding and action in a multiplicity of situations of use. Within such a perspective context is viewed as a core component of the organization of language. A very striking, and profound, example of these two positions toward language, and the dynamic tensions that exist between them, can be found in the work of a single person: Ludwig Wittgenstein. In the early part of his career (in work that culminated in his *Tractatus Logico-Philosophicus* [1922]) Wittgenstein proposed a theory of language based on the assumption of a one-to-one correspondence between parts of speech and aspects of the context or activity that was being described. This approach still paid homage to the predominantly "referential" or –reflectionist view" (cf. Silverstein 1979) of language and thus continued the earlier philosophical tradition of favoring declarative sentences (e.g. *The boy hit the ball*) over other kinds of linguistic expressions (e.g. imperatives, questions). However, in the *Philosophical Investigations* (Wittgenstein (1958) countered his own earlier work by arguing that emphasis on the development of a logically coherent, self-contained formal system had to be replaced by an approach focused on language as a form of action (or "form of life," as he wrote) and thus used context as a point of departure for uncovering the multifaceted variety of thought and action made available by the different **language games** that human beings engage in. Thus, just as a coin can mean one thing when offered to a storekeeper after taking a candy bar, and quite another when used to replace a missing piece in a game of checkers, so the same utterance can mean quite different things when it is embedded within different natural activities. Study of decontextualized sentences must therefore be replaced by investigation that goes beyond the talk itself to analyze the larger activities within which the talk is embedded, and through which it becomes meaningful (for discussion of how activities are relevant to the analysis of talk see Duranti 1981, 1984, this volume; Goodwin and Goodwin 1989; and Levinson 1979).

A second philosopher who has had major influence on the analysis of language as a mode of action is J. L. Austin. In order to describe how people use words to accomplish action, Austin (1962) turned to the cultural and social conventions that provide for the interpretability and efficacy of performative utterances. Thus a statement such as "I now pronounce you man and wife" (when spoken in an appropriate civil or religious ceremony) is able to change the marital status of its addressees because of a surrounding framework of social conventions about what constitutes marriage and how it is validly entered into. The context, in the sense of a set of recognizable conventions, provides the infrastructure through which the utterance gains its force as a particular type of action. Rather than speaking of grammaticality conditions (or their logical equivalent, "well-formedness conditions"), Austin introduced the concept of "felicity conditions." Thus a speech act is not "grammatical" or "ungrammatical," rather it works or misfires (if the conditions are not appropriate or if they change). The felicity conditions he proposed for the speech acts he discussed were in fact categorizations of contexts (e.g. the range of participants necessary for a marriage ceremony, the manifest or implicit knowledge and attitude of speaker and hearer(s), etc.). Moreover, with his notion of "uptake" Austin emphasized interactive aspects of both speech acts and the context that encompasses them.

One of the main differences between Austin's theory and generative grammar lies in his emphasis on conventions as opposed to innate structures or internalized knowledge (Griffin and Mehan 1981, Strawson 1964), a point echoed by Wittgenstein's (1958) concern with community norms as opposed to the speaker's state of mind in the definition of meaning. Later work on speech acts (for example Searle 1969) was, in our view, influenced by the "cognitive turn" of linguistic studies characteristic of Chomskyan and post-Chomskyan linguistics. Such a turn was originally a reaction to crude behavioristic models of verbal behavior, but had the effect of facilitating the reintroduction of psychologism in the philosophical literature on linguistic competence. Interest shifted from conventions and context to focus on intentionality and speakers' inner psychological states. This turned into a methodology that avoids discussing those aspects of meaning that could not be immediately traced back to the speaker's state of mind (cf. Bach and Harnish 1979, Searle 1983). Whatever needs reference to societal norms or conventions that may exist outside of the speaker's conscious intentions to communicate is seen as problematic for a theory that explicitly takes the speaker as the sole originator of the meaning making process. This is demonstrated quite vividly by the way in which the hearer is treated in some versions of speech act theory. Although both speaker and hearer often enter in the representation of speech acts and speech act types, they have unequal status. The hearer is often but a projection of the speaker's wants or attitudes, and rarely an active (co-)participant in the utterance event (cf. the exchange between Clark 1982 and Sperber and Wilson 1982a, 1982b; and the exchange between Clark and Carlson 1982 and Allan 1986, with Clark's 1986 reply). That is, the hearer exists as an Internalized Other, but not as an actual additional participant who could guide the interaction (and the interpretation of talk) toward directions unforeseen by the speaker. More recent work in speech act theory has moved beyond some of these limitations by paying attention to effects as well as intentions, and by devoting attention to speech act sequences and the behavior of speech acts in conversational sequences (see Streeck 1980, 1984; Verschueren 1983).

The issue of where actions are situated, and what actions these are, becomes much more complex when the power of recipients, as well as speakers, to constitute what actions are occurring is given serious attention. Despite the importance accorded intentionality in speech act analysis, not all societies grant such primacy to the intentions of the speaker, but instead allow recipients considerable power to determine what act an utterance will be officially heard to constitute (Duranti 1988a, Rosaldo 1982). Even in our own society there is now clear evidence that the action that a strip of speech embodies is mutable and capable of change and negotiation within multi-turn sequences.[10] Both the constitution of acts by different individuals across different turns (Ochs, Schieffelin, and Platt 1979; Duranti 1981, in press), and recipient negotiation of what an act will eventually be seen to be (C. Goodwin 1979, 1981) demonstrate that situations exist in which actions emerge not from the speaker alone in a single turn, but rather are collaboratively defined through a process of interaction in which recipients play a very active role. In the present volume, Kendon ties the question of intentionality to the problem of achieving coordinated social action, and his analysis reveals how the structure of intentionality, rather than being situated within the mind of a single individual, might be distributed within the interactive context. Lindstrom's chapter, on the other hand, taking inspiration from Foucault's work on technologies of power, suggests that the very act of interpretation, the evoking of some specific frame or context, is an act of power whereby participants try to establish what is acceptable evidence or truth, and what could be meant at any given time. Intentionality in this perspective is deeply embedded within local practices for political action. The idea that one could build a theory of human action with the speaker's intentions at its center becomes highly problematic when we look at actual interactions, and when we try to place acts of interpretation within the context of political struggle.

5.3   The Bakhtin Circle and Vygotsky

The intellectual ferment following the Russian revolution of 1917 produced two quite separate, though complementary, research programs built on the idea that language and context were interdependent phenomena that must be analyzed in concert with each other.

First, the Bakhtin Circle, in a critique that was most clearly articulated in Vološinov (1973),[11] argued that Saussure's view of language as an abstract system internalized in the minds of individual speakers was inadequate:

Verbal communication can never be understood and explained outside of . . . connection with a concrete situation . . . Language acquires life and historically evolves . . . in concrete verbal communication, and not in the abstract linguistic system of language forms, nor in the individual psyche of speakers.
(Vološinov 1973: 95)

This perspective is quite consistent with the "early" Marx and with the dialectical materialist program for the construction of a philosophy of human praxis (cf. also Gramsci's work), where there is an interplay between subjective (namely psychological) and objective (namely historical) processes and where language as a relatively autonomous manifestation of superstructure can play an important role in the constitution of both the individual and society.

Rather than constituting a formal system that can be safely extracted for independent analysis, for Vološinov (1973: 98) "Language is a continuous generative process implemented in the social-verbal interaction of speakers." Vološinov opposed what he called the "isolated monologic utterance" (Vološinov 1973: 94), emphasized the ways in which language must be conceptualized as embedded within a matrix of human interaction, and produced ground breaking work on the contextualizing power of reported speech (cf. Bakhtin 1981, 1984).

Central to the work of Bakhtin is the notion of the **dialogic** organization of language. That term can be somewhat misleading since it immediately conjures up visions of multi-party talk, i.e. a dialogue between different speakers. This is not what Bakhtin meant by **dialogic**. Rather he wanted to call attention to how a single strip of talk (utterance, text, story, etc.) can juxtapose language drawn from, and invoking, alternative cultural, social, and linguistic home environments, the interpenetration of multiple voices and forms of utterance. An example of such dialogic use of language is provided in Dostoyevsky's novels:

Dostoyevsky's novel is dialogic. It is constructed not as the whole of a single consciousness, absorbing other consciousnesses as objects into itself, but as a whole formed by the interaction of several consciousnesses, none of which entirely becomes an object for the other; this interaction provides no support for the viewer who would objectify an entire event according to some ordinary monologic category [. . .] and this consequently makes the viewer also a participant. [. . .] everything in the novel is structured to make dialogic opposition inescapable.

(Bakhtin 1984: 18)

A prototypical example of the way in which dialogical oppositions are created is found in **reported speech** in which the quoted talk of one party is embedded within the speech of another. Vološinov discussed several ways in which the author's or a character's voice can infiltrate the speech of another. As developed in Silverstein's notion of metapragmatics (Silverstein 1985a, 1985b), verbs of saying are ideal framing devices for expressing local linguistic ideologies and can thus be equally exploited by authors/speakers and analysts for getting at the interplay of alternative interpretations of text or talk. Speech genres vary in the extent to which they permit dialogic organization (narrative vs. scientific writing). In this volume, Bauman uses Bakhtin as point of departure to rethink how folklorists have traditionally analyzed both genres and the concept of tradition itself.

Bakhtin's perspective on the relationship between language and context insightfully anticipates many of the contemporary theoretical concerns that animate current attempts to rethink context in fields as varied as conversation analysis, Goffman's (1974) frame analysis, Habermas' (1970) critique of the monologic competence embedded within Chomskyan linguistics, and the current interest in developing a Bakhtinian, dialogic perspective within linguistics and anthropology (cf. Brenneis 1986, Duranti 1988a, Duranti and Brenneis 1986, Hanks 1987, Hill 1985, Macaulay 1987, Tedlock 1983).

A second attempt to place the genesis of thought and language within a context constituted through dynamic processes of social interaction can be found in the work of Vygotsky (1962, 1978)[12] and his two closest associates, Luria (1979) and Leont'ev (1981a, 1981b).

Focusing on the development of language and cognition, Vygosky took strong issue with Piaget's (1959) claim that before using speech **socially** children first passed through a stage characterized by **egocentric** speech. Vygotsky opposed Piaget through an ingenious series of experiments in which he demonstrated that "egocentric" speech was strongly influenced by the social context in which it occurred. As Emerson (1983: 10–11) observes:

Vygotsky concluded that egocentric speech was not, as Piaget had suggested, a compromise between primary autism and reluctant socialization, but rather the direct outgrowth (or better, ingrowth) of speech which had been from the start socially and environmentally oriented. Piaget was correct when he observed that private and socialized speech did indeed intersect at this stage, but development was proceeding not along the lines of Piaget's scenario, but in the opposite direction. The child was not externalizing his internal thoughts, but internalizing his external verbal interactions.

For Vygotsky, replacing autistic egocentric speech with a focus on the social context of language acquisition was but part of a much larger endeavor: demonstrating that language and consciousness were both lodged within a matrix of **social activity**, and that this **activity system**, rather than the isolated individual, should be the primary focus of study. Thus, when he turned to study intelligence he did not focus on measurements of the individual child, as most Western psychologists do, but rather on the process of interaction between the child and its teacher. For Vygotsky, what should be measured is not what the child knows before the test, but rather the ability of the child to interact with its caretakers so as to extend its present knowledge toward new frontiers. The difference between what the child can do on his or her own, and what he or she can do under adult collaboration is what constitutes the "zone of proximal development." Vygotsky argued that "what is the zone of proximal development today will be the actual developmental level tomorrow" (Vygotsky 1978: 87). In this framework, intrapsychological (i.e. internal) processes typically arise, first, at the interpsychological (i.e. social) level. It is in the coordination with the environment and other, more competent members of their community that children come to take advantage of tools, a most important class of tools being symbols. Words are thus seen as but one example of tools that function as mediating devices. In this scheme, language is, from the beginning, part of an interaction, an activity system, whereby development can take place.

If indeed language development starts as part of a social matrix and the child's egocentric speech is in fact internalized social speech, we should be questioning the adequacy of child language acquisition models based on a notion of linguistic structure as an independent level, not affected, in its most basic nature, by the conditions of linguistic performance. Indeed, it would seem that any kind of language acquisition device would have to be able to both read, i.e. interpret, and reformulate (or filter) some aspects of the context that give meaning and form to speech signals. A device only aimed at decoding context-free forms may not be able to decode the relevant input.

The ideas and theoretical perspective of Vygotsky remain very much alive today and are currently having new influence, not only in the Soviet Union, but also in the United States where the approach to issues of language, intelligence, learning, and technology he originated is being pursued by scholars interested in investigating cognition, language, and education as phenomena embedded within social contexts. The influence of context on cognitive operations is well illustrated by Scribner's (1984) study of how the spatial organization of material in a warehouse is utilized in the mathematical operations that workers perform in taking inventory, by Scribner and Cole's (1981) work on the acquisition of literacy (cf. also Cole 1985, Cole and Griffin 1987, Laboratory of Comparative Human Cognition 1983, Newman, Griffin, and Cole 1984), and by Suchman's (1987) research into the organization of situated activity. Lave (1988) contrasts a contextually embedded, practice-based approach to mathematical operations with traditional accounts of cognition in both psychology and anthropology. The role of context is also central to the approach to the analysis of educational processes developed by McDermott (McDermott 1976, McDermott and Gospodinoff 1979, McDermott, Gospodinoff, and Aron 1978), Erickson (Erickson 1979, 1982; Erickson and Shultz 1981), Cook-Gumperz (1986, Cook-Gumperz, Corsaro, and Streeck 1986) and John Gumperz and his students (Gumperz 1982b).

5.4   Human interaction

The organization of human interaction is central to the analysis of context in a number of different ways. First, face-to-face interaction provides the primordial locus for the production of talk. The features of face-to-face interaction thus constitute a primary examplar of context. Second, in so far as face-to-face interaction is accomplished through the collaborative work of separate individuals it provides an elementary example of human social organization. Talk spoken there is thus inescapably a form of social action. Moreover, the way in which talk-in-interaction is designed for, and shaped by, the social properties of its interactive environment sheds light on the basic organization of language itself (Schegloff, this volume). Treating human interaction as a central context for speech provides an expanded view of language, one that ties the production of talk to systematic social organization. Third, within interaction participants are faced with the task of accomplishing understanding and, as part of this process, displaying to each other their understanding of the events in progress at a particular moment (see for example the chapters by the Goodwins and by Cicourel in this volume). Accomplishing such shared agreement about the events that members of a society encounter in their phenomenal world is central both to what anthropologists have traditionally analyzed as culture and to the social organization of cognition and intersubjectivity that has been a main topic of ethnomethodology (Cicourel 1973, this volume; Garfinkel 1967; Heritage 1984). Finally, face-to-face interaction is inherently dynamic. Each subsequent utterance, and indeed events within a single utterance, change in subtle but profound ways the operative context of the moment (see Heritage 1984, and the chapters by Duranti, the Goodwins, Gumperz, Hanks, Kendon, Lindstrom, and Schegloff in this volume). Face-to-face interaction thus provides an opportunity to analyze language, culture, and social organization as integrated components of a single system of action, and moreover deal with such processes as dynamic, intrinsically time-bound phenomena. No comprehensive view of context can ignore analysis of this topic.

Important early research into the properties of face-to-face interaction can be found in the work of the anthropologist Gregory Bateson (an important collection of his essays can be found in Bateson 1972). Bateson helped formulate some of the most basic theory and methodology for the study of human communication. For example he was one of the founders of the field of cybernetics. While doing fieldwork in Bali with Margaret Mead he pioneered the use of film as a research tool for the analysis of human interaction. Later he organized the Bateson Project on Human Communication, a research group which produced work that had far-reaching consequences for subsequent studies of face-to-face interaction. One process that they analyzed was therapy. Their work led them to reconceptualize "mental illness," which had previously been treated as something located inside the individual (e.g. by Freud, etc.), as an interactive phenomenon. Early work on the theory that they called the "double bind" led them to shift both analysis and therapy from the psychiatrist–patient dyad to encompass the relevant social units that the "patient" was embedded within, and in particular the family. This work helped found the field of Family Therapy and had great influence on other social approaches to psychiatric phenomena. As part of this research Bateson organized an interdisciplinary team, including linguists, anthro-pologists, and psychiatrists, to intensively analyze films of interaction. Though publication of the final report of this team was delayed for many years, work on the project produced a range of seminal insights about the organization of face-to-face interaction, including recognition of the importance of meta-communication, the development of kinesics as a discipline, intensive study of how talk, paralanguage, and body movement were related to each other, etc. A similar close analysis of films of therapy sessions was undertaken by Albert Scheflen at Bronx State Hospital and led to important insights about how participants used the spatial alignment of their bodies to communicate about their interaction (Scheflen 1963, 1964, 1966, 1971, 1973). One of Scheflen's collaborators was Adam Kendon, whose chapter in this volume provides a good example of how spatial orientation, and a range of other phenomena in a "disattend track", provide organization for the events that are the official focus of their attention. In subsequent work Scheflen investigated how features of settings (for example the type of event in progress, the arrangement of furniture in a room, etc.) shape interaction, and performed an extensive cross-cultural study of how members of different ethnic groups use the space in their homes. The work on visual materials of both Bateson and

Scheflen had considerable influence on the research of subsequent scholars.

Bateson's interests were by no means restricted to therapeutic discourse. Looking at otters playing in a zoo he made the crucial observation that they were capable of **framing** their behavior, so that actions that in other circumstances would be treated as quite hostile and aggressive – nips and bites for example – were here recognized as not serious but playful. Building from such observations, Bateson called attention to the crucial role that **framing** plays in the organization of interaction in general. Indeed, framing provides a prototypical example of context (consider for example how the narrator frames his story in Bauman's chapter, the way in which postural configurations frame spates of talk in Kendon's analysis, the framing provided by discourse genres in Lindstrom's chapter, etc.). Bateson laid the groundwork for an ecological, contextual view of phenomena as diverse as play, family structure, art, and the mind itself. His work had a strong influence on the approach to context, keying, and frame analysis developed by Erving Goffman (1974).

A number of different, major analytical perspectives for the analysis of face-to-face interaction can be found in the work of Erving Goffman. With respect to the chapters in this volume it is useful to distinguish two distinct strands in Goffman's work. The first, most prominent in his early work (especially Goffman 1961, 1963, 1967, but also 1974), provides a variety of analytical frameworks for the description and analysis of all types of multi-party interaction. Goffman starts by differentiating **unfocused inter- action** (which occurs whenever two or more individuals are mutually accessible to each other, for example when strangers pass each other on the street) from **focused interaction**, "the kind of interaction that occurs when persons gather close together and openly cooperate to sustain a single focus of attention" (Goffman 1963: 24), for example conversations, card games, surgical operations, etc. He then offers a range of analytical categories to describe the structural features of each of these types of situations, for example primary and subordinate involvements, involvement shields, rules governing accessibility and leave taking, different types of spatial regions, information structures, communication boundaries, situational properties, etc. Goffman is careful to take into account both the physical and the social setting of interaction (for example in Goffman 1971 he devotes considerable attention to the distinction between public and private space in our society), and indeed on one level his work provides a powerful ethnography of middle-class society. Of particular relevance to the work in the present volume is the analysis of participant structures he provides, differentiating for example those within an encounter from those outside it (ratified participants vs. overhearers), and a range of different types of participants within an encounter (speaker, addressee, hearer, etc.). The themes found in this strand of Goffman's work are most explicitly addressed in Kendon's chapter in this volume, which investigates how the defining characteristic of a focused encounter, the collaborative organization of a moving focus of attention, is accomplished within face-to-face interaction (other analysis of the collaborative organization of mutual involvement can be found in the Goodwins' chapter).

A second theoretical strand in Goffman's work investigates frames that can be invoked by a single speaker within talk itself. A good example is provided by Goffman's analysis, in both "The Frame Analysis of Talk" (one of the concluding chapters of *Frame Analysis*, Goffman 1974) and "Footing" (Goffman 1981), of the different entities that can be invoked by a speaker within a strip of talk: (a) the **author** of the words being spoken; (b) a **principal** or party officially responsible for what is being said (who might, as in the case of a President and press spokesman, be quite different from the person who is actually speaking); (c) the **animator** or entity who is actually speaking; (d) a **figure** or protagonist animated by the speaker, for example a character in a story, though the speaker can of course animate him- or herself as a figure and does so when using the pronoun "I". Note that such framing can be performed by a single speaker within a single strip of talk. It is "dialogic" in the Bakhtinian sense (and indeed Goffman's formulation of these distinctions was influenced by the work of Vološinov [1973] on reported speech) rather than dialogue in the conversational sense of a state of talk sustained through the collaborative action of multiple participants. Though Goffman included various types of recipients in his analysis of **participation status** (1981: 131–7), the way in which his conceptual apparatus provides resources for describing how speakers build participant frameworks has had the most influence on subsequent research (Hanks 1990, Levinson 1987), with only a few scholars focusing empirical investigation on what recipients as well as speakers actually do to constitute a state of talk (see the Goodwins' chapter in this volume for an example of such an approach).

5.5   The ethnography of speaking

Following up on Malinowski's notion of "context of situation" and Jakobson's (1960) speech event scheme, Hymes' SPEAKING model (1972) represents a major shift in the choice of units of analysis: for the first time (see also Hymes 1965) a non-linguistic unit, the event, becomes the frame of reference for interpreting speech. This has several consequences for the scope of context, the most important one being that context is not defined on the basis of what is needed to interpret a particular set of linguistic phenomena. Rather, the ethnographer attempts a description of what seem the most important dimensions of the event, on the basis of culturally defined categories, before or while engaging in linguistic interpretation. The native taxonomies for the communicative event inform the analysis of talk and vice versa (Bauman 1977, 1986; Bauman and Sherzer 1974; Duranti 1981; Sherzer 1983).

The grid proposed by Hymes defines a wide range of phenomena under the rubric of "context." With respect to the grammatical studies and philosophical approaches mentioned earlier, the most striking difference is the introduction of the category "participant" in the analysis. This means going beyond the dyad speaker–hearer and taking more subtle distinctions into consideration. The study of oratorical discourse has taught us, for instance, that at times the speaker may need to be differentiated from the addressor and that the hearer may need to be differentiated from the addressee (cf. the articles in Bloch 1975 and Brenneis and Myers 1984) – or that different kinds of addressees may need to be taken into consideration (see for example the extensive deconstruction of the terms "speaker" and "hearer" in Goffman's analysis of "Footing" [1981: 124–69]; and Levinson 1987). In the last few years, research within anthropological linguistics and conversational analysis has developed these concepts in an attempt to define the collaborative albeit differentiated work done by participants in a public verbal performance (cf. Brenneis 1978, 1986, 1987; Du Bois 1987; Duranti 1986, 1988b; C. Goodwin 1986; Haviland 1986).

Whereas in speech act theory context usually does not go beyond speaker and hearer, in the ethnographic approach, several other aspects of the speech event are taken into consideration, for example the spatial and the temporal dimensions of the event (cf. also Duranti 1981, 1985). This is particularly the case for the study of ritual and institutional activities (e.g. classroom interactions, political meetings), which tend to use linguistic markers to define the spatio-temporal scope of phenomena that are locally relevant to the ongoing talk.

Other elements of the SPEAKING model also offered an alternative to the more limited notion of context proposed within speech act theory. For instance, the study of genres implied an attention to units of discourse larger than the sentence (cf. Bauman 1977, 1986; Sherzer 1983). The very notion of genre assumes a complexity of linguistic and extralinguistic factors that can be exploited for an integrated analysis of speech performance as inherently dialogical and constitutive of social reality. This is indeed the direction of the study of genres recently inspired by the work of Bakhtin and his Circle (see for example Bauman's chapter in this volume and Hanks 1987). The attention to larger units of analysis and the contexts of their production also questions the cross-contextual and cross-cultural validity of taken-for-granted speech acts such as **promising** and **praising**. The more we pay attention to actual acts of speaking and their embedded practices, the more we realize that any act of interpretation is indeed a social act and participants must continuously negotiate what is being said and what the appropriate, namely acceptable, interpretation is (see Lindstrom, this volume; Duranti 1988a; Rosaldo 1982). A given speech act, e.g. **praising** or **promising**, is seen within the wider context of a speech performed on a given occasion, within particular sociocultural expectations. The focus on **keys** – an aspect of communicative behavior analyzed as well by Bateson (1972) and Goffman (1974) – also stressed the need to consider multifunctional aspects of linguistic expressions, whereby the same utterance may carry several messages at once, namely a given proposition and the locally appropriate interpretation, e.g. serious, ironic, etc.

The attention to all of these factors has been very important in expanding current notions of context and making them more receptive to culture-specific norms and expectations.

The approach to the ethnography of communication established by Gumperz and Hymes now includes several flourishing lines of research. For example Gumperz and his collaborators (Gumperz 1982a, 1982b) have devoted considerable attention to analysis of **context as a process of inference**, the study of the **contextualization cues** through which context is invoked (see also Basso, this volume), and how the cultural loading of such cues can lead to **miscommunication in cross-cultural settings**, issues discussed in some detail by Gumperz in his chapter in this volume. For a more detailed view of research produced by Hymes and his students see Duranti (1988b).

5.6　Ethnomethodology

An important perspective on context emerges not from the study of language itself but rather from sociologists interested in systematic analysis of how members of a society build the events they participate in. **Ethnomethodologists** including Aaron Cicourel (Cicourel 1964, 1968, 1973, 1974; Cicourel and Kitsuse 1963; Cicourel *et al.* 1974) and Harold Garfinkel (Garfinkel 1967, Garfinkel and Sacks 1970, Garfinkel, Lynch, and Livingston 1981) are interested in the most basic of all social phenomena: the way in which social order and social organization are constituted. In order for separate individuals to engage in coordinated social action they must recognize in common what activities are in progress and what those present must do to perform the activity. The central question of intersubjectivity (how separate individuals are able to know or act within a common world) is thus raised as a constitutive feature of social action. What ethnomethodology (from Husserl and via Schutz) defined as the problem of intersubjectivity can be seen as an attempt at answering the question about how members negotiate or achieve a common context. Many traditional social theorists essentially bypass this problem by assuming that through psychological processes such as internalization members of a society will automatically recognize the scenes they confront and be motivated to play their parts within them. Analysis can then focus on larger aspects of the social system while the cognitive activity of actual actors is treated as either epiphenomenal or defective (Heritage 1984). Mundane social actors are conceptualized as "judgmental dopes" (Garfinkel 1967) embedded within a matrix of action that exceeds their comprehension. The context of their understanding exists prior to their acting in the world. By way of contrast, ethnomethodologists argue that both intersubjectivity and the social order visible in coordinated action are accomplished through ongoing, moment-by-moment social and cognitive work; participants display to each other their understanding of the events they are engaged in as part of the process through which these very same events are performed and constituted as social activities. Instead of judgmental dopes the ethnomethodologist finds actors who are reflexively aware of the social events they are producing and who are possessed of a rich and immensely varied, socially organized cognitive life. Part of this richness arises from the way in which social action is embedded within the settings and institutions of a society from mundane talk to abstract science (Knorr-Cetina, Mulkay, and Mulkay 1983; Lynch 1982, 1988; Lynch, Livingston, and Garfinkel 1983). Analysis of how participants accomplish social order requires detailed investigation, from the inside out, of the indigenous settings and activities of a society. Within ethnomethodology strong disputes exist about a variety of issues, including the relevance of ethnographic fieldwork. In his chapter in this volume, Aaron Cicourel, one of the founders of ethnomethodology, addresses some of these questions and demonstrates how vast an array of members' knowledge, situated within specific settings and activities, must be deployed to understand even a very short stretch of talk.

5.7   Conversation analysis

Conversation analysis is a field of study that emerged within sociology through the work of Harvey Sacks, Gail Jefferson, Emanuel Schegloff, and their colleagues. It accords primary importance to the analysis of talk as a body of situated social practices.[13] This work emerged from a larger ethnomethodological tradition. The central place that language occupies in the organization of human social phenomena is recognized by Garfinkel and Sacks (1970: 342) when they equate the basic social actor with **mastery of natural language**. Such mastery includes the ability to understand more than is explicitly said within a strip of talk by situating it both within indigenous frameworks of commonsense knowledge, and within the practical circumstances and particular activities that parties to the talk are engaged in. Analysis thus shifts from the isolated sentence that is the focus of study within linguistics to the utterance embedded within a **context**:

A speaker's action is context-shaped in that its contribution to an on-going sequence of actions cannot adequately be understood except by reference to the context – including, especially, the immediately preceding configuration of actions – in which it participates. This contextualization of utterances is a major, and unavoidable, procedure which hearers use and rely on to interpret conversational contributions and it is also something which speakers pervasively attend to in the design of what they say.

(Heritage 1984: 242)

Indeed the production of talk is **doubly contextual** (Heritage 1984: 242) in that a subsequent utterance not only relies upon existing context for its production and interpretation, but that utterance is in its own right an event that shapes a new context for the action that will follow it. Consider for example the way in which a **question** makes producing an answer to that question the appropriate thing to do next. As a mode of action an utterance invokes for its interpretation the social field from which it emerges while simultaneously creating a new arena for subsequent action.[14]

When viewed from this perspective, talk is analyzed, not as a syntactic code, or a medium that reports events in some external world, but rather as a mode of action embedded within human interaction. Conversation analysts seek to describe the procedures used by participants in conversation to produce and understand that behavior. A key focus of research by conversation analysts has been the **sequential organization**, the larger sequences of talk, within which utterances and speech acts emerge and are interpreted (Sacks, Schegloff, and Jefferson 1974). As Heritage and Atkinson (1984: 6) note:

no empirically occurring utterance ever occurs outside, or external to, some specific sequence. Whatever is said will be said in some sequential context, and its illocutionary force will be determined by reference to what it accomplishes in relation to some sequentially prior utterance or set of utterances. As long as a state of talk prevails, there will be no escape or timeout from these considerations. And, insofar as unfolding sequences and their constituent turns are unavoidable analytic concerns for interactants, they provide a powerful and readily accessible point of entry in the unavoidable contextedness of actual talk.

Such an approach to the study of face-to-face behavior has much to contribute to a range of theoretical and methodological issues of interest to cultural anthropologists (cf. M. H. Goodwin 1990, Moerman 1988). For example, participants in conversation have the job of providing next moves to ongoing talk which demonstrate what sense they make of that talk. It is therefore possible to see how group members themselves **interpret** the interaction they are engaged in without having to rely on accounts they pass on to anthropologists through interviews or an analyst's rendition of speakers' intentions. Moreover this indigenous process of interpretation links cultural and social phenomena; the analysis participants are engaged in is itself a constitutive element of the social organization achieved and manifested through interactive talk. Conversational structure thus provides a powerful proof procedure that is quite relevant to some of the major theoretical issues that have long been the focus of ethnographic theory.

Conversation analysis is represented most clearly in the present volume in the chapters by Schegloff and the Goodwins. In these chapters the analysis of context, and of sequential organization, is explored on a variety of different levels. Thus the first part of the Goodwins' chapter focuses on the interactive organization of activities occurring within a single utterance. By way of contrast, Schegloff investigates how events which seem to disattend their local context when examined on a micro level, can in fact be found to be organized by their placement in much larger sequences. Finally, the Goodwins' analysis of **instigating** describes how the internal structure of stories is shaped by the larger social projects within which the production of narrative is embedded (for example, by telling a story in which recipient is a principal character, speaker can incite recipient to a future confrontation with someone who is portrayed as having committed offenses against him or her). In brief, conversation analysis provides a thoroughgoing analysis of language as a mode of interaction which relies upon context for the interpretation of action that at the very same time shapes, expands and changes that context.

5.8   Foucault

Finally, we want to turn to another major trend of analytical thought in the Western tradition that has had an impact on our current notions of context, namely the work of the French historian and polymath Michel Foucault. Through a number of extremely original and thought-provoking series of lectures and publications, Foucault reexamined the history of human sciences, prisons, madness, and public health, and how such varied institutions affect individuals and their perception of themselves, their sexuality, and the meaning of their existence. Foucault's contribution was to highlight vast domains of power that are mostly sub-institutional and therefore hidden. These are often unconscious cultural conditions, rules, and practices that govern what people do with their bodies, how they communicate and otherwise relate among themselves, how they desire and fear, and so on. All "knowledge" – or what we might call cultural "domains" – carries within it sub-institutional power networks in which we become enmeshed as soon as we begin to learn and to use that knowledge socially. Following post-structuralist practice, Foucault calls a cultural domain of knowledge a "discourse." Discourse, here, should not be confused with its usage in other analytical traditions in which it means simply the flow of conversation, or a text longer than a sentence. Rather, for Foucault, a discourse is a cultural complex of signs and practices that regulates how we live socially. As such, Foucault's "discourse" has many similarities with Bourdieu's "habitus" – mostly unthought but still learned ways of thinking, feeling, and acting.

As in Bourdieu's case, Foucault was interested in providing a solution to the dichotomy between the predetermined socio-historical and economic conditions of existence and its emergent, and socially negotiated properties. The realm of discourse practices discovered by Foucault provides the analytical link between more subjective, emotional experience and the objective constraints of the institutions. As pointed out in Lindstrom's chapter, what is relevant from the point of view of our rethinking the notion of context is the stress that Foucault places on the intricate and subtle relationship between the interpretive frames we use in everyday life (within and across various activities and institutional roles) and the implicit power relations that each frame implies, exploits, and, at the same time, helps reproduce (in a different vein, similar themes are discussed by Cicourel in this volume). Thus, for instance, Foucault discusses how domains of scientific knowledge are protected by the operation of "disciplinal" policing – by the operation of rules that limit who can "talk" science, who can use it publicly, and that make some talk seem scientifically true, some seem false, and some just "silent," not even audible. We realize then that the discourse of science is not necessarily different from the discourse of politics. They are both concerned with the definition of "truth." But truth, Foucault reminds us, is a socio-historical construction, mediated by particular discourse practices. The role of the historian, or of any other social or human scientist interested in such practices, is to systematically unveil the hidden processes whereby a potentially undifferentiated stream of sounds or sets of continuous behaviors are channeled into systematic oppositions of figures and grounds, visible and less visible elements, focused and unfocused interaction, talk and its surrounding context.

6   Conclusion

Recent work in a number of different fields has called into question the adequacy of earlier definitions of context in favor of a more dynamic view of the relationship between linguistic and non-linguistic dimensions of communicative events. Instead of viewing context as a set of variables that statically surround strips of talk, context and talk are now argued to stand in a mutually reflexive relationship to each other, with talk, and the interpretive work it generates, shaping context as much as context shapes talk. On the one hand the traditional variables of ethnographic and sociological analysis have to be supplemented by study of participant attributes and patterns of social organization that are intrinsic to the activity of talk itself. On the other, the characteristics of language as an interactive phenomenon have challenged traditional notions of linguistic structure and linguistic rules, suggesting a view of the relationship between language and context as a process that emerges and changes through time and space. To rethink something means to recontextualize it, to take it out of earlier frames and place it in a new set of relationships and expectations. The notion of context stands at the cutting edge of much contemporary research into the relationship between language, culture, and social organization, as well as into the study of how language is structured in the way that is is. The essays in this volume represent a variety of viewpoints on this new concept of context. They draw upon a wide range of methodological and theoretical expertise. Each one describes some complex phenomenon involving the role of context in linguistic interpretation and offers suggestions for the relevance of such phenomena to the understanding of other aspects of speech as social action. We offer these chapters as a bridge between the past and the future in an area of study that is relevant to much of contemporary cognitive and social sciences.

Notes

1 See for example Morris (1938), Carnap (1942), Bar-Hillel (1954), Gazdar (1979), Ochs (1979), Levinson (1983), Leech (1983).
2 See for example Malinowski (1923, 1935), Jakobson (1960), Gumperz and Hymes (1972), Hymes (1972, 1974), Bauman and Sherzer 1974.
3 See for example Labov (1966, 1972a, 1972b), Romaine (1982), Sankoff (1980).
4 However, there have been attempts at clarifying the terms and notions necessary for handling the different kinds of relations that linguistic signs entertain or establish with their context of use. The semiotically informed work by Silverstein (1985a, 1985b) on metapragmatics is one such example.
5 Describing what is being contextualized as the **focal event** implies that it is in some sense more salient and noticeable than its **context**, and indeed, as analyzed in some detail by Hanks and Kendon in this volume, there does seem to be a fundamental **figure–ground** relationship implicated in the organization of context, with the **figure**, what we are calling the focal event, standing out from a more amorphous ground as the official focus of attention. This will be discussed in more detail below.
6 For a review of the scope of pragmatics that encompasses interactive as well as linguistic and philosophic approaches, see Levinson (1983).
7 The importance of the dichotomy foreground vs. background information has long been accepted within discourse-based grammatical studies, as shown by such contributions as Cooreman (1987), Givón (1983), Hopper and Thompson (1980), among others.
8 Indeed literacy, and writing in particular, is one of the main procedures through which the **ground** within which language emerges is systematically erased, made invisible, and excluded from analysis. This has enormous consequences for how the linguistic phenomena that become objects of study within particular paradigms are in fact constituted. Though work in the linguistic traditions flowing from generative grammar is based on spoken examples, the utterances studied are not spontaneous but rather built by the analyst in terms of specific theoretical problems. The utterances are in fact dealt with as **printed samples of**

language possibilities whose natural home is other printed language (either in an article by the researcher or on a handout for a talk). The linguistic context for these very specialized samples of language thus consists of either talk by the linguistic **about** the written sentences (rather than responses to them as embodied social action) or juxtaposition with other written samples in an organized "data set." The effect of all this is to focus grammatical analysis on language samples that exist only within a very unusual, highly specialized context. Moreover, this context is not usually attended to explicitly by the analyst, but instead sentences are studied as though context were irrelevant (a problem that becomes especially serious in speech act analysis).

9 The asymmetry between figure and ground has dramatic consequences for special populations such as deaf people when they try to fully participate in interactions where the simultaneous use of both verbal and nonverbal information is necessary (e.g. a teacher talking while writing on the blackboard). Both channels cannot be accessed via an interpreter who typically chooses to translate verbal over nonverbal information. However, the verbal information requires almost exclusive visual access in order for it to be understood (Johnson 1989).

10 For example Jefferson (1979) has demonstrated that outbreaths and other paralinguistic cues are redefined as "laughter" or "invitations to laughter" only after the recipient has given hints that that interpretation is acceptable.

11 We will not here enter into the dispute about whether, and to what extent, Bakhtin was in fact the author of *Marxism and the Philosophy of Language* (cf. Clark and Holquist 1984). Many groundbreaking attempts to explore new phenomena emerge from the intense collaboration of a small group of individuals, and efforts to unequivocally assign ideas to unique individuals seem rather to reflect a Western prejudice about the importance of the individual (carried to an extreme in America) than to provide a relevant guide to the body of ideas being examined, especially for a group so committed to the social nature of language and thought as the Bakhtin Circle. Both Vološinov and Medvedev suffered the consequences of publishing the work of the Bakhtin Circle under their names (Medvedev to the death) and we agree with Todorov (1984: 10) that "in such a context I would be most loath to deny him even partial authorship of works for which he died." Furthermore, Bakhtin's theory recognizes any meaning-making process as always cooperative and, therefore, his co-authors and friends deserve from us the credit that his recognizes.

12 For more detailed commentary on Vygotsky, and his relevance to contemporary social theory, see Cole (1985), Laboratory of Comparative Human Cognition (1983), Wertsch (1979a, 1979b, 1981a, 1981b, 1985a, 1985b). For explicit comparison of the perspectives of Vygotsky and Bakhtin see Emerson (1983), Wertsch (1985b), and the special issue of the *Quarterly Newsletter of the Laboratory of Comparative Human Cognition* 5(1) (1983).

13 Important collections of research in conversation analysis can be found in Atkinson and Heritage (1984), Button and Lee (1987), Schenkein (1978), the special double issue of *Sociological Inquiry* edited by Zimmerman and West (1980), and a special issue of *Human Studies* (1986) edited by Button, Drew, and Heritage. Turn-taking is most extensively analyzed in Sacks, Schegloff, and Jefferson (1974). The investigation of phenomena within the turn, including the interdigitation of verbal and nonverbal behavior in that process, is dealt with at

length in C. Goodwin (1981) and Heath (1986). For an analysis both of basic ideas in ethnomethodology and of work in conversation analysis that grows from it see Heritage (1984). Levinson (1983) provides a review of conversation analysis that focuses on its contributions to pragmatics. For examples of how conversation analysis can be applied to the analysis of larger institutions see Atkinson (1984), Atkinson and Drew (1979) and Maynard (1984).

14 For more detailed exposition of how an action in conversation creates a framework of expectations that constrains and provides for the interpretation of subsequent action see Schegloff's (1968) discussion of **conditional relevance** and the reviews of work in conversation analysis provided in Heritage (1984, 1985) and Levinson (1983).

Acknowledgments

We are deeply indebted to Aaron Cicourel, Michael Cole, John Gumperz, Candy Goodwin, Dell Hymes, Adam Kendon, Stephen Levinson, Ronald Macaulay, Yutaka Sayeki, and members of a seminar at the Laboratory of Comparative Human Cognition, and two anonymous reviewers for comments on an earlier version of this chapter.

References

Allan, Keith. 1986. Hearers, Overhearers, and Clark & Carlson's Informative Analysis. *Language* 62: 509–17.

Ashby, W. Ross. 1956. *An Introduction to Cybernetics*. New York: John Wiley. 1960. *Design for a Brain*. New York: John Wiley.

Atkinson, J. Maxwell. 1984. *Our Masters' Voices: The Language and Body Language of Politics*. London: Methuen.

Atkinson, J. Maxwell, and Paul Drew. 1979. *Order in Court: The Organisation of Verbal Interaction in Judicial Settings*. London: Macmillan.

Atkinson, J. Maxwell, and John Heritage (eds.). 1984. *Structures of Social Action*. Cambridge: Cambridge University Press.

Austin, J. L. 1962. *How To Do Things With Words*. Oxford: Clarendon Press.

Bach, Kent, and Robert M. Harnish. 1979. *Linguistic Communication and Speech Acts*. Cambridge, Mass.: MIT Press.

Baker, G. P., and P. M. S. Hacker. 1984. *Language, Sense & Nonsense*. Oxford: Blackwell.

Bakhtin, Mikhail. 1981. *The Dialogic Imagination: Four Essays*, ed. M. Holquist, trans. C. Emerson and M. Holquist. Austin: University of Texas Press.
    1984. *Problems of Dostoevsky's Poetics*. Ed. and trans. C. Emerson. Introduction by Wayne C. Booth. Minneapolis: University of Minnesota Press.

Bar-Hillel, Yehoshua. 1954. Indexical Expressions. *Mind* 63: 359–79.

Bateson, Gregory. 1972. *Steps to an Ecology of Mind*. New York: Ballantine Books.

Bauman, Richard. 1977. *Verbal Art as Performance*. Rowley, Mass.: Newbury House.
    1986. *Story, Performance, and Event*. Cambridge: Cambridge University Press.

Bauman, Richard, and Joel Sherzer. 1974. *Explorations in the Ethnography of Speaking*. Cambridge: Cambridge University Press.
Bloch, M. 1975. *Political Language and Oratory in Traditional Society*. New York: Academic Press.
Bloomfield, Leonard. 1946. *Language*. New York: Henry Holt and Company.
Brenneis, Donald. 1978. The Matter of Talk: Political Performance in Bhatgaon. *Language in Society* 7: 159–70.
   1986. The Fiji Pancayat as Therapeutic Discourse. *IPrA Papers in Pragmatics* 1 (1): 55–78.
   1987. Discourse and the Definition of Dispute. Paper presented at the 1987 conference of the International Pragmatics Association, Antwerp.
Brenneis, Donald Lawrence, and Fred R. Myers. 1984. *Dangerous Words: Language and Politics in the Pacific*. New York: New York University Press.
Buckley, Walter (ed.). 1968. *Modern Systems Research for the Behavioral Scientist*. Chicago: Aldine Publishing Company.
Button, Graham, Paul Drew, and John Heritage (eds.). 1986. *Human Studies: Special Issue*. Dordrecht, the Netherlands: Martinus Nijhoff.
Button, Graham, and John R. Lee (eds.). 1987. *Talk and Social Organisation*. Clevedon, England: Multilingual Matters.
Carnap, Rudolf. 1942. *Introduction to Semantics*. Cambridge, Mass.: Harvard University Press.
Cicourel, Aaron V. 1964. *Method and Measurement in Sociology*. New York: Free Press.
   1968. *The Social Organization of Juvenile Justice*. New York: Wiley.
   1973. *Cognitive Sociology*. Harmondsworth: Penguin.
   1974. *Theory and Method in a Study of Argentine Fertility*. New York: Wiley.
Cicourel, Aaron V., and J. I. Kitsuse. 1963. *The Educational Decision Makers*. New York: Bobbs Merrill.
Cicourel, Aaron *et al.* 1974. *Language Use and School Performance*. New York: Academic Press.
Clark, Herbert H. 1982. The Relevance of Common Ground: Comments on Sperber and Wilson's Paper, in *Mutual Knowledge*, ed. Neil V. Smith, pp. 124–7. New York: Academic Press.
   1986. What is Said to Whom: A Rejoinder to Allan. *Language* 62: 518–29.
Clark, Herbert H., and Thomas B. Carlson. 1982. Hearers and Speech Acts. *Language* 58: 332–73.
Clark, Katerina, and Michael Holquist. 1984. *Mikhail Bakhtin*. Cambridge, Mass.: Harvard University Press.
Cole, Michael. 1985. The Zone of Proximal Development: Where Culture and Cognition Create Each Other, in Wertsch (1985a), pp. 146–161.
Cole, Michael and Peg Griffin (eds.). 1987. *Contextual Factors in Education: Improving Science and Mathematics Education for Minorities and Women*. Madison, Wisconsin: Wisconsin Center for Education Research, School of Education, University of Wisconsin-Madison.
Cook-Gumperz, Jenny (ed.). 1986. *The Social Construction of Literacy*. Cambridge: Cambridge University Press.
Cook-Gumperz, Jenny, William A. Corsaro, and Jurgen Streeck (eds.). 1986. *Children's Worlds and Children's Language*. Berlin: Mouton de Gruyter.
Cooreman, A. M. 1987. *Transitivity and Discourse Continuity*. Berlin: Mouton de Gruyter.
Du Bois, John W. 1987. Meaning Without Intention: Lessons from Divination. *IPrA Papers in Pragmatics* 1(2): 80–122.

Duranti, Alessandro. 1981. *The Samoan Fono: A Sociolinguistic Study*. Pacific Linguistics Monographs, Series B, Vol. 80. Canberra: Australian National University, Department of Linguistics.

1984. *Lauga* and *Talanoaga*: Two Speech Genres in a Samoan Political Event, in Brenneis and Myers (1984), pp. 217–37.

1985. Sociocultural Dimensions of Discourse, in *Handbook of Discourse Analysis*. Vol. 1: Disciplines of Discourse, ed. Teun A. Van Dijk, pp. 193–230. New York: Academic Press.

1986. The Audience as Co-Author: An Introduction. *Text* 6(3) 239–47.

1988a. Intentions, Language and Social Action in a Samoan Context. *Journal of Pragmatics* 12: 13–33.

1988b. The Ethnography of Speaking: Toward a Linguistics of the Praxis, in *Linguistics: The Cambridge Survey. Vol. IV; Language: The Socio-Cultural Context*, ed. T. Newmeyer, pp. 210–28. Cambridge: Cambridge University Press.

In press. Four Properties of Speech-in-Interaction and the Notion of Translocutionary Act, in *Proceedings of the 1987 International Pragmatics Conference*, ed. Jef Verschueren. Amsterdam: Benjamins.

Duranti, Alessandro, and Donald Brenneis (eds.). 1986. *The Audience as Co-Author, Special Issue of Text* (6[3]). New York: Mouton de Gruyter.

Dyer, M. G. 1983. *In-Depth Understanding: A Computer Model of Integrated Processing for Narrative Comprehension*. Cambridge, Mass.: MIT Press.

Emerson, Caryl. 1983, Bakhtin and Vygotsky on Internalization in Language. *The Quarterly Newsletter of the Laboratory of Comparative Human Cognition* 5(1): 9–13.

Erickson, Frederick. 1979. Talking Down: Some Cultural Sources of Miscommunication in Interracial Interviews, in *Nonverbal Communication*, ed. Aaron Wolfgang, pp. 99–126. New York: Academic Press.

1982. Classroom Discourse as Improvisation: Relationships between Academic Task and Structure and Social Participation Structure in Lessons, in *Communicating in the Classroom*, ed. L. C. Wilkinson, pp. 153–81. New York: Academic Press.

Erickson, Frederick, and Jeffrey Shultz. 1981. *The Counselor as Gatekeeper: Social Interaction in Interviews*. New York: Academic Press.

Firth, J. R. 1957. *Papers in Linguistics*. Oxford: Oxford University Press.

Garfinkel, Harold. 1967. *Studies in Ethnomethodology*. Englewood Cliffs, N. J.: Prentice-Hall.

Garfinkel, Harold, Michael Lynch, and Eric Livingston. 1981. The Work of a Discovering Science Construed with Materials from the Optically Discovered Pulsar. *Phil. Soc. Sci.* 11: 131–58.

Garfinkel, Harold, and Harvey Sacks. 1970. On Formal Structures of Practical Actions, in *Theoretical Sociology*, ed. J. D. McKinney and E. A. Tiryakian, pp. 337–66. New York: Appleton-Century-Crofts.

Gazdar, Gerald. 1979. *Pragmatics: Implicature, Presupposition, and Logical Form*. London: Academic Press.

Givón, Talmy. 1983. *Topic Continuity in Discourse: A Quantitative Cross-Language Study*. Amsterdam: Benjamins.

Goffman, Erving. 1961. *Encounters: Two Studies in the Sociology of Interaction*. Indianapolis: Bobbs-Merrill.

1963. *Behaviour in Public Places: Notes on the Social Organization of Gatherings*. New York: Free Press.

1967. *Interaction Ritual: Essays in Face to Face Behavior*. Garden City, New York: Doubleday.

1971. *Relations in Public: Microstudies of the Public Order*. New York: Harper and Row.

1974. *Frame Analysis: An Essay on the Organization of Experience*. New York: Harper and Row.

1981. *Forms of Talk*. Philadelphia: University of Pennsylvania Press.

Goodwin, Charles. 1979. The Interactive Construction of a Sentence in Natural Conversation, in *Everyday Language: Studies in Ethnomethodology*, ed. George Psathas, pp. 97–121. New York: Irvington Publishers.

1981. *Conversational Organization: Interaction Between Speakers and Hearers*. New York: Academic Press.

1984. Notes on Story Structure and the Organization of Participation, in Atkinson and Heritage (1984), pp. 225–46.

1986. Audience Diversity, Participation and Interpretation. *Text* 6(3): 283–316.

1987. Unilateral Departure, in Button and Lee (1987), pp. 206–16.

Goodwin, Charles, and Marjorie Harness Goodwin. 1989. Context, Activity and Participation, in *The Contextualization of Language*, ed. Peter Auer and Aldo di Luzio. Amsterdam: Benjamins.

Goodwin, Marjorie Harness. 1982a. Processes of Dispute Management Among Urban Black Children. *American Ethnologist* 9: 76–96.

1982b. 'Instigating': Storytelling as a Social Process. *American Ethnologist* 9: 799–819.

1990. *He-Said-She-Said: Talk as Social Organization among Black Children*. Bloomington: Indiana University Press.

Griffin, Peg, and Hugh Mehan. 1981. Sense and Ritual in Classroom Discourse, in *Conversational Routine: Explorations in Standardized Communication Situations and Prepatterned Speech*, ed. F. Coulmas. The Hague: Mouton.

Gumperz, John J. 1982a. *Discourse Strategies*. Cambridge: Cambridge University Press.

(ed.). 1982b. *Language and Social Identity*. Cambridge: Cambridge University Press.

Gumperz, John J., and Dell Hymes (eds.). 1972. *Directions in Sociolinguistics: The Ethnography of Communication*. New York: Holt, Rinehart and Winston.

Habermas, Jurgen. 1970. Toward a Theory of Communicative Competence, in *Recent Sociology No. 2*, ed. Hans Peter Dreitzel, pp. 114–48. New York: Macmillan.

Halliday, M. A. K. 1973. *Explorations in the Functions of Language*. London: Arnold.

Halliday, M. A. K., and Ruqaiya Hasan. 1976. *Cohesion in English*. London: Longman.

Hanks, William F. 1987. Discourse Genres in a Theory of Practice. *American Ethnologist* 14(4): 668–92.

1990. *Referential Practice: Language and Lived Space among the Maya*. Chicago: University of Chicago Press.

Haviland, John B. 1986. 'Con Buenos Chiles': Talk, Targets and Teasing in Zinacantan. *Text* 6(3): 249–82.

Heath, Christian. 1984. Talk and Recipiency: Sequential Organization in Speech and Body Movement, in Atkinson and Heritage (1984), pp. 247–265.

1986. *Body Movement and Speech in Medical Interaction*. Cambridge: Cambridge University Press.

Heim, I. R. 1981. The Semantics of Definite and Indefinite Noun Phrases. Ph. D. dissertation, Department of Linguistics, University of Massachusetts, Amherst (reproduced by the graduate students association, University of Massachusetts at Amherst).

Heritage, John. 1984. *Garfinkel and Ethnomethodology.* Cambridge: Polity Press.
    1985. Recent Developments in Conversation Analysis. *Sociolinguistics News-
    letter* 15 (1): 1–19.
Heritage, John, and J. Maxwell Atkinson. 1984. Introduction to Atkinson and
    Heritage (1984), pp. 1–16.
Hill, Jane H. 1985. The Grammar of Consciousness and the Consciousness of
    Grammar. *American Ethnologist* 12: 725–37.
Hopper, Paul, and Sandra A. Thompson. 1980. Transivitity in Grammar and
    Discourse. *Language* 56: 251–99.
Hymes, Dell. 1964. *Language in Culture and Society.* New York: Harper and Row.
    1972. Models of the Interaction of Language and Social Life, in Gumperz and
    Hymes (1972), pp. 35–71. New York: Holt, Rinehart and Winston.
    1974. *Foundations in Sociolinguistics: An Ethnographic Approach.* Philadelphia:
    University of Pennsylvania Press.
Jakobson, Roman. 1960. Concluding Statement: Linguistics and Poetics, in *Style in
    Language*, ed. Thomas A. Sebeok, pp. 350–77. Cambridge, Mass.: MIT Press.
Jefferson, Gail. 1978. Sequential Aspects of Storytelling in Conversation, in
    Schenkein (1978), pp. 219–48. New York: Academic Press.
    1979. A Technique for Inviting Laughter and its Subsequent Acceptance/
    Declination, in *Everyday Language: Studies in Ethnomethodology*, ed.
    George Psathas, pp. 79–96. New York: Irvington Publishers.
Johnson, K. 1989. Miscommunication between Hearing and Deaf Participants (via
    the Interpreter) in a College Classroom Setting. MA thesis, Department of
    Anthropology, UCLA.
Kamp, Hans. 1981. A Theory of Truth and Semantic Interpretation, in *Formal
    Methods in the Studies of Language, Vol. 1*, ed. Groenendijk, T. Janssen, and
    M. Stokhof. Amsterdam: Mathematical Centre.
Kendon, Adam. 1982. The Organization of Behavior in Face-to-Face Interaction:
    Observations on the Development of a Methodology, in *Handbook of
    Methods in Nonverbal Behavior Research*, ed. Klaus R. Scherer and Paul
    Ekman, pp. 440–505. Cambridge: Cambridge University Press.
Knorr-Cetina, Karin D. Mulkay, and Michael Mulkay (eds.). 1983. *Science
    Observed: Perspectives on the Social Study of Science.* Beverly Hills: Sage.
Kristeva, Julia. 1981. *Desire in Language: A Semiotic Approach to Literature and
    Art*, trans. T. Gora, A. Jardine, and L. S. Roudiez. New York: Columbia
    University Press.
Laboratory of Comparative Human Cognition. 1983. Culture and Cognitive
    Development, in *Handbook of Child Psychology, Vol. 1: History, Theory and
    Method*, ed. W. Kessen. New York: Wiley.
Labov, William. 1966. *The Social Stratification of English in New York City.*
    Washington, D.C: Center for Applied Linguistics.
    1970. *The Study of Nonstandard English.* Champaign, Ill.: National Council of
    Teachers.
    1972a. *Language in the Inner City: Studies in the Black English Vernacular.*
    Philadelphia: University of Pennsylvania Press.
    1972b. *Sociolinguistic Patterns.* Philadelphia: University of Pennsylvania Press.
Lave, Jean. 1988. *Cognition in Practice.* Cambridge: Cambridge University Press.
Leech, Geoffrey N. 1983. *Principles of Pragmatics.* London: Longman.
Leont'ev, A. N. 1981a. The Problem of Activity in Psychology, in *The Concept of
    Activity in Soviet Psychology*, ed. James V. Wertsch, pp. 37–71. Armonk, NY:
    M. E. Sharpe.
    1981b. *Problems of the Development of the Mind.* Moscow: Progress Publishers.

Levinson, Stephen. 1979. Activity Types and Language. *Linguistics* 17: 365–99.
  1983. *Pragmatics*. Cambridge: Cambridge University Press.
  1987. Putting Linguistics on a Proper Footing: Explorations in Goffman's Concepts of Participation, in *Goffman: An Interdisciplinary Appreciation*, ed. Paul Drew and Anthony J. Wootton, pp. 161–227. Cambridge: Polity Press.
Levi-Strauss, Claude. 1963. *Structural Anthropology*. New York: Basic Books.
Lewis, D. 1973. *Counterfactuals*. Oxford: Blackwell.
  1986, *On the Plurality of Worlds*. Oxford: Blackwell.
Luria, A. R. 1979. *The Making of Mind: A Personal Account of Soviet Psychology*, ed. M. Cole and S. Cole. Cambridge Mass.: Harvard University Press.
Lynch, Michael E. 1982. Technical Work and Critical Inquiry: Investigations in a Scientific Laboratory. *Social Studies of Science* 12: 499–533.
  1988. The Externalized Retina: Selection and Mathematization in the Visual Documentation of Objects in the Life Sciences. *Human Studies* 11: 201–34.
Lynch, Michael E., Eric Livingston and Harold Garfinkel. 1983. Temporal Order in Laboratory Work, in Knorr-Cetina, Mulkay and Mulkay (1983), pp. 205–38.
Macaulay, Ronald. 1987. Polyphonic Monologues: Quoted Direct Speech in Oral Narratives. *IPrA Papers in Pragmatics* 1 (2): 1–34.
Malinowski, Bronislaw. 1923. The Problem of Meaning in Primitive Languages, in *The Meaning of Meaning*, ed. C. K. Ogden and I. A. Richards, pp. 296–336. New York: Harcourt, Brace and World, Inc.
  1935. *Coral Gardens and their magic*, 2 vols. London: Allen and Unwin.
Mandler, J. H. 1979. Categorical and Schematic Organization in Memory, in *Memory Organization and Structure*, ed. C. K. Puff, New York: Academic Press.
Maynard, Douglas W. 1984. The Structure of Discourse in Misdemeanor Plea Bargaining. *Law & Society Review* 18(1): 75–104.
McDermott, R. P. 1976. Kids Make Sense: An Ethnographic Account of the Interactional Management of Success and Failure of One First-Grade Classroom. Unpublished Ph.D. dissertation, Stanford University.
McDermott, R. P., and K. Gospodinoff. 1979. Social Contexts for Ethnic Borders and School Failure, in *Nonverbal Behavior: Applications and Cultural Implications*, ed. A. Wolfgang, pp. 175–96. New York: Academic Press.
McDermott, R. P., K. Gospodinoff, and J. Aron. 1978. Criteria for an Ethnographically Adequate Description of Concerted Activities and their Contexts. *Semiotica* 24: 245–75.
Moerman, Michael. 1988. *Talking Culture: Ethnography and Conversation Analysis*. Philadelphia: University of Pennsylvania Press.
Morris, C. W. 1938. Foundations of the Theory of Signs, in *International Encyclopedia of Unified Science*, ed. O. Neurath, R. Carnap, and C. Morris, pp. 77–138. Chicago: University of Chicago Press.
Nelson, K. 1978. How Young Children Represent Knowledge of their World in and out of Language, in *Children's Thinking: What Develops?*, ed. R. S. Siegler. Hillsdale, NJ: Erlbaum.
  1981. Social Cognition in a Script Framework, in *Social Cognitive Development*, ed. J. H. Flavell and L. Ross. Cambridge: Cambridge University Press.
Newman, Denis, Peg Griffin and Michael Cole. 1984. Social Constraints in Laboratory and Classroom Tasks. In *Everyday Cognition: Its Development in Social Context*, ed. Barbara Rogoff and Jean Lave, pp. 172–93. Cambridge, Mass.: Harvard University Press.

Ochs, Elinor. 1979. Introduction: What Child Language Can Contribute to Pragmatics, in *Developmental Pragmatics*, ed. Elinor Ochs and Bambi B. Schieffelin, pp. 1–17. New York: Academic Press.
   1983. Cultural Dimensions of Language Acquisition, in *Acquiring Conversational Competence*, ed. Elinor Ochs and Bambi B. Schieffelin, pp. 185–191. Boston: Routledge and Kegan Paul.
   1986. Introduction to *Language Socialization across Cultures*, ed. Bambi B. Schieffelin and Elinor Ochs, pp. 1–13. New York: Cambridge University Press.
   1988. *Culture and Language Development: Language Acquisition and Language Socialization in a Samoan Village*. Cambridge: Cambridge University Press.
Ochs, Elinor, and Bambi B. Schieffelin. 1984. Language Socialization: Three Developmental Stories, in *Culture Theory: Essays on Mind, Self, and Emotion*, ed. Richard A. Shweder and R. A. LeVine, pp. 276–320. Cambridge: Cambridge University Press.
Ochs, Elinor, Bambi B. Schieffelin, and Martha Platt. 1979. Propositions across Utterances and Speakers, in *Developmental Pragmatics*, ed. Elinor Ochs and Bambi Schieffelin, pp. 251–68. New York: Academic Press.
Ochs, Elinor, Ruth Smith, and Carolyn Taylor. 1988. Detective Stories at Dinnertime: Problem-Solving through Co-Narration. Prepared for the American Ethnological Society Annual Meetings, Symposium on Narrative Resources for the Creation of Order and Disorder, St. Louis, Missouri, March 25, 1988.
Parisi, Domenico, and Cristiano Castelfranchi. 1976. *Discourse as a Hierarchy of Goals*. Working Paper no. 54–5. Urbino: Centro Internazionale di Semiotica e Linguistica.
Piaget, Jean. 1959. *The Language and Thought of the Child*. London: Routledge and Kegan Paul. Originally published in 1926.
Romaine, Suzanne. 1982. *Sociolinguistic Variation in Speech Communities*. London: Arnold.
Rosaldo, Michelle Z. 1982. The Things We Do with Words: Ilongot Speech Acts and Speech Act Theory in Philosophy. *Language in Society* 11: 203–37.
Sacks, Harvey. 1974. An Analysis of the Course of a Joke's Telling in Conversation, in Bauman and Sherzer (1974), pp. 337–53.
Sacks, Harvey, Emanuel A. Schegloff, and Gail Jefferson. 1974. A Simplest Systematics for the Organization of Turn-Taking for Conversation. *Language* 50: 696–735.
Sankoff, Gillian. 1980. *The Social Life of Language*. Philadelphia: University of Pennsylvania Press.
Schank, R. C., and R. P. Abelson. 1977. *Scripts, Plans, Goals, and Understanding*. Hillsdale, NJ: Erlbaum.
Schank, R. C., and C. K. Riesbeck. 1981. *Inside Computer Understanding: Five Programs Plus Miniatures*. Hillsdale, NJ: Erlbaum.
Scheflen, Albert E. 1963. Communication and Regulation in Psychotherapy. *Psychiatry* 26: 126–36.
   1964. The Significance of Posture in Communication Systems. *Psychiatry* 27: 316–31.
   1966. Natural History Method in Psychotherapy, in *Methods of Research in Psychotherapy*, ed. L. A. Gottschalk and A. H. Auerbach. New York: Appleton-Century-Crofts.
   1971. Living Space in an Urban Ghetto. *Family Processes* 10(4): 429–50.
   1973. *Communicational Structure: Analysis of a Psychotherapy Transaction*. Bloomington: Indiana University Press.

Schegloff, Emanuel A. 1968. Sequencing in Conversational Openings. *American Anthropologist* 70: 1075–95.

1987. Between Macro and Micro: Contexts and Other Connections, in *The Micro-Macro Link*, ed. J. Alexander, B. Giesen, R. Munch and N. Smelser, pp. 207–34. Berkeley: University of California Press.

Schenkein, Jim (ed.). 1978. *Studies in the Organization of Conversational Interaction*. New York: Academic Press.

Schieffelin, Bambi B. 1986. Context and Interpretation in Kaluli Story Telling. Paper presented at the invited session on Rethinking Context at the 1986 Annual Meeting of the American Anthropological Association.

Schieffelin, Bambi B., and Elinor Ochs (eds.). 1986. *Language Socialization across Cultures*. New York: Cambridge University Press.

Scribner, Sylvia. 1984. Studying Working Intelligence, in *Everyday Cognition: Its Development in Social Context*, ed. Barbara Rogoff and Jean Lave, pp. 9–40. Cambridge, Mass.: Harvard University Press.

Scribner, Sylvia, and Michael Cole. 1981. *Psychology of Literacy*. Cambridge, Mass.: Harvard University Press.

Searle, John R. 1969. *Speech Acts*. Cambridge: Cambridge University Press.

1983. *Intentionality: An Essay in the Philosophy of Mind*. Cambridge: Cambridge University Press.

Sherzer, Joel. 1983. *Kuna Ways of Speaking: An Ethnographic Perspective*. Austin: University of Texas Press.

Silverstein, Michael. 1979. Language Structure and Linguistic Ideology, in *The Elements: A Parasession on Linguistic Units and Levels*, ed. P. R. Clyne, W. F. Hanks, and C. L. Hofbauer, pp. 193–247. Chicago: Chicago Linguistic Society.

1985a. The Culture of Language in Chinookan Narrative Texts: or, On saying that . . . in Chinookan, in *Grammar Inside and Outside the Clause*, ed. J. Nichols and A. Woodbury. Cambridge: Cambridge University Press.

1985b. The Functional Stratification of Language and Ontogenesis, in Wertsch (1985a), pp. 205–235.

Sperber, Dan, and Deidre Wilson. 1982a. Mutual Knowledge and Relevance in Theories of Comprehension, in *Mutual Knowledge*, ed. Neil V. Smith, pp. 61–85. New York: Academic Press.

1982b. Reply to Clark, in *Mutual Knowledge*, ed. Neil V. Smith, pp. 128–31. New York: Academic Press.

Stalnaker, R. C. 1979. Assertion, in *Syntax and Semantics. Vol. 9: Pragmatics*, ed. P. Cole, pp. 315–32. New York: Academic Press.

Strawson, P. F. 1964. Intention and Convention in Speech Acts. *Philosophical Review* 73: 439–60.

Streeck, Jürgen. 1980. Speech Acts in Interaction: A Critique of Searle. *Discourse Processes* 3: 133–54.

1984. Embodied Contexts, Transcontextuals, and the Timing of Speech Acts. *Journal of Pragmatics* 8: 113–37.

Suchman, Lucy A. 1987. *Plans and Situated Actions: The Problem of Human Machine Communication*. Cambridge: Cambridge University Press.

Tedlock, Dennis. 1983. *The Spoken Word and the Work of Interpretation*. Philadelphia: University of Pennsylvania Press.

Todorov, Tzvetan. 1984. *Mikhail Bakhtin: The Dialogical Principle*, trans. Wlad Godzich. Minneapolis: University of Minnesota Press.

Tompkins, Jane P. (ed.). 1980. *Reader–Response Criticism: From Formalism to Post-Structuralism*. Baltimore: The Johns-Hopkins University Press.

Verschueren, Jef. 1983. On Bugaslawski on Promise. *Journal of Pragmatics* 7: 629–32.

Vološinov, Valentin Nikolaevic. 1973. *Marxism and the Philosophy of Language*, trans. Ladislav Matejka and I. R. Titunik. New York: Seminar Press. (First published 1929 and 1930.)

Vygotsky, Lev Semenovich, 1962. *Thought and Language*, trans. Eugenia Hanfmann and Gertrude Vaker, Cambridge, Mass.: M.I.T. Press.

1978. *Mind in Society*. Cambridge, Mass.: Harvard University Press.

Wertsch, James V. 1979a. The Regulation of Human Action and the Origins of Inner Speech, in *The Development of Self-Regulation Through Speech*, ed. G. Zivin. New York: Wiley.

1979b. From Social Interaction to Higher Psychological Processes: A Clarification and Application of Vygotsky's Theory. Human Development 22: 1–22.

1981a. The Concept of Activity in Soviet Psychology: An Introduction, in *The Concept of Activity in Soviet Psychology*, ed. James V. Wertsch, pp. 3–36. Armonk, NY: M. E. Sharpe.

1981b. Trends in Soviet Cognitive Psychology. *Storia e critica della psicologia* 2(2).

1985a. *Culture, Communication, and Cognition: Vygotskian Perspectives.* Cambridge: Cambridge University Press.

1985b. *Vygotsky and the Social Formation of Mind*. Cambridge Mass.: Harvard University Press.

Wittgenstein, Ludwig. 1922. *Tractatus Logico-Philosophicus*, reprinted in 1961 in a new translation by D. F. Pears and B. F. McGuinnes. London: Routledge and Kegan Paul.

1958. *Philosophical Investigations*, ed. G. E. M. Anscombe and R. Rhees, trans. G. E. M. Anscombe, 2nd edition, Oxford: Blackwell.

Zimmerman, Don H., and Candace West (eds.). 1980. *Sociological Inquiry: Special Double Issue on Language and Social Interaction*.

2 The indexical ground of deictic reference

WILLIAM F. HANKS

Editors' introduction

William F. Hanks received a joint Ph.D. in Anthropology and Linguistics from the University of Chicago, where he is currently Associate Professor of Anthropology. His research interests encompass both contemporary and classical Mayan languages. In his work Hanks has attempted to incorporate central processes implicated in the organization of human interaction into the description and analysis of both cultural phenomena and linguistic structure, investigating for example the interactive basis of Maya divination (1984, 1988, 1990). He also has a strong interest in the social and historical constitution of speech forms. For example, drawing on the work of both Bakhtin and Bourdieu, he has investigated how new language genres were constituted in Mayan society just after the Spanish conquest as part of the process through which Mayan leaders adapted to the new social conditions created by the conquest (Hanks 1987).

Much of Hanks' analysis of language structure has focused on **deixis**. Deictic expressions are terms such as "here" and "over there" which point to features of the surrounding context. In that deictic terms act as pointers they are sometimes called "indexical expressions." The referents of deictic expressions are constantly shifting as the relationship between utterance and context changes. For example, within a conversation the person identified as "I" changes as speakers change (and in much more complex ways when a speaker quotes the talk of another – see Goffman 1974, 1981; Hanks 1990; and Vološinov 1973 for analysis of the framing issues involved in such reported speech). The term "shifter" is thus also used to refer to deictic expressions. The properties of shifters, and their relevance to basic questions about how language is organized, have received extensive analysis in the work of Michael Silverstein (1976, 1985). The existence of deictic expressions within language raises questions about the extent to which it is proper or appropriate to analyze language as a self-contained autonomous system. The early Greeks recognized that the truthfulness of a sentence such as "I am an initiate" could not be determined just by examining the sentence itself but required additional knowledge about who was speaking, etc., and that indeed even for a single speaker the sentence might be true at some points in his or her life (after he or she had undergone the initiation ceremony) but not at others (when he or she was a young child). Such issues apply even to the semantic interpretation of individual words. Thus Heritage (1984) notes that the sense of "nice" in the

43

expression "That's a nice one" changes radically if the entity being talked about is a head of lettuce in a greengrocer's shop as opposed to a diamond ring in a jeweler's window, or a photograph of one's host. In each of these different situations a listener fills in the sense of "nice" with a very different array of features (e.g. while freshness is quite relevant to how the lettuce is being assessed it is completely irrelevant to the evaluation of a diamond ring). Deictic expressions thus pose with particular clarity the issue of how analysis of language requires that features of context be taken into consideration. Indeed alternative approaches to the study of language sometimes diverge most sharply on precisely this issue. Thus for some formal linguists and philosophers the contextual issues raised by indexical expressions are treated as simply a troublesome residue of problems that can be safely ignored while research proceeds on the analysis of language as a formal, autonomous system. On the other hand, for ethnomethodologists (Cicourel 1973, this volume; Garfinkel 1967; Garfinkel and Sacks 1970; Heritage 1984) indexicality is central to the organization of language, something that can never be erased or overcome, and precisely what constitutes language as an essentially context-bound, interactively organized phenomenon. Though ethnomethodology and conversation analysis take the social articulation of natural language as their core subject matter (indeed for Garfinkel and Sacks [1970] mastery of natural language constitutes the defining attribute of a competent social actor), these research enterprises have their roots in sociology not linguistics. The effect of this is that the field of linguistics itself has remained largely immune to the argument that interactive phenomena are central to the organization of language (indeed this possibility was rather vehemently rejected by Saussure [1959] when he delimited the subject matter of modern linguistics).

   In the present chapter Hanks provides a major rethinking of deixis, one that integrates basic properties of human interaction into the analysis of core elements of language structure. Indeed he demonstrates that "verbal deixis is a central aspect of the social matrix of orientation and perception through which speakers produce context." Moreover Hanks' development of the figure/ground contrast for the analysis of deixis provides important new conceptual tools for the study of context (cf. Chapter 1). The notion of indexical ground elaborated by Hanks is dynamic, subtle, and productive. The indexical ground is intimately tied to basic processes of human interaction and participant frameworks. The relationships that are encoded in deictic usage "make up what might be called an implicit playing field for interaction – a set of positions in deictic space, along with expectations about how actors occupy these positions over the course of talk." However, while the deictic properties of this field provide a template for interaction, the indexical ground itself is constituted and deployed by participants in a dynamic fashion through their ongoing interaction with each other. The indexical ground thus both shapes interaction, and is shaped by those very same interactive processes that it helps to constitute. This field is capable of systematic transformation, a process illustrated quite clearly in **reported speech** (the phenomenon of reported speech is also given considerable attention from a variety of perspectives in a number of other chapters in this volume, including Bauman, Basso, the Goodwins, and Lindstrom). The analysis Hanks makes in this chapter of how participant frameworks within the indexical ground can be transformed is elaborated considerably in his recent book, *Referential Practice* (1990). In its analysis of how linguistic choices can both define context and be defined by it, Hanks' chapter has clear ties to Duranti's in this volume. A key property of the indexical ground is the way in which it encompasses and encodes the differential **access** that participants have to relevant events (see also the Goodwins' chapter in this volume): "What the relational features in deictics categorize is this accessibility of referents, in terms of interactants' knowledge, orientation of attention, spatial and temporal location, prior speech, and current sensory awareness . . ." The notions of symmetry and asymmetry in perspectives developed by Hanks here, and the way in which this provides a framework for investigating what participants assume each other knows and is known in common, is quite relevant to analysis of reciprocity in participants' perspectives and the organization of shared background knowledge, topics which are central themes in phenomenological sociology and ethnomethodology (cf. Cicourel 1973, this volume; Garfinkel 1967; Heritage 1984; Schutz 1971). In common with this tradition, and almost all of the chapters in this volume, Hanks draws attention to the dynamic character of both the indexical ground and the context constituted through it.

References

Cicourel, Aaron V. 1973. *Cognitive Sociology*. Harmondsworth: Penguin.

Garfinkel, Harold. 1967. *Studies in Ethnomethodology*. Englewood Cliffs, NJ: Prentice-Hall.

Garfinkel, Harold, and Harvey Sacks. 1970. On Formal Structures of Practical Actions, in *Theoretical Sociology*, ed. J. D. McKinney and E. A. Tiryakian, pp. 337–66. New York: Appleton-Century-Crofts.

Goffman, Erving. 1974. *Frame Analysis: An Essay on the Organization of Experience*. New York: Harper and Row.

1981. *Forms of Talk*. Philadelphia: University of Pennsylvania Press.

Hanks, William F. 1984. Sanctification, Structure, and Experience in a Yucatec Ritual Event. *Journal of American Folklore* 97 (384): 131–66.

1987. Discourse Genres in a Theory of Practice. *American Ethnologist* 14(4): 668–92.

1988. Word and Image in a Semiotic Perspective, in *Word and Image in Mayan Culture: Explorations in Language, Writing and Representation*, ed. William F. Hanks and Don S. Rice, Salt Lake City: University of Utah Press.

1990. *Referential Practice: Language and Lived Space among the Maya*. Chicago: University of Chicago Press.

Heritage, John. 1984. *Garfinkel and Ethnomethodology*. Cambridge: Polity Press.

Saussure, Ferdinand de. 1959. *Course in General Linguistics*, ed. Charles Bally and Albert Sechehaye, in collaboration with Albert Riedlinger, trans. from the French by Wade Baskin. New York: Philosophical Library.

Schutz, Alfred. 1971. *Collected Papers I: The Problem of Social Reality*, ed. and introduced by Maurice Natanson. The Hague: Martinus Nijhoff.

Silverstein, Michael. 1976. Shifters, Linguistic Categories, and Cultural Description, in *Meaning in Anthropology*, ed. Keith H. Basso and Henry A. Selby, pp. 11–56. Albuquerque: University of New Mexico Press.

1985. The Functional Stratification of Language and Ontogenesis, in *Culture, Communication and Cognition: Vygotskian Perspectives*, ed. James V. Wertsch, pp. 205–35. Cambridge: Cambridge University Press.

Vološinov, Valentin Nikolaevic. 1973. *Marxism and the Philosophy of Language*, trans. Ladislav Matejka and I. R. Titunik. New York: Seminar Press. (First published 1929 and 1930.)

The indexical ground of deictic reference

1   Introduction

When viewed as transcriptions of typical American English utterances, the sentences in (1–5) illustrate what is commonly called verbal "deixis," and the items in boldface belong to the class of linguistic forms called "deictics."

(1) **You** and **I** could meet **here** Tuesday.
(2) **Now you** tell **me this**?
(3) **Here**, take **it**.
(4) **He** told **her** about **it over there**.
(5) **There**, does **that** make **you** happy?

There is widespread agreement in the literature that deixis and the linguistic forms that subserve it play a central role in the routine use and understanding of language. Levinson (1983: 54) described it as "[the] single most obvious way in which the relationship between language and context is reflected in the structures of languages themselves . . ." In a similar vein, Horn (1988: 116) notes that "the interaction between the context of utterance of an expression and the formal interpretation of elements within that expression constitutes a central domain of pragmatics, variously labelled deixis, indexicality or token-reflexivity."

Whereas both Levinson and Horn define deixis in such a way as to encompass an entire range of referential and non-referential functions of speech, from pronouns to regional accents, this chapter focuses on the more restricted class of referential usages of lexical deictics, such as the ones in (1-5). To see the difference, imagine that any of (1–5) is pronounced in an accent that identifies its speaker as being from a certain region or social stratum, or that (2) is rendered with prosody appropriate to an angry response, or that (1) were coded for deference to addressee as it might be in Javanese. All of these codings are indexical, but none is deictic for the purposes of this chapter. Rather, "deixis" designates a special variety of reference, sometimes called "demonstrative reference," which is limited both formally and functionally.

Formally, whereas Levinson's (1983) "social deixis" can be signaled by any aspect of utterance form whatsoever, deictics in the present sense are morphemes (or strings of morphemes) that in most languages make up closed paradigmatic sets. Standard examples include pronouns (1-5), demonstratives and articles (2, 4, 5), spatial adverbs (1, 4, 5), temporal adverbs (2), and presentative adverbs (3). In functional terms, these are what Jespersen (1965[1924]: 219) and Jakobson (1971[1957]) called "shifters", and Silverstein (1976) defined as "referential indexicals." Their basic communicative function is to individuate or single out objects of reference or address in terms of their relation to the current interactive context in which the utterance occurs. So a shifter such as "here" denotes a region of space by indicating that this region is proximal (or otherwise immediate) to the place in which the form is uttered. For Silverstein (1976) this relationship of correspondence was to be accounted for through rules of use linking contextual variables with deictic tokens, a formulation consistent with Horn's (1988: 116) "shifters or indexicals, [are] expressions whose meaning can best be viewed as a function from context to individual by assigning values to variables for speaker, hearer, time and place of utterance, style or register, purpose of speech act, etc."

But what are these contextual variables and how exactly are they related to the denotata picked out in deictic usage? If deictic context is segmentable in this way, how does it hang together as a whole? How is interactive context linguistically structured in acts of reference? It is noteworthy that Horn's list ends in an "etc.," suggesting that there might be an open-ended list of such variables. In similar fashion, ethnographies of speaking, as in Hymes (1974) and Silverstein (1976), have long proposed that speech events be decomposed into a number of segmentable components, typically symbolized as **Es** → {**Spkr, Adr, Loc, Time, Key. . . .**}. The problem is that such open-ended lists suggest that the components are coordinate and independent, and they leave us with the nagging uncertainty of never knowing whether the list is complete or whether yet more components are needed (cf. for instance Levinson's 1987 expansion of the set of participant roles, and decomposition of roles into features along the lines of distinctive features in phonology). Do components differ from utterance to utterance, context to context, language to language, or all of these? In examining individual utterances, how should one think of the relations between the components? A good description of deixis could help answer these questions.

It is widely recognized that all natural languages have deictics (Anderson and Keenan 1985, Benveniste 1974, Kuryłowicz 1972, Weinreich 1980), and that these forms constitute key points of juncture between grammar and context. Yet there has been relatively little in-depth description of actual usage, and available descriptive frameworks are partial and relatively coarse (cf. Levinson 1983). One result of this is that it is difficult if not impossible to do comparative research on deixis. As Irvine (1985: 574) observed in relation to studies of honorifics, indexical features tend to be erratically handled in standard descriptions, with inconsistencies and lack of appropriate data getting in the way of systematic comparison between languages (or even contexts in a single language).

Table 2.1. *Functional components of deixis*

Type	Role	Typical exemplar
Communicative	signal speech act value	Presentative, Directive, Referential, Phatic, Expressive
Characterizing	describe referent	Human, Animate, Regional/Extended, Punctual/Restricted, Static, Kinetic
Relational	signal relation referent-to-origo	Immediate, non-Immediate, Visible, Tactual, Inclusive, Exclusive, Discourse
Indexical	ground reference to origo in speech event	Speaker, Addressee, Speaker & Addressee, Anaphoric

In this chapter I try to show that deictics (under the present definition) share a distinctive semantic structure, which sets them apart from non-referential indexicals (such as status indicators) and also from other kinds of expressions that do combine reference with indexicality, but are nonetheless not deictics.[1] My aim is to get a clearer picture of the semantic and pragmatic mechanisms of deixis, and to contribute to a better metalanguage for pragmatic description and cross-linguistic comparison. Because deixis links language to context in distinguishable ways, the better we understand it, the more we know about context. In effect, the study of deixis provides privileged evidence for the ways that natural languages define interactive context by encoding pragmatic categories and forms of interaction in the grammar itself.

1.1   Functional heterogeneity of deixis

It is helpful by way of starting to summarize the kinds of information encoded in deictic forms. The first fact one confronts in trying to describe the conventional meanings of these forms is their functional heterogeneity. Table 2.1 displays in rough outline what I take to be the main types of information encoded in standard deictics.[2]

In saying that the information in Table 2.1 is **encoded**, I do not wish to assert that for any form it is possible to state a set of invariant features that remains constant across all of its uses. The features are not necessary and sufficient conditions on the proper usage of forms. Rather, they are defeasible aspects that conjointly characterize the range within which proper usage varies, and therefore the conventional **potential** of forms. Consider the different uses of "here" in (6–10).

(6)   Oh, it's just beautiful here! (sweeping arm gesture to countryside)
(7)   Here's a good one for ya'. (embarking on narrative)
(8)   John lives over here, but we live here. (pointing to small map)
(9)   Oh doctor, it hurts here. (hand on abdomen)
(10)   I'm over here! (shouted to companion through the woods)

Notice that whatever else is going on in these utterances, the word "here" in each contributes to an act of reference, and yet these acts seem quite different. The region referred to in (6) is of broad extent and includes both interlocutors, whereas the one in (10) is restricted to the speaker's place and excludes that of the addressee. Example (9) refers to a small segment of the body of its speaker, whereas (8) is a deferred ostension using a map in the common perceptual field of the interactants. Notice that (8) could well be used to refer to a spatial region that actually excludes both interlocutors at the time of utterance, and the two regions contrasted could be actually very close together or very far apart depending on the scale of the map.

Rather than attempting to reduce all of these to a single abstract feature bundle, a revealing description of deixis must maintain these distinctions and try to explain why they fall within the range of a single lexical form in English, whereas the paraphrase equivalents in another language might require distinct forms.[3] For instance, in Yucatec Maya, examples (6) and (10) require what I have called the Egocentric Inclusive locative adverb *way e?* "here," whereas (7) requires the Presentative Evidential *hé?el a?* "here it is," as in *hé?el ump'eél a?* "here's one (take it)," and (8-9) correspond to yet a third form, the Sociocentric Restricted locative adverb *té?el a?* "right here (where we can perceive)" (see Table 2.3). The descriptive challenge for a comparative theory of deixis is to provide a sufficiently delicate vocabulary to give a consistent account of such a range of pragmatic effects.

The Communicative functions of deictic types are speech act values that specify what kinds of act are performed in routine proper usage of the deictic. Presentative designates the kind of act illustrated in (3). Directive designates the act performed when one speaker points out a referent, as in "There it is (look!)." The Referential function is the contribution of deictics to acts in which referential objects are individuated, as in (1-10) (with the possible exception of (7)). The term Phatic is the standard label for what speakers do in managing their contact with interlocutors, including what Yngve (1970) called backchannel, as well as the participation procedures described by C. Goodwin (1981). In Maya the adverbial deictic *b'èey* "thus, so, like (that)" is commonly uttered *sotto voce* by addressees listening to a speaker, as a way of signaling attentiveness and comprehension (not necessarily agreement). This is a Phatic use. Expressivity is the foregrounding of a speaker's own involvement in an utterance, including

subjective evaluation, special emphasis, surprise, admiration, etc. Expressive functions of deictics in Maya include these and others signaled by
special foregrounded constructions in which only deictics occur (Hanks
1984, 1990).

It is occasionally observed that deictics differ from semantic descriptions
in that they denote referents without actually describing them, as in (11)
vs. (12):

(11)   I work here.
(12)   I work in my office on Wilton Avenue in Chicago.

While this observation captures what is indeed a different blend of
information in the semantics of deictic and non-deictic expressions, it is not
strictly accurate. Deictics regularly encode features such as Human,
Animate, Regional/Extended vs. Punctate/Restricted, Concrete vs. Abstract, and Static vs. Kinetic. These do describe aspects of the objects to
which they refer, and they therefore make up a dimension of Characterizing features. Contrast these with the true Relational features, which
specify the relation between the object of reference and the current
utterance framework in which the act takes place. Typical ones include
Proximal vs. Distal, Immediate vs. non-Immediate, Visible, Inclusive vs.
Exclusive, Up vs. Down, Centripetal vs. Centrifugal. The distinctive
property of these is that they all presuppose an origo relative to which they
are computed. That is, they describe not the referent itself, but the relation
between the utterance framework and the referent.

If the Relational features specify the deictic relation, the Indexical ones
specify the origo to which the relation attaches. In (6) the Indexical
function is what grounds the reference to the interlocutors in the countryside at the time of utterance. In (7) it includes the state of the discourse and
interaction leading up to the utterance, and in (8) it includes both the
proximity of the interactants to each other and to the map, as well as the
fact that this is a deferred or transposed deictic reference. Although all of
these examples are cited as single utterances, for the sake of brevity, they
should all be understood as interactive moves in a chain of moves, and this
too is an aspect of the indexical ground of reference.

It is this plurality of features that I point to in saying that deictics are
functionally heterogeneous. While studies may focus on one or another
subset of the functions, a general account must provide a way of integrating
them. What is the organization of all this information in the semantics of
individual utterances, deictic types, given classes of deictics, and deixis in
general? Where do gestures fit in the semantics of deixis? As diacritics of
Communicative functions? As special constraints, as aspects of the indexical ground, or as independent signs with their own semantic structures?
How do the different features bundle in languages? Are there patterns of
cooccurrence that would allow us to predict likely combinations? The first

step towards answering such questions is to clarify the relational structure of deictic reference.

2   Relational structure of deictic reference

Consider the glosses in (13–17), which are alternative attempts at defining what I call the relational structure of deictic reference.

(13) "This" is equivalent to "what I-now notice."

(Russell 1951[1940]: 114)

(14) "I" means the person who utters ↓ this token ↓ .

(Reichenbach 1947: 284)

(15) "The [substitution] types of *this, here, now* and *that, there, then* represent relations of distance from the speaker or from the speaker and the hearer."

(Bloomfield 1933: 248)

(16) "This book" is equivalent to "the book which is near the speaker."

(Lyons 1977: 646)

(17) "This" indicates that its object is nearest to the present communication, dominant in the field of perception or attention, focused in the center.

(Collinson 1937: 43ff)

Russell's treatment of egocentric particulars was an attempt to reduce deixis to the experience of the speaking subject, whereas Reichenbach sought to reduce it to the token reflexivity of deictic form (hence the diacritic arrows in (14)). Bloomfield states the classic proximity-based gloss recapitulated by Lyons, whereas Collinson combines proximity with perception and cognitive focus. What they all share is that they posit as fundamental to deixis a relation between some part of the speech event and the object of reference.

This basic observation can be rephrased by saying that each deictic category encodes a relation between the referent and the indexical framework in which the act of reference takes place. Thus, a single deictic word stands for minimally two objects: the referent is the thing, individual, event, spatial or temporal location denoted; and the indexical framework is the origo ("pivot" or zero-point) relative to which the referent is identified (the speech event in which the act of reference is performed, or some part of this event). We can see that where (13-17) differ is on the nature of the origo (the speaker, the token sign, the present communication) and the quality of the relation (proximity, perceptibility, cognitive focus). Table 2.2 shows an array of hypothetical paraphrases for English usages.

Notice that the column labeled "denotatum type" shows distinctions between objects, regions, persons and times. This list (surely incomplete) reflects the differences among the classes of referents typically individuated by different categories of deictic. This portion of the gloss incorporates what were called Characterizing features in Table 2.1, since

Table 2.2. *Some relational structures of deictic reference*

Form		Denotatum type	Relational type	Indexical type*
this	=	"the one	Proximal to	me"
that	=	"the one	Distal to	you"
that	=	"the one	Distal to	you and me"
this	=	"the one	Visible to	me
that	=	"the one	Visible to	you and me"
here	=	"the region	Immediate to	you"
there	=	"the region	non-Immediate to	you and me"
I	=	"the person	Speaker of	this utterance"
you	=	"the person	Addressee of	this utterance"
now	=	"the time	Immediate to	this utterance"

* Indexical types are abbreviated and stand for participation configurations
realized in the utterance and actually occupied in the interactive situation.

regionality, individuality, and so forth are taken to be inherent features of
the referent, like shape, animacy, and other more familiar features.

The relationship types in the middle column localize the referent relative
to the origo. The most important point regarding these at this stage in the
discussion is that they may be multiple. That is, we need not assume that
any of the glosses in (13-17) is correct to the exclusion of the others. Any
language contains more than one type of Relational feature, and languages
differ significantly on which ones they encode. The standard assumption
that space is always foundational in deixis is an inconvenient fiction not
borne out comparatively (Frei 1944, Levinson 1983, Anderson and Keenan
1985).

Whereas Table 2.2 shows only a few possible Indexical types, this
portion of the relational structure is susceptible of significant variation as
well. The problem is that it is simply not known which aspects of
interactive events can serve as the ground of reference. In clear cases one
or another of the participants serves as origo, as assumed in (13, 15, 17).
Instances of speaker-grounded reference appear to be what justifies
Russell (1940) and Lyons (1977: 646, 1982: 121) when they assert that
deixis is egocentric, and others when they assert that it is "subjective." But
as Bühler (1982[1934]: 105) pointed out, this subjectivity is based in the
fact that all indicators require an origo in order to be interpreted, whether
or not the origo is the speaking subject. It may be that the location,
knowledge and orientation of participants are inherently more central to
reference than other aspects of the situation, but Reichenbach (14) and

Collinson (17) pose a challenge to this assumption. In theory at least, one could imagine any number of alternative indexical pivots, logocentric, person-centric, event-centric, and so forth. Given that acts of reference are interactively accomplished, a sociocentric approach is certain to be more productive than an egocentric one, even when the speaker is the primary ground of reference.

The paraphrases in Table 2.2 incorporate the Characterizing, Relational and Indexical features from Table 2.1, but they leave out the extra-referential Communicative functions. These could be represented heuristically as predicative elements in paraphrases such as (18-19):

(18) "Take the one Tactually available to me right now." (Presentative)
(19) "Look at the one Visible to you and me right now." (Directive)

As incomplete as these paraphrases are, they allow us to sketch out an important part of the referential apparatus encoded in deictic systems. As a heuristic device, they are productive in two ways. They can be read off as mini-descriptions of interactive contexts in which deixis occurs, thus setting a direction for pragmatic research. And, by varying the three components independently, one can raise questions regarding how features from each component combine. Do certain Relational features require certain types of indexical context, or occur only in certain grammatical categories?

Table 2.3 presents a sketch of part of the deictic system in Yucatec Maya, a native American language spoken in Mexico. The first three forms are Ostensive Evidential adverbs. OSTEVs form a special series of adverbs whose Communicative functions range from Presentative to Directive, while the deictic modal *hé?ele?* "indeed, for sure" is an Expressive indexing speaker certainty. The modal is not a referring item at all, while the OSTEVs subsume reference within a complex communicative act. The remaining five forms are locative adverbs (DLOCs) which share the primary function of reference, but differ in terms of their Relational and Indexical features.

2.1   Transformations of the Indexical ground

A basic property of the indexical context of interaction is that it is dynamic. As interactants move through space, shift topics, exchange information, coordinate their respective orientations, and establish common grounds as well as non-commonalities, the indexical framework of reference changes. Patterns of deictic usage reflect these changes, and thereby provide us with a powerful tool for investigating them. Consider a situation in which two Maya interactants are physically separated from each other in the forest, looking for a misplaced tool. One speaker calls out to the other, asking whether he has found it, and the other responds that he has.

Table 2.3. *Synopsis of Maya deictics (partial)*

Form	Gloss	Paraphrase	Features
héʔelaʔ	"Here it is"	"Take the one in my hand"	Presentative, Tactual/Spkr
héʔel oʔ	"There it is"	"Look at the one visible to us"	Directive, Visual/Spkr&Adr
héʔeb'eʔ	"There it is"	"Listen to the one audible to us"	Directive, Auditory/Spkr&Adr
héʔel eʔ	"Indeed"	"for sure, affirmative"	Expressive, Certain
téʔel aʔ	"There, here"	"at this very place immediate to us"	Referential Immediate/Spkr&Adr
téʔel oʔ	"There"	"at that place non-immediate to us"	Referential, ØImmediate/Spkr&Adr
way eʔ	"Here"	"at this place including me"	Referential, Inclusive/Spkr
tol oʔ	"There"	"at that place excluding me"	Referential, Exclusive/Spkr
tíʔiʔ	"There"	"at that place known to us"	Referential, Anaphoric/Discourse

(20)   A.   *tíʔ an wá tol oʔ?*
              "Is it over there?"
        B.   *hàah, way yan eʔ.*
              "Yeah, it's here (where I am)."

Notice that A codes B's location with the Exclusive DLOC *tol oʔ*, which always refers to a place removed from its speaker, whereas B makes reference to the same place by using the Inclusive DLOC *way eʔ*, which always refers to a region that includes its speaker. Wherever B is, the tool is with him, and A can simply follow the voice to find it. Schematically, the two deictic references can be contrasted as in Figure 2.1.[4]

The inversion in their positions is a canonical case of an Indexical difference: A and B stand in different actual relations to the object (the location of the tool) at the moment of the exchange, and they must therefore code it differently. The same phenomenon arises in the exchange of participant deictics and nominal demonstratives: A and B are both "I" to themselves but "you" to each other; A's "this" is B's "that" (more or less). If in (20), B follows the voice and goes to A, then he too would refer to the tool with the Inclusive form *way eʔ* "here." Once he has joined A at the tool site, he can no longer describe its location as *tol oʔ* "out there,"

tol o? "there (excluding me now)"

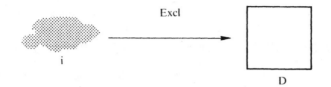

way e? "here (including me now)"

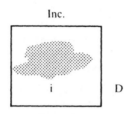

Key

Excl, Incl	Relational types
i	Indexical origo, always entails Spr
D	Donotatum

Figure 2.1 *Relational schemas for way e?* "here" *and tol o?* "there"

any more than he could switch the participant roles at his pleasure, describing himself in the second person and his interlocutor in the first.[5] These rudimentary details of usage make up what might be called an implicit playing field for interaction – a set of positions in deictic space, along with expectations about how actors occupy these positions over the course of talk. In their deictic systems, languages provide irreplaceable resources for this process.

Consider now a slightly less simple but equally mundane example, in which an interactant uses quoted speech. A and B are working in a corn field, squatting down, weeding nearby sections. The two are loosely engaged in talk, but separated by ten feet or so, each paying attention to his own work. A recounts a strip of interaction he had with C, a mutual friend, in the market the day before, and says at one point,

(21)   . . . *ká tuún tuyá?alah ten, kó?oten way e? kih, ká hb'inen i?.*
   . . . so then he says to me, **"Come here (to me)"** he says, so I went to him.

Notice that the portion of (21) in boldface is quoted speech. Although A utters the standard directive for summoning an addressee in Maya, B understands immediately that A is not calling him to his side. He also understands that the referent of *way e?* does not refer to A's current locus, but to C's locus at the time of the original utterance. Thus, if either A or B were to make reference to C's locus in the subsequent discourse, as A does in the final clause of (21), then they do so using Distal or Anaphoric deictics *tí?i* "there (where we said)" or perhaps *té?el o?* "there (where we both know)."

Thus one and the same place is referred to with the Inclusive deictic in quoted discourse but with the Distal or Anaphoric one in direct talk. This shift is well known and typical of all deictic categories. It is what motivated Jespersen's original description of these forms as "shifters." It follows that one and the same deictic is interpreted in one way in quoted discourse, but quite differently in direct. This does not mean, however, that the relational values reverse from use to use, *way e?* encodes Inclusive in (21) just as it does in (20). Rather, the shift can be accounted for by saying that quotation involves a transposition of the indexical ground of reference. The Relational features of the forms remain constant in both types of discourse, but the **origo** is projected in quoted speech from the actual utterance framework into a narrated one. This projection is an important part of what is signaled in the phrases that often mark quotation, 'he said, she said' (for extensive discussion of this, see M. H. Goodwin 1990, Hanks 1990, Lucy, in press).

The information status of referents changes over discourse even when the interactants sit still and speak entirely in direct talk. This change is a third example of the dynamic character of the indexical framework, and it is reflected systematically in the distribution of deictics in text. To take another very simple example, consider (22), in which Francisco explained to me that his nephew teaches English in a nearby town called Yotholim.

(22) *yáan untuúl insobrino té? yot'olim a?, yohe ?íngles [. . .]*
I have a nephew **right here in Yotholim** (who) knows English [. . .]
té? yot'olim o? k u ¢'ik klàases.
There in Yotholim he gives classes.

[BB.5.56]

At the time of this utterance, we were sitting in Francisco's store some twenty miles from the place to which the phrases in boldface refer, and in uttering both phrases, he made vague pointing motions in the direction of the town. Notice that he has shifted from the DLOC *té?el a?* "(right) there" in the first reference to *té?el o?* "there" in the second.[6] Extensive research on Maya usage confirms that this shift is a standard one, motivated by the fact that in the first case, Francisco is introducing a new referent into the discourse (compare Leonard 1985). He knows that I am familiar with Yotholim, and that it is generally considered to be a neighboring town, but he is introducing it into the talk for the first time. In the second case he is maintaining a reference already established. This difference pertains to the indexical ground, in particular to the state of knowledge and attention focus of the interactants.

In general, because indexical frameworks change more or less constantly in talk, the deictic forms that make for proper reference to objects change as well. Thus whereas the Relational features associated with deictics may remain relatively consistent across uses, the indexical framework of interaction is in constant flux. This may be due to a variety of factors, including the adjustments in bodily orientation of the participants, any motion they may be engaged in, the arrival of new participants on the scene, as well as background frames that may be activated. Because of its relational structure, deixis is perhaps the clearest linguistic indicator of the interactive transformations involved in producing context. General statements about indexical centering can only be evaluated in relation to distinct tokens and distinct types, not to the entire phenomenon of deixis as a whole.

2.2   The focality of the referent

The referential and indexical poles in the deictic relation are not coordinate, but are actually in a foreground–background relation. The referent (denotatum) is the figure and the indexical origo is the ground. This disparity is evident both in the grammatical structures of deixis and in its interactive production.

Regarding grammaticalization, recall the Characterizing and Relational features from Table 2.1. It is the denotatum that these features describe, as illustrated in (23–7).

(23)   *wuna:-'ga:-'=garan^{g}ga:-'*   *nu:-'ba-gi-yun^g*
      3Pl/3MSg-Rdp-Ben=look-Pa2   M-Anaph-MSg-Abs
      They looked for that one   (Heath 1980: 18)

(24)   *ma-na-ri*
      NClass-NonProx-Immed
      that   (Heath 1978: 59)

(25)   *ṇi-na-ri-tu*   *ṇarguni-ga-bidič-yaw*
      MaSg-that-Imm-Erg 3MSg/2Pl-Sub-nearly-spear
      That one almost spears you
                                   (Heath 1978: 227)

(26)   *les voi-ci*
      ArtMaPl Adv-Prox
      Here they are

(27)   *héʔel-óʔob-aʔ*
       OSTEV-Pl-Tact
       Here they are (take them!)

Example (23) is from a collection of Nunggubuyu texts. It illustrates a nominal deictic composed of four morphemes which encode masculine gender, Anaphoric function, singular number and absolutive case. Gender, noun class and number categories subcategorize the denotatum of the deictic, whereas what Heath labels the Anaphoric function is, by my reckoning, a Relational function. It encodes the fact that the denotatum is in a relation of being known (cognitively accessible) to the interactants. Similarly, (24-5) are from Ngandi, another Australian language in which deictics are composed of morphemes signaling noun class, number and case (among other things). In so far as case markers specify the role of the denotatum in the event described, they too apply to the denotational pole of the deictic relation, rather than to the indexical one.

The Ngandi deictic stems (24-5) are composed of two morphemes which conjointly specify the Relational value of the expression: *-na-* encodes non-Proximal (in opposition to *-ni-* "Proximal"), and *-ri* encodes Immediate (in opposition to *-ʔ* "non-Immediate"). While the precise nuances of these features are not clear from Heath's description, it is clear that they have to do with distinct kinds of relations to the indexical origo. In (26), Characterizing information is encoded primarily in the article (Masculine, Plural), while the adverbial deictic encodes the Immediate relation and Presentative/Directive Communicative function. In (27) the Yucatec Ostensive Evidential encodes the Tactual relation with Presentative function. The only Characterizing feature is the plurality encoded in the suffix. These are all instances of grammaticalized information bearing primarily on the denotatum.

Relational features function in deictic reference to foreground the denotatum, but they do so in a way different from the Characterizing features. The latter apply directly to the denotatum, describing it or its role in the proposition. Relational features, by contrast, subcategorize the link between the denotatum and the indexical origo. Thus relations such as Proximal and Distal may appear to offer no evidence for the focality of the referent over the ground. After all, proximity is reversible: if A is close to B, then B is close to A, and the two poles of the relation are coordinate. However, in deictic systems, the relation to ground is heavily weighted toward the referent, even when the link is spatial proximity. The referent is essentially a target rather than a mere end-point.

Consider (28), in which A asks B where he left the hammer they had been working with, and B tells him it is at the worksite (several kilometers from the location of the exchange).

(28)   A: *túʔuš yàan martiyòo?*
            'Where's (the) hammer?'

B: *tol o?*
   there (vague point towards worksite)

B's response encodes that the place referred to is Exclusive relative to the location of utterance (see Figure 2.1). That is, it is outside the boundaries of the current interactive field, however broadly or narrowly this is conceived. In order to successfully interpret the reference, A must have sufficient background knowledge to infer which place B has in mind. Both the location of the exchange and the background knowledge A and B share are part of the indexical origo of the reference. It would be clearly incorrect to say that B's utterance **refers to** his own location or to the shared background knowledge, yet the reference cannot be computed without these factors. The correct description is that the shared spatial and cognitive field of interaction is the background relative to which the worksite is individuated as a referential foreground.

Predicative and so-called "modifying" uses of deictics provide further indications of the salience of the Referential component. Consider (29-32).

(29)   *tí? an tol o?.*
      It's (out) there.
(30)   *way yan e?.*
      It's here.
(31)   *to nukuč k' aáš o?*
      (out) there (in the) old forest
(32)   *le pak'b'i nah o?*
      that cement-construction house

The element in boldface in (29-30) is the locative existential verb "to be (in a place)." This is the standard way of deriving a predicate from a spatial deictic in Yucatec. Both sentences would make appropriate responses to A's question in (28), conditions permitting, since both assert the location of the object (in this case the hammer). Thus (29) might be paraphrased roughly "it is located in the place Exclusive in relation to me" and (3) "it is located in the place Inclusive in relation to me." Notice that they could **not** be paraphrased even roughly as "it is in relation to me that its location is Exclusive" or "it is relative to me that it is close at hand." The problem with these would-be paraphrases is that they reverse the Figure–Ground relation encoded in the deictics, focalizing the indexical ground rather than the denotatum. Predicative uses of deictics retain the Figure–Ground structure of referential uses. They assert the Relational feature, not the Indexical one.

Similarly, phrases in which deictics function as modifiers to lexical descriptions, such as (31-2), usually elaborate the Relational or Characterizing features, not the Indexical ones. So in (31) the place referred to by the Exclusive deictic is described as "high forest," and in (32) the referent is described as a "cement-construction house." In other words, lexical description combines very productively with deictics to individuate the denotata more precisely. By contrast, attempts to further specify or make explicit the indexical origo of the reference in the same phrase with the deictic are usually odd or require special interactive contexts for proper use: ?"Out there relative to me," ?"This in relation to us right now," ?"That relative to our visual field," ?"Over there from me", and so forth.

Thus the Characterizing and Relational features of deictics serve to focalize the referential pole in the deictic relation. Lexical descriptions and predicative derivations preserve the Figure–Ground asymmetry between the two poles. This is of course related to the fact that in referential usage, it is the denotatum and not the indexical ground that is uniquely identified. Languages provide sometimes elaborate semantic resources for deictic reference in the form of large inventories of Relational and Characterizing features, as in Yucatec Maya (Hanks 1990), Malagasy (Dez 1980), Santali (Zide 1972) and Inuktitut Eskimo (Denny 1982). We summarize this information with cover labels such as "relative proximity," but it is clear that this proximity is not a matter of reversible spatial contiguity. Instead, what is basic to deixis is the access (cognitive, perceptual, spatiotemporal) that participants have to objects of reference in the current speech event. Access, like awareness, is an intensional arc from participants to objects, and this inherently orients deixis towards the denotatum.

So far as can be determined from published descriptions, most languages encode more distinctions among types of referents than among types of indexical origos. Elaborate inventories of Characterizing or Relational features are offset by minimal and often vague indexical grounds. This holds even for many "person oriented" languages (Anderson and Keenan 1985), in which the origo is subcategorized by distinct speaker-grounded vs. addressee-grounded vs. other-grounded deictic types. A possible counter-example is Japanese, for which Anderson and Keenan (1985) cite the three-way distinction: *kono* "near speaker" vs. *ano* "far from speaker and addressee" vs. *sono* "near addressee." Note that the three terms have three distinct indexical grounds, but only two Relational features. According to Boas (1917: 113), Tlingit has only a single Relational feature, "Near," paired with several distinct indexical grounds (relative to me, to you, to him), while Lower Chinook has an analogous three way split (Boas 1911: Section 44).[7] If these descriptions are accurate, then Japanese, Tlingit and Lower Chinook are atypical in that the indexical ground is more finely subcategorized than the referential focus. Usually, the inverse is the case, in accord with the greater salience of the referent.[8]

3   Figure and Ground in the semantics of deixis

The discreteness, individuation, definiteness, and singularity that are the hallmarks of deictic reference are all typical figure characteristics. The diffuseness, variability, and background character of the indexical origo are due to its being, in fact, the ground upon which the referential figure is defined. The Figure–Ground relation, as invoked here, organizes visual perception. Deictic reference is by no means limited to visual, or even perceptual access to referents, but perceptual distinctions are encoded in deictics in a variety of languages, including Yucatec (Hanks 1984), Crow (Graczyk 1986), Malagasy (Dez 1980) and Santali (Bodding 1929, Zide 1972). Even in languages such as German and English, in which apparently no perceptual distinctions are encoded in deictics, the perceptual corollaries of spatial or cognitive immediacy may still be fundamental to the actual use of the forms (Bühler 1982[1934], Lakoff 1987). One advantage of the analogy to Figure–Ground is exactly that it focuses our attention on the fact that deixis is a framework for organizing the actor's **access** to the context of speech at the moment of utterance. Deictic reference organizes the field of interaction into a foreground upon a background, as figure and ground organize the visual field.

3.1   Figure and ground in linguistic systems

A number of linguists have proposed applications of the Figure–Ground concept to linguistic categories. Starting from examination of spatial prepositions, as in "the pen rolled off the table," Talmy (1978) distinguished the figure object (the pen) from the ground (the table). The figure is conceptually movable and localized relative to the ground, which is stationary within a frame. Talmy noted that such "relative referencing" functions in a broad range of linguistic contexts, including non-locational sentences (X resembles Y, where X is figure and Y is ground), equational sentences (X is Y, cf, figure is ground), temporal reference, assertion (figure) as opposed to presupposition (ground), cause (figure) as opposed to result (ground) and temporal sequence of events (ground is prior). More recently, Talmy (1983) investigated verbal descriptions of spatial scenes and considerably refined the Figure-Ground analysis. Starting from the selectivity of linguistic representation, he argues that language imposes a primary–secondary division among portions of spatial scenes, thereby laying the basis for a Figure–Ground relation in speech. The corollaries of the primary–secondary division are consistent with this correspondence, and include: movable/more permanently located; smaller/larger; geometrically simpler (point-like)/more geometrically complex (with extent, shape, dimensionality); more salient/more backgrounded; and more recently in awareness/earlier in scene or memory (Talmy 1983: 231). To these can be added another, anticipated (forward path)/recalled (behind, path already covered) (Hanks 1983). Hence, in linguistic systems, and particularly in spatial reference, a broad variety of asymmetric oppositions among objects are encoded according to a consistent division between figure and ground.

Recent linguistic research on discourse has contained further applications of the distinction, to explain the relations among a still broader spectrum of grammatical categories. Summarizing work by a number of scholars, Wallace (1982: 212) organized categories of nouns, verbs, clauses and sentences into paradigmatic oppositions, as in {human, animate, proper, singular, definite, and referential}, which are salient, as opposed to their non-salient counterparts {non-human, inanimate, common, non-singular, indefinite, and non-referential}. Similarly, {perfective, present-immediate tense} are the more salient counterparts of {non-perfective, non-present-remote tense} within the verb.

It is important to bear in mind that the proposals summarized by Wallace are focused on the paradigmatic relations among different grammatical categories, assigning each category a single coefficient of relative salience. Hence, when linked to an analysis of information structure in narrative, the salience coefficients of each category condition its distribution in foregrounded vs. backgrounded portions of the discourse. In this kind of system, a speaker selects either the more or less focal term for use at a specific point in discourse.

The basic proposal of this paper is different in that I am applying the Figure–Ground dichotomy to the internal semantic structure of individual grammatical forms. A term such as "this" incorporates within its own relational structure both figure (denotatum) and ground (indexical origo). Whereas speakers must choose between perfective and imperfective aspect, or proper vs. common nouns, they do not choose between an indexical and a referential object. Rather, they identify the referential in relation to the indexical. Whereas the asymmetric relations among categories that Wallace treats can be described in terms of markedness oppositions, the linkage between Relational and Indexical components of reference is a matter of combination, not opposition. The difference becomes quite obvious in light of the different generalizations about deixis that arise from the two perspectives. Consider first the classification of distinct deictic categories by their relative salience coefficients.

3.1.1   *Relative salience of distinct deictic categories*

In a number of languages, including Yucatec and Malagasy, there are lexical distinctions among the Communicative functions in Table 2.1. Presentative-Directive adverbial deictics make up a distinct series from merely Referential ones. The former are typically associated with actual gestural presentation of the referent, as opposed to merely indicating it, and may be used as the sole predicate in "minor" sentences, as opposed to a modifier within a noun or adverbial phrase. In Yucatec, Presentative and Directive forms (first three in Table 2.3) are all subject to a number of special grammatical constraints (Hanks 1984). Most of the remaining forms, by contrast, are typically used to make reference, not to assert the presence of the referent. In Yucatec, these other deictics do not encode perceptual distinctions, nor are they typically used to actually present a referent, nor are they predicative unless derived grammatically, nor, finally, are they subject to the same set of grammatical constraints (Hanks 1984). The Presentative and Directive forms are relatively more salient and figure-like than the others, and their grammatical and pragmatic features reflect this.

The distinction between categories that encode perceptual features and those that do not could be viewed as another relation of relative figure-like as opposed to ground-like forms. Perceptual deictics single out the referent according to the mode of perceptual access by which it is available to interactants. In Yucatec, perceptual individuation combines with presentative force (Table 2.3) to make a series of deictics whose central interactive function is to direct the addressee's perceptual focus to the referent. Figure-like values cluster together in this case. In Malagasy, by contrast, nominal, adverbial and presentative bases all encode perception (Dez 1980), while Crow deictics distinguish visible from invisible in the nominal series, but lack a distinct presentative (Graczyk 1986).

It is intuitively obvious that Proximal deictics such as *way eʔ* "here" and *téʔel aʔ* "right here" in Yucatec are more figure-like than Distal ones such as *tol oʔ* "out there" and *téʔel oʔ* "there" (Table 2.3). As such they tend to be more Punctual (as opposed to regional), more canonically Referential (as opposed to Anaphoric or non-Referential), more likely to take on presentative or directive force and to be used in reference to concrete as opposed to abstract objects. Some tokens of deictics are non-referential in that they fail to individuate any existent object, "referring" instead to some vague or hypothetical object. The forms in question tend to be non-Proximal and non-Punctuate. The Exclusive locative *toloʔ* may be used to convey that the speaker does not know where something is located, as in *tinsatah wá túuš toloʔ* "I lost it somewhere out there." Compare (33-5):

(33) W: *má tawáal ten yàan abin?*
      Didn't you tell me you're going?
   E: *niŋ káʔa→ pero máa č im bin **to naáč** oʔ.*
      I'm going, but I don't go **way out there**.

[BB.5.48]

(34) *un-ani*
   there, somewhere down there (Extended, Subord, AT)

(Denny 1982: 361)

(35) *n-ɔ̃-k'ɔ̃+e*
   this (Prox, Inan, Intensive)

(Zide 1972: 268)

In (33), taken from my field notes, E was explaining to me that she goes to collect firewood only at the edge of the planted fied by her house, rarely

Table 2.4. *Relative salience of opposed deictic categories (partial)*

Higher salience	Lower salience
Presentative	non-Presentative
Directive	non-Directive
Predicative	non-Predicative
Perceptual	non-Perceptual
Proximal	Remote
Anticipated	Recalled
Punctual	Regional
Concrete	Abstract
Referential	non-Referential

straying into the forest. The spatial expression (in boldface) refers vaguely to the outback of the woods. Example (34) is taken from Denny's (1982) discussion of Inuktitut Eskimo, where he reports that the distal extended deictic is used to indicate that the speaker does not know the precise whereabouts of the object. Canonically referential usages are more figure-like than such non-specific, only marginally referential ones. In Santali, the inverse case arises. According to Zide (1972) and Bodding (1929: 125), there is an "intensive" or "particularizing" infix -Vk'+ that restricts deictic reference, glossable roughly as "the very one." This infix occurs only on Proximal bases. These divisions are summarized in Table 2.4.

The hierarchy summarized in Table 2.4 can help answer the question of how information is linguistically organized in the encoded structure of deixis. On the assumption that figural properties tend to cluster, Table 2.4 generates a number of interesting predictions that can help motivate facts of structure and use that appear otherwise arbitrary. For instance,

- If a language has both Presentative and Perceptual features in the deictics, they will tend to be lumped in the same forms.
- Directives are more likely to individuate points than regions of broad extent.
- Proximal forms lend themselves readily to anticipatory reference (as in "this one [coming up]") whereas Remote ones do not.
- Remote forms tend to be used for anaphora and reference to discourse.
- Forms used for non-specific reference to vague zones will be the same ones used for non-punctuate, remote, and recalled referents.

3.1.2   *Relative salience of simultaneous components*

These uses of the Figure–Ground relation as a way of classifying grammatical categories necessarily involve a logical transposition. Whereas the members of a paradigm are opposed according to their respective salience coefficients, figure and ground elements of perception are syntagmatically combined in the organization of the visual field. The syntactic combination of elements in discourse corresponds more directly to the Figure-Ground concept than does the assignment of coefficients inherent in individual categories. What actually makes a member of a paradigm figure-like is that it tends to be used in reference to figural objects in discourse. The considerable generality of this approach derives partly from its linking up of discourse with grammar. We would expect such a linkage to interact in detailed ways with markedness oppositions which account for many of the same distributional facts.

In applying figure and ground to the internal structure of deictics, on the other hand, there is also a linking together of discourse with grammar, but there is no transposition. The two simultaneous components of deictic reference combine in just the way the two components of perception do: as asymmetric parts of a single event. When a speaker utters (36), he creates **both** a figure (the one moving) and the ground upon which it is individuated (the shared perceptual and orientational field).[9]

(36) *héʔ kubin oʔ.*
      (Look!) There he goes. (pointing)

The duality of the referential focus as against the indexical background in deictic usage fits into a larger series of Figure–Ground relations among components in a single utterance. Consider the routine Maya utterance in (37).

(37) *héʔel aʔ p'oʔ ak'ab' iʔ iʔ.*
      Here! Wash your hands here.

[BB.4.80]

Margot was filling a water basin with a hose in the back yard when I walked towards her, looking for a place to wash my hands. Although we were not engaged in talk, she was aware of my intention. Holding the running hose out to me, she uttered (37). The deictic in boldface is presentative, and individuates the running hose as a maximal figure. This entails a directive to me to focus on the referent, walk to it and touch it. Observe that in (36) the directivity was also in force (hence the finger-pointing gesture), but there was no presentation, since the object was not available in the tactual field. Presentative and Directive further entail the distinct act of singular definite reference to the object. While the three functions are laminated in (37), there are clearly cases of deictic reference that are neither Directive nor Presentative (20, 22, 28). Reference in turn entails the indexical origo.

The Presentative, Directive, Referential and Indexical components of (37) are scaled from the most figural to the most backgrounded. Presentative is maximally focal and entails all of the other functions. The indexical origo is the interactive ground on which all of the others rest. The focality

Table 2.5. *Relative salience of simultaneous components of deictic utterances*

Figural	Backgrounded
Presentative	Directive
Directive	Referential
Referential	Expressive
Expressive	Phatic
Relation-to-referent	Indexical origo
Characterizing features	Indexical features
Newly introduced	Already part of common ground

of the Presentative is well reflected on native-speaker metalinguistic glosses of this form, which consistently associate it with acts of manually handing the referent to the addressee (Hanks 1984, in press). In general, those components of deictic acts which are new in context (Leonard 1985), or which effect a change in the orientations of participants, are the most figural. These generalizations are summarized in Table 2.5.[10]

3.2   Interactive emergence of the indexical ground

In so far as it alters discourse context, deixis has a creative or "constitutive" function. Even when interlocutors can presuppose a common context rich with shared information, the individuation of the referent may be new (cf. 33, 36, 37). To point out or present an object to an interlocutor is to orient his attention. In some situations, the change may be relatively radical, as in (38), a quote taken from a personal narrative told by DC, a Maya speaker. When he was just a boy, DC once locked his grandfather out of his house, by accident. The old man returned at night wanting to get in, and had to guide DC, who was inside, disoriented in the pitch darkness. DC groped along the inner wall towards the door as the old man rapped his cane, saying:

(38)   *hé?el a? hé?el a? way a tàal e?*
        Here it is! Here it is! Come here (to me)

[BB.4.87]

This utterance alters its own context by localizing the door for DC, and summoning him to it (cf. Bühler 1982[1934]: 109 on the importance of voice as an auditory signal of the origo).

Locative deictics in Maya are commonly used in utterances that initiate interactions. This is another case of constitutive reference, in which a participant relation is created and the parties to it arrive at mutual orientation. For instance, (39) is a standard greeting that Maya speakers call out to announce their arrival at the home of another.

(39) *tàa téeloóo!*
      Coming in there!

[BB.4.66]

In this example a woman arrived at DC's gate and called out before slowly entering, waiting for a response of acknowledgment from within the house. DC's daughter-in-law (his neighbor within the homestead) responded with (40), an equally routine utterance.

(40) *ʔòoken iʔ!*
      Enter there!

[BB.4.66]

Occurring without prior interaction, from a perceptually and spatially remote location, from outside the boundaries of the homestead, (39) rests on a relatively lean indexical framework. Rather, it creates a framework, producing an interactive relation that did not exist prior to the utterance.

Speakers routinely interact across boundaries of various kinds, talking from one room to another in the homestead, one corner to another at a work site, through the vegetation in the woods, orchards and fields. In such situations, deictic reference has the potential to reorient participants to a relatively great degree, creating a reciprocal or common focus of attention and bringing about physical proximity (see Kendon 1985). These uses are what Collinson (1937: 17ff) called "points," as opposed to "markers," and more recent studies have called "creative" as opposed to "presupposing" (Errington 1988; Friedrich 1979[1966]: 96; Hanks 1984; Silverstein 1976). Creative deixis significantly alters its own indexical origo. Thus (39) creates the engagement that functions as indexical ground from which the speaker "points" into the homestead, while the response in (40) presupposes the ground and "marks" the spatial referent relative to it (anaphorically).

The play between creative and presupposing aspects of usage is an ongoing one, which means that the indexical origo is a dynamic ground, rather than a fixed object. In many deictic acts, an already constituted indexical framework is presupposed, in which interlocutors share certain relevant knowledge, immediate experience and engagement (22, 28, 37, 40). The origo is already in place. For instance, a directive utterance such as "There he goes (pointing)" is most likely to be used when interactants are already mutually oriented, close together, and perhaps awaiting the motion of a particular individual. Even in highly creative uses, the object may recede to the status of a given, being introduced as a referential figure, and thereafter presupposed as common indexical ground.

3.3   Indexical symmetry and referential salience

A central aspect of the indexical origo is the degree to which the interactants share, or fail to share, a common framework. It is convenient to distinguish between the specific fields of participant access (spatial, perceptual, cognitive), and the participant domains relative to which reference is made. Typical participant domains are the Common ground (Sociocentric), Speaker (Egocentric), Addressee (Altercentric) and Other (non-Participant in current speech event). Ego- and Altercentric grounds are pragmatically asymmetric because they split the Speaker from the Addressee, while the Common ground is pragmatically symmetric, because it joins the two and puts them on roughly equal footing relative to the referent. This use of "symmetry" is consistent with its use by Brown and Gillman (1960) and Friedrich (1979[1966]) in their classic studies of address, and is analogous to Labov's (1972[1970]: 299ff) A vs. B vs. AB events in discourse. The participant relation is negotiated in an ongoing fashion, and the relative symmetry of context is gradient rather than all or nothing (cf. Clark and Wilkes-Gibbs 1986, Goffman 1981, C. Goodwin 1981, M. H. Goodwin 1990).

The indexical origo of deictic reference is bound up crucially in the interaction between participants, and relative symmetry provides a limited way to talk about this interaction. By lumping together many different aspects of the interactive origo into the single dimension of symmetry, it provides a unifying framework in which interactive contexts can be compared and scaled. Examples (28) and (37) illustrate relatively symmetric indexical grounds, whereas (20) was relatively asymmetric. Other aspects of social symmetry and asymmetry have been shown to play a fundamental role in the use of "pronouns of address" (Brown and Gillman 1960, Friedrich 1979[1966], Silverstein 1976), as well as verbal etiquette (Errington 1988) and forms of conversational inference (Gumperz 1982). What we see in deixis is the same social relation among participants, this time as a backgrounded origo for reference and presentation.

A more concrete view of symmetry focuses on the specific parameters in which the interactive origo is embodied. As Friedrich (1979 [1966]) showed for Russian pronoun usage, the indexical ground consists in a number of distinct dimensions, not just an abstract dichotomy (or continuum). Participants can be separated spatially and perceptually, but share highly determinate knowledge of the referent based on experience prior to the speech event. Hence two indexical contexts could be equally asymmetric, but qualitatively distinct in terms of **what** is shared and unshared. This is significant because different deictic forms rely on different aspects of the indexical field. Whether or not interactants share background knowledge of a referent is largely irrelevant to the usage of presentatives, which require immediate sensory access (cf. 18, 27, 37). On the other hand, reference to a place empirically remote requires proportionately more background knowledge (28, 31). Given a sufficiently rich common knowledge of a place, even reference to it from a great distance can be accomplished with normally punctate, proximal forms (22).

The overall symmetry of a speech context, therefore, has a central impact on deictic usage. There are relatively few deictic forms that can be used appropriately in highly asymmetric contexts, when interactants fail to share basic information and orientation.[11] Presentatives, punctual immediate reference and manual demonstration, for instance, mean little to an addressee who cannot see the speaker and share in his perceptual field. Thus while creative reference can transform indexical context, indexical context also constrains reference. There is a simple proportion between the two, which says the greater the symmetry of the indexical ground, the greater the possibilities for individuated reference. This is equivalent to saying that the more information participants already share in the indexical origo, the more precisely they can individuate referents. When they are face to face, engaged, mutually oriented, and share detailed background knowledge of referents, they can mobilize potentially any shifter in the language. Proper and successful reference can be based on the presupposition that the interlocutor will accurately identify the object (even a remote one), given only the relational description. The less they share, on the other hand, the leaner the indexical origo and the fewer the referential oppositions available to individuate objects. Under very asymmetric circumstances, it is more difficult to succeed at deictic reference without further lexical description or collaborative work of the sort analyzed by Clark and Wilkes-Gibbs (1986). This proportion can be summarized in a principle of relative symmetry, which says simply:

The more symmetric the indexical origo (the more fully constituted the ground), the greater the range of deictic oppositions available for making reference (the more differentiated the possibilities for denoting figures).

This principle has among its interactive corollaries two which I will state here in the form of generalizations for further research. Relatively **symmetric** indexical frameworks, where interactants share a current orientation, experiential field, and background knowledge, can be treated in reference as though they were asymmetric. Interlocutors can and routinely do "distance" themselves from one another, and from aspects of their immediate situation, through their choices of deictic forms. What is commonly called the "proximal" zone of interaction is not merely contiguous, but is maximally available to participants for subdivision by distinct deictic acts. The more richly defined the origo, the more possibilities there are for deictic use.

Under **asymmetric** circumstances, where interactants fail to share a common experiential field, less can be presupposed and relatively fewer alternative deictic acts can be performed. Asymmetric frameworks are not typically treated in reference as though they were symmetric. That is, it is relatively difficult for interlocutors who are in fact separated to successfully use deictics whose interpretation requires a common ground. Non-deictic lexical description becomes necessary in the absence of a common ground.[12]

The principal of relative symmetry also has structural concomitants that may help motivate the observed configurations of deictic categories in the world's languages. Relatively more focal deictic categories, which are used to individuate maximally figural referents, require a symmetric indexical ground in order to be fully interpretable. The more focal the deictic reference, the more likely it is that the act requires a symmetric origo in relation to which the object is identified. Hence, "proximal" deictic categories tend to presuppose indexical frameworks in which mutual access among participants is already established. Furthermore, deictic systems should tend to be skewed towards symmetric contexts. That is, they should tend to have a greater number of relatively figural forms than background ones (Table 2.4).

4   Conclusion

Verbal deixis is a central aspect of the social matrix of orientation and perception through which speakers produce context. Many communicative effects are fused with or achieved through indexical reference as shown in Table 2.1. At the heart of deixis is the unique relational structure whereby the referent is identified through its relation to the indexical origo.

Although part of grammar, Relational features are inherently embodied in communicative contexts and cannot be reduced to any set of would-be objective dimensions, such as spatial contiguity. Each relation is paired with indexical conditions that link modes of access to actual sets of actors under concrete conditions. The Indexical component of deixis is the processual background of interaction within which the act of reference takes place. Hence, the generalized structure of shifters conjoins the two poles of practical action in an interactive "conjuncture," which we might call the "conjuncture of indexical reference."

Deixis entails at least three further kinds of relations. The first are the **paradigmatic oppositions** between categories, of which some are inherently more figural than others. This leads to a classification of functions by relative figurality, analogous to markedness, although not identical to it (Table 2.4). Presentatives, for example, are inherently more focal than merely Referential deictics, as Proximate, Punctate forms are inherently more focal than Remote, Regional ones. The second relation is the **syntagmatic contrasts** between different components of discourse, in terms of their being interactively focal or backgrounded (Table 2.5). The third relation is the **relative symmetry of the indexical origo**. The origo consists of the social relation between participants, and symmetry is a way of describing the degree to which their respective orientations overlap. The greater the mutuality, reciprocity and commonality between participants, the more symmetric the origo. The more symmetric the origo, the greater the range of paradigmatic selections available to a speaker for the purpose of reference.

By joining together these different orders of context in the semantics of individual linguistic forms, deixis illustrates a special case of a more general phenomenon in natural language, whereby the meanings of individual lexical items may be of the same order of complexity as those of sentences. The indexical-referential structure of "this" or "here" is a formally condensed case of the more global interplay between grammar and discourse, which is central to communication as an interactive phenomenon.

Acknowledgments

The research and writing of this chapter were made possible in part by a grant from the Division of Research Programs of the National Endowment for the Humanities. I am grateful for this support. Earlier versions were presented at the 1986 Annual Meeting of the American Anthropological Association (Philadelphia), the Conference on Discourse in Sociocultural Context at University of Texas, Austin in April, 1987, and at the December 1988 monthly meeting of the Chicago Linguistic Society. The chapter in its present form was presented as a paper at the Parasession on Language in Context of the 1989 Chicago Linguistic Society, and appeared in the Papers from the Parasession. I am grateful to the participants in these meetings for their questions and critical remarks. In particular thanks to Chuck Goodwin for extensive and very helpful written comments, as well as to Joe Errington for written comments. Thanks to Lynn MacLeod for editorial assistance.

Notes

1 Indexicals are traditionally defined as signs that stand in a relation of contiguity with their objects (Morris 1971: 31; Peirce 1955[1940]: 107). In more recent works, this contiguity may be more or less abstract, depending on the theorist. In a framework like Putnam's in which the extension of terms is fixed by local standards, even natural kind terms like 'lemon' and 'gold' have indexical components (1975: 233ff), just as Searle's (1979) treatment of literal meaning generalizes indexicality to virtually all of language. Schutz (1967), Cicourel (1972), Garfinkel (1972) and Schegloff (1982) are among sociologists who have noted the pervasiveness of indexicality in everyday language use. One consequence of the progressive indexicalization of semantics is that deictics can no longer be called merely "indexicals," as they have been in the past. We must look elsewhere for their distinctive features.

2 In this chapter I concentrate exclusively on the referential–pragmatic aspects of deixis, and there are several kinds of information conspicuously missing from Table 2.1 that would need to be specified in a fuller treatment. These include

major category features (e.g. NP, ADV, PARTICIPANT); **semantic roles** (e.g. Agent, Object, Location, Path, etc.); and **special constraints** on distribution (e.g. main clauses only, restrictions on derivation, inflection, cooccurrence).

3 It would be possible to claim that these are all different lexical forms that happen to be homophonous, but the problem of variable usage of a single form would arise ultimately anyway.

4 The deictic is split into discontinuous portions that circumfix the place name, according to the standard grammatical pattern (Hanks 1990).

5 This is oversimplified for brevity. The Exclusive zone may be quite close physically, and there are usually more deictic alternatives available to speakers than the ones I cite. Transpositions are also common, particularly in status asymmetric exchanges. See Errington (1988: 160ff) on the transposed speech style in Javanese known as *mbasakaké*.

6 *Té?el-* is one of several initial deictic bases that participate in a morphophonemic alternation involving the omission of the *-l-* of the base form in certain environments. The *-l-* is obligatorily present when the deictic form is continuous or when the initial deictic is followed by a vowel-initial suffix, but it is obligatorily omitted when the initial deictic base is followed by a suffix that is consonant-initial. When an independent word (whether consonant- or vowel-initial) follows the initial deictic, the base-final *-l-* is optional (Hanks 1990: 20).

7 Although see Swanton (1911: 172) and Story and Naish (1973: 387), both of which cite more standard glosses for the Tlingit, with three distinct Relational features and the standard range of grounds.

8 I do not discuss here the linguistic resources that languages do provide for transforming the indexical ground by way of transposition, quotation (see above) and special foregrounding constructions (Hanks 1984). Languages with elaborate speech levels, such as Javanese (Errington 1988) or with honorifics, such as Japanese, also subcategorize the indexical origo by signaling aspects of the social relations among participants and referents. Moreover, bundles of Relational and Characterizing features can function as indexes of social relations within the origo, as in the usage of Tu and Vous forms (and their analogs) in address and person reference systems (Errington 1988, Friedrich 1979[1966], Silverstein 1976). These facts notwithstanding, the origo of the referential relation is typically less differentiated than the figural object.

9 Taking into account the combination of utterance, directed gaze and manual indication, the example actually illustrates the creation of three focal objects, one by each signal. Speakers assume that the three objects coincide, and they typically do, but examples are easy enough to imagine in which they would not, in Maya as well as English. The speaker could be intently observing the addressee or some other portion of the immediate field other than the referent, or the pointing gesture could be omitted, or shrugged off. In canonical events of ostensive reference with *hé?*, all signals reinforce the individuation of a single focal referent.

10 The hierarchy in Table 2.5 can be rearranged through foregrounding. For instance, the expressive force of a Maya presentative utterance can be boosted into focus through reduplication of the deictic base, yielding *hé? yàan hé?el a?* "here it is (take it!!)" from simple *hé?el a?* "here it is (take it)." Such foregrounded constructions are fairly elaborate in Maya and cannot be treated here.

11 This generalization does not apply to other types of social asymmetry, such as the status differences coded in honorifics and address forms. A language such as Javanese elaborately codes status asymmetry, especially in the deictic paradigms (Errington 1988: 96, 205ff). The kind of symmetry I am most concerned with is the commonalities of participant access to referents distinct from the participants themselves. The emphasis I place on shared access is motivated by the requirement that, for interactively successful reference to take place, both participants must identify what counts as the same object.
12 These generalizations all assume that no major status asymmetry exists between interactants which licenses one of them to make exceptional presuppositions that the other must be able to fill in.

References

Anderson, S. R., and E. L. Keenan. 1985. Deixis, in *Language Typology and Syntactic description*, Vol. 3: *Grammatical Categories and the Lexicon*, ed. T. Shopen, pp. 259-308. Cambridge: Cambridge University Press.

Bauman, R. 1977. *Verbal Art as Performance*. Prospect Heights, Ill.: Waveland Press.

Bauman, R., and J. Sherzer (eds.). 1974. *Explorations in the Ethnography of Speaking*. Cambridge: Cambridge University Press.

Benveniste, E. 1966a. La Nature des pronoms, in *Problèmes de linguistique générale*, Vol. 1, pp. 251–8. Paris: Editions Gallimard.

1966b. De la subjectivité dans le langage, in *Problèmes de linguistique générale*, Vol. 1, pp. 258–66. Paris: Editions Gallimard.

1974. Le Langage et l'expérience humaine, in *Problèmes de linguistique générale*, Vol. 2, pp. 67–78. Paris: Editions Gallimard.

Bloomfield, L. 1933. *Language*. New York: Holt.

Boas, F. 1911. Chinook, in *Handbook of American Indian languages*, ed. F. Boas, BAE Bulletin 40, Part 1, pp. 559–677.

1917. Grammatical Notes on the Language of the Tlingit Indians. *Anthropological Publications*, Vol. 8.1. Philadelphia: University of Pennsylvania Museum.

Bodding, P. O. 1929. *Materials for Santali Grammar II, Mostly Morphological*. Dumka. Bengaria: The Santal Mission Press.

Brown, R., and A. Gillman. 1960. The Pronouns of Power and Solidarity, in *Style in Language*, ed. T. Sebeok, pp. 253–76. Cambridge, Mass.: MIT Press.

Bühler, K. 1982 [1934]. *Sprachtheorie, die Darstellungsfunktion der Sprache*. Stuttgart: Gustav Fischer Verlag.

Cicourel, A. 1972. Basic and Normative Rules in the Negotiation of Status and Role, in Sudnow (1972), pp. 229–59.

Clark, H., and D. Wilkes-Gibbs. 1986. Referring as a Collaborative Process. *Cognition* 22(1): 1–39.

Collinson, W. 1937. Indication, a Study of Demonstratives, Articles and Other 'Indicators'. *Language*, monograph no. 17, April–June.

Denny, J. P. 1982. Semantics of the Inuktitut (Eskimo) Spatial Deictics. *International Journal of American Linguistics* 48(4): 359–84.

Dez, J. 1980. Structures de la langue malgache. Éléments de grammaire à l'usage des francophones. *Publications des Orientalistes de France*. Paris: Institut national des langues et civilisations orientales de l'Université de Paris VII.

Errington, J. J. 1988. *Structure and Style in Javanese: A Semiotic View of Linguistic Etiquette.* Philadelphia: University of Pennsylvania Press.

Fillmore, C. 1982. Towards a Descriptive Framework for Spatial Deixis, in *Speech, place and action: Studies in deixis and related topics*, ed. R. Jarvella and W. Klein, pp. 31–59. New York: John Wiley.

Frei, H. 1944. Systèmes de déictiques. *Acta Linguistica* 4: 111–29.

Friedrich, P. 1979[1966]. *Language, Context and the Imagination: Essays by Paul Friedrich.* Stanford: Stanford University Press.

Garfinkel, H. 1972. Studies of the Routine Grounds of Everyday Activities, in Sudnow (1972), pp. 1–30.

Goffman, E. 1981. *Forms of Talk.* Philadelphia: University of Pennsylvania Press.

Goodwin, C. 1981. *Conversational organization: Interaction between speakers and hearers.* New York: Academic Press.

Goodwin, M. H. 1988. Retellings, Pretellings and Hypothetical Stories. Paper presented at the 87th Annual Meeting of the American Anthropological Association, Phoenix.

   1990. *He-Said-She-Said: Talk as Social Organization among Black Children.* Bloomington, Ind.: Indiana University Press.

Graczyk, R. 1986. Crow Deixis. Unpublished ms., Department of Linguistics, University of Chicago.

Gumperz, J. 1982. *Discourse Strategies.* Cambridge: Cambridge University Press.

Hanks, W. F. 1983. *Deixis and the Organization of Interactive Context in Yucatec Maya.* Unpublished Ph.D. thesis, Department of Anthropology, Department of Linguistics, University of Chicago.

   1984. The Evidential Core of Deixis in Yucatec Maya, in *Papers from the Twentieth Regional Meeting of the Chicago Linguistic Society*, ed. J. Drogo et al., pp. 154–72. Chicago: Chicago Linguistic Society.

   1987. Markedness and Category Interactions in the Malagasy Deictic System. *University of Chicago Working Papers in Linguistics* 3: 109–36.

   1990. *Referential Practice: Language and Lived Space among the Maya.* Chicago: University of Chicago Press.

   In press. Metalanguage and Pragmatics of Deixis. In Lucy (in press).

Heath, J. 1978. *Ngandi Grammar, Texts and Dictionary.* Canberra: Australian Institute of Aboriginal Studies.

   1980. *Nunggubuyu Myths and Ethnographic Texts.* Canberra: Australian Institute of Aboriginal Studies.

Hopper, P. J. 1982. *Tense–Aspect: Between Semantics and Pragmatics.* Amsterdam/Philadelphia: John Benjamins Publishing Company.

Horn, L. R. 1988. Pragmatic Theory, in *Linguistics: The Cambridge Survey*, Vol. 1: *Linguistic Theory*, ed. F. J. Newmeyer, pp. 113–45. Cambridge: Cambridge University Press.

Hymes, D. 1974. *Foundations in Sociolinguistics: An Ethnographic Approach.* Philadelphia: University of Pennsylvania Press.

Irvine, J. 1985. Review article: Status and Style in Language. *Annual Review of Anthropology* 14: 557–81.

Jakobson, R. 1971 [1957]. Shifters, Verbal Categories and the Russian Verb, in *Selected Writings of Roman Jakobson*, Vol. 2. The Hague: Mouton.

Jespersen, O. 1965 [1924]. *The Philosophy of Grammar.* New York: W. Norton.

Kendon, A. 1985. Behavioural Foundations for the Process of Frame Attunement in Face-to-Face Interaction, in *Discovery Strategies in the Psychology of Action*, ed. G. P. Ginsberg et al., pp. 229–53. London: Academic Press.

Kuryłowicz, J. 1972. Universaux linguistiques, in *Proceedings of the Eleventh International Congress of Linguists*, ed. L. Heilman. Bologna.

Labov, W. 1972[1970]. The Study of Language in its Social Context, in *Language and Social context*, ed. P. P. Giglio, pp. 283–308. New York: Penguin.

Lakoff, G. 1987. *Women, Fire and Dangerous Things*. Chicago: University of Chicago Press.

Leonard, R. A. 1985. Swahili Demonstratives: Evaluating the Validity of Competing Semantic Hypotheses. *Studies in African Linguistics* 16(3): 281–95.

Levinson, S. 1983. *Pragmatics*. Cambridge: Cambridge University Press.

  1987. Putting Linguistics on a Proper Footing: Explorations in Goffman's Concepts of Participation, in *Goffman: An Interdisciplinary Appreciation*, ed. P. Drew and A. Woolton, pp. 161–227. Oxford: Polity Press.

Lucy, J. (ed.). In press. *Reflexive Language: Reported Speech and Metapragmatics*. Cambridge: Cambridge University Press.

Lyons, J. 1977. *Semantics*, Vols. 1 and 2. Cambridge: Cambridge University Press.

  1982. Deixis and Subjectivity: Loquor, Ergo Sum?, in *Speech, Place and Action: Studies in Deixis and Related Topics*, ed. R. Jarvella and W. Klein, pp. 101–24. New York: John Wiley.

Morris, C. W. 1971. *Writings on the General Theory of Signs*. The Hague: Mouton.

Peirce, C. S. 1955 [1940]. *Philosophical Writings of Peirce*, ed. J. Buchler. New York: Dover Publications.

Putnam, H. 1975. The Meaning of Meaning, in *Mind, Language and Reality: Philosophical Papers II*, pp. 215–71. Cambridge: Cambridge University Press.

Reichenbach, H. 1947. *Elements of Symbolic Logic*. New York: Macmillan.

Russell, B. 1951[1940]. *An Inquiry into Meaning and Truth*. London: Allen and Unwin.

Schegloff, E. A. 1982. Discourse as an interactive achievement, in *Analyzing Discourse: Text and Talk*, ed. D. Tannen, pp. 71–94. 1981 Georgetown University Round Table on Languages and Linguistics. Washington, DC: Georgetown University Press.

Schutz, A. 1967. *The Phenomenology of the Social World*, trans. G. Walsh and F. Lehnert. Evanston: Northwestern University Press.

Searle, J. 1969. *Speech Acts: An Essay in the Philosophy of Language*. Cambridge: Cambridge University Press.

  1979. *Expression and Meaning*. Cambridge: Cambridge University Press.

Silverstein, M. 1976. Shifters, Verbal Categories and Cultural Description, in *Meaning in anthropology*, ed. K. Basso and H. Selby, pp. 11–55. Albuquerque: School of American Research.

Story, G. L. and Naish, C. M. 1973. *Tlingit Verb Dictionary*. Fairbanks: University of Alaska, Alaska Native Language Center.

Sudnow, D. (ed.). 1972. *Studies in Social Interaction*. New York: The Free Press.

Swanton, J. R. 1911. Tlingit, in *Handbook of American Indian languages*, ed. F. Boas, BAE Bulletin 40, Part 1, pp. 159–204.

Talmy, L. 1978. Figure and Ground in Complex Sentences, in *Universals of Human Language*, Vol. 4, ed. J. Greenberg *et al.* Stanford: Stanford University Press.

  1983. How Language Structures Space, in *Spatial Orientation: Theory, Research and Application*, ed. H. L. Pick and L. P. Acredolo, pp. 225–82. New York and London: Plenum Press.

Timberlake, A. 1982. Invariance and the Syntax of Russian Aspect, in Hopper (1982), pp. 305–34.

Vološinov, V. N. 1986 [1929]. *Marxism and the Philosophy of Language*, trans. L. Matejka and I. R. Titunik. Cambridge, Mass.: Harvard University Press.

Wallace, S. 1982. Figure and Ground: The Interrelationships of Linguistic Categories, in Hopper (1982), pp. 201–26.

Weinreich, U. 1980. *On Semantics, ed.* W. Labov and B. Weinreich. Philadelphia: University of Pennsylvania Press.

Yngve, V. 1970. On Getting a Word in Edgewise, in *Papers from the Sixth Regional Meeting of the Chicago Linguistic Society*, ed. M. A. Campbell *et al.*, pp. 567–78. Chicago: Chicago Linguistic Society.

Zide, N. 1972. A Munda Demonstrative System: Santali, in *Melanges Haudricourt*, Vol. 1, ed. J. M. C. Thomas and L. Bernot, pp. 267–72. Paris: Editions Klincksieck.

3　Language in context and language as context: the Samoan respect vocabulary

ALESSANDRO DURANTI

Editors' introduction

Alessandro Duranti is Associate Professor of Anthropology at the University of California, Los Angeles. Originally trained in typological linguistics and discourse analysis, Duranti became interested in integrating grammatical analysis with ethnography during his first fieldwork experience in Western Samoa, in 1978–9. Since then, he has been involved in several projects centered around the documentation of communicative competence in a traditional Samoan village. In his research, Duranti has often focused on political discourse, which he sees as embedded in and at the same time constitutive of specific social activities. In this chapter, he examines one of the lexical features of oratory, respect vocabulary, across a number of settings. Like Philips (this volume), Duranti is concerned with recurrent patterns as used by the same speakers across contexts. Like Cicourel (this volume), he relied on ethnography for making hypotheses about what is relevant for the participants themselves.

Linguistic taxonomies have been used by ethnographers all over the world as a window on the universe of social and psychological relations that make human action meaningful and hence unique. Through the study of the words dedicated to a particular domain, e.g. colors, or to particular kinds of human relationships, e.g. kinship, researchers have the opportunity to test hypotheses about both the universality and the specificity of perceptually and socially salient distinctions. Among the various linguistic taxonomies found in the world languages, honorific lexical systems, e.g. the Javanese speech levels (Geertz 1960) and the "in-laws" languages of Australia (cf. Dixon 1972; Haviland 1979a, 1979b), have captured not only anthropologists' but also linguists' interest. One of the linguists' concerns has been how to formally characterize the linguistic and contextual features that "trigger" the use of a particular lexical or morphological choice. Several types of analytical distinctions have been proposed to describe the different kinds of relationships indexed by lexical choices in honorific registers. In each case, one or more components of the speech event are said to be relevant to the choice of honorific terms. Distinctions among systems and choices have been made in terms of referent honorifics, speaker's honorifics, addressee's honorifics, and bystander's honorifics (cf. Comrie 1976, Levinson 1983).

In this chapter, after examining the use of a special set of Samoan words (nouns and verbs) describing actions, feelings, possessions, and relations involving high status individuals, Duranti concludes that, based on transcripts of spontaneous interactions both in casual and formal encounters, the use of respectful terms cannot be simply predicted on the basis of referent or addressee, but must be related to the kind of activity and the kinds of social relationships and social personae that the lexical items are used to activate. In other words, linguistic choices are shown to be both context-defined and context-defining, while the status and rank distinctions they presuppose are constituted in the constant struggle to reassert or challenge the existing social order. Duranti shows that these character-istics make the Samoan honorific terms perfect candidates for the pragmatic uses of speech that Brown and Levinson (1978, 1987) have labeled "politeness." Respect-ful words recognize the addressee's high status and hence suggest virtual immunity from imposition. By providing "deference" to the addressee (or to a third party), they can be employed to diffuse potentially face-threatenings acts such as requests and denials. Duranti, however, also proposes another, if not alternative, parallel function of these honorifics – a function that is shown to be frequent in the recorded interactions and consistent with Samoan beliefs. The notion of "respect" (*fa'aaloalo*), for Samoans, is not only linked to what we might call "politeness," but also to "tradition" and hence to culturally specific obligations such as the dignified, controlled behavior expected from high-status individuals. In this view, respectful words are activated not only to defer to another's authority but also to coerce, or to oblige the recipient(s) or target(s) of the speech act to behave according to the expectations dictated, through tradition, to the social persona indexed by the honorific term. As shown by some of the studies of similar phenomena cited by Duranti, such use of "polite" language is perhaps quite common around the world. The evoking of a particular context through lexical choice can thus be seen not only as a politeness strategy but also as an instrument of power which sets the tone for what can be said, done, and understood by the participants (on these themes, see also the chapter by Lindstrom in this volume).

References

Brown, Penelope, and Stephen C. Levinson. 1978. Universals of Language Usage: Politeness Phenomena, in *Questions and Politeness Strategies in Social Interaction*, ed. Esther N. Goody, pp. 56–311. Cambridge: Cambridge University Press.
    1987. *Politeness: Some Universals in Language Usage*. Cambridge: Cambridge University Press.
Comrie, B. 1976. Linguistic Politeness Axes: Speaker–Addressee, Speaker–Reference, Speaker–Bystander. *Pragmatics Microfiche* 1(7): A3–B1.
Dixon, R. M. W. 1972. *The Dyirbal Language of North Queensland*. Cambridge: Cambridge University Press.
Geertz, Clifford. 1960. *The Religion of Java*. Glencoe, Ill.: Free Press.
Havilland, John B. 1979a. How to Talk to Your Brother-in-Law in Guugu Yimidhirr, in *Languages and their Speakers*, ed. T. Shopen. Cambridge, Mass.: Winthrop.

1979b. Guugu Yimidhirr Brother-in-Law Language. *Language in Society* 8: 365–93.

Levinson, Stephen C. 1983. *Pragmatics*. Cambridge: Cambridge University Press.

Language in context and language as context: the Samoan respect vocabulary

1   Introduction

As shown by the chapters in this collection, scholars from different disciplines concerned with human interaction and human communication are faced with the problem of defining a theory and methodology able to capture the inherently dynamic character of human action and human understanding. While linguists have been productively experimenting with analytical tools for the description of structural properties of linguistic codes, anthropologists, sociologists, and other social scientists have been stressing the need to understand human interaction as a set of practices that cannot be completely defined prior to the emergent semiotic activities in which they are embodied. Those working on language have been moving to larger and larger units of analysis – namely from the word to the sentence, from the sentence to discourse – and across qualitatively different domains – namely from linguistic texts to social events. As suggested by hermeneutics some time ago (see Gadamer 1976), the challenge is to reproduce in our accounts the sometimes harmonious sometimes conflicting links between the parts and the whole, which, for linguistic anthropologists, consist respectively of linguistic structures and the psycho-social systems giving them content.

In this chapter, I engage in this enterprise and select a linguistic subsystem – a special set of words, or lexical register – as a window on a universe of forms that are both defined by and are used to shape social activities and human understanding of such activities. By combining ethnographic and structural methods of description, I propose a characterization of the Samoan Respect Vocabulary which assumes and goes beyond an instrumental model of the relationship between language and context (see Bühler 1934, Malinowski 1923, Vygotsky 1978). I will demonstrate that a feature analysis of a particular classificatory system can be a useful tool in a first description of the phenomenon, but is too crude for an understanding of the sociocultural implications and assumptions related to the use of such a subsystem in daily interaction. Feature analysis of the kind used to describe selectional restrictions on lexical items – e.g. the generalization that the English verb *eat* needs an animate being as the referent of its subject – assumes a causal relation between context and language, with the former "explaining" the latter. When we look at the actual use of specific lexical items within everyday discourse, however, we find that the relation between words and the context of their use is a much more complex and dynamic one. In particular, we realize that words do not simply reflect a taken-for-granted world "out there," they also help constitute such a world by defining relations between speaker, hearer, referents, and social activities. Furthermore, if we are truly interested in the meaning that such linguistic forms have in people's daily lives, we must take into consideration local theories of their use as instantiated through linguistic and other communicative practices. Within the context of this chapter, it is such a local perspective which forces us to reconsider the notion of respect as used by Brown and Levinson (1978) in their study of politeness phenomena. In particular, rather than paying back the addressee for potential loss of face, respect can be used as an emergent pragmatic force that constrains human behavior and makes recipients do what they might not otherwise do. In this sense, the offer of "respect" does not stand for "freedom of action," – as suggested by Brown and Levinson's model – but, on the contrary, for control and imposition.

2   A structural description of the phenomenon

In Samoan, as in many languages of the world (cf. Geertz 1960, Dixon 1972, Haviland 1979, etc.) one finds that certain words are considered to be part of a "special" set, to be distinguished from other, more ordinary or "common" words. These words in Samoa are called *'upu fa'aaloalo* "respectful words" (RWs) and are said to be associated with a particular class of people, namely, titled individuals (*matai*), including chiefs (*ali'i*) and orators (*tulaafale*).

RWs are nouns and verbs that describe individuals, groups, relations, as well as a certain range of their actions, attributes, and possessions. Figure 3.1 contrasts some RWs with common words. I should mention here that there is no Samoan term for "common word" to be contrasted with "respectful word." However, the pairing of the two sets of Samoan words in Figure 3.1 (and Figure 3.2) represents common native metalinguistic strategies to explain or paraphrase the meaning of RWs; some of these pairings are also found in the poetic parallelism typical of oratorical speeches (see Duranti 1981, 1984a), whereby both an RW and a common word are found within the same sentence.[1]

Figure 3.1 shows a number of characteristics that the Samoan RWs share with special lexicons in other languages. Thus, for instance, as in the "in-law" languages of Australia (Dixon 1972; Havilland 1979a, 1979b), in several cases, the Samoan Respect Vocabulary conflates in one word what in ordinary lexicon is represented by several distinct lexemes: e.g. both *vae* "leg, foot" and *lima* "hand, arm" are expressed by one term, *'a'ao* "limb"; while three different parts of the human face – mouth, nose, and eyes – are

Figure 3.1 *Examples of respectful words (spelled in "bad speech") with English translation and with Samoan paraphrases in common words*

Common words	English translation	Respectful words
lima	arm, hand ⎱	*aʻao*
vae	leg, foot ⎰	
maʻi	sick	*gasegase*
iloa	know	*silafia*
vaʻai	see, look	*silasila*
magaʻo	want, need	*figagalo*
ola	live	*soifua*
olaga	life	*soifuaga*
ʻai	eat	*kaumafa*
guku	mouth ⎱	
isu	nose ⎬	*fofoga*
maka	eye ⎰	

Figure 3.2 *Examples of respectful words (spelled in "bad speech") which show further distinctions in terms of status and rank*

Common	Translation	Chiefs	Orators	High orator
fale	house	*maoka*	*laoa*	
koʻalua	spouse ⎱	*falekua*	*kausi*	
aavaa	wife ⎰			
kaukala	speak	*saugoa*	*fekalai*	*vagaga*
sau	come	*afio mai*	*maliu mai*	
alu	go	*afio aku*	*maliu aku*	

all conveyed by one RW, i.e. *fofoga*. However, as shown in Figure 3.2, the opposite situation is also quite common, namely, cases in which the Respect Vocabulary makes more subtle distinctions than the common lexicon. Thus, for some terms, a single common word can be "translated" into different RWs depending on the specific status or rank of the referent, e.g. instead of the common word *fale* "house," a distinction must be made between *laoa* and *maoka* when talking about an orator's house or a chief's house respectively.

In the course of gathering material for his Samoan dictionary, G. B. Milner collected some 450 RWs and provided a description of their use (Milner 1961). Both Milner's description and the way in which Samoans tend to gloss RWs for outsiders encourage accounts of RWs in terms of lexical choice associated with particular referent types. The rules for the **use** of such lexical items are also defined in terms of features of the referent, with some additional considerations about the relationship between the speaker and the referent:

> when there is a polite equivalent or equivalents for a given ordinary word, the use of a common word is almost ruled out when a speaker addresses (and usually when he refers to) chiefs [a term which includes here titled chiefs, orators, and certain high status individuals, A. D.]. If he is referring to himself, his kinsmen, or his possessions, then no matter how high his own rank may be, the use of ordinary words is, conversely, obligatory.

> (p. 297)

Although both referent and addressee are mentioned in Milner's account as important factors, Samoan RWs are described as examples of what Comrie (1976) and Levinson (1983) call **referent honorifics**, namely, lexical items that show respect by referring to the "target" of the respect. This informal description can be easily translated into a formal account based on semantic features. We can thus classify Samoan nouns and verbs according to the features [+titled], which characterizes *matai* in general (both chief and orators), and [-titled] which characterizes untitled people (*taulele'a*). Further distinctions could be made between [+chief] and [−chief], with the latter covering the orator set (the lexically most marked group), and with the standard implication that if [+chief] then [+titled]. For a few items, the feature [+high] will be needed, in those cases where certain RWs are restricted to either very high chiefs or very high orators (e.g. the term *vagaga* in Figure 3.2).

Here are a few examples of RWs as defined by this small set of features:

iloa	"know"	Nom Arg_1 [−titled]
silafia	"know"	Nom Arg_1 [+titled]
sau	"come"	Nom Arg_1 [−titled]
afio mai	"come"	Nom Arg_1 [+chief]
maliu mai	"come"	Nom Arg_1 [+titled, −chief]
vagaga	"speak"	Nom Arg_1 [+titled, −chief, +high]
fale	"house"	[__ *o*("of") −titled]
maoka	"house"	[__ *o*("of") +chief]
laoa	"house"	[__ *o*("of") +titled, −chief]

(Nom Arg_1 for transitive verbs = Agent NP; for intransitive verbs = Absolutive NP.)

All of the RWs will have the conventional implicatures that they could not refer to either the speaker or a close kin, given that, according to Samoans and as reported by Milner, it is considered inappropriate to use an RW in talking about oneself or one's close relatives (but see below for an apparent violation of such a constraint).

Typically, feature analysis is not intended to provide predictions on performance. It simply describes certain kinds of regularities in people's knowledge of lexical items. However, if we took the nature of the referent to the crucial factor in selecting RWs, feature analysis could be used as a predictor of performance. Thus, for instance, we could predict that, given a certain referent *A* with the feature [+chief], and given the existence of a lexical item *I* with the feature [+titled], speakers would select the item *I* over an item *J* which had the same semantic specification but the feature [−titled].

This characterization of RWs is nothing more than a simple formalization of Milner's description and it has the advantage of being easy to test. At the same time, it also employs a particular conception of the relationship between language and context, i.e. one in which language is seen as acting within an independently established social world and as mirroring some of its characteristics – this is what Silverstein (1977, 1979) has characterized as the "reflectionist point of view." In this case, the choice of certain lexical items, namely, RWs, is seen as causally defined by certain (language-independent) properties of the context such as the referent's social status and/or rank. This view is schematically represented in Figure 3.3.

CONTEXT   LANGUAGE

⟶

feature(s) {X}   feature(s) {x}

Figure 3.3 *Context determines language*

Note: The arrow should be interpreted as "triggers."

Can this view of the relationship between language and context, with the latter determining the former, account for how RWs are actually used in everyday verbal interaction? That is, can a causally interpreted feature analysis (with status/rank features constituting the independently established "context") be adequately used for (1) making predictions on **when** speakers are going to use RWs; (2) explaining **how** they are used, i.e. with which communicative/social functions?

3   Looking at language use

When we test the accuracy of status/rank features alone to account for the actual use of RWs in everyday interaction, we realize that such features of the context are good predictors of performance **only in some contexts**.

Thus, for instance, in a *fono*, a judiciary-political event attended only by titled people (Duranti 1981, Shore 1982), RWs are used quite consistently in talking about titled people. In example (1), the orator Fanua expresses his unwillingness to give an opinion on the first agenda of the meeting, given that the highest chief of his subvillage, Lealaisalanoa – shortened form: Salanoa – has not expressed his opinion. We find here the RWs *afio mai* "arrive, come" and *koofaa* "opinion" when the chief is understood as the referent about which the description is given or predication made:

(1) (*Fono* April 7, 1979)

> Fanua: *e ui fo'i ga 'o legaa e afio mai Lealaisalagoa*
> although Lealaisalanoa **has arrived** [+chief]
>
> *e le 'i 'aumaia se koofaa iaa Salagoa ma-*
> no **opinion** [+chief] has been given from (Lealai)salanoa and–

The same can be seen in (2), where, in turn, the high chief Lealaisalanoa acknowledges the arrival of one of the senior orators and the term *maliu mai* "come" (see Figure 3.2) is used:

(2) (*Fono* April 7, 1979)

> Salanoa: *ia 'o le maliu mai laa o le Makua,*
> So the senior orator has **arrived** [+titled, −chief].

On other social occasions such as informal meetings or visits, however, the use of RWs is much less "consistent" and the referent condition is often violated. In the following conversation, for instance, in talking about the same chiefly title (Salanoa), one speaker, A, uses the RW *afio mai* [+chief] "come, arrive" but the other speaker, F, paraphrases with the common word *'o'o aku*, literally "reach (there)":

(3) (Pastor and deacon)

> 147 A: *ia 'o le afio aku legaa o Salagoa.*
> So then there **arrives** [+chief] Salanoa.
>
> 148   *kau fa 'amakala 'ae ua leaga maakou ua-*
> (I/we?) try to explain but we are bad-
>
> 149 F: *ga- ga o'o aku laa Salagoa?=*
> did- did Salanoa himself **get there** [−titled]?

It should be pointed out that F is not related to the chief Salanoa and in fact later on in the conversation, in quoting his own direct speech to the chief, he uses the RWs *figagalo* "want" and *lau afioga* "your highness (said of/to a chief)." However, even in this discourse context, F refers to Salanoa as *si koiga* (short for *si koea'iga* "dear/poor old man"), which, without being disrespectful – it does convey some positive affect toward him – is not a respectful term:

(4) (Pastor and deacon)

160 F: *'ou fai aku i si koiga o Salagoa. "ia'."=*
I said to the dear old man Salanoa. "Well."

161 A: *=faiuiga lelei mEa.*
Interpret things well.

162 F: ***"Figagalo** maalie ia." (.3)*
"(If your) **wish** [+chief] agrees (with this)." (.3)

163 A: (?)

164:   *"lau **afioga** ma- (...)"*
"Your **Highness** [+chief] (...)"

These apparent "inconsistencies" are not restricted to casual conversational settings. Even when title holders are gathered to have a *fono*, there are cases in which the same individual is identified by a common word at one time and by an RW at another (Duranti 1984a: 226):

(5) (*Fono*, April 7, 1979. Before the meeting starts, the chairman Moe'ono asks about the people who are likely to attend. Mata'afa is an orator from the Falelua subvillage.)

Moe'ono: *Ga'o Maka'afa a le Falelua ga **sau**?*
Only Mata'afa has **come** from Falelua?

(. . .)

(Later on during the meeting)

Moe'ono: *(. . .) ia. 'o lea 'ua lua **afio** mai Kevaseu **maliu** mai fo'i Maka'afa*
. . . So, now you Tevaseu have **come** [+chief] (and) Mata'afa has also **come** [+title, −chief]

Finally, there are also cases in which a party uses an RW when the referent condition would predict a common word. In the following example, Tafili, an orator, talks about her brother Savea, a chief, using the RW *figagalo* "want," (but also "mind, opinion"). This instance violates the constraint against the use of RWs for kin.

(6) (*Fono*, April 7, 1979. Tafili speaks up in defence of her brother Savea.)

Tafili: *'a 'o legei kaimi, lelei aa le maalamalama uaa 'o le makaa'upu, 'o le makaa'upu o lea 'ua- 'ua lafo kaaofi iai le kalosaga iaa Savea iga ia kakala loga- . . . **figagalo** i laga kagi.*

> But at this point, it is better to clarify because the agenda, the agenda of this- it is- (since) Savea has already filed the suit could he change his . . . **mind** [+chief] about the suit.

Given that the unexpected absence of RWs in examples (3) and (5) is not perceived as "lack" of respect, and the presence of an RW term in (6) is not interpreted as ostentatious (or ludicrous), these examples show that **the referent's status/rank alone cannot be used to predict the lexical choice made**.

One option we have in trying to explain these apparent inconsistencies in language use is to expand our notion of "context" beyond the nature of the referent and think in terms of speech events (Hymes 1972), activity types (Levinson 1979), or levels of interactions. This is in fact what Shore suggested several years ago:

In Samoa, despite the use of the term "chiefly language" to refer to the polite lexical forms, common or polite forms are appropriate more clearly to levels of discourses and interaction than to levels of persons. With the exception of young children, polite forms can be employed by and with anyone when the intention is to signal or support a formal interaction. Conversely, the use of everyday vocabulary signals intimacy and commonness in encounters and not so much in persons.

(Shore 1977: 457)

As I will show next, by improving our notion of what constitutes context, and in particular by reconsidering the relationship between context and language, we will in fact be able to improve our understanding of these phenomena at least in terms of the accuracy with which we can predict or justify the actual use of RWs.

3   Respectful words as markers of public, positional identities

In analyzing the *fono* interactions, we are reminded of Goffman's work on behavior in public places and the notion of **back stage** behavior (Goffman 1959). For instance, common words tend to occur in conversation **before** the *fono* starts, or in the breaks of the *fono* proceedings – Goffman's (1974) "time-outs" from a given frame – as in example (5). There is indeed a tendency for RWs to be more consistently used in the more public or "formal" parts of such events, when participants are "on stage" and when cooccurrence restrictions are stricter (Ervin-Tripp 1972, Irvine 1979). A more refined notion of context, one for instance in which we make crucial use of such notions as **temporal** and **spatial boundaries** (Duranti 1981, 1985; Goffman 1974), might indeed allow us to make more precise predictions on the use of RWs.

However, we still need to explain cases such as (6) above, where a speaker uses an RW in talking about her brother, and cases such as those in examples (3) and (4), where, during the same conversation, only a few seconds apart, speakers switch from one set of terms to another in referring to the same individual.

4   Language defines context

In trying to understand these phenomena we may be guided by Samoan ideology, which stresses the high level of context-sensitivity in social interaction and communication. We thus know from previous accounts (Mead 1937; Shore 1982; Duranti 1984b, 1988) that the notion of Self as conceived in the Western analytical tradition is not shared by Samoans, who are not as committed as most Westerners are to the ideology of permanency of individual characteristics and social values across social contexts. In Samoan society, the individual is defined as a composite persona with several "sides" (*ituu*), which are – often consciously so – foregrounded or backgrounded according to the situation, the use of RWs being no exception to this theory and practice. Indeed, a given social actor deserves respect according to his or her role/status in a given context. In (6), for instance, we could say that Tafili is referring to Savea **as a chief** and not **as her brother** (something similar was at work when Robert Kennedy in his public speeches used to refer to John Kennedy as "President Kennedy"). The lexical choice made by the speaker helps define which "side" of the referent's social persona or which particular relationship is relevant in the ongoing interaction. In other words, the linguistic choice partly defines some aspects of the "context" to be presupposed or entailed in the interaction (cf. Silverstein 1985a, 1985b). That is, once we start saying that RWs can be used to evoke particular "sides," we are moving toward a different characterization of the relationship between context and language. It is no longer context alone (be it the referent's status/rank or the speech event) that determines the language used. It is also the language, namely RWs, that helps define what the context is. In some cases, in fact, **language is the context**. The consistency of RW uses in a *fono* during the discussion could thus be explained as a common strategy for defining, over an extended period of time, a context in which certain particular social personae (those of certain titles, with their associated rights and duties) must count and must be evoked. The role of language as defining context is schematically represented in Figure 3.4.

The most obvious cases covered by this scheme are those in which RWs are used with individuals who do not hold a title but are, on some particular occasion, asked to act **as if** they did.

5   Language and context: a reflexive relationship

In fact, both Figures 3.3 and 3.4 are oversimplifications of an ongoing dialogical process in which language and context mutually feed into one

LANGUAGE   CONTEXT

$\longrightarrow$

feature(s) {x}   feature(s) {X}

Figure 3.4 *Language defines context*

another. To better explain this point, we will have to go beyond the question of the distribution of the RWs and consider more specifically the question of their social meaning. Rather than talking about specific referents or speech events determining the use of RWs or about RWs defining the nature of the referents, it might be helpful to consider RWs as indices (Peirce 1955, Silverstein 1976) of particular roles and relationships among participants in the speech event that could or should be activated at a given point in the interaction. RWs can thus function as keys (Hymes 1972) or contextualization cues (Gumperz 1977, this volume) that trigger a certain set of expectations, attitudes, and inferential processes associated to the kind of referent or activity they index. They can be used (or interpreted) as mediating devices that define the relationship between a referent and an activity, between the speaker and the referent, or between the speaker and the activity – the activity itself can of course be further analyzed into several components.

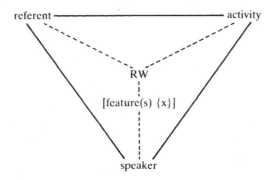

Figure 3.5 *Mediating role of RWs*

As illustrated in Figure 3.5, the feature set {x} of the RW triggers a particular set of expectations and attitudes *vis-à-vis* the relationship among the three corners of the triangle (dotted lines). In some cases, the features in {x} may override the preexisting (e.g. language-independent) relationship among speaker, referent, and activity (marked by solid lines). The term "activity" in Figure 3.5 includes addressee(s) and any other members in the so-called "participant structure" of the event (Goodwin 1986, Haviland 1986, Philips 1983).

The apparent **inconsistency** of lexical choice in referring to titled persons (as well as to their belongings, actions, and properties) can thus be partly explained by taking into consideration the potentially **reflexive relationship** between words and social reality. If we conceive of words not only as labels for an already existing reality but also as ideologically loaded tools for defining the situations in which speakers *qua* social actors co-construct their context, we can better appreciate the social (hence pragmatic) function of linguistic subsystems such as the Samoan RWs.

Within this framework, the intermittent use of RWs in examples (3), (4), and (5) will have to be understood over against the background of the speaker's relationship with both the referent and his addressee (feature of the ongoing activity) and by making hypotheses on what his – conscious? unconscious? – goals may be in redefining such relationships in the course of the interaction (e.g. he pays tribute/honor to the chief when the situation calls for it – e.g. face-to-face – but can also informally afford to speak of him as "the dear old man," and by so doing distinguish himself from A, who does not do so, etc.). In such cases, only a very fine ethnographically grounded analysis will allow us to come up with hypotheses that might go beyond the realm of hazardous, albeit suggestive, speculations.

As an example of the kind of phenomena and analysis I am thinking of, I will briefly reconsider the use of RWs in cooccurence with so-called **face-threatening acts** (FTAs).

6   RWs and face-threatening acts

In Brown and Levinson's (1978) cross-linguistic research on politeness, giving deference is described as one of the strategies for compensating for FTAs. (I will assume hereafter that "deference" and "respect" are synonymous in their theory.)

There are two sides to the coin in the realization of deferences: one in which S[peaker] humbles and abases himself, and another where S raises H[earer] (pays him positive face of a particular kind, namely that which satisfies H's want to be treated as superior). In both cases what is conveyed is that H is of higher social status than S. By conveying directly the perception of a high P[ower] differential, deference serves to defuse potential face-threatening acts by indicating that the addressee's rights to relative immunity from imposition are recognized – and moreover that S is certainly not in a position to coerce H's compliance in any way.

(Brown and Levinson 1978: 183)

This notion of deference/respect as a way of recognizing relative immunity from imposition seems at first confirmed by our Samoan data. We do find several cases where RWs are used in what seem to be attempts to mitigate some FTA.

For example, in (7), taken from a transcript of a conversation recorded during our first month in the village, A, the elderly deacon, has come to the pastor in whose compound we were living to cancel an invitation to our research group (Alesana and the "family") to go over for dinner at his house. In listing the people to whom, with the help of the pastor, he wants to explain the reason for not being able to keep his invitation, speaker A uses the RW *falekua* ("wife" [+chief]) in referring to my wife (Elinor Ochs). The common term *to'alua* could have also been used.

(7) (Pastor and Deacon. Participants: F, the pastor, A, the deacon, Alesana, the researcher.)

347 A: *-hh e iai le mea ga 'ou afe mai ai.*
         -hh there is a thing I came for.

348   (.5)

349 F: *ia'. lelei.*
         Okay. good (go ahead).

350 A: *go'u afe mai iaa ke 'oe e fa'amaalie aku.*
         I came to you to apologize.

351   *ia' e fa'amaalamalama lelei iaa- (.3)*
         to explain carefully to- (.3)

352   *Alesana ma le 'aaiga.*
         Alesana and (his) family.

353   (1.)

354   *i fo'i lele- i le falekua o le ali'i.*
         also to the- to **wife** [+chief] of the gentleman.

355   (1.)

356   *uaa o le maakou kalagoaga o gagei*
         because of our talk about later today

357   *e oo aku- koe kaafafao.*
         (when) they were going to visit (us) again.

358 F: *mm.*
         mm.

         (. . .)

This use of the RW *falekua* (see Figure 3.2) can indeed be seen as a way of giving deference to both of us and can therefore be analyzed as a mitigating device before an FTA. At the same time, this exchange brings out the problematic nature of the categories Speaker and Hearer in the analysis of strategic verbal interaction and shows that in fact there might be simultaneous "targets" (Brenneis 1978, Haviland 1986) of the RW. In this, as well as in many other instances that have been discussed in the literature (Hymes 1972, Duranti 1985, Levinson 1986), a more sophisticated notion of **participant** is needed. Although I was sitting next to A and F, I was at the time (a few weeks after arriving in the village) unable to follow their conversation. I was then both a **hearer** and one of the **recipients** of the message but not a fully fledged participant. One could say that the apology was intended for me but the message was directed to the pastor, who later on had to translate it for me, first in Samoan foreigner talk and then in English. We might then say that the expressed respect was also indirectly addressed to the pastor, who was not only part of the audience but the locally alleged head of our extended family and our mentor in the eyes of the villagers.

With this in mind, let's move to another example. In this case as well, RWs seem to be used to reassure a hearer that his actions or wishes are not being coerced by someone else's actions (in this case, mine). The scene here is a *fono*. The meeting is over and Moeʻono, the senior orator who also acts as the chairman of the meeting, has just been told that there is no more *kava*[2] left for a closing ceremony. He then turns to me and says:

(8) (*Fono*, April 7, 1978 [p. 103, ms.])

> Moeʻono: *ia Alesaga (le) Sili, uaa ua ʻuma ga kusikusi?*
> So, Alexander the Great, well, is all the writing done?
> *ʻo aa ea ga mea e kusikusi (e) ʻoe?*
> what is that you keep writing down?

> Others: (laughter) *hehehehe.*

> Fuimaono: *ʻo a kou **vagaga** aa ma **saugoaga** lea*
> it's your **speech** [+high orator] (see Figure 3.2) and the **speech** [+chief] that
>
> *ua- (.3) kusikusi uma lava e le kama.*
> the (.3) boy has been writing down word by word
> [
> [
> Moeʻono: *oh.*
> Oh!

We find here two RWs: *vagaga* and *saugoaga* (a nominalization from *saugoa*) (see Figure 3.2), both of which mean "speech," with the first one being restricted to the highest ranking orators (Moeʻono being one of the two in the village) and the second being appropriate for chiefs. The utterance freely translates as "it is the speech of you holy senior orators and honorable chiefs that the boy has been writing." On the other hand, the use of the word *kama* "boy" in talking about me can be seen as an example of **other-abasement**. This way of characterizing my person is quite a contrast with the respect I was shown on other occasions, see for example segment (7) above. What is happening then? In a very Samoan fashion, what we find here is the attempt by a third party (the chief Fuimaono) to both downplay my role and diffuse Moeʻono's potentially antagonistic remark (notice Moeʻono's use of the locution "Alexander the Great", which is a way of indexing my lack of chiefly status – that is, the only title he can think of is a blatantly fake one, which invites laughter). The chief Fuimaono successfully gets me off the hook (and probably saves my dissertation) by reassuring Moeʻono of Moeʻono's superiority as against my (contextually defined) low status. What could a "boy" do to such a powerful man? He (that is, I) could only take notes and learn from the old man's high eloquence.

This interpretation is based on Brown and Levinson's concept of respect as a way of reassuring the addressee that someone else (the speaker or a third party) is not coercing them. However, the principle on which this interpretation is based might be very context-specific. That higher status is something that anyone would want or prefer is not always apparent across sociocultural contexts. Studies of the strategic behavior centered around greeting exchanges in highly stratified African societies, for example, have stressed the coercive effect of verbal formulae that both foreground status differential and imply financial obligations among members of a given community (Goody 1972, Irvine 1974). Thus, in her study of Wolof greetings, Irvine points out:

It should not be assumed that a person, whatever his or her caste, will necessarily wish to take the position of higher status. Although high status implies prestige, respect, and political power, it also implies the obligation to contribute to the support of low-status persons. Thus high rank means a financial burden, while low rank has its financial compensations.

(Irvine 1974: 175)

Similar considerations could be made about the use of Samoan RWs. Samoan speakers as well often worry when they are addressed with RWs and may try to avoid being put in a higher-ranking position.

By linking these observations with the function of RWs as context-creating devices, it might be argued that in fact **one of the functions of RWs is not to recognize the recipients' immunity from imposition, but, on the**

contrary, to coerce, to oblige them to behave in a certain way (e.g. with generosity, with a controlling demeanour), as appropriate to the social status (and rank) entailed by the RWs.

As I will show next, the potentially coercive and obliging nature of the act of giving "respect" is frequently recognized in people's conversations and seems to be part of the local theory of emotions and social action.

7   The Samoan notion of respect

I will show now that Samoans see respect as something that, once evoked, can force people to do things they would not otherwise do. I will start by examining two examples from the same conversation between a pastor and a deacon mentioned above. In this segment, the elderly deacon is recounting to the village's young pastor the visit of our research group to his house the night before. He lists all the good foods that had been prepared for us and then expresses satisfaction about the event (line 33). At this point, the pastor challenges that statement by asking whether in fact we had eaten. By so doing, he displays access to privileged information, namely, the fact that we had already eaten at his house before going to visit the deacon's family. The deacon's response clarifies that we were forced to eat some of the food because of the respect (*fa'aaloalo*).

(9) (Pastor and deacon)

33 A: *fiaFIia lava agapoo. -hh 'ai maa'Ona.*
         Very happy last night. -hh (we/they) ate a lot!

34 (?)

35 F: *ga 'a 'ai laa le vaaega?=*
         Did the gang eat?

36 A: *=Ioe. (.3) maakou 'a 'ai.*
         Yes. (.3) we (all) ate.

37 (.5)

38 F: *hh.*

39 A: *'a e le 'i lava- le 'i kele laga le mea-*
         but not much–   not much because the thin-

40 F: *le 'i kele laga-*
                  not much because–

41 F: *laga 'ua 'uma oga ('a 'ai).*
         because (they) already (ate).

42 A: *'ae lee mafai laa leaga 'ou faku-*
          But (they) couldn't (refuse) because I say=

43   = *'o le fa'aaloalo. (.3) fa'aaloalo.*
          it's (for) the respect. (.3) respect.

44 F: *'o le fa'aaloalo,*
          (it's) the respect

45 A   *fa'aaloalo*
          respect.

The second example is taken from a point in the conversation where the deacon recounts an incident in which some members of the church congregation were being hosted at someone's house but were not sure whether they should be there or somewhere else. When they tried to leave, the story says, they couldn't because they were "caught by the respect":

(10) (Pastor and deacon)

107 A: *ia'. 'ae 'o le uma aku legaa o Vaekolu*
          So, when Vaetolu had finished eating,

108   *faimai ga lavea la 'ua ma Salagoa i le fa'aaloalo.*
          (she) said (that) she and Salanoa were caught by the respect.

These two examples are representative of attitudes and beliefs that we recurrently encountered during our fieldwork: "respect" (*fa'aaloalo*) is not just something that people "have" in their minds or their hearts (e.g. in the US one might "have respect" for another person without ever telling or showing him or her) but rather a set of behaviors and constraints on behaviors (see also Gerber 1985). Respect is something that is done to people, like forcing them to eat when they are not hungry – see example (9) – or stopping them from leaving too soon – see example (10).

Like other such systems or special terms (cf. the Kaluli kin term *ade* discussed by Schieffelin 1984), Samoan RWs can be a powerful means to evoke feelings and attitudes that trap recipients into behavioral patterns that they might not otherwise endorse or sustain. Thus, for instance, in (8) above, the chief Fuimaono was able to diffuse Moe'ono's attempt to question the legitimacy of my work by defining his status as disproportionately high *vis-à-vis* such a young untitled person like myself.

Furthermore, we should also seriously consider the connection established in Samoan ideology between "respect" and "tradition" (*aganu'u*) – a link which is absent in contemporary synchronically oriented models of politeness. In this perspective, the Samoan notion of respect ties individuals, situations, the here and now, as it were, to the past, and its projection into the present, hence defining the way the world **should** be, namely the accepted and acceptable social order. The occurrence of "respectful" behavior (words being one example) is talked about by

Samoans as something that can make people do things they might not do otherwise as a way of complying with a system of relations and social obligations that can maintain and help reproduce the social system – with its hierarchies, mutual obligations, and worldview – intact and unaffected by the continuous threat of change. This link with tradition may suggest that the use of RWs described in this chapter supports Bloch's (1975) characterization of traditional oratory as an ideological tool that forces individuals to accept the status quo – especially in light of the fact that the most pervasive use of RWs in Samoa is found in speechmaking. RWs can certainly be used to impose traditional solutions and support and traditional political apparatus. On the other hand, as examples such as (8) show, it is also possible to use RWs to get around the system and introduce new elements in the political arena, e.g. a foreign observer who writes down and tape-records what is being said.[3] The weakness in Bloch's argument is to assume that homage to tradition necessarily implies a conservative stand. In reality, this is often but not always the case.

8   Conclusions

To capture the uses and functions of lexical choices we must conceive of context and language as a dynamic and evolving relation in which words mediate between different versions of the world and often let more than one version coexist in the act of speaking. The Samoan respect vocabulary offers a potentially perfect match between language and the social world. The Samoan hierarchical system, with its distinctions between untitled and titled individuals, chiefs and orators, ordinary and high-ranking title holders, is reified by lexical distinctions that faithfully and routinely remind everyone of who-is-who in the sociopolitical arena. At the same time, the availability of such a taxonomy makes such a simple task as lexical choice into an art, unconscious at times, cunning on some occasions, merciless on others.

A feature analysis of the kind illustrated at the beginning of this chapter can be a useful tool in a first description of the phenomenon at hand. At the same time, it needs to be integrated with more sophisticated notions of "context" to capture a fuller range of variation in the social meaning of the use of RWs across and within social activities.

I have suggested that at least in some cases, the use of RWs in cooccurrence with FTAs should not be interpreted only as a way of paying back the addressee for what the addressee may be losing, i.e. face. What the Samoan case (as well as the Wolof, Gonja, Kaluli, etc.) demonstrates is that speakers use certain respectful lexical items and descriptions to make sure that addressees will comply with what they are expected to do. Thus, respect is not only given **in exchange** for something (e.g. request, impositions of various kinds), it is also a **pragmatic force** that coerces certain behaviors or actions upon people and thus indexes speakers' control over addressees rather than addressees' "freedom" of action. As any Samoan knows, RWs are not just means to say "sorry, but I must ask you x"; they are strategically powerful tools that can force others to assume particular social personae, to wear social masks from behind which it will be very hard to refuse what is requested.

Acknowledgments

For the study of the Samoan Respect Vocabulary and more generally of Samoan language use and ideology, I am particularly indebted to the Samoan orators and chiefs who, with great patience, let me record their interactions and spent many hours trying to make me into a knowledgeable participant: 'Alo Eti, Iuli Lua Veni, Iuli Sefo, Savea Savelio, Fulumu'a (Tavo) Utulei For his friendship, help, and understanding, I am also grateful to Rev. Fa'atauoloa Mauala, pastor of the Congregational Christian Church in the village of Falefa. I am also indebted to the members of the 1980–1 Working Group on Language and Cultural Context at the Research School of Pacific Studies, the Australian National University, for providing encouragement and insightful comments on the matters discussed in this chapter; in particular, I benefited from discussions with Penny Brown, Steve Levinson, John Haviland, Judy Irvine, and Robert van Valin. Finally, I would like to thank Aaron Cicourel, Chuck Goodwin, Bill Hanks, John Haviland, and Elinor Ochs for detailed comments on earlier drafts of this chapter. The research on Samoan language and culture on which this chapter is based was supported by the National Science Foundation and the Australian National University. The writing of this chapter has been partly supported by NSF Grant no. 53-4028-4129 (A. Duranti and E. Ochs principal investigators).

This chapter is dedicated to the memory of 'Alo Eti, orator, deacon, and friend, and Iuli Lua Veni, the best speechmaker I ever met. These two men's words and wisdom I have extensively borrowed throughout this chapter and on many other occasions.

Notes

1 To make things easier for the reader, in the following figures I have used the same phonological register found in the examples used in the text (e.g. *figagalo* instead of *finagalo* or *kausi* instead of *tausi*). This is an unconventional choice, given that this register, called by Samoans "bad speech" (Duranti 1981, Duranti and Ochs 1986, Shore 1982), is not found in literacy activities (such as school instruction or writing), but is very common in most of daily speech, in both formal and informal interactions. It should be also noted that I have here used traditional Samoan orthography (e.g. *g* stands for a velar nasal and the inverted apostrophe ['] for a glottal stop), with the exception of vowel length, which I have marked phonemically, namely, with two identical vowels. For the

computerized version of my transcripts, I have used a program for personal computer prepared by John B. Haviland and mostly based on the conventions introduced in Conversation Analysis by Gail Jefferson. The hyphen "-" indicates the cut-off point; an equals sign indicates that there is no break between turns; a square bracket connecting the talk of different speakers shows where overlap begins; numbers in parentheses indicate length of pause in minutes (3.) in tens of seconds (.3).

2 *Kava* is a pan-Pacific nonalcoholic beverage prepared by mixing water with the pounded or pulverized dry roots of a pepper plant (*Piper methysticum*). In Samoa, ceremonial kava drinking is traditionally restricted to titled individuals, although I observed informal kava drinking by both titled and untitled men during collective projects requiring hard physical labour.

3 The potential effects of such technological innovations were well understood by an emerging young leader who asked me to use my audio-tapes of the meetings as evidence in a court case against more powerful parties. But that's another story.

References

Bloch, M. 1975. Introduction to *Political Language and Oratory in Traditional Society*, ed. M. Bloch. London: Academic Press.

Brenneis, D. 1978. The Matter of Talk: Political Performances in Bhatgaon. *Language in Society* 7: 159–70.

Brown, P., and S. Levinson. 1978. Universals in Language Usage: Politeness Phenomena, in *Questions and Politeness*, ed. E. Goody, pp. 56–310. Cambridge: Cambridge University Press.

Bühler, K. 1934. *Sprachtheorie: Die Darstellungsfunktion der Sprache*. Stuttgart: G. Fisher.

Comrie, B. 1976. Linguistic Politeness Axes: Speaker–Addressee, Speaker–Reference, Speaker–Bystander. *Pragmatics Microfiche* 1 (7) A3-B1.

Dixon, R. M. W. 1972. *The Dyirbal Language of North Queensland*. Cambridge: Cambridge University Press.

Duranti, A. 1981. *The Samoan Fono: A Sociolinguistic Analysis*. Pacific Linguistics Monographs, Series B, Vol. 80. Canberra: Australian National University, Department of Linguistics.

1984a. *Lauga* and *Talanoaga:* Two Speech Genres in a Samoan Political Event, in *Dangerous Words: Language and Politics in the Pacific*, D. L. Brenneis and F. Myers (eds.), pp. 218–42. New York: New York University Press.

1984b. *Intentions, Self, and Local Theories of Meaning: Words and Social Action in a Samoan Context*. Center for Human Information Processing, Report No. 122. La Jolla: University of California, San Diego.

1985. Sociocultural Dimensions of Discourse, in *Handbook of Discourse Analysis, Vol. I: Disciplines of Discourse*, ed. T. A. V. Dijk, pp. 193–230. New York: Academic Press.

1988. Intentions, Language, and Social Action in a Samoan Context. *Journal of Pragmatics* 12: 13–33.

Duranti, A., and E. Ochs. 1986. Literacy Instruction in a Samoan Village, in *The Acquisition of Literacy: Ethnographic Perspectives*, eds. B. B. Schieffelin and P. Gilmore, pp. 213–32. Norwood, NJ: Ablex.

Ervin-Tripp, A. 1972. On Sociolinguistic Rules: Alternation and Cooccurrence, in *Directions in Sociolinguistics: The Ethnography of Communication*, ed. J. J. Gumperz and D. Hymes, pp. 213–50. New York: Holt, Rinehart and Winston.

Gadamer, H.-G. 1976. *Philosophical Hermeneutics*, trans. and ed. D. E. Linge. Berkeley: University of California Press.

Geertz, C. 1960. *The Religion of Java*. Glencoe, Ill.: The Free Press.

Gerber, E. R. 1985. Rage and Obligation: Samoan Emotion in Conflict, in *Person, Self, and Experience: Exploring Pacific Ethnopsychologies*, ed. G.M. White and J. Kirkpatrick. Berkeley: University of California Press.

Goffman, Erving. 1959. *The Presentation of Self in Everyday Life*. Garden City, New York: Doubleday Anchor Books.

1974. *Frame Analysis: An Essay on the Organization of Experience*. New York: Harper and Row.

Goodwin, C. 1986. Audience Diversity, Participation and Interpretation. *Text* 6 (3): 283–316.

Goody, E. 1972. 'Greeting', 'Begging', and the Presentation of Respect, in *The Interpretation of Ritual*, ed. J. S. LaFontaine, pp. 39–72. London: Tavistock.

Gumperz, J. 1977. Sociocultural Knowledge in Conversational Inference, in *Georgetown University Round Table on Languages and Linguistics 1977*, ed. M. Saville-Troike. Washington, DC: Georgetown University Press.

Haviland, John B. (1979a). How to Talk to Your Brother-in-Law in Guugu Yimidhirr, in *Languages and their Speakers*, ed. T. Shopen. Cambridge, Mass.: Winthrop.

1979b. Guugu Yimidhirr Brother-in-Law Language. *Language in Society* 8: 365–93.

1986. 'Con Buenos Chiles': Talk, Targets and Teasing in Zinacantan. *Text* 6(3): 249–282.

Hymes, D. 1972. Models of the Interaction of Language and Social Life, in *Directions in Sociolinguistics: The Ethnography of Communication* ed. J. J. Gumperz and D. Hymes, pp. 35–71. New York: Holt, Rinehart and Winston.

Irvine, J. 1974. Strategies of Status Manipulation in the Wolof Greeting, in *Explorations in the Ethnography of Speaking*, ed. R. Bauman and J. Sherzer, pp. 167–91. Cambridge: Cambridge University Press.

1979. Formality and Informality in Communicative Events. *American Anthropologist* 81: 773–90.

Levinson, S. C. 1979. Activity Types and Language. *Linguistics* 17: 365–99.

1983. *Pragmatics*. Cambridge: Cambridge University Press.

1986. Putting Linguistic on a Proper Footing: Explorations in Goffman's Concepts of Participation. Paper delivered to the conference "Erving Goffman: An Interdisciplinary Appreciation," York, July 1986.

Malinowski, B. 1923. The Problem of Meaning in Primitive Languages, in C. K. Ogden and I. A. Richards *The Meaning of Meaning*, ed. C. K. Ogden and I. A. Richards. New York: Harcourt, Brace and World, Inc.

Mead, M. 1937. The Samoans, in *Cooperation and Competition among Primitive People*, ed. M. Mead, pp. 282–312. Boston: Beacon Press.

Milner, G. B. 1961. The Samoan Vocabulary of Respect. *Journal of the Royal Anthropological Institute* 91: 296–317.

Peirce, C. S. 1955. *Philosophical Writings of Peirce*, ed. J. Buchler. New York: Dover Publications.

Philips, S. U. 1983. *The Invisible Culture: Communication in Classroom and Community on the Warm Spring Indian Reservation*. New York: Longman.

Schieffelin, B. 1984. Ade: A Sociolinguistic Analysis of a Relationship, in *Language in Use: Readings in Sociolinguistics*, ed. J. Baugh and J. Scherzer, pp. 229–43. Englewood Cliffs, NJ: Prentice-Hall.

Shore, B. 1977. A Samoan Theory of Action: Social Control and Social Order in a Polynesian Paradox. Unpublished Ph. dissertation, University of Chicago.

1982. *Sala'ilua: A Samoan Mystery*. New York: Columbia University Press.

Silverstein, M. 1976. Shifters: Linguistic Categories and Cultural Description, in *Meaning in Anthropology*, ed. K. Basso and H. Sleby, pp. 11–55. Albuquerque: University of New Mexico Press.

1977. Cultural Prerequisites in Grammatical Analysis, in *Georgetown University Round Table on Languages and Linguistics 1977*, ed. M. Saville-Troike. Washington, DC: Georgetown University Press.

1979. Language Structure and Linguistic Ideology, in *The Elements: A Parasession on Linguistic Units and Levels,* ed. P. R. Clyne, W. F. Hanks, and C. L. Hofbauer. Chicago: Chicago Linguistic Society.

1985a. The Culture of Language in Chinookan Narrative Texts; or, On Saying That . . . in Chinookan, in *Grammar Inside and Outside the Clause: Some Approaches to Theory from the Field*, ed. J. Nichols and A. Woodburg. Cambridge: Cambridge University Press.

1985b. The Functional Stratification of Language and Ontogenesis, in *Culture, Communication and Cognition: Vygotskian Perspectives,* ed. J. V. Wertsch. Cambridge: Cambridge University Press.

Vygotsky, L. S. 1978. *Mind in Society: The Development of Higher Psychological Processes*, ed. M. Cole, V. John-Steiner, S. Scribner and E. Souberman. Cambridge, Mass.: Harvard University Press.

4   Context contests: debatable truth statements on Tanna (Vanuatu)

LAMONT LINDSTROM

Editors' introduction

Lamont Lindstrom is Associate Professor of Anthropology at the University of Tulsa. Drawing on several years' research in Vanuatu, he has published on Pacific ethnohistory, traditional oratory, and drug uses. In this chapter, Lindstrom directly addresses the limits of formal treatments of verbal interaction of the kind evoked by such notions as "frame" (Bateson, Goffman) or "speech event" (Hymes). Taking inspiration from Foucault's work, he argues that such analytical concepts are not value-free, but instead are strictly connected with local norms about what can be said by whom and how to interpret. Starting from a detailed analysis of a dispute between a father and a son on the Melanesian island of Tanna, Vanuatu, Lindstrom shows that much of the talk in conflict-management settings is about defining truth, and that the ability to establish what is true and what is false is but an instrument of power. Where does the power reside? Precisely in the ability to evoke and use the relevant domains of knowledge that link certain individuals with particular rights, duties, and responsibilities. The authority of one's voice is thus conveyed and realized by relying on culturally acceptable discourse procedures, which can reshape the ongoing context or challenge what might have been taken for granted before talk occurred.

Lindstrom's chapter thus relates and complements a number of perspectives taken in other contributions to this volume. In particular, the criticism of the neutrality of context echoes some of the points made by Cicourel on the need to be aware of the institutional constraints on what counts as relevant background information in any given context (e.g. among the staff in a medical setting). Just as Melanesian bigmen and their in-laws can, in making their points during a public debate, rely upon a variety of local rules or taboos on what constitutes evidence for a given claim, whose voice can be heard, and which topic can be publicly discussed, Ciccourel shows us that within the culture of medical facility different terms (e.g. patient, liver, eye) can evoke technical knowledge and experience that give authority to one voice over another, and provide evidence for a given set of procedures over others.

Conversation analysis has taught us to pay attention first to the details of what is actually said, and has developed some powerful analytical tools for doing it. The ethnographically oriented research of the type carried on by Lindstrom, Cicourel, and Philips (in this volume) teaches us not to hide what the participants themselves must know in order to interact at all in the way they do. The multi-level model that emerges from these different contributions and perspectives is one in which the formal properties of the communicative system can be seen through a variety of filtering devices, with power being one of them.

Context contests: debatable truth statements on Tanna (Vanuatu)

On June 15, 1983, around seventy-five people on Tanna Island, Vanuatu, met to resolve a dispute between a father and son.[1] The meeting went badly. Talk degenerated into a fist fight and general melee. Subsequent debate failed to clear the air and repair the dispute. The meeting ended without a consensual resolution.

To understand what people said to each other at this meeting, why they failed to resolve their problem, and why talk led to violence, we obviously need to know about "context." Reading a transcript of what people said during debate is not enough. Context informs the text. This island meeting, like any speech event, needs to be situated within the actors' cultural horizons. But how can we be more specific? What aspects of the cultural context should we notice? In this chapter, I use an approach to context I borrow from Foucault (1981). In this, the context of talk consists of "orders of discourse." Context is a set of cultural rules, conditions, and practices that govern how people talk. People have to attend to local conditions for talking in order to converse in ways that sound authentic, meaningful, and worth saying. They also have to pay attention to existing, surrounding "discourses" – or bodies of organized, local knowledge. The term "discourse" sometimes refers to conversation – what in this chapter I instead call "talk." This talk takes place in the context of cultural "discourses," or "complexes of signs and practices which organize social existence and social reproduction" (Terdiman 1985: 54).

This approach to discursive context demands that we pay attention to several kinds of power. First, there is the power of culture (or context) itself. It is difficult to converse authentically unless one talks by the rules. Already existing discourses and already existing conditions for talking set limits on what can be said and how it can be said. Secondly, these surrounding discourses and these conditions for talking empower people unequally. Some have rights to talk. Some do not. Some people may claim expertise over important bodies of knowledge; some are ignorant of those discourses. When people come together to talk, they arrive endowed with different conversational rights and resources.

Context is a field of power relations. It is not, however, a frozen field. Context rolls as people talk. Preexisting discourses and discursive conditions do set limits on talk, but they are never totally determinant. People can occasionally say the unsayable. They can contest the context, by evoking available alternative or competing discourses. There is an inter-relation between talk and context. If context informs the text, so can a text inform its context. Orders of discourse are not monolithic (Foucault 1978: 95–6; Terdiman 1985; see also Bakhtin 1981: 271–3). Even within the most hegemonic culture, possibilities for counter-discourses exist. Furthermore, the various discourses within a culture may be contradictory. Talk that is true in the context of one may be construed false in the context of a second.

During the debate analyzed here, the contextual background was not fixed. People played with its loose ends and its contradictions in order to win the debate: to add value to what they said; to devalue the talk of their opponents. As some speakers strove to establish the truth of what they said in terms of one local island discourse, others labored to decontextualize this, revealing its falsity in the terms of a second. Disputants, furthermore, sometimes refused to recognize the value, or "seriousness," of some of the statements of their rivals. They avoided hearing, for example, the subtextual meanings of metaphors, allegories, or other indirect speech, finessing their rivals' statements as mere trivia or nonsense (see McKellin 1990). Although context/culture/orders of discourse largely determine the limits of what can be said, people talking in context nonetheless find room to negotiate and resist, given the "dynamic character of human action and human understanding" (Duranti, this volume, p. 79).

1   Context as a discursive order

As Ochs (1979) and others have observed, there exist two principal analytics of context: the one, stemming from the cognitive sciences, focuses on information-processing structures in our heads that help us understand talk. The other, more sociological, breaks down those features of interpersonal speech events that influence our production of talk. Both approaches bundle up cognitive and/or social aspects of context into packages labeled frames, schema, schemata, scripts, or speech events (see Tannen 1979). Talk occurs in this manner within frames; in terms of a mental schema or script; or is embedded within the several constituent elements of a speech event.

These concepts of "frame" (Bateson 1972; Goffman 1974), "schema," and "speech event" have been dominant models for thinking about context. Context is often further sorted and broken down into various component elements such as settings, scenes, participants, ends, topics, tones, channels, codes, norms, genres, and so on (see Hymes 1967: 20–5). However plotted, these models of context often grant context an inert neutrality: context is a neutral field for the play of speech events, or is the cumulation of cognitive schemata that are cued to foreground past understanding.[2]

Foucault's "orders of discourse," on the other hand, spotlight the relations of power, and of resistance, inherent in context. People converse in a context full of conditions that govern authentic, "audible" forms of talk and, furthermore, that organize who may talk. This, Foucault calls a "rarefaction" of speaking subjects: "none may enter the order of discourse if he does not satisfy certain requirements or if he is not, from the outset, qualified to do so" (1981: 61–2). Secondly, an order of discourse establishes conditions under which talk is heard to be true or false. "It is always possible that one might speak the truth in the space of a wild exteriority, but one is 'in the true' only by obeying the rules of a discursive 'policing' which one has to reactivate in each of one's discourses" (1981: 61).

Abandoning the neutrality of schema, frame, and speech event, contextual analysis begins instead by asking what kinds of talk can be heard and understood, and what kinds of talk cannot. Are all participants qualified to speak and to speak the truth? Can talk carry all meanings? Let's take context, instead, to be an apparatus by which our talk most of the time is organized and controlled: A set of devices and procedures that protect ruling powers and truths, in Foucault's terms. Instead of speech event personnel, let's look for disparately qualified "subjects"; instead of contextual ends, let's look for relations of power and truth; instead of contextual norms, let's look for rules, devices, and procedures of discourse control.

Let's define the context of talk to be sets of discursive procedures and conditions that organize the qualifications and opportunities of speakers to make statements, and that establish conditions under which those statements are heard as authentic or true. Foucault (1981: 52–61) identifies three general kinds of discourse control procedures. Some endow certain people with better rights and opportunities to talk than others. In the debate analyzed here, for example, a wife's beating was at issue. Although the injured woman was present, she did not speak. Under the conditions of Tanna's discursive order, women's talk is muted. Secondly, some procedures establish areas of taboo or "silence" by making certain kinds of talk appear inauthentic, mad, irrational, or false. Finally, other conditions working from within a discourse serve to protect and reproduce that discourse. An example here is the "discipline" (Foucault 1981: 61). Disciplines organize knowledge by confirming which statements are true, which are false, and which are inaudible: "in order to be part of a discipline, a proposition has to be able to be inscribed on a certain type of theoretical horizon . . . within its own limits, each discipline recognizes true and false propositions; but it also pushes back a whole teratology of knowledge beyond its margins" (1981: 60).

In sum, people talk in a context of existing discursive orders that (1) endow people with different qualifications and opportunities to talk, and with different rights to tell the truth; (2) establish regions of knowledge and regions of "silence"; (3) set truth conditions – a "regime of truth"; and (4) link that regime of truth "in a circular relation with systems of power which produce and sustain it, and to effects of power which it induces and which extend it" (Foucault 1980: 133). To analyze the reflexive relationship of debate to its context, therefore, I have in mind a context full of discursive devices and procedures, not one composed of disinterested cognitive schemata or the comfortable furniture of speech events.

2   Debates on Tanna

The debate, or dispute-settlement meeting, is the main institutionalized forum for the resolution of social problems on Tanna (see Lindstrom 1981). Concerned leading men set the date for a meeting and send messages of invitation to third parties to come "witness" the proceedings. Witnesses tend to be older, powerful leaders of local groups, and also leaders of the several politico-religious organizations on the island.

Debates take place at forest clearings shaded by magnificent banyan trees. Here, men also convene daily to prepare and drink *kava* (*Piper methysticum*). People attending a debate sit along the periphery of these circular clearings. Disputants, consistent with island dualism, sit at anti-podal points, facing one another across the clearing. The third parties who witness debate mediate this dualism, positioning themselves between the two sides.

To speak, men stand and enter the center of the clearing. They hold the center until they are done expositing and then return to the periphery to sit. Debate rarely takes the form of question/answer or other sorts of adjacency pairs, as it does in the Fijian Indian Pancayat (Brenneis 1990; see also Goldman 1983: 19). Instead, speakers deliver statements. These statements may be terse or extensive; devoted to one point, or addressed to a number of points and fellow speakers. Debaters do refer to statements made by previous speakers. As the floor is self-acquired, however, topical and speaker interactions often are not adjacent. One to several subsequent statements by other speakers may have occupied the floor in the mean-while. Direct questioning or accusation of others is uncommon; speakers address their statements to the audience in general, or to important witnesses uninvolved in the dispute itself. If disputants do confront one another directly, nervous others hasten to interrupt and redirect the debate.

Speaking continues until about 4 p.m., when men need to begin the day's kava preparation, or their journeys to reach home villages before nightfall. People ordinarily pretend that a decision will be found, or a dispute settled, in one day's meeting – before dusk, in fact, so that kava preparation may properly begin. Shared kava between antagonists at the end of the day symbolizes the achievement of a consensus and the at least apparent resolution of dispute.

The debate I analyze in this chapter was convened to resolve a familial dispute between Misiuaren and his son Kara Ouihi. Long-standing ill feelings existed between father and son. These had, in part, grown out of problems in Kara Ouihi's and his brothers' marital arrangements. Tannese marriage practice is one of sister-exchange. When a man marries he gives up one of his sisters or other female relatives in exchange for his wife. Marriage agreements are often complex and difficult to organize. Most men rely on the goodwill and expertise of their fathers to carry out negotiations, but Misiuaren had been less than helpful and generous. Kara Ouihi was also angry that his father, as yet, had refused to bestow any of the family's set of traditional personal names on his grandchildren, all of whom were still known by European appellations. Personal names, on Tanna, give boys specific rights to various land plots in a locale (Lindstrom 1985).

Friction between Misiuaren and his son had worsened following the death of Kara Ouihi's infant boy. When Kara Ouihi brought his son's body home from the island's hospital (where he had been taken in a last-ditch effort – typical on the island – after traditional medicines had failed to cure a serious case of malaria), Misiuaren refused to let a grave for his grandson be dug in his village. Misiuaren also struck his wife Seroki for reasons that were muddied in later recountings of the event.

This was the dispute that about sixty men and fifteen women (including the abused Seroki) gathered to resolve. The most important point at issue was the cause of Kara Ouihi's son's demise. People, according to island discourses about kinship relations, took this death as an index of the family's discord, and of the necessity to settle this conflict quickly, lest angry ancestors kill off anyone else. The second important point concerned the facts of Seroki's beating. Why had Misiuaren clubbed his wife, and with what instrument? Misiuaren, Kara Ouihi, supporters, and witnesses all made statements about these events. In so doing, each side evoked several alternative island disciplines in order to dislocate the truth value of the statements of the other.

After ninety minutes or so of dispute, debate took a dangerous turn. Misiuaren and Kara Ouihi began addressing each other directly. Misiuaren, not dissuaded by witnesses' attempts to redirect talk along safer channels, then crossed to his son's side of the kava-drinking ground to strike him. Kara Ouihi's brothers and supporters managed to shield him from the blow, and other participants dashed to get hold of Misiuaren, who had grabbed a log as an impromptu club. In the meanwhile, however, one of Misiuaren's younger allies snuck up behind Kenat, Kara Ouihi's classificatory brother, and knocked him unconscious with a blow. Women keened and milled about. Most of the rest of the men rushed into the center in the clearing to secure both Misiuaren and Kara Ouihi, and to put a stop to several side-fights between supporters of each.

After Kenat had been revived by a pounding on his chest and a dousing of cold water, important witnesses managed to convince everyone to find their places again on the periphery of the clearing in order to keep debate alive. If talk had collapsed, and antagonists departed, the deepened social fissure would have been even more difficult to repair. An hour's additional discussion resulted in the typical Tannese response to serious conflict. A revived Kenat and his assailant would exchange a pig and a kava root. Misiuaren, on the one hand, and Kara Ouihi, on the other, would do likewise. The latter exchange, however, went awry. Only Kara Ouihi and his supporters drank kava together that night. Misiuaren went off with his allies and stayed away from home for a number of days until tempers had cooled to some degree. The debate's dramatis personae, to summarize, included the following:

The Father	Misiuaren (MI)
The Beaten Wife	Seroki
The Bereaved Son	Kara Ouihi (KO)
The Son's Main Supporter	Kieri (KI)
The Assaulted Brother	Kenat
Some Witnesses	Kauke (KA); Narua (NA); Nouar (NO)

To illustrate relations between talk and context, I excerpt statements made by some of these people during their debate. (Speakers are identified by the abbreviations listed above.) Following Foucault (1972: 80, 87), I take the "statement" to be the basic unit, or "function," of discourse. As Dreyfus and Rabinow (1982: 48) read Foucault, these statements are best understood as "serious speech acts" – the sort of talk produced by persons who "speak with authority beyond the range of their merely personal situation and power." These are statements whose claims to be true of reality take place "in a context in which truth and falsity have serious social consequences."[3] This is perhaps especially characteristic of the sort of truth statements produced during a dispute-settling debate.

Tanna's discursive order conditioned the form, the truth value, and the meaning of the statements made in debate, but so did these statements conjure up and occasionally shift the contextual order, as people contested context to their advantage. In the rest of the chapter, I explore these relations between discursive context, on the one hand, and debate statement meaning, and statement truth value, on the other.[4] Discussing statement meaning, I will be most concerned with discourse procedures that "rarefy" the speaking subject. Given Tanna's discursive context, what are peoples' rights to talk and to mean what they say? Discussing statement truth, I will be most concerned with discourse procedures, such as the "discipline," that determine whether talk rings true or if it sounds false notes.

3   Context and statement meaning

It is clear that the context informs the meaning of what people say. Conversely, people can shift or manipulate context by talking in the right way. A statement may directly evoke a new context (e.g. "let's be serious now"), or its linguistic features indirectly may "cue" (Gumperz 1982) or "key" (Goffman 1974) a contextual frame in which a speaker means his or her statement to be understood. I focus on this contextual keying and cuing first. Discussion of the other side of the story – context's effects on meaning – follows below.

In debate, disputants are obviously interested to control the discursive frame. Misiuaren's opening statements, for example, attempted to fix the limits of both debate personnel and debate topic. In his attempt to control who could participate in the debate, Misiuaren keyed local discursive conditions that endow older men with best rights and opportunities to talk. Stating that "everything rests with us bigmen" (line 7), he highlighted the weaker rights to talk of those younger men present – most of whom supported Kara Ouihi's position – and thus devalued somewhat what they could later say in debate. In fact, given this discursive rarefaction of speakers, of the sixty men in attendance only a dozen or so leading figures made statements during debate.

Misiuaren also tried to limit debate participation by claiming that the problem was an internal family problem, and therefore out of bounds for public discussion (lines 2–3). He stated that he had already had a private meeting with important classificatory brothers, implying that the problem was settled. Although this was a valid ploy in terms of local discourses of kinship that establish the private rights of fathers to talk about family problems, and to represent in that talk the positions of their wives and children, the seriousness of this particular conflict mostly vitiated his claims. People also recognized Kara Ouihi's competing fatherly rights to talk about his dead child.

Opening debate, therefore, Misiuaren stated that he was perturbed to find himself in front of a large audience that included his classificatory brothers-in-law, that is, a less friendly crowd:

> 1 MI: *Si rivi **kampani** takwtakwnu? Si rivi **kampani** tawktakwnu?*[5]
> Who pulled together the audience today? Who pulled together the audience today?
> 2   *Kimaha iahino sakimaha fwe ia rukwanu iakuvni iakua, nima me naha iraha nipigi nenimen me.*
> I've said we've already had a talk in the village, the men there

were "pupils of the eye" (exchange-partners related as classifactory brothers).

3   *Hamaiu ia kwopɨn u, ruvehe, mhavahag mɨ kɨmaha. Ik nah.*
    They ran here, he came, and advised us. You were there.
4   *Mata takwtakwnu iakata mwi nɨmahan me havehe nah takwtakwnu.*
    But now I see also "beds" (exchange-partners related as brothers-in-law) who have come now.

What is typical of Tanna's discursive order is that Misiuaren's strategy focused on stifling the talk of his son and his son's supporters, rather than that of his wife Seroki. Although Seroki was sitting, bandaged, on the sidelines of debate, no one asked her for her version of the affair. One might think she would have something to say. Under the conditions of island discourse, however, women have no qualifications to speak in public debate fora – although Seroki no doubt talked plenty in private. It is thus no good appealing to female victims to testify, and Misiuaren had no worries about any public backtalk from his battered wife.

In addition to these attempts to limit debate participation, Misiuaren's opening statements also attempted to restrict the debate's agenda to safe issues, such as the disappointing results of national independence (line 8).

5 MI: *Iou iama asori u, ua.*
       I am the bigman here.
6
       Iakata hiaruvahi nɨkuar takwtakwnu, kwanahan anan.
       I see that you have filled (the debate ground) now, many exchange-partners.
7   *Nari rara pam ia rukwanu me, nari rara pam fwe ia kɨtaha nɨma asori me.*
       Things rest in the village, everything rests with us bigmen.
8   *Sairapw mhamagkiari ia kwopɨn u nɨpɨn me tɨ nɨkava sanmwutaha mɨne **indipendens** sakɨtaha mata samenouenou iermama. Samenouenou iermama.*
       We've talked here many times about our kava and about our independence which ignores us. Ignores us.

Kieri, speaking second, swiftly countered by invoking a different agenda: men had gathered specifically to resolve a familial dispute in the course of which Misiuaren had beaten his wife Seroki:

9 KI: *Nɨma asori me iakokeikei ianhu i mua kua in ramagkiari nah mata iankarei **kes** rosi pranema rokeikei mua truvahi na pwah saukupwɨn raka marupwi savanrau, savanrau.*
       Bigmen, I suggest that although he states as he does, the other side of the case is that his old woman wants that we first pursue their two troubles, their two troubles.
10   *Nɨfe rɨnosi pranema tukwe?*
       Why did he hit his old woman?

At various turns throughout the debate, Misiuaren continued his attempts to change the topic. He returned a number of times to his statement that the meeting should address problems of national independence. He sidetracked debate in other ways too, attempting to open more general discussion about the value of European versus traditional personal names, and about the universal problems of sorcery and cursing. His supporters also cued inapposite topics with extended asides.

These statements, however, remained asides. Misiuaren's antagonists succeeded for ninety minutes in reframing the debate, keeping it "on track" by parrying these attempts to deframe. Witness Kauke, for example, in some exasperation stated:

> 11 KA: *Kimaha iahanapwah nuveheien ti nahag me sikimiaha me mua so* **wok** *ira ipwet.*
> We didn't come here today to worry over your personal names.
> 12   *Ramara naha ia nakwai inwarim.*
> That rests inside the kava-drinking ground group.
> 13   *Mata kimaha iahamregi mua ia nagkiariien ouihi kwara sikimiaha, iahamuvehe tukwe.*
> We are listening to this small talk (problem) of yours, we came for this.
> 14   *Iahamuvehe mua taharegi ro mua hiino* **stat**; *nukunen rifo ira?*
> We came to listen why you started; what was the cause of it?
> 15   *Men mesite pen* **trabol** *naha pranema; rifo ira?*
> It continued until the trouble with the old woman; what was it about?

The competition in dispute-settlement meetings of this sort to deframe and reframe transgresses (at least on the surface) Griceian maxims of conversational cooperation. Disputants violate conversational rules of quantity by revealing too little; they violate principles of conversational relevance by veering off on tangents or making statements about topics having little to do with preceding talk; they violate principles of manner by hiding behind obscure and ambiguous language; and they violate principles of quality by insisting on alternative truths, as discussed below. Disputatious talk needs to be analyzed not only for devices that ensure coherence and cohesion (see Tannen 1984), but also for those mechanisms by which speakers achieve sudden shifts and underminings of context, and thereby of unpalatable meanings and truths, and how they bring about breakdowns of conversational coherence. It does not always pay to be understood, particularly where someone else has established the contextual limits of understanding.

Shifts and lack of cohesion in debate frustrated more witnesses than just Kauke (lines 11–15), in that reframing attempts occurred frequently. The competition to frame and deframe perhaps helps us understand the debate's transformation into a fight. Violence has strong decontextualizing effects. Misiuaren's statements (we can count nonverbal signs such as grabbing a club as statements too) transformed talk's context from debate to brawl. The transition occurred thus:

16 KO: *Nagkiariien savani rukupwin mier.*
His (Misiuaren's) talk (curse) preceded (the child's death).

17 *Na nari nah ramni mini mua trap ia kwopin u rino.*
What he said was for him (the child) to get out of here.

18 MI: *Kara Ouihi. Apwah ra nagkiariien, mua ikino rong!*
Kara Ouihi. Stop talking, you are wrong!

19 KO: *Imri nei! Imri nei!*
Put down the club! Put down the club!

20 MI: *Mua ikurkurin mua ikino rong!*
You know that you did wrong!

21 KO: *Imri nei! Imri nei!*
Put down the club! Put down the club!

22 MI: *Mua ikino nukwanek rinamisa ti mwipwuk ua, a?*
You made my head sore regarding my grandchildren, huh?

23 *Mua iakuvni iakua tikapwah. Mua iakuvni mua si rouraha nas? Si rouraha nas? A, a, a? Si rouraha nas?*
I asked you to stop. I asked who ruined the milk? Who ruined the milk? Huh, huh, huh? Who ruined the milk?

24 KI: *Haouasi, haouasi, haouasi ira!*
Beat, beat, beat him with it!
[melee]

This unusual series of adjacency pairs signaled the recontextualization of debate into fracas. Misiuaren's demand that Kara Ouihi "stop talking" (line 18) and Kieri's call for an attack on Misiuaren (line 24), along with parallel nonverbal statements – Misiuaren's picking up a club – transformed the context and the identities of those in attendance: "witnesses" became "fighters" or "referees."

If talk cues new contexts and transforms existing ones, it is also clear that the contextual order informs the meaning of statements. In this regard, Duranti (1984) has criticized Grice's location of meaning in an independent speaker's intention that his statements induce an understanding in an audience (intending also that this audience recognize that intention). With Samoan data, Duranti argues that a speaker-centred approach of this sort builds on Western, culturally specific theories of the speaking person. Situation of meaning within an individual's intentions neglects active audience contributions to the determination of the meaning of a statement. Does an audience merely recognize a speaker's intentions, or is its contribution to a statement's meaning greater than this?

Given Samoan contextual and relational theories of the person and of social action, Duranti suggests that meaning in Samoa "is seen as the product of an interaction (words included) and not necessarily as something that is contained in someone's mind" (1984: 14). Scollon and Scollon (1984: 182–4), in a similar analysis of Athabaskan story-telling, distinguish "focused" from "nonfocused" discourses. In the latter, "no participant is assumed to have the right to make his or her own sense of the situation 'stick' for all other participants" (1984: 183). They correlate this with Athabaskan respect for "individual human difference."

Discursive orders in which all interacting personnel have equal rights to take part in meaning production are probably rare. Duranti, for example, notes the effects of Samoan political hierarchy on contextual determinations of statement meaning: a high chief, unlike other subjects, can "'own' the meaning of his words. . . lower ranking individuals have more limited control over the interpretation of their utterances" (1984: 17). Orders of discourse establish invidious qualifications to have intentions that an audience is willing to recognize (see Foucault 1978: 66–7; McKellin 1990).

As noted above, not all participants in a Tannese debate have equal discursive qualifications to make statements. They also do not have equal qualifications to mean what they say. Rather, leading bigmen possess both best rights to talk and best rights to find the public sense of talk. Powerful debate witnesses more easily enunciate this joint, public reading to the extent that "meaning is not conceived of as owned by the individual" (Duranti 1984: 14). Tanna's discursive order mutes the recognition of individual intentionality in meaning construction. Since interlocutors establish meaning interactionally, individuals have less control of how their words are publicly taken.

This is particularly true of the emergent "sense" of speech events as wholes. The Tannese, for example, presume that their debates ought to construct a public accounting of a particular conflict and how this is to be resolved (see Lindstrom 1990b; Brenneis 1984: 79; Weiner 1983: 163). In debates, people work to make common knowledge, a singular public version of events, a consensus. This production of consensus ordinarily also requires enunciation. Someone must enunciate what the emergent sense of the debate is, in order to make it public. Witnesses often provide "summary" statements and exhortations for future public action as debates wind up before the kava hour. It is here that some individual interest and intention may creep back in and, by shaping emergent meaning, effect the reproduction of social relations of power. Here, the powerful – as in Samoa – manage to represent women, children, and politically insignificant men who have fewer rights to possess a publicly recognized intentionality in these sorts of debate fora.

People's use of devices of indirection – common throughout Oceania – also facilitates the capture and enunciation of truth by the discursively powerful (Brenneis 1984: 78; Strathern 1975: 199; Weiner 1983: 700). Such devices, including indefinite pronominals, metaphor, ambiguity, etc., weaken an individual speaker's control over the public sense of his words. Statements are thus more amenable to appropriation, interpretation, and reenunciation by others. Moreover, reported speech is very common in Tannese debate (see lines 31, 36, 51, 53). In Vološinov's (1971) terms, many statements are thus reported "indirectly." They are inserted into a second statement by means of the framing verb *-ua* ("say, aver, believe"). The opportunity to manipulate a reported statement's form, meaning, and truth value obviously exists here: "Language devises means for infiltrating reported speech with auctorial retort and commentary in deft and subtle ways" (Vološinov 1971: 155).

Where the powerful enunciate a public interpretation of the "sense" of a meeting, indirection is redirected. An interactive construction of meaning necessarily implies at least some degree of individual estrangement from self-meaning and self-intention. This is, however, an unequal estrangement. Interactional meaning construction proceeds in the context of existing "rarefying" procedures and conditions in which people have variable qualifications to mean.

The received meaning of **single** statements, in addition to the sense of a debate as a whole, may also be interactively construed – particularly in cases where the statement maker is an ordinary man, woman, or child, or in situations of dispute (Lindstrom 1990b). One example: after an hour's debate, or so, Misiuaren confessed to being sorry for beating his wife, called for the end of discussion, and stated that he was ready to receive punishment (typically, a fine of a pig):

25 MI: *Na pranema naha iou iakni atukwatukw; rerɨk ramisa puk tɨ*
nagkiariien saiou, iakuasi praena tukwe, mata nari auar a. . .
Now about the old woman I state straightly; my heart is sore because of my words, the reason I beat the old women, but this is nothing . . .

26 *Hauvurkurɨn nah i navisaien sakɨmrau, apwah ra nagkiariien.*
They all know the fight between us, stop the talk.

27 *Saiou nah iakni. Hapwah ra nagkiariien. Rɨno sampam.*
This is what I say. Stop the debate. Finish it.

28 *Hauvurkurɨn navisaien sakɨmrau.*
They all know the fight between us.

29 *Hio **panis** ianrak. Hio **panis** ianrak. Mapwah ra nagkiariien.*
Punish me. Punish me. Stop talking.

Although Misiuaren, increasingly desperate, restated his demand at least twelve more times before the debate transformed into brawl, audience contributions to the sense of his statement ignored his confession of sorrow and his request to be fined. Only two interlocutors replied specifically to Misiuaren. Narua immediately pronounced the profession of sorrow a meaningless falsehood:

30 NA: *Ik Misiuaren ik iama asori mata nermama hinata pam raka **kona**
    saim Himata **kona** saim takwtakwnu.*
    You Misiuaren you are a bigman but people have seen all of your
    tricks (corners). They see your tricks now.

Nouar, a witness, reworked Misiuaren's statement that the problem was
"nothing" (line 25) and called, instead, for more debate:

31 NO: *Na iakni a mua **tauian** rinasisig raka nagkiariien, ruvkure; nasisig
    raka mua nermama tuapwah ra negkiariien.*
    Now I say that brother-in-law has closed the debate and sat down;
    closed the debate so that people stop talking.

32   *Na mata in nah nermama pam hamregi noien u sarino ia mwipwuk
    u ramakure, mesite pam nermama.*
    But everyone has heard of the thing we three did to my grandson
    (Kara Ouihi) sitting here, news reached everyone.

33   *Ikata nermama hamagkiari. Tiko irouapwah ninien mua tiko,
    kimirau **tauien**, irouapwah nasisigien nagkiariien.*
    You see everyone still talking. Don't you two say that you will,
    you and brother-in-law, don't you two close the debate.

34   *Pwah nermama heua pam.*
    Let people spill everything out.

Although, in this case, the audience did not reformulate Misiuaren's
locutionary act, it did determine its illocutionary force. The confession was
not a confession; sorrow not sorrow; debate not closed. Whether statement
meanings are anchored principally to speaker intentions or to audience
recognition depends upon the sort of subjectivity known within local
discursive orders – on local discourses about the "person." These orders,
moreover, establish differential qualifications to talk and to mean what one
says. They, furthermore, endow certain subjects with best rights and
opportunities to control the public hearing of what is said. Discursive
contexts that inform talk meaning are not innocent.

4   Context and statement truth

Theories of the truth of statements often locate that truth in the relationship of a statement to its context. If context is the "real world," truth
depends upon the accuracy of a statement's reflection of facts in that
world. If context, however, is the way in which the world is culturally
perceived, and discursively ordered and communicated, a statement's truth
then depends on its relationship to the procedures and devices of its
formulation and enunciation: on how people are able to compose and utter
that statement. In disputes and in other sorts of discourse where a
statement's truth is directly at stake, debaters take pains to invoke
"friendly" aspects of context in which to fix their talk and inform its truth.

Debate antagonists at Iamanuapen, for example, enunciated contradictory statements about two principal issues:

A.   *Why did the baby die?*

35 MI: *Takifi raka nari ira pwah irouata ia saed sai famli planing.*
I'll open up something for you two to see about the issue of family planning (breaking postpartum sexual taboos, which poisons mothers' milk).

36   *Na mata trimua hiani mua hiamreirei iou takwtakwnu takuvahi irapw nagkiariien mimri takwtakwnu.*
If you say that you disregard me now, I'll bring out this talk and place it (into discussion) now.

37   *Hiap nieri!*
Run away brothers-in-law!

38   . . . *Irnifo rouarahi afafa mwipwuk roueiuaiu ianmai nari? A? A?*
. . . Why did you two secretly carry my grandchild and go down into the bush (have sexual intercourse)? Huh? Huh?

39   *Rouavahi rouaiu afafa ianmai nari.*
You two went secretly into the bush.

Misiuaren stated that his son and daughter-in-law's sexual intercourse spoiled her milk, a recognized cause of illness in island etiological discourse. Kara Ouihi and his supporters, in opposition, accused Misiuaren of cursing the child:

40 KO: *Ik makwein reraha ira mua trakeikei memha.*
You (Misiuaren) cursed him that he must die.

41 KI: *Iakunouihi rameses ramasan mata saik kwarumrum ramen ti iakunouihi.*
The baby was nursing well but your bad words went into the child.

B.   *Why was Seroki beaten?*

42 KI: *Ia nipnipin ro faet nah puta, Seroki ramiri pehe Reva tukw iou naha pesu.*
The morning of the fight up there, Seroki sent Reva to me down south.

43   *Ruvehe mata "Rinamosi anan iou."*
He came (with her message) "He has just begun to really beat me."

44 KO: *Saiou nataien, iakamata, iakinata ia taem naha mata mama ruvehe.*
I was a witness, I was seeing, I saw at that time mother came.

45   *Iarouasak ia nipnipin Tus, e, Wensde ia nipnipin.*
We two wailed on Tuesday morning, uh, Wednesday morning.

46   *Ikata ikua ripikokeikei mha mua mama truvehe mukurira ianrak.*
You see he (Misiuaren) didn't want mother to come to me.

47   *Mua mama trukurira ia savani fasin, savani fasin nife tro, pranema traukurira i.*
He wants mother to follow his (bad) ways, whatever his fashion is, the old woman must follow.

Here, Kieri and Kara Ouihi claimed that Misiuaren was angered by his wife Seroki's desire to see her dead grandson and her son staying a quarter mile away or so in Kieri's hamlet (lines 46–7). Misiuaren, on the other hand, gave a couple of reasons for why he beat his wife. The first was that he and Seroki fell into an argument regarding transportation of goods exchanged with Seroki's brother the day of the child's funeral:

48 MI: *Na mata in rino niamaha miou ti trak nahe mua iakinasitu ia niruk sinaha iti.*
Now she was angry with me over the truck, wanting that I help my son.

49   *Na ruvsini makure matipare nah; na ripiko mha iakamuasi tukwe mata iakinarari maropen muvahi nari nah kamakure.*
She turned away sitting looking towards the mountain; it isn't that I struck her because of this but I turned around and went over to fetch that thing (a club) sitting there.

50   *Murupwi sinaha sarouihi.*
Knocked (her) with that small one.

51   *Iakua, "Rifo iakni nari irouakure?"*
I said, "Why do you two sit down when I've asked something?"

52   *Na sinaha in nah no sampam ia kwopin nah.*
Now that's all there was to it.

Misiuaren, later, also claimed that it was simply the death of his grandchild which angered him enough to beat Seroki.

Who was telling the truth? The disputants put forward contradictory statements. How did each side work within the context of island discourses to assert that they were telling the truth? First, islanders recognize that serious statements can be true; island discourses admit the possibility of truth. Debate commentators, for example, frequently challenged the truth (*niparhienien*) of statements uttered by disputants. Narua, for example, a supporter of Kara Ouihi, stood to demand the real truth behind Misiuaren's statement regarding the child's demise:

53 NA: *Misiuaren mi Reva u krauakure rosi mua krouagkiari mua nas reraha, mua nas reraha.*
Misiuaren and Reva sitting here seem to say that the milk was bad, that the milk was bad.

54   *Kini kitaha u samakure kini sin ratukwatukw?; kimirau sin ro ratukwatukw ro ansa ia nagkiariien?*

But we sitting here asking who is right? Of you two, whose
answer is straight talk?

I have argued elsewhere (Lindstrom 1990a) that the "will to truth" on
Tanna differs from that which operates in orders of discourse elsewhere.
To take "falsity" as truth's principal opposite mistranslates local evaluative
sensibilities. Untrue statements are lies, more than they are false.
Nifefeien, the island term that comes closest to notions of objective falsity
in Western orders of discourse, builds on a semantic core meaning of
"hypocrisy." As a procedure of statement evaluation, Tannese falsehood
thus implicates and accuses a statement's maker as much as it does its
meaningful content. The compulsively familiar apparatus of objective
referential truth and falsity belongs to regimes of discourse alien to the
island. In island discursive orders, a statement's truth value depends
greatly on who said it, and how it was said.

With this in mind, we can understand why people, in this debate,
attempted to devalue the statements of antagonists by challenging the
conversational qualifications of those who made statements, as well as the
"justness" of their act of stating (Foucault 1981: 54). To drain truth value
from an unfriendly statement, local strategy demands that antagonists aim
their fire at the statement maker (as liar). This is more effective than
criticizing the referential fit between a statement's content and the posited
real world. Narua, therefore, accused Misiuaren of having "corners" (line
30); Kieri denounced him as a "radio" (i.e., notoriously untruthful).
Misiuaren, in turn, when Kieri brought forward an armload of hefty clubs
and dumped these onto the ground of the forum, also complained of
"tricks." That is, he questioned the justness of Kieri's act of stating in
addition to his statement's referential truth value:

55 KI: *Nima asori hiata niperi nei nah ramosi pranema i!*
        Bigmen, look at these pieces of wood he beat his old women with!
56 MI: *Pwah iakni atukwatukw siu. Trik nah, **trik** u hino. **Trik** u hino.*
        Let me state correctly about this. This is a trick, a trick they did.
        This is a trick they did.
57   *Mata sa iakamuasi pranema ira u, sa iakamuasi ira u.*
        But that one is the one I beat the old woman with, that one I beat
        her with.
58   *Ko iakuvahi niperi nei u muasi pranema ira saiou ko ravin muvehe
        naha ia kwopin u takwtakwnu?*
        If I had used this club to beat my old woman with, would she be
        able to walk to this place today?
59   *. . .Maewad takosi saiou pranema takosi mosi apune; nife **trabol**
        sakimirau?*
        . . . My word, if I were to beat my old woman (with that) I'd kill
        her; what trouble are you two up to?

He also accused Kieri of being a kingfisher, calling foolishly in the forest, and a banded rail, running haphazardly about the bush.

Given that people discursively recognize a continuum of truth value (running from the truth to the lie), the task is to attach positive truth value to one's statements. This is particularly necessary in a debate. If truth is an "ensemble of rules according to which the true and the false are separated and specific effects of power attached to the true" (Foucault 1980: 132), a disputant must cue these rules in order to justify or authenticate his statement, his qualifications to state, and the act of his stating. As noted above, Foucault names the "discipline" as the discursive procedure that in particular regulates what counts as true. Disputing statement makers, therefore, in order to fix the truth or authenticity of their talk, cue strategic local disciplines that contextualize the truth of their statements and the justness of their act of stating.

Why did the baby die? Why was Seroki beaten? To authenticate talk about these matters, Misiuaren and his antagonists evoked several island disciplines. These included geography, sex, medicine, and kinship. Disputants also foregrounded more general understandings of the nature of men and women. Truthful context shifted as one or another of these disciplines were evoked. Within the terms of each, any given statement appeared more-or-less true or, conversely, its stater more-or-less a liar.

At the beginning of debate, Misiuaren foregrounded island "geographic" discourse that unites knowledge of place, knowledge of ancestors, sets of personal names, personal qualifications to repeat local ancestral stories, myths, and song, and rights to control the public construction of statement truth in one's own place (see Lindstrom 1984). Misiuaren attempted to contextualize his talk by calling attention to the fact that this was taking place at **his** kava-drinking ground. Here, he had best rights to speak the truth, given his geographic subjectivity.

60 MI: *Plis iakni pehe ti kimiaha mua nieri me tapu tiapwah nagkiariien, tapu tiapwah nagkiariien.*
Please, I say to you that you brothers-in-law are forbidden to talk, you must not talk.

61   *Saiou **kastom** iakamni, saiou **kastom** iakamni. . .Iou iama asori, u, ua.*
It's my custom I'm stating, my custom I'm stating. . .I'm the bigman here.

62   *. . . Iakni nipik u; nieri rini naha mata iakni nipik u.*
. . . I speak the banyan tree here (control the place); brother-in-law talks over there but I speak the banyan tree here.

63   *Iakni atukwatukw kamaspau matagi trerieri kwopin u; kwasuahi Nikia, Mopse nah ramakure pesu.*
I say straightly that one will see the wind shake this place; an oath on my sisters Nikia and Mopse living to the south.

Misiuaren jockeyed to lend truth to his statements by foregrounding numerous times his personal qualification to tell the truth, given the location of debate at his kava-drinking ground, and by taking an oath on the names of his sisters (line 63). Applying a similar discursive geographic truth-fixing device, he also chopped notches into the trunks of the banyan trees shading the kava-drinking ground as he uttered important talk. An invocation of geography, however, only diffusely constrains the truth value of statements such as those regarding the cause of a child's death or the reasons behind a wife's beating. Other island disciplines ordinarily have closer connections to the truth of these sorts of events.

Kara Ouihi, in opposition, therefore invoked the local disciplines of "kinship" and "medicine" in order to authenticate what he said about the cause of his son's death. His rights to speak here were impeccable in kinship discursive terms: he was the child's father, giving him best rights of representation of the child (Lindstrom 1990b). Local etiology links serious illnesses (particularly of children themselves not directly involved) to intrafamilial imbalance and dispute. It also recognizes the power of the word to injure. Kara Ouihi called attention to the ongoing friction between his father and himself; he also claimed that a number of people had heard his father say that the child "must die" (line 40). Kara Ouihi's statement that the cause of his son's death was a grandfatherly curse in the midst of a familial dispute met discursively established local truth conditions.

In the tangential discussion about Misiuaren's grasp upon the family's heritage of male personal names, and his refusal to bestow traditional names upon his grandsons, Kara Ouihi also evoked "geographical" discourse to foreground a rationale behind the curse. He intimated that Misiuaren wanted no additional grandsons who would eventually require names. In the act of naming a boy, a greedy Misiuaren would thereby have to transfer rights to valuable coconut plantations and other lands to an heir.

Misiuaren attempted to dislocate the truth claims of his son's statement by evoking instead local discourses of "sex" to tell a different truth about the baby's death (lines 35–9). This was an astute move. Misiuaren's discursive qualifications to talk publicly about sex were stronger than Kara Ouihi's. As a father, his was the responsibility to advise his children including Kara Ouihi about proper sex. Island medical discourse also recognizes that parental intercourse during the two or three years that a mother nurses a child can cause illness (although less commonly death). Misiuaren's statement that the baby died of spoiled milk (line 23) thus minimally met the truth conditions of the local discipline of medicine.

Furthermore, Tanna's discursive order establishes certain "silences" around sexuality (Foucault 1981: 52). For Misiuaren, these silences were useful contextual resources he could hide behind. People who stand towards each other as cross-cousins – that is, as real or potential brothers-in-law and sisters-in-law – ought not to discuss sex together in public. In this manner, Misiuaren had the advantage of contextualizing his statement about cause of death in sexual terms, without having to provide details of the supposed sex act itself. Whereas Kara Ouihi and his supporters had to support in some detail their claim that Misiuaren indeed cursed his grandson into the grave, Misiuaren merely had to foreground sex. To do this he used, not surprisingly, the code-mixed Bislama term *famli planing* (family planning, line 35), which sanitized somewhat the sexual reference. He did not have to give details. In fact, discursive silence here required that he not give details, given the presence of his classificatory brothers-in law in the audience.

Misiuaren, playing with these conditions, threatened several times to go into the sordid facts about the sex act between his son and daughter-in-law. He cued this by warning his brothers-in-law to "run away" (line 37). They remonstrated uneasily that talk about sex ought to occur in private:

64 NA: *Navahagien nah Misiuaren ikni, nari ia nakwai nimwa ua.*
      That sort of advice, Misiuaren, is something for inside the house.
65   *Nari ia nakwai nimwa fwe; ikamavahag mɨ saik me nɨkwarakwara.*
      Something inside the house; there you advise your children (not to have postpartum sex).
66   *Ikakeikei mua tikuvahi nari ia nakwai nimwa; rapwah namwhenien mua tikuvahi muvehe ia **kampani** fa rɨfe takwtakwni.*
      You must bring that up privately; it isn't seemly that you bring it to the company here and reveal it now.
67   *Ro naurɨsien i ua.*
      It causes shame.

Kara Ouihi responded to each of Misiuaren's threats to violate discursive rules of prohibition by telling his father to go ahead and "spill it out" – to show his hand and make explicit his insinuations. Misiuaren, however, avoided the particulars until he at last stated (still without much detail) that he had spied Kara Ouihi and his wife sneaking off into the bush (lines 38–9). This violation of discursive silence occurred immediately before debate became brawl, and no doubt was one of the cues serving to effect this contextual transformation.

The truth of the first query – why the baby died – was somewhat more disputed than that of the second – why Misiuaren beat his wife Seroki. Here, everyone including Misiuaren agreed that he had, in fact, struck her although they argued over the exact instrument of her chastisement. The significant point was why. Was it because she had angered Misiuaren by meddling in the arrangements for distribution of the funeral meats (lines 48–9)? Was it because she had angered him by her desire to go to Kieri's hamlet in order to perform her grandmotherly duties of holding and wailing over her grandson's corpse (line 46)? Or was it that Misiuaren was maddened by the death of his grandchild, which resulted from the fact that his rascal son had neglected good advice about postpartum sex (line 22)? Both sides appealed to local discourses about the nature of men and women, and how relations between the sexes are properly constituted, to authenticate their rival statements.

Misiuaren, to add truth to his talk, keyed these wider discourses that qualify men's rights to dominate and instruct (even by beating) wives and children. He observed:

> 68 MI: *Ko ikni nagkiariien saim, tamarua ran pen ianram iakreirei mua iko noien u ua rikam.*
> If you gave advice, but the young man ignored you I don't know if you'd do this thing (beating) or not.
>
> 69   *Kitaham pam nima reraha ua.*
> We are all bad men.
>
> 70   *Mata kua iou iermama iti; iakni pehe atukwatukw ti kimiaha me mua iakamwhen ia Souarim nah.*
> But I am one man; I say truly to you all that I am like Souarim.

Here he also foregrounds geography. Souarim was a notoriously violent local ancestor; Misiuaren calls attention to the geographic truth that descendants inherit ancestral personalities.

Misiuaren's antagonists also evoked discourses of gender relations, but they did so in order to dislocate the truth of his statement. Various witnesses and antagonists made the point that men manage relations with dependants without having to beat them up, whether these involve ordering them to distribute feast goods, advising them about sex, or whatever. Kara Ouihi's supporters, in this way, authenticated their alternative statement that Misiuaren's anger with Seroki stemmed instead from animus towards his son and grandson. It was not a pernicious rebellion of Misiuaren's dependants that sparked his anger, but his unreasonable demand that his wife not visit her son and dead grandson (lines 46–7). Kara Ouihi, substantiating this, also observed that, contrary to local expectation, neither his father nor his mother had prepared any traditional medicines, indulged and carried or otherwise attempted to cure the child while he was dying. Each side thus evoked available island disciplines in the context of which their statements, and their acts of stating, were infused with truth value.

5   Conclusion

I have suggested that Foucault's analysis of orders of discourse helps reveal the contextual effects of power and truth on talk. Rather than situating talk within a context of more-or-less neutral frames, speech events, or schemata, we might instead attempt to uncover the discursive procedures and conditions in terms of which some people have better qualification and opportunity to make meaningful truth statements. Cognitive schemata, originating in previous shared experience, and interpersonal qualities of speech events certainly comprise talk's context; but so do discursive conditions, devices, and procedures that regulate and organize talking and saying.

Secondly, existing discursive orders often comprise multiple lines of power that allow contradictory truths. In a dispute, therefore, a person can add meaning and truth value to his statements by evoking favorable discourses in whose terms his talk finds authenticity, or in whose terms he has better personal qualifications to speak, and to speak the truth. Conversely, others can resist or negate a statement's truth value, in a decontextualization process, by foregrounding alternative disciplines, or other discursive conditions that undermine a disputant's right to speak, or that dislocate the truth claims of his statement. If context imposes limits upon the sense and the truth of talk, talk informs and talkers maneuver within that context nevertheless.

Notes

1 I thank the Fulbright Hays program, the English Speaking Union of the United States, the Department of Anthropology of the Research School of Pacific Studies, Australian National University, the University of Tulsa, and all friends in southeast Tanna for the assistance I received and the welcome I experienced during several periods of research on Tanna. I also thank C. Goodwin, W. McKellin, and A. Duranti for advice and comment on an earlier version of this chapter.

2 Goffman does identify "ritual constraints" on talk, noting that these vary cross-culturally (1981: 16, 25). Along perhaps similar lines, Sacks (1984: 428) describes "regulations" on a person's entitlement to make claims about experience. These conversational constraints and regulations parallel some of the discourse control procedures that Foucault describes.

3 "Serious" truth statements need not be serious in the ordinary sense of the word. Jokes, riddles, allegories, insults, etc. may all be "serious" in Dreyfus and Rabinow's terms if they have potentially important social consequences.

4 There are also clear co-determining relations between context and talk form that I do not discuss in this chapter. For example, when people engage in activities including church services, political meetings, and soccer games, they often shift to Bislama (Vanuatu Pidgin English). Here, the context influences how people encode what they say. Conversely, a speaker's choice of one talk form over another can shift context, and cue alternative discursive orders. The mixing of Bislama lexemes into a debate statement, for example, evokes authoritative discourses (e.g. of Christianity and of national development). These then become an available context for reinterpreting the meaning or truth of what has been said (cf. Gumperz 1982: 97).

5 In these statement transcriptions of SE Tanna's Kwamera language, the symbol [ɨ] represents a mid central vowel. Forms in boldface are code-mixed Bislama (Vanuatu Pidgin English) terms. Ellipses indicate that intervening statements have been omitted.

References

Bakhtin, M. 1981. *The Dialogic Imagination: Four Essays*, ed. M. Holquist, trans. C. Emerson and M. Holquist. Austin: University of Texas Press.

Bateson, G. 1972. *Steps to an Ecology of Mind*. New York: Ballantine Books.

Brenneis, D. 1984. Straight Talk and Sweet Talk: Political Discourses in an Occasionally Egalitarian Community, in *Dangerous Words: Language and Politics in the Pacific*, ed. D. Brenneis and F. Myers, pp. 69–84. New York: New York University Press.

1990. Dramatic Gestures: The Fiji Indian Pancayat as Therapeutic Event, in *Disentangling: Conflict Discourse in Pacific Societies*, ed. K. Watson-Gegeo and G. White, pp. 214–38. Stanford: Stanford University Press.

Dreyfus, H., and P. Rabinow. 1982. *Michel Foucault: Beyond Structuralism and Hermeneutics*. Chicago: University of Chicago Press.

Duranti, A. 1984. *Intentions, Self, and Local Theories of Meaning: Words and Social Action in a Samoan Context*. San Diego: Center for Information Processing, University of California, San Diego.

Foucault, M. 1972. *The Archaeology of Knowledge*. New York: Pantheon Books.

1978. *The History of Sexuality, Volume I: An Introduction*. New York: Vintage Books.

1980. *Power/Knowledge: Selected Interviews and Other Writings, 1972–1977*. New York: Pantheon Books.

1981. The Order of Discourse, in *Untying the Text: A Post Structuralist Reader*, ed. R. Young, pp. 48–78. Boston: Routledge and Kegan Paul.

Goffman, E. 1974. *Frame Analysis: An Essay on the Organization of Experience*. Cambridge, Mass.: Harvard University Press.

1981. *Forms of Talk*. Philadelphia: University of Pennsylvania Press.

Goldman, L. 1983. *Talk Never Dies: The Language of Huli Disputes*. London: Tavistock.

Gumperz, J. 1982. *Discourse Strategies*. Cambridge: Cambridge University Press.

Hymes, D. 1967. Models of the Interaction of Language and Social Setting. *Journal of Social Issues* 23(2): 8–28.

Lindstrom, L. 1981. Speech and Kava on Tanna, in *Vanuatu: Politics, Economics and Ritual in Island Melanesia,* ed. M. Allen, pp. 379–93. New York: Academic Press.

1984. Doctor, Lawyer, Wise Man, Priest: Big-Men and Knowledge in Melanesia. *Man* 19: 291–309.

1985. Personal Names and Social Reproduction on Tanna, Vanuatu. *Journal of the Polynesian Society* 94: 27–45.

1990a. *Knowledge and Power in a South Pacific Society*. Washington: Smithsonian Institution Press.

1990b. Straight Talk on Tanna, in *Disentangling: Conflict Discourse in Pacific Societies*, ed. K. Watson-Gegeo and G. White, pp. 373–411. Stanford: Stanford University Press.

McKellin, W. 1990. Self and Inference: Intentional Ambiguity in Managalase Negotiations, in *Disentangling: Conflict Discourse in Pacific Societies*, ed. K. Watson-Gegeo and G. White, pp. 335–70. Stanford: Stanford University Press.

Ochs, E. 1979. Social Foundations of Language, in *New Directions in Discourse Processing*, ed. R. Freedle, pp. 207–21. Norwood, NJ: Ablex Publishing.

Sacks, H. 1984. On Doing "Being Ordinary," in *Structures of Social Action: Studies in Conversation Analysis*, ed. J. Atkinson and J. Heritage, pp. 412–29. Cambridge: Cambridge University Press.

Scollon, R., and S. Scollon. 1984. Cooking it Up and Boiling it Down: Abstracts in Athabaskan Children's Story Retellings, in *Coherence in Spoken and Written Discourse*, ed. D. Tannen. Norwood: Ablex Publishing, pp. 173–197.

Strathern, A. 1975. Veiled Speech in Mount Hagen, in *Political Language and Oratory in Traditional Society*, ed. M. Bloch, pp. 185–204. New York: Academic Press.

Tannen, D. 1979. What's in a Frame? Surface Evidence for Underlying Expectations, in *New Directions in Discourse Processing*, ed. R. Freedle, pp. 137–81. Norwood, NJ: Ablex Publishing.

　　1984. *Coherence in Spoken and Written Discourse*. Norwood, NJ: Ablex Publishing.

Terdiman, R. 1985. *Discourse/Counter-Discourse: The Theory and Practice of Symbolic Resistance in Nineteenth-Century France*. Ithaca, NY: Cornell University Press.

Vološinov, V. 1971. Reported Speech, in *Readings in Russian Poetics: Formalist and Structuralist Views*, ed. L. Matejka and K. Pomorska, pp. 149–75. Cambridge. Mass.: MIT Press.

Weiner, A. 1983. From Words to Objectives to Magic: Hard Words and the Boundaries of Social Interaction. *Man* 18: 690–709.

5 Contextualization, tradition, and the dialogue of genres: Icelandic legends of the *kraftaskáld*

RICHARD BAUMAN

Editors' introduction

Richard Bauman is Professor of Folklore and Anthropology at Indiana University. He received his doctorate in American Civilization from the University of Pennsylvania. While there he was part of a small group of graduate students working under Dell Hymes who were actively involved in the seminal development of the field that became known as the Ethnography of Speaking. Before moving to Indiana to head its folklore program he taught for many years at the University of Texas. He is a former editor of the *Journal of American Folklore*.

In this chapter Bauman rethinks not only how **context** is relevant to the study of the speech genres (stories and verse for example) that have been a principal focus of folklore research, but uses a participant-centred, dynamic view of context to simultaneously rethink some of the core analytical concepts that underlie folklore, including **tradition** and **genre**. While doing this he also provides a very lucid exposition of how the work of the Russian semiotician and literary theorist Mikhail Bakhtin can be used to develop new understanding of how language is organized as a cultural and social phenomenon. Bakhtin has become an increasingly influential figure in anthropological linguistics (in recent years several sessions have been devoted to his work at the annual meetings of the American Anthropological Association). Bauman tempers his genuine appreciation of what Bakhtin has to offer with recognition of some limitations in the analytic framework he has left us.[1] "As suggestive as they are, however, Bakhtin's writings engender a certain amount of frustration in the analysis of dialogic forms; his perspective seems to demand a dimension of formal analysis, but he never provides it." In the present chapter Bauman combines an approach influenced by Bakhtin with formal analysis of the speech forms being examined.

Central to the work of Bakhtin is the notion of the **dialogic** organization of language. The term **dialogic** can be somewhat misleading since it immediately conjures up visions of multi-party talk, i.e. a dialogue between different speakers. This is not what Bakhtin meant by **dialogic**. Rather he wanted to call attention to how a single strip of talk (utterance, text, story, etc.) can juxtapose language drawn from, and invoking, alternative cultural, social and linguistic home environments, the interpenetration of multiple voices and forms of utterance. A prototypical example is provided by the phenomenon of **reported speech**, in which the quoted talk of one party is embedded within the speech of another (Bakhtin's most complete exposition of reported speech can be found in Vološinov 1973, which was written in conjunction with, indeed possibly by, Bakhtin). Speech genres vary in the extent to which they permit dialogic organization. "Frozen" genres, poetry with a fixed format for example, provide only limited opportunities for the incorporation of other speech forms, while the possibilities for dialogic embedding offered by the novel are almost endless. In the present chapter Bauman focuses his analysis on a particular kind of text, a story about a nineteenth-century Icelandic "magical poet" that was told by an old man to someone who was collecting folk materials in the 1960s. The text being analyzed contains a number of different types of speech embedded within other speech. Most striking is the prophetic curse of the poet, which takes the form of verse embedded within a framing narrative. One genre (verse) is thus embedded within another (narrative) which contextualizes it, thus generating what Bauman analyzes as a "dialogue of genres." Formal analysis of how the verse and narrative are linked to, and differentiated from, each other enables Bauman to draw on seminal insights of Bakhtin while overcoming some of their limitations. Such analysis is relevant to theory and practice in folklore in another way as well: it creates the possibility of moving beyond a somewhat problematic taxonomy of stable genres to explore the creative constitution of dialogic genres, in which a single text places one genre in dynamic juxtaposition to another. What Bauman has done here would seem to open the door to a new line of very productive scholarship within folklore.

The verse within the story is not however the only type of embedded speech found within this text. Before getting to the story proper, the teller provides a genealogy of previous tellers, locating "his discourse in relation to a sequential series of other discourses." Bauman uses such talk to radically rethink the notion of **tradition** by arguing that the teller is actively involved in a process of **traditionalization:** systematically linking the present talk to a meaningful past, while at the same time authenticating his story (much like an art or antique dealer) by "tracing its provenience." Instead of being treated as a static feature of the past, "a quality of traditionality that is considered to inhere in a cultural form conceived of as akin to a persistent natural object," tradition becomes an aspect of situated practice, work that members of a society actively perform to constitute objects as traditional. Such a framework shifts the analysis of context from events surrounding the object being examined to "the inside . . . using the text itself as a point of departure, and allowing it to index dimensions as the narrator himself forges links of contextualization to give shape and meaning to his expression." The contrast that Bauman notes between context viewed from the "outside in" vs. a view from the "inside" looking outward is in fact one major place where different approaches to the analysis of context actively challenge each other. For example, conversation analysis works from the "inside out", starting from the talk itself and insisting that all proposed contextual variables be shown to articulate within the data being examined (the work of the Goodwins in this volume provides an example of conversational analysis), a position that is actively challenged by Cicourel's chapter in this volume.

Bauman also notes that while citing past speakers the teller has the capacity to distance himself from what they say, and indeed from the story itself. Such analysis is quite relevant to the arguments made by Erving Goffman from *Asylums* (1961) to "Footing" (1981) about how the individual has to be analyzed as a "stance-taking entity."

Note

1 Bauman's critique of Bakhtin is elaborated in more detail in a paper presented at the 1988 meetings of the American Anthropological Association

References

Goffman, Erving. 1961. *Asylums: Essays on the Social Situation of Mental Patients and Other Inmates*. Garden City, New York: Anchor Books, Doubleday.
1981. *Forms of Talk*. Philadelphia: University of Pennsylvania Press.
Vološinov, Valentin Nikolaevic. 1973. *Marixsm and the Philosophy of Language*, trans. Ladislav Matejka and I. R. Titunik. New York: Seminar Press. (First published 1929 and 1930.)

Contextualization, tradition, and the dialogue of genres: Icelandic legends of the *kraftaskáld*

1   Introduction

The field of folklore is currently in the midst of a highly charged period of critical reexamination of some of its most foundational concepts. Energized by the performance-centred approaches developed by folklorists themselves and related reorientations in adjacent disciplines, there is a movement in current folklore theory toward counterbalancing established structural, institutional, collective orientations toward expressive forms with more agent- and practice-centered perspectives that emphasize individual agency and the emergent aspects of performance in the accomplishment of social life.[1]

In regard to genre, for example, the emphasis of the late 1960s through the mid 1970s was on structural definitions of individual genres, stimulated by the translation into English of Propp's *Morphology of the Folktale* (1968) and the burgeoning of interest in the work of Lévi-Strauss, and on culturally established systems of classification discovered through the techniques of ethnoscience.[2] More recently, these concerns have been tempered by a conception of genre as a dynamic expressive resource, in which the conventional expectations and associations that attach to generically marked stylistic features are available for further combination and recombination in the production of varying forms and meanings (Hymes 1975a, Sherzer 1979, Urban 1985).

Tradition, long considered a criterial attribute of folklore, is coming to be seen less as an inherent quality of old and persistent items or genres passed on from generation to generation, and more as a symbolic construction by which people in the present establish connections with a meaningful past and endow particular cultural forms with value and authority.[3] Thus, the focus of attention is the strategic process of traditionalization rather than a quality of traditionality that is considered to inhere in a cultural form conceived of as akin to a persistent natural object.

Likewise, we are seeing a shift away from context, understood as the conventional, normative anchoring of an item or form within institutional structures, event structures, or general patterns of cultural or psychological meaning, and toward the active process of contextualization in which individuals situate what they do in networks of interrelationship and association in the act of expressive production (Bauman 1983, Bauman and Briggs 1990, Briggs 1985, Young 1985). Indeed, so conceived, contextualization appears to be the most general process of them all, but that is too large a topic to undertake here. Rather, my purpose in this chapter is to suggest some of the ways in which the communicative exploration of genre, the act of traditionalization, and the situated management of contextualization may be seen as parts of a unified expressive accomplishment. This chapter is intended as a prolegomenon to a more extensive study of the materials on which it is focused.

2   Legends of the kraftaskáld

The corpus of materials I will examine in the full study is a set of Icelandic legends about magical poets. Many of the world's cultures attribute magical power to poets and magical efficacy to poetry. The theme is especially resonant in Nordic tradition: the poetic skill of the skaldic poets, for example, was seen as a divine gift (Almqvist 1965: 209); continuities have been suggested between skaldic poetry and shamanism (Kabell 1980); and the damaging effects of the shaming *nið* verses, best known from the famous episodes in *Egils Saga*, appear in at least some instances to have been attributed to their magical qualities (Almqvist 1974: 185–6). In Iceland, one of the expressive foci of this theme is the figure of the *kraftaskáld* or *ákvæðaskáld*. Kraftaskáld, the more commonly used term, is perhaps most literally translated as "power poet," but commentators also use the term "magical poet" to render kraftaskáld in English (Sigurðsson 1983: 437). *Ákvæði*, meaning "uttered opinion" (Cleasby, Vigfusson, and Craigie 1957: 42), "decision, verdict" (Zoëga 1910: 33), is also used in popular tales and superstitions in the more marked sense of "spell," or "charm." An ákvæðaskáld is thus a spell-poet, whose verse has magical power. The two terms are often cited as synonyms (Cleasby, Vigfusson, and Craigie 1957: 42; Almqvist 1961: 73), though ákvæðaskáld may suggest the use of magical verse for more negative ends.

The kraftaskáld is an individual – most are men, but some are women – who has the capacity in problem situations to improvise verses which have magical efficacy: they may turn inclement weather, drive away predators, procure food and other provisions in time of need, or vanquish adversaries. It is important to emphasize that the verses of the kraftaskáld are not traditional, ready-made incantations, charms, magical formulae, or the like, but are composed spontaneously for a single occasion only. All of the approximately two hundred kraftaskálds[4] documented by Bo Almqvist in his historical searches (1961) were known to compose other poetry as well and for the most part they appear to be people of uncommon character and ability, strong-minded, passionate, and quick to anger (1961: 77). Three factors are worth noting with regard to the source of the magical power of the kraftaskálds and their verses. First, many of the kraftaskálds were ministers, with special spiritual powers. In addition, it appears that the artistic excellence of the kraftaskáld's verses was independent of their magical efficacy: it is said of one Þorsteinn from Varmavatnsholar that "Although Þorsteinn was a bad poet, he seemed to have in him a trace of the kraftaskáld" (Almqvist 1961: 76). Finally, the verses of the kraftaskáld are characteristically composed in moments of strong feeling. Taken together, these factors indicate that the magical power of the kraftaskáld's verses is the combined product of poetic formalization of the utterance and the charismatic power of the kraftaskáld's character – both seem necessary.

There are numerous legends about kraftaskálds in the classic Icelandic folktale literature, with the oldest documentary records stemming from around 1600, though the earliest mention of the terms kraftaskáld and ákvæðaskáld occurs only around 1830 (Almqvist 1961: 73–4). But this legend tradition is now moribund, if not fully dead, in contemporary Icelandic oral tradition. I am fortunate, though, to have a number of recorded texts, made available to me by Hallfreður Örn Eiríksson, Icelandic folklorist, from his own collection. These stories were recorded in the late 1960s from quite elderly informants in old-age homes. I will base this preliminary discussion on one of these narratives, a story about a well-known kraftaskáld of the nineteenth century, the Reverend Páll Jonsson (1779–1846) of the Westman Islands, widely called Páll skáldi, Páll the Poet. Páll was a difficult and quick-tempered man, who drank heavily and lived the last ten years or so of his life without a position in the church. Nevertheless, he was known to be a man of intelligence and a talented poet (Sigfússon 1946: 60). The story was recorded by Eiríksson from the telling of Jón Norðmann, in Reykjavík, November 10, 1968. A transcription and translation of the text are given below. Line breaks mark breath pauses, though not all breath pauses in the delivery of the text mark the beginning of new lines; I have also taken account of syntactic structures in rendering the printed text.

Páll skáldi/Páll the Poet

HÖE 1   *Voru nokkrir fleiri . . . voru fleiri kraftaskáld talin þarna í Skagafirði?*
Were any others . . . were others reputed to be kraftaskálds in Skagafjord?

JN   2   *Ég man að nú ekki núna í augnabliki,*
I don't remember that now, just now at the moment,

3   *en eitt ég nú sagt þér ef . . . ef þú kærir þig um.*
but I can tell you now if . . . if you care (to hear it).

4   *það er nú ekki beint úr Skagafirði,*
It is, now, not exactly from Skagafjord

5   *og þó, það er í sambandi við Gudrúnu,*
although it is connected with Gudrún,

6   *dóttur séra Páls skálda í Vestmannaeeyjum.*
daughter of Reverend Páll the Poet in the Westman Islands.

7   *Páll skáldi þótti nú kraftaskáld,*
Páll the Poet was thought, now, to be a kraftaskáld

8   *og það þótti nú ganga eftir einu sinni, honum lenti eitthavð saman við*
and that was thought, now, to prove true one time he had something of a conflict with

9   *einhvern vertíðarmann þarna í Vestmannaeyjum,*
some seasonal fishermen there in the Westman Islands,

10   *og . . . og hann . . . þessi vertíðarmaður, hann kvað einhverja vísu um . . . um Pál*
and . . . and he . . . this seasonal fisherman, he spoke some verse about . . . about Páll

11   *þar sem hann spáir honum því að hann muni drukkna.*
where he prophesies about him that he will drown.

12   *Og Páll reiddist og gerir vísu.*
And Páll got angry and makes a verse.

13   *þetta var á vertíðinni.*
This was in the fishing season.

14   *Og sú vísa er svona:*
And the verse is thus:

15   *Fari það svo að fyrir lok*   Should it turn out that in the end

16   *fáirðu að rata í sandinn,*   you get to fall into the sand,

17 *ætti að skerast ofan í kok,* may it cut itself down in your
throat,

18 *úr þér tungufjandinn.*   out of you, the tongue-devil.

19 *En það fór nú svo að þessi maður*
And it turned out, now, such that this man

20 *þegar hann var að fara í land,*
as soon as he was going to the mainland,

21 *þá drukknaði hann við Landeyjasandur*
that he drowned by Land-Isles Sand

22 *og þegar hann fannst, hafði marfló étið úr honum tunguna.*
and when he was found, a shrimp had eaten his tongue out.

23 *Og . . . ja* (laugh) *. . . etta gat nú vel allt hafa skeð án ess að visan
hefði komið,*
And . . . well (laugh) . . . that could, now, all well have happened
without the verse having occurred,

24 *en þetta hittist nú svona á.*
but that is how it turned out, now.

25 *Nú Gudrún dottir hans sagði föður minum þessa sögu.*
Now Gudrún, his daughter, told my father this story.

Kraftaskáld legends, as I suggested earlier, recount an instance in which
the poet, confronting a situation of adversity, gains mastery by means of a
magical verse, composed on the moment. In other words, what we have
here are stories about poems, or better, narrating about versifying. One of
the things going on in them, then, is the creation of a narrative context for
reporting a poem, a problem in the interaction of genres. In addition to
contextualizing the verse, the narrator also contextualizes the narrative
itself, weaving a complex web of verbal anchorings for his discourse that
link it to a range of other situations and other discourses, endowing it with
traditional authority in the process. What I want to do is trace the strands
of this web through the text before us to illuminate the ways in which
contextualization in its various dimensions may be accomplished in the act
of recounting these legends.

The story of Páll and the seasonal fisherman illustrates clearly the
general structure of kraftaskáld legends. While the narrative may open and
close with framing matter, as this one does (of which more later), the plots
characteristically begin with the situation of adversity confronting the poet,
here the prophetic verse attack on Páll the Poet by the fisherman. The poet
then composes a verse to counteract the problem situation, which is recited
by the narrator as part of the narration. The third structural plot element,
following the verse, recounts the overturning or reversal of the adverse

circumstance – from the poet's point of view – a transformation of state brought about by the magical verse. In the story before us, the seasonal fisherman drowns and, to make Páll's victory still more complete, his adversary's villainous tongue is eaten out by a shrimp.

3   The dialogue of genres

Let us look first at the problem of contextualization in terms of genres, that is, the interplay of the two genres, verse and story, in the text. This is an instance, *par excellence*, of a Bakhtinian dialogue of genres, resting not primarily on dialogue in the turn-taking social interactional sense, as in riddles or knock-knock jokes, for example, but on the interplay of two (or more) primary genres, each with its own formal and functional characteristics (Bakhtin 1986: 60–102). That we are dealing here with the juxtaposition of two locally recognized primary genres within a more complex text is evidenced by the actual naming of the two generic forms within the text itself: *vísa*, or verse (lines 12, 14, 23), and *saga*, or story (line 25). Even a preliminary reading – or hearing – of the text reveals that the verse is contained by the story. Accordingly, we have at least a preliminary warrant to approach the interplay of genres in terms of the contextualization of the verse by the surrounding narrative. And indeed, the formal analysis of the text sustains this procedure.

Lines 1–6 in the transcript are framing matter, and I will return to them later. The actual recounting of the narrated event – the conflict between Páll the Poet and the fisherman and its resolution – begins with line 8, marked by the adverbial formula *einu sinni*, "one time," that marks the onset of the narrative action in so many Icelandic folktales. However, line 7 – "Páll the Poet was thought, now, to be a kraftaskáld" – is the opening step in the process that moves toward the presentation of the verse, by anticipating what is most reportable about a kraftaskáld, that is, the exercise of his magical powers. This process is further advanced by line 8 – "and that was thought, now, to prove true one time . . ." – which reinforces the expectation set up in line 7 that we will hear an account of an actual incident confirming Páll's status as a kraftaskáld. The mention of the conflict in line 8 establishes the situation of adversity that Páll will overcome with his magical verse.

In lines 10 and 11, the seasonal fisherman, also a poet, attacks Páll with a verse, identified as a prophecy, which means, importantly, that it is merely a prediction of the future, lacking the performative power actually to bring about the happening it foretells. Knowing already that Páll is a kraftaskáld and that this represents an incident in which his magical power was used, we begin to recognize a nascent parallel being set up by the narrator: the fisherman spoke a verse predicting Páll's drowning, but without the power to bring it about, while Páll will produce a verse about the fisherman's fate that will actually cause it to happen. Note too that the fisherman's verse is merely reported in the narrator's voice, not quoted.

In immediate response to the fisherman's challenge, "Páll got angry and makes a verse" of his own (line 12), thus beginning the fulfillment of the anticipated parallel. It is worth observing that while the fisherman **spoke** his verse, Páll **makes** his, suggesting more agency, power, and immediacy in regard to the latter. Páll's anger represents the motivational impetus for him to employ the full force of his magical power; the magical verses of the kraftaskáld are commonly called forth by strong emotion.

Finally, line 14, culminating in the demonstrative adverb *svona*, thus, is the quotative frame that directly offers up the verse itself as direct discourse. Note the shift of tense here. To this point, the recounting of the narrated event leading up to the verse has been in the past tense or the historical present (line 11: "prophesies," line 12: "makes"), but in line 14 the narrator shifts to the present tense: "And the verse is thus." That is, the verb forms in lines 7–13 index the narrated event, the event told about, while the verb form in line 14 indexes the narrative event, the event in which the story is told. Line 14, then, accomplishes that merger of narrated event and narrative event that is characteristic of quoted speech, which does not merely recount, but re-presents the quoted discourse. The two instances of historical present tense mediate the transition. In this first part of the legend, then, we may observe that much of the narrative work in the text is in the service of the verse to follow, building a structure of anticipation for its presentation and ultimately (in line 14) pointing directly to it.

We arrive, then, at the verse itself, which is heavily set off from the surrounding discourse by formal contrasts, including the following:

- meter, with alternating 4 and 3 stress lines;
- rhyme, in an abab pattern;
- loudness, with the poem delivered more loudly than the surrounding narrative;
- figurative language, in the personification of the "tongue-devil";
- mode, marked by the subjunctive verb forms at the head of the first three lines, contrasting with the indicative mood of the surrounding narrative;
- temporal dynamic, shifting from the linear progression that moves from the more distant to the more proximal past in lines 7–12, to the future orientation of the verse;
- syntax, marked by the unconventional form of lines 17–18, which would more normally be *"ætti að tungufjandinn ur þér skerast ofan í kok."*

In general, with the advent of the verse the narrator takes on the voice of the poet, serving as a kind of surrogate for him. While the verse is performed as Páll ostensibly performed it, with Páll at the deictic center of the utterance (note the second person pronouns in the verse which index the fisherman, not the folklorist), the narrator is not making the verse but re-presenting it and the verse is shorn of its performative power; it will not cause the person to whom it is directed in the narrative event to drown and lose his tongue.

When the verse is completed, the style shifts back to that of the preceding narrative, in the past tense, less heavily marked in formal terms, and so on. Stylistic contrast notwithstanding, however, there is marked cohesion established between lines 19–22, which follow the verse, and the verse itself. There is, first of all, a parallelism of action sequence, in which the drowning of the fisherman and the cutting out of his tongue, recounted in the narrative past tense, correspond to the anticipation of these events in the verse, delivered in the subjunctive mood. We may also observe the use of lexical cohesion through the use in lines 19, 21, and 22 of grammatical variants of the words used in the verse:

- *Fari það* (15) vs. *það fór* (19) = "Should it turn out" (subjunctive) vs. "it turned out" (preterite);
- *sandinn* (16) vs. *-sandur* (21) = *sand-* + definite article suffix vs. *-sand* + accusative case marker;
- *tungu-* (18) vs. *tunguna* (22) = *tung-* + genitive case marker vs. *tung-* + accusative case marker.

We can see clearly, then, in lines 19–22, that the verse has a strong formative influence on the narrative discourse that follows it; it has the capacity to shape and permeate the narrative beyond its own formal boundaries.

If we examine the verse in functional as well as formal terms, we can see why this should be so. In his analysis of magical discourse, Tzvetan Todorov has suggested that "the magical formula is a micro-narrative" (1973: 44, my translation), resting his contention on the essential presence in such formulae of a verb form that signifies a change of state, a necessary condition for the existence of a narrative. He goes on to point out, however, that the narrative of the magical formula is different from other narratives insofar as it designates a virtual action, not an actual one, an action that is not yet accomplished but must be. While I would reserve the term "narrative" for accounts of action reported as accomplished, I believe Todorov's observation of the structural relationship between magical discourse and narrative is very acute, holding the key to the relationship between the verse and the ensuing narrative in our legend text. The magical verse sets forth virtual action – the drowning of the seasonal fisherman and the cutting out of his tongue in the subjunctive mood – while the subsequent narrative portion of the text recounts the realization of that virtual action in the past tense. Hence the power of the verse over the narrative, its formative effect on the narrative discourse that follows it. The verse itself, however, is formally impenetrable, as we have seen. The preceding narrative stops short at the initial boundary of the verse, and the subsequent narrative picks up again immediately after it, but the narrative exercises no shaping influence at all in formal terms on the verse. Performative efficacy resides in the form of the verse; the narrative merely describes the external circumstances of the verse and reports on the realization of the change of state that it effects.

In this generic dialogue, then, the narrative is formally and functionally subordinate to the verse. While in one general functional sense we might perhaps say that there is a mutual process of contextualization going on since there are ties of cohesion linking the story and the verse together, the point I want to emphasize is that it is through the framing narrative that all the work of contextualization is accomplished. The narrative is accommodated to the verse at the end, while the verse retains its unitary integrity, if not its performative power. Note, however, that this is not a necessary consequence of merging narrative and verse. That narrative can take over and subordinate verse is clearly evidenced by line 11, in which the fisherman's verse is merely reported, preserving only a reference to its general poetic form and illocutionary force. It is Páll's verse, with its magical efficacy, that is the point of the story, hence its dominant position in the interplay of genres.

4   Traditionalization

Thus far in the analysis, I have focused my discussion on lines 7–22 of the text, which constitute the narrative portion of Jón Norðmann's discourse in the formal and functional senses I indicated earlier. Let me turn now to the other portions of the text to examine the dynamics of contextualization at work within them. There are, in fact, several kinds of contextualizing work evidenced in these opening and closing sections, including a small negotiation by which Mr Norðmann shifts the discussion from kraftaskálds in Skagafjord, his own region in the very north of Iceland, to Páll the Poet, a kraftaskáld from the Westman Islands off the south coast, a little job of contextualizing this story *vis-à-vis* the preceding discourse between himself and the folklorist. For present purposes, however, I am more concerned with a different order of business accomplished in the lines at the beginning and end of the transcript, in particular lines 5–8 and 23–5. First, lines 5, 6, and 25: "although it is connected with Gudrún, daughter of the Reverend Páll the Poet in the Westman Islands," and "Now Gudrún, his daughter, told my father this story." What I want to suggest is that this linking of his story to the antecedent tellings of his father and Gudrún represents the work of traditionalization, traditionalization in practice.

Now, in conventional folkloric terms, the story would be reckoned to be traditional by several interconnected measures. The tale can be documented in what is recognizably the same plot, though with some variation, in texts in the folktale collections, all gathered from "oral tradition," so called, meaning the oral storytelling of narrators who heard them aurally from other narrators. In one of the more interesting of these, for example (Sigfússon 1946: 59–60), Páll's adversary is not a seasonal fisherman, but one Jón Torfabróður, a rival poet with whom Páll engaged in heated verse battles. Páll's magical verse is given as follows, clearly a variant of the verse in our text:

> það færi betur fyrir þitt sprok
> þu fengir að rata í sandinn.
> það ætti að skerast uppvið kok
> úr þer tungu-fjandinn!

> It would be better for (all) your talk
> (if) you got to fall into the sand.
> That may it cut itself up (out of) your throat
> out of you, the tongue-devil!

Interestingly, in this version both verses are successful: Jón drowns and his body is found with its tongue missing, but Páll drowns also. Thus, this story would be considered a traditional item on two standard grounds: it is handed down orally from generation to generation and it exists in different versions in the social group within which it is current. This is a kind of objective and analytical conception of tradition, in the sense that it views folklore items essentially as persistent objects, rooted in the past and passed on from person to person through time and space. And, indeed, Mr. Norðmann's testimony may be viewed from this vantage point as corroborative recognition by the folk of this handing down of the story from Gudrún, Páll's daughter, to Mr. Norðmann's father, to Mr. Norðmann, and ultimately to the folklorist.

From an agent-centered point of view, however, looking at Mr. Norðmann's storytelling as social practice, other questions must arise. What we have in this text is Mr. Norðmann directly and explicitly engaged in an act of symbolic construction, drawing the links of continuity by which he may tie his story to past discourses as part of his own recounting of it. This is the act of traditionalization, and it is part of the process of endowing the story with situated meaning. "The traditional begins with the personal" (Hymes 1975b: 354) and the immediate here, not with some objective quality of pastness that inheres in a cultural object but with the active construction of connections that link the present with a meaningful past. When examined, this process of traditionalization in the text before us manifests itself as a species of contextualization. Mr. Norðmann locates his discourse in relation to a sequential series of other discourses, starting in fact with Pall's own and proceeding through those of Gudrún and his father, so that his story, in effect, contains them all. That Gudrún told the story to his father, who told it to him, constitutes one dimension of the story's social meaning and value in the situational context of Mr. Norðmann's telling of it to Eiríksson. Specifically, traditionalization here is an act of authentication, akin to the art or antique dealer's authentication of an object by tracing its provenience. Mr. Norðmann establishes both the genuineness of his story as a reliable account and the legitimacy and strength of his claim to it by locating himself in a direct line of transmission, including lines of descent through kinship, that reaches back to Páll himself, the original speaker of those reportable words that constitute the point of the narrative. By orienting his talk to his father's talk, to Gudrún's talk, to Páll's talk, Norðmann endows his discourse with a dimension of traditional authority in a Weberian sense. If the original event is reportable, Mr. Norðmann's direct connection with it through the links with his father and Páll's daughter establishes and enhances the legitimacy of his claim to report it himself.

It is important to establish, though, that Norðmann's claims about the authenticity of the story, his argument for it as the real thing truly told about Páll by people with a strong claim to reliable knowledge, is not also an argument for the validity of others' interpretations of the story. In fact, Mr. Norðmann leaves open the possibility of calling into question certain aspects of others' tellings of the story. Observe, for example, his statements in lines 7–8 that Páll was "thought" to be a kraftaskáld, and that this was "thought" to prove true in the events narrated in the story, picking up on the framing of Eiríksson's question about those who were "reputed to be" (*talin*) kraftaskálds. This does not question the external events recounted in the narrative, but it certainly leaves open the question of whether Páll's verse actually did have the magical efficacy attributed to it. Even stronger is Mr. Norðmann's meta-narrational comment in line 23: "that could, now, all well have happened without the verse having occurred." This raises the question of alternative explanations quite directly; others may interpret the fisherman's drowning and loss of his tongue as brought about by Páll's verse, but Mr. Norðmann acknowledges that it might have happened anyway. Thus, his traditionalization of the narrative by contextualizing it *vis-à-vis* others' discourse has a dual thrust: it authenticates the story as a significant piece of discourse, strengthening its claim – and his own – on our attention, but it questions the authority of others' expressed interpretations of the story. In the process, then, he reframes the story by taking a different line toward its meaning, though one at least partially set up by the framing of the folklorist's question to him. The plot is accepted – even valorized – in terms of its connection with certain talk that preceded it but the meaning of the story, as also given expression in earlier talk, is subjected to question. This is an active engagement with tradition, the use of traditionalization to endow the story with dimensions of personal and social meaning; it is not simply a recognition of an inherent quality of traditionality in a particular cultural object.

5   **Discussion: contextualization, genre, and tradition**

This recounting of the legend of Páll the Poet, then, emerges from our examination as a structure of multiply embedded acts of contextualization in which talk is oriented to other talk: Páll's verse, Gudrún's story, Mr. Norðmann's father's story, the interpretive talk of those who commented on the story, and Mr. Norðmann's own recounting of it to the folklorist. I have intended in my examination of the text to suggest how an analysis of the management of these contextualizations may illuminate certain other foundational concepts beyond context itself, specifically genre and tradition.

Genre is a classificatory concept, a way of sorting out conventionalized discourse forms on the basis of form, function, content, or some other factor or set of factors. Scholarly thinking about verbal genres, both in folklore and linguistic anthropology, has been much influenced by canons of scientific taxonomy, whether from an etic or an emic point of view: genre classifications must be based on the application of consistent sorting principles throughout, they must be exhaustive, the categories must be mutually exclusive, and so on. But even in the enthusiasms of ethnoscience, there were constant reminders from the data that human expression doesn't fit so neatly into taxonomic categories. Gary Gossen (1974), in the most elegant of the elucidations of verbal genres in native terms, noted that he could only get agreement – more or less – from his Chamula sources down to five taxonomic levels, below which agreement on what went in which category was not to be achieved. And, in folklore scholarship, there has always been some unease about those anomalous, blended forms that do not fit neatly into systems of genre classification, such as neck riddle, riddle ballad, cante fable, and the like, that serve as nagging reminders that genres leak. These are themselves conventional forms of folkloric expression in which what are analytically considered as primary genres are brought into dialogue with each other.

Kraftaskáld legends represent another instance of such dialogic genres in Bakhtin's sense of the term, not necessarily involving two or more interlocutors but rather the interpenetration of multiple voices and forms of utterance. My use of Bakhtinian terminology here indicates the potential usefulness of Bakhtin's ideas in the elucidation of such compound forms, and, indeed, I have been much stimulated by his dialogic perspective (especially Bakhtin 1981, 1986; Medvedev/Bakhtin 1978; Vološinov 1973). As suggestive as they are, however, Bakhtin's writings engender a certain amount of frustration in the analysis of dialogic forms; his perspective seems to demand a dimension of formal analysis, but he never provides it. **How** are genres brought into dialogue? **How** is dialogization actually accomplished? What I have tried to suggest in this chapter is the productiveness of such formal analysis, framed as a problem in the mutual contextualization of primary genres. In order to accomplish a telling of a kraftaskáld legend, the narrator must accomplish the management of contextualization, determined to a significant degree by the formal and functional capacities of the genres brought into dialogue, here *saga* and *vísa*, story and verse. My analysis has been meant to show for this one dialogic form how that generic contextualization gets done. For other mergers, it would have to be accomplished differently. One value of the kind of formal and functional analysis I have attempted, I believe, is its potential for establishing a basis for the comparative investigation of such hitherto poorly understood dialogic genres as a key to a significant dimension of generic creativity. Let me suggest some of the possibilities in a very preliminary way by reference to a few examples.

Consider, for instance, the class of epics known as shamanic epics (Oinas 1978: 293), such as the Finnish *Kalevala* (Lönnröt 1963), which deal in significant part with deeds that are accomplished by magical means. Throughout the *Kalevala* narrative, we find the heroes and heroines employing magical charms. Not surprisingly, in light of our examination of kraftaskáld legends, the virtual transformations given expression in the charms are subsequently reported as having been realized, with the charms pointing ahead and giving shape to these narrative reports. In the *Kalevala*, however, all is in verse. Thus, by contrast with the parallelism of action sequence and occasional lexical cohesion that we observed between the magical verse and the ensuing narrative prose in the story of Páll the Poet, we find a far tighter line-by-line parallelism allowed for in the *Kalevala* between the magical charm and the account of its working:

> Make a cloud spring up in the east, raise up a cloudbank in the northwest
> send others from the west, drive others from the south.
> Shed rain gently from the heavens, sprinkle honey from the clouds
> on the sprouting shoots, on the murmuring crops.

> He made a cloud spring up in the east, raised a cloudbank in the northwest,
> sent another from the west, drove one from the south.
> He pushed them right together, banged them against one another.
> He shed rain gently from the heavens, sprinkled honey from the clouds
> on the sprouting shoots, on the murmuring crops.

> (Lönnröt 1963: 12–13)

Or, take the tale often cited as the prototype of the cante fable, "The Singing Bone" (Grimm no. 28, AT 780), summarized thus by Thompson: "The brother kills his brother (sister) and buries him in the earth. From the bones a shepherd makes a flute which brings the secret to light" (1961: 269). The secret is brought to light by means of a verse sung by the bone flute (hence **cante fable**, singing tale). Here, once again, we have the merger of story and verse, but in this case it is the preceding narrative that has at least a partial determinative effect on the embedded verse, as the verse recapitulates the preceding action. In "The Singing Bone," the verse, far from being impenetrable as it is in our legend text, is shaped into a narrative sequence of its own by the prose that precedes it.

A similar process is at work in the dialogic form known as the neck riddle, blending narrative and riddle (Abrahams 1980, 1985; Dorst 1983). The term "neck riddle" derives from the common framing of such narratives in terms of a man who saves his neck by propounding a riddle that his executioner cannot answer, but the form also includes the strategic use of unanswerable riddles as a kind of test or wager. According to Abrahams and Dundes (1972: 133), "The essential characteristic of this type is that the riddle must be based on some experience that only the riddler has undergone or witnessed." Perhaps the most widely known example is Samson's riddle (Judges 14: 14) "Out of the eater came forth meat, and out of the strong came forth sweetness," referring to a lion he had earlier killed by rending it apart and in whose carcass a swarm of bees later nested and produced honey. As in "The Singing Bone," the antecedent narrative gives shape to the inset form, here the riddle, but while the bone flute's verse is meant to reveal what has transpired, the riddle is meant to obscure it, hence the opaque language of the riddle.

These three brief examples represent the merest scratching of the surface of the possibilities suggested by an exploration of dialogic genres. Nor is this process confined to conventional blending alone; there is always the potential of bringing genres into dialogue in more spontaneous and emergent ways (e.g. Sherzer 1979). Ultimately, the exploration of how such generic blendings are accomplished in performance will highlight a creative dimension of human verbal expression that has tended to be obscured by established notions of genre, revealing more closely how people use verbal art in the conduct of their social lives.

Now this illumination of the problem of genre is but one of the outcomes of an examination of this text in terms of the contextualization of discourse by other discourse. Beyond the contextualization of the verse by the story, the other task accomplished by the narrator is the outward contextualization of his story by situating it in a lineage of other tellings or commentaries. This act of contextualization, I have suggested, represents traditionalization in practice. What is accomplished thereby is the authentication of his discourse, the endowing of it and himself with a species of authority, a claim on our attention and interest. Tradition here is a rhetorical resource, not an inherent quality of a story. To be sure, tradition is always such a resource, but in folklore and anthropology traditionalization has overwhelmingly been a resource of intellectual outsiders, a means of selectively and analytically valorizing, legitimizing, and managing aspects of culture frequently not their own by establishing them within lineages of descent and patterns of distribution for scholarly rhetorical and analytical

purposes. Examination of this text highlights the significance of a complementary strategy at the folk level, the active construction of links tying the
present to the past. Oral tradition, in these active and local terms, is a
particular strategic form of the contextualization of speech *vis-à-vis* other
speech, a way that those who use spoken art forms as equipment for living
invest what they say with social meaning, efficacy, and value.

There are many implications here for written literature as well, but that
would carry me far beyond the scope of this chapter. I will confine myself
to one especially relevant example. Devices that establish a linkage
between current discourse and earlier discourses have been a prominent
focus of discussion in the scholarship devoted to the classic Icelandic sagas,
with special reference to saga origins (see, for example, Andersson 1966;
Bell 1976; Liestøl 1974 [1930]: 33–4). Proponents of the "freeprose"
argument that the sagas are deeply rooted in oral narrative tradition point
to the frequent use of such oral "source references" as "*svá er sagt*" (so is
said), "*frá því er sagt*" (it is related), "*þat segja menn*" (so men say), or "*er
þat flestra manna sǫgn*" (it is the report of most men) as evidence of an
active oral tradition antecedent to the written sagas, while adherents of the
more literary "bookprose" position tend to dismiss such devices as mere
stylistic convention.

While the written sagas as we have them unquestionably represent a
literary genre, no one familiar with the dynamics of an oral tradition can
doubt that the sagas are strongly tied to such a tradition in Commonwealth
Iceland. Debates over origins aside, however, I would maintain that the
findings of this chapter concerning the dynamics of traditionalization offer
a useful vantage point from which to consider the "source references" of
the classic sagas. Like the intertextual linkages forged by the narrator of
our kraftaskáld legend, the establishment of ties to other discourses by the
writers of the sagas represents traditionalization in action, the active
process of contextualizing the saga narratives in a socially constituted field
of verbal production that endows them with traditional authority in a
society that relied centrally on such authority in the conduct of social life.
The source references are stylistic devices in the service of rendering the
saga accounts in which they are employed socially authoritative. Whether
or not they point to what someone really said in every instance is to this
extent beside the point. The rhetorical effect of traditionalization through
the weaving of inter-discursive ties is what is significant; this process
endows the sagas, like our kraftaskáld legend, with a distinctive element of
social groundedness and force.

6   Conclusion

The analysis of folklore in context directs attention to the anchoring of
folklore in the social and cultural worlds of its users, to the complex,

multidimensional web of interrelationships that link folklore to culturally defined systems of meaning and interpretation and to socially organized systems of social relations. In the general usage of folklorists, however, the notion of context invokes three principal dimensions of such interrelationships: (1) the context of cultural meaning, that is, what it is one needs to know about a culture to make sense of its folklore; (2) the functional context, social or psychological, that is, how folklore operates to validate social institutions, maintain social solidarity, socialize children, alleviate psychological conflict, and the like; and (3) the situational context, focusing on the social use of folklore in the conduct of social life, within culturally defined scenes and events. If I may venture a generalized, but still, I think, accurate, characterization of these three contextual perspectives, they tend largely to approach folklore from the outside in, constructing a kind of contextual surround for the foklore forms and texts under examination which is seen to have a formative influence upon them. I have endeavored in this chapter, by pursuing a more agent-centered line of analysis, to explore a perspective on context from the inside, as it were, using the text itself as a point of departure, and allowing it to index dimensions of context as the narrator himself forges links of contextualization to give shape and meaning to his expression. The aim is not to dismiss the more collective, institutional, conventional dimensions of context, but ultimately to provide an analytical counterweight to them in the service of moving us closer to a balanced understanding of that most fundamental of all anthropological problems, the dynamic interplay of the social and the individual, the ready-made and the emergent, in human life.

Acknowledgements

I am grateful to Hallfreður Örn Eiríksson of the Stofnun Árna Magnússonar, Reykjavík, for making available to me the kraftaskáld legend analyzed in this chapter and for many other collegial kindnesses; to Birna Arnbjörnsdóttir for assistance with transcription and translation; and to Roger Abrahams, Roberta Frank, Jeffrey Kittay, Jennifer Livesay, and the members of the Text as Social Action collective of the Center for Psychosocial Studies for many helpful comments on earlier presentations of this material. Thanks also to Jesse Byock for his encouragement of my Icelandic ventures.

Notes

1 For discussion of these trends see Bauman (1986, 1987) and Limón and Young (1986).
2 Prominent examples of structural definitions of genre, comprehending both formal structures and the structure of logical relations, include Dundes (1964),

Georges and Dundes (1963), Maranda (1971), and Maranda and Maranda (1971). On culturally established systems of genre classification see Abrahams and Bauman (1971), Ben–Amos (1976), and Gossen (1974).
3 Ben–Amos (1984) is a comprehensive review of folkloric conceptions of tradition. Handler and Linnekin (1984), Hobsbawm and Ranger (1983), Hymes (1975b: 353–5), MacCannell (1976), and Williams (1977) have been influential in the reorientation from tradition as persistent cultural objects to tradition as symbolic construction.
4 In Icelandic, kraftaskáld is the same in singular and plural; in this chapter, I have anglicized the plural form.

References

Abrahams, Roger D. 1980. Between the Living and the Dead. FFC 225. Helsinki: Suomalainen Tiedeakatemia.
   1985. A Note on Neck-Riddles in the West Indies as They Comment on Emergent Genre Theory. *Journal of American Folklore* 98: 85–94.
Abrahams, Roger D., and Richard Bauman. 1971. Sense and Nonsense in St. Vincent. *American Anthropologist* 73: 762–72.
Abrahams, Roger D., and Alan Dundes. 1972. Riddles, in *Folklore and Folklife: An Introduction*, ed. Richard M. Dorson, pp. 129–43. Chicago: University of Chicago Press.
Almqvist, Bo. 1961. Um Ákvæðaskáld. *Skirnir* 135: 72–98.
   1965. *Norrön Niddiktning 1*. Stockholm: Almqvist and Wiksell.
   1974. *Norrön Niddiktning 2*. Stockholm: Almqvist and Wiksell.
Andersson, Theodore M. 1966. The Textual Evidence for an Oral Family Saga. *Arkiv för Nordisk Filologi* 81: 1–23.
Bakhtin, Mikhail M. 1981. The Dialogic Imagination, ed. Michael Holquist, trans. Caryl Emerson and Michael Holquist. Austin: University of Texas Press.
   1986. *Speech Genres and Other Late Essays*, ed. Caryl Emerson and Michael Holquist, trans. Vern McGee. Austin: University of Texas Press.
Bauman, Richard. 1983. The Field Study of Folklore in Context, in *Handbook of American Folklore*, ed. Richard M. Dorson, pp. 362–8. Bloomington: Indiana University Press.
   1986. Performance and Honor in 13th-Century Iceland. *Journal of American Folklore* 99: 131–50.
   1987. The Role of Performance in the Ethnography of Speaking. *Working Papers and Proceedings of the Center for Psychosocial Studies* 11: 3–12.
Bauman, Richard, and Charles L. Briggs. 1990. Poetics and Performance as Critical Perspectives on Social Life. *Annual Review of Anthropology*, vol. 19, ed. Bernard J. Siegel, pp. 59–88. Palo Alto: Annual Reviews Inc.
Bell, L. Michael. 1976. Oral Allusion in *Egils saga Skalla-Grímssoner:* A Computer-Aided Approach. *Arkiv för Nordisk Filologi* 81: 1–23.
Ben–Amos, Dan. 1976. Analytic Categories and Ethnic Genres, in *Folklore Genres*, ed. Dan Ben–Amos, pp. 215–42. Austin: University of Texas Press.
   1984. The Seven Strands of *Tradition. Journal of Folklore Research* 21: 97–131.
Briggs, Charles L. 1985. Treasure Tales and Pedagogical Discourse in *Mexicano* New Mexico. *Journal of American Folklore* 98: 287–314.
Cleasby, Richard, Gudbrand Vigfusson, and William Craigie. 1957. An Icelandic--English Dictionary. 2nd edn. Oxford: Clarendon Press.

Dorst, John. 1983. Neck-Riddle as a Dialogue of Genres. *Journal of American Folklore* 96: 413–33.

Dundes, Alan. 1964. The Morphology of North American Indian Folktales. FFC 195. Helsinki: Suomalainen Tiedeakatemia.

Georges, Robert, and Alan Dundes. 1963. Toward a Structural Definition of the Riddle. *Journal of American Folklore* 76: 111–18.

Gossen, Gary. 1974. *Chamulas in the World of the Sun*. Cambridge, Mass.: Harvard University Press.

Handler, Richard, and Jocelyn Linnekin. 1984. Tradition, Genuine or Spurious. *Journal of American Folklore* 97: 273–90.

Hobsbawm, Eric, and Terence Ranger (eds.). 1983. *The Invention of Tradition*. Cambridge: Cambridge University Press.

Hymes, Dell H. 1975a. Breakthrough Into Performance, in *Folklore: Performance and Communication*, ed. Dan Ben–Amos and Kenneth Goldstein, pp. 11–74. The Hague: Mouton.

1975b. Folklore's Nature and the Sun's Myth. *Journal of American Folklore* 88: 345–69.

Kabell, Aage. 1980. Skalden und Schamanen. FFC 227. Helsinki: Suomalainen Tiedeakatemia.

Liestøl, Knut. 1974 [1930]. *The Origin of the Icelandic Family Sagas*. Westport, CT: Greenwood Press.

Limón, José, and M. Jane Young. 1986. Frontiers, Settlements, and Development in Folklore Studies, 1972–1985. *Annual Review of Anthropolgy*, vol. 15, ed. Bernard J. Siegel, pp. 437–60. Palo Alto: Annual Reviews Inc.

Lönnröt, Elias. 1963. *The Kalevala*, trans. Francis P. Magoun. Cambridge, Mass.: Harvard University Press.

MacCannell, Dean. 1976. *The Tourist*. New York: Schocken Books.

Manhire, W. 1975–6. The Narrative Functions of Source–References in the Sagas of Icelanders. *Saga–Book of the Viking Society for Northern Research* 19(2–3): 170–90.

Maranda, Elli Köngäs. 1971. The Logic of Riddles, in *Structural Analysis of Oral Tradition*, ed. Pierre Maranda and Elli Köngäs Maranda, pp. 189–232. Philadelphia: University of Pennsylvania Press.

Maranda, Elli Köngäs, and Pierre Maranda. 1971. *Structural Models in Folklore and Transformational Essays*. The Hague: Mouton.

Medvedev, P. N./M. M. Bakhtin. 1978. *The Formal Method in Literary Scholarship*. Baltimore: Johns Hopkins University Press.

Oinas, Felix J. 1978. The Balto–Finnic Epics, in *Heroic Epic and Saga*, ed. Felix J. Oinas, pp. 286–309. Bloomington: Indiana University Press.

Propp, Vladimir. 1968. *The Morphology of the Folktale*. Austin: University of Texas Press.

Sherzer, Joel. 1979. Strategies in Text and Context. *Journal of American Folklore* 92: 145–63.

Sigfússon, Sigfus. 1946. *Íslenzkar þjóð-Sögur og -Sagnir*, vol. 8. Reykjavík: Víkingsútgafan.

Sigurðsson, Arngrimur. 1983. *Íslenzk-Ensk Orðabók*. Reykjavík: Ísafoldarprentsmiðja H. F.

Thompson, Stith. 1961. The Types of the Folktale. FFC 184. Helsinki: Suomalainen Tiedeakatemia.

Todorov, Tzvetan. 1973. Le discours de la magie. *L'Homme* 13(4): 38–65.

Urban, Greg. 1985. The Semiotics of Two Speech Styles in Shokleng, in *Semiotic Mediation*, ed. Elizabeth Mertz and Richard Parmentier, pp. 311–29. New York: Academic Press.

Vološinov, V. N. 1973. *Marxism and the Philosophy of Language*. New York: Seminar Press.
Williams, Raymond. 1977. *Marxism and Literature*. Oxford: Oxford University Press.
Young, Katherine. 1985. The Notion of Context. *Western Folklore* 44: 115–22.
Zoëga, G. T. 1910. *A Concise Dictionary of Old Icelandic*. Oxford: Clarendon Press.

6 Assessments and the construction of context

CHARLES GOODWIN and MARJORIE HARNESS GOODWIN

Editors' introduction

Charles and Marjorie Harness Goodwin are both Professors of Anthropology at the University of South Carolina. Both received their Ph.D.s from the University of Pennsylvania – Charles in Communications and Marjorie in Anthropology – where they worked closely with Erving Goffman, Gail Jefferson, and William Labov. Their primary research interest is the analysis of how talk is organized as a phenomenon embedded within human interaction, and more generally the systemic resources and procedures used by human beings to organize their interaction with each other. As anthropologists they want to investigate interaction in the endogenous situations where people actually live their everyday lives. Moreover, because of their belief that talk is intrinsically interactive, and thus shaped as much by recipients as by speakers, as well as by the activity within which the talk and its participants are embedded, the Goodwins want to focus their analysis on the talk that members of a society **produce for each other** within the **activities** that constitute their culture, rather than relying on interviews, collected stories, or other texts produced for the anthropologist or other outsiders.

In pursuit of such goals Marjorie Harness Goodwin tape-recorded the conversations of a group of urban black children over a period of a year and a half as they played on the street. In analyzing these materials she has been especially interested in how the children use talk to build social organization in the midst of moment-to-moment interaction. The length of time she spent in this setting enabled her to track how the children moved from activity to activity, while the fact that she recorded everything that they said permitted fine-grained analysis of how the activity of the moment was being constituted through their talk. Boys and girls were able to build different types of social organization within their same-sex peer groups (hierarchical for the boys, and egalitarian with extensive coalition formation for the girls) through alternative ways of formatting, and responding to, speech actions such as directives (M. H. Goodwin 1980c). However, when activities shifted, and girls and boys interacted with each other, the girls were fully competent in forms of speech typically associated with males, and indeed were frequently able to outdo the boys in activities such as argument and ritual insult (M. H. Goodwin and C. Goodwin 1987). These findings challenge current perceptions about how women speak with an inherently different voice (Gilligan 1982), while

147

demonstrating the importance of tracking interaction across a range of different types of events. Other speech activities of the children included stories (M. H. Goodwin 1982a, 1982b), disputes (M. H. Goodwin 1983), and a particular type of gossip that the children called "he-said-she-said" (M. H. Goodwin 1980a). In all of these events, talk was shaped in fine detail by the activity in progress, carefully designed for its particular recipients, and it provided resources for both constituting and transforming the social organization of the moment. None of this analysis, with its focus on the design of talk for its recipients and the events it is helping to constitute, could have been pursued if talk had not been recorded within endogenous activities that the participants were organizing, not for the researcher, but for each other. Marjorie Harness Goodwin's analysis of how the children used talk to collaboratively build the events of their lifeworld is the subject of her recent book *He-Said-She-Said: Talk as Social Organization among Black Children* (1990b). In other work she has used video-recordings to investigate interaction within the turn in assessment sequences, and **byplay** (1990a) – collusive commentary on the extended talk of another speaker.

Talk is typically viewed as an activity that **speakers** perform. Thus one might imagine a division of labor in which the exchange of turns at talk was an interactive phenomenon (as is clearly demonstrated in Sacks, Schegloff, and Jefferson 1974), but the production of talk **within** the turn was not. Instead it rested in the hands of a single individual, the speaker. Study of how individual utterances were shaped and produced could then be safely left to psychologists and linguists, with analysis of interaction beginning at the boundaries of the turn. In his research Charles Goodwin has been interested in demonstrating that in fact talk emerges through **systematic processes of interaction in which recipients are very active co-participants**. By using videotapes of conversation he was able to investigate **processes of interaction that occur within the turn itself** (cf. C. Goodwin 1981). Most basically a speaker needs a hearer, and the availability and orientation of a recipient is something that participants actively accomplish and negotiate as an utterance unfolds. Thus a speaker who brings her gaze to an addressee who is not gazing back toward her frequently produces a restart in her talk at precisely that point. Such action both marks the talk then in progress as defective (i.e. the sentence is aborted without being brought to completion), and acts as a request for the recipient's gaze; right after the restart the recipient typically starts to move her gaze to the speaker. Such phrasal breaks are not manifestations of the speaker's defective performance, or the product of purely psychological processes restricted to a single individual, but instead interactive phenomena that demonstrate the active work that speakers perform to produce sentences that are attended to as coherent wholes by their recipients. Similarly, in order to coordinate their actions with appropriate reciprocal actions of their recipients, speakers frequently add new segments to emerging utterances, and change the meaning of an emerging sentence as they move their gaze from one addressee to another so that it maintains its appropriateness for its recipient of the moment. The utterance actually spoken within the turn, and the sentence manifested through it, thus emerge not from the actions of the speaker alone, but rather as the product of a process of interaction in which the recipient is a very active co-participant. In other work Charles Goodwin has investigated the interactive organization of gesture (1986b), displays of forgetfulness (1987), and stories (1984, 1986a), showing for example how the telling of a story creates a multi-party field of action in which alternative types of participants are differentially positioned, each with their own tasks to perform, as they collaboratively constitute the telling as a social event.

The events that occur within a turn at talk are quite heterogeneous, encompassing a range of both vocal and nonvocal behavior, as well as a variety of different types of action. This poses the question of how such disparate phenomena can be studied as integrated, coherent systems of action. In this chapter, the Goodwins argue that investigating **the interactive organization of activity systems** and the **participation frameworks** they include is one way of doing this.[1] They focus their analysis on a specific activity: **assessments**. Activities provide context that guides the interpretation of events lodged within them, and indeed when collaboratively producing assessments different participants can calibrate their separate evaluations of events in their phenomenal world and intricately demonstrate how their minds are in tune with each other. However, while such interpretive issues are important, they do not provide a comprehensive picture of the social and cognitive phenomena relevant to the organization of activities. While using activities as interpretive resources participants are simultaneously faced with the task of building these very same activities. This process is accomplished through a complex deployment of inference, action, and behavior which is situated within time and space. Within such a framework individual behavior is transformed into meaningful social action, and affect, action, and cognition can be analyzed as socially distributed phenomena. The analysis of **participation within activities** makes it possible to view actors as not simply embedded within context, but actively involved in the process of building context through intricate collaborative articulation of the events they are engaged in.

The phenomena investigated here are relevant to themes addressed in a number of other chapters in this volume, including the analysis of contextualization cues (Gumperz), the study of how larger social frameworks can be invoked within small strips of talk (Duranti, Hanks, Gaik, and Cicourel), the analysis of stories (Bauman, Lindstrom, and Basso), and the collaborative organization of participation (Kendon and Hanks).

Note

1 Indeed scholars in a number of different disciplines have independently advocated the central relevance of activities to the study of a range of interactive phenomena including the acquisition of language in its sociocultural matrix (Ochs 1988: 14–17), the analysis of discourse (Levinson 1979), the study of language acquisition and learning processes from a Vygotskian perspective (Wertsch 1981, 1985), and the analysis of cognition as a situated process (Lave 1988). Within the field of face-to-face interaction, Goffman (1961: 96) proposed that a basic unit of study should be the "situated activity system": a "somewhat closed, self-compensating, self-terminating circuit of interdependent actions." Such a framework has close affinity with Hymes's (1972) sociolinguistic notion of

"speech event," an interactive unit above the level of speech act "which is to the analysis of verbal interaction what the sentence is to grammar" (Gumperz 1972: 17). Both Goffman and Hymes formulate a unit of analysis which emphasizes the interactive meshing of the actions of separate participants into joint social projects. Participation frameworks have been the topic of recent study by Goffman 1981; C. Goodwin 1981, 1984: C. Goodwin and M. H. Goodwin (1990), M. H. Goodwin (1980b, 1990a), Hanks (1990), Heath (1986), Kendon (1990, this volume), and Levinson (1987).

References

Gilligan, Carol. 1982. *In a Different Voice: Psychological Theory and Women's Development*. Cambridge, MA: Harvard University Press.

Goffman, Erving. 1961. *Encounters: Two Studies in the Sociology of Interaction*. Indianapolis: Bobbs–Merrill.

1981. *Forms of Talk*. Philadelphia: University of Pennsylvania Press.

Goodwin, Charles. 1981. *Conversational Organization: Interaction Between Speakers and Hearers*. New York: Academic Press.

1984. Notes on Story Structure and the Organization of Participation, in *Structures of Social Action*, ed. Max Atkinson and John Heritage, pp. 225–46. Cambridge: Cambridge University Press.

1986a. Audience Diversity, Participation and Interpretation. *Text* 6(3): 283–316.

1986b. Gesture as a Resource for the Organization of Mutual Orientation. *Semiotica* 62(1/2): 29–49.

1987. Forgetfulness as an Interactive Resource. *Social Psychology Quarterly* 50 (2): 115–30.

Goodwin, Charles, and Marjorie Harness Goodwin. 1990. Interstitial Argument, in *Conflict Talk*, ed. Allen Grimshaw, pp. 85–117. Cambridge: Cambridge University Press.

Goodwin, Marjorie Harness. 1980a. He-Said-She-Said: Formal Cultural Procedures for the Construction of a Gossip Dispute Activity. *American Ethnologist* 7: 674–95.

1980b. Processes of Mutual Monitoring Implicated in the Production of Description Sequences. *Sociological Inquiry* 50: 303–17.

1980c. Directive/Response Speech Sequences in Girls' and Boys' Task Activities, in *Women and Language in Literature and Society*, ed. Sally McConnell–Ginet, Ruth Borker, and Nelly Furman, pp. 157–73. New York: Praeger.

1982a. Processes of Dispute Management Among Urban Black Children. *American Ethnologist* 9: 76–96.

1982b. 'Instigating': Storytelling as Social Process. *American Ethnologist* 9: 799–819.

1983. Aggravated Correction and Disagreement in Children's Conversations. *Journal of Pragmatics* 7: 657–77.

1990a. Byplay: Participant Structure and the Framing of Collaborative Collusion, in *Les Formes de La Conversation*, Vol. 2, ed. B. Conein, M. de Fornel and L. Quéré, pp. 155–80. Paris: CNET.

1990b. *He-Said-She-Said: Talk as Social Organization among Black Children*. Bloomington: Indiana University Press.

Goodwin, Marjorie Harness, and Charles Goodwin. 1987. Children's Arguing, in *Language, Gender, and Sex in Comparative Perspective*, ed. Susan Philips, Susan Steele, and Christina Tanz, pp. 200–48. Cambridge: Cambridge University Press.

Gumperz, John J. 1972. Introduction, in *Directions in Sociolinguistics: The Ethnography of Communication*, ed. John J. Gumperz and Dell Hymes, pp. 1–25. New York: Holt, Rinehart and Winston.

Hanks, William F. 1990. *Referential Practice: Language and Lived Space among the Maya*. Chicago: University of Chicago Press.

Heath, Christian. 1986. *Body Movement and Speech in Medical Interaction*. Cambridge: Cambridge University Press.

Kendon, Adam. 1990. *Conducting Interaction: Patterns of Behaviour in Focused Encounters*. Cambridge: Cambridge University Press.

Lave, Jean. 1988. *Cognition in Practice*. Cambridge: Cambridge University Press.

Levinson, Stephen. 1979. Activity Types and Language. *Linguistics* 17: 365–99.

  1987. Putting Linguistics on a Proper Footing: Explorations in Goffman's Concepts of Participation, in *Goffman: An Interdisciplinary Appreciation*, ed. Paul Drew and Anthony J. Wootton, pp. 161–227. Cambridge: Polity Press.

Ochs, Elinor. 1988. *Culture and Language Development: Language Acquisition and Language Socialization in a Samoan Village*. Cambridge: Cambridge University Press.

Sacks, Harvey, Emanuel A. Schegloff, and Gail Jefferson. 1974. A Simplest Systematics for the Organization of Turn-Taking for Conversation. *Language* 50: 696–735.

Wertsch, James V. 1981. The Concept of Activity in Soviet Psychology: An Introduction. In *The Concept of Activity in Soviet Psychology*. James V. Wertsch, ed. pp. 3–36. Armonk, N.Y.: M. E. Sharpe.

  1985 (ed.). *Culture, Communication, and Cognition: Vygotskian Perspectives*. Cambridge: Cambridge University Press.

Assessments and the construction of context

This chapter will investigate some of the ways in which context is attended to and constituted as a dynamic phenomenon within the turn at talk in conversation. Two processes that occur within the turn will be investigated:

(1) **The activity of performing assessments or evaluations of events being discussed within talk**

This process is relevant to the issue of how context is organized within the turn in a number of different ways. For example, examining it will enable us to look at how participants attend to the emerging structure of the stream of speech as both context to their actions and a resource for the achievement of coordinated action within the turn, and to investigate coherent social activity systems that provide participants with resources for displaying to each other a congruent view of the events they encounter in their phenomenal world. We will thus be able to study how both social organization and shared understanding can be negotiated and accomplished within the boundaries of the turn at talk.

(2) **Instigating**

> A process situated within a gossip-dispute activity in which one girl tells
> another that a third was talking about her behind her back. Examination
> of the talk used to build this activity will enable us to investigate how
> assessments and evaluations can be used to build structures within the
> turn that both attend to and help shape activities that extend far beyond it.

The present chapter is able to focus on specific activities within the turn
at talk in large part because of other research which has provided extensive
analysis of how context is constituted in larger processes of interaction that
surround the turn. Of particular importance are Goffman's work on the
organization of talk in interaction (see for example Goffman 1953, 1964,
1974, 1981), Kendon's analysis of the role played by body behavior and
spatial organization in framing encounters in which talk occurs (for an
excellent review of much of this research see Kendon 1990), and work of
anthropological linguists such as Gumperz (1982) on such phenomena as
contextualization cues. The work that is most relevant to the issues being
investigated in the present study is the research initiated by Harvey Sacks
and his colleagues into the sequential organization of conversation (see for
example Atkinson and Heritage 1984; Jefferson 1973; Pomerantz 1978;
Sacks 1963; Sacks, Schegloff, and Jefferson 1974; Schegloff 1968, 1986b).
Indeed, this research contrasts with other approaches to discourse (speech
act theory for example) in its sustained effort to investigate how participants utilize context, and in particular sequential organization, to both
understand and produce the talk they are engaged in. Thus Schegloff
(1988: 61) argues that

What a rudimentary speech act theoretic analysis misses, and I suspect a
sophisticated one will miss as well, is that parties to real conversations are
always talking in some sequential context. I refer here not to social contexts like
offices, classrooms or families, but sequential contexts formulated in terms of
more or less proximately preceding talk and the real jobs of projecting further
talk which utterances can do, for which they can be inspected by their recipients, an inspection to which speakers must therefore be reflexively attentive.
Such prior and prospective contexts are inescapably implicated in the real life
projects, however humble or exalted, which are being prosecuted through the
talk. These real life projects, and the sequential infrastructure of talk-in interaction, are involved in the production and analysis of talk by the parties in such
intimate detail that we are only beginning to understand it. But it is clear that
temporality and sequentiality are inescapable; utterances are in turns, and turns
are parts of sequences; sequences and the projects done through them enter
constitutively into utterances like the warp in a woven fabric.

Similarly Atkinson and Heritage (1984: 11) note that in examining
conversation

the analyst is immediately confronted with an organization which is implemented
on a turn-by-turn basis, and through which a context of publicly displayed and

continuously updated intersubjective understanding is systematically sustained. It is through this turn-by-turn character of talk that the participants display their understandings of the state of the talk for one another . . .

While much of this research has focused on how turns are sequenced to each other, C. Goodwin (1981), M. H. Goodwin (1980b), and Heath (1986) have demonstrated how such sequential organization is constitutive of the turn itself. This research constitutes the point of departure for the present study.

1   Data and transcription

We will investigate in some detail sequences of conversation recorded on audio- and videotape. The tapes are from a larger sample of data recorded in a range of natural settings. The data to be examined here are drawn from talk between two women at a July 4th block party, a phone call between two teenage girls, and a group of urban black children playing on the street in front of their homes.[1] Talk is transcribed using the Jefferson transcription system (Sacks, Schegloff, and Jefferson 1974: 731–3). The following are the features most relevant to the present analysis:

- **Boldface** indicates some form of emphasis, which may be signaled by changes in pitch and/or amplitude.
- A **left bracket** connecting talk on separate lines marks the point at which one speaker's talk overlaps the talk of another.
- A **right bracket** marks the place where the overlap ends.
- **Double slashes** provide an alternative method of marking overlap. When they are used the overlapping talk is not indented to the point of overlap.
- **Tildes** between words are used to mark rapid speech.
- **Colons** indicate that the sound just before the colon has been noticeably lengthened.
- A **dash** marks a sudden cut-off of the current sound.
- Intonation: punctuation symbols are used to mark intonation changes rather than as grammatical symbols:

  - A **period** marks a falling contour.
  - A **question mark** indicates a rising contour.
  - A **comma** indicates a falling–rising contour.

- **Numbers in parentheses** mark silences in seconds and tenths of seconds.
- A **series of "h"s preceded by an asterisk** marks an inbreath.
- **Italics in double parentheses** indicate material that is not part of the talk being transcribed, for example a comment by the transcriber if the talk was spoken in some special way.
- A **degree sign** (°) indicates that the talk following it is spoken with noticeably lowered volume.
- An **arrow** is used to mark specific lines of talk being discussed in the text.

- An **equals sign** is used to indicate "latching"; there is no interval between the end of a prior unit and the start of a next piece of talk.
- **Capitals** indicate increased volume.

2   Assessments

One activity that both speakers and recipients perform within the turn at talk is evaluating in some fashion persons and events being described within their talk. The following provide clear and simple examples of assessments performed by speakers in the midst of their talk.[2] In both cases speakers preface descriptive nouns with the word "beautiful" and thus evaluate the phenomena referenced by those nouns (i.e. in [1] Eileen **assesses** the "Irish Setter" she is talking about by describing it as "beautiful"):

(1) Eileen: Paul en I got ta the first green,
                         (0.6)
→   An this beautiful, (0.2) Irish Setter.
                         (0.8)
                  Came tearin up on ta the first **gree**(h)n
                  an tried ta steal Pau(h)l's go(h)lf ball. *hh

(2) Curt: **Th**is guy had, a beautiful, thirty two O:lds.

The word "assessment" can in fact be used to refer to a range of events that exist on analytically distinct levels of organization. In view of this some definitional issues arise:

  (i) The term can be used to describe a structural unit that occurs at a specific place in the stream of speech, for example the adjective "beautiful." For clarity this sense of the term, which is used to designate a specific, segmental unit in the stream of speech, can be called an **assessment segment**. Though we will quickly see that not all assessment signals are limited to specific segmental phenomena in this way (and moreover that segments that precede the explicit assessment term, for example intensifiers, might also be part of the activity of assessment), being able to talk about an assessment occurring at a particular place offers great advantages for starting analysis of the larger activity of performing assessments – e.g. once an **assessment segment** is located an analyst can look in detail at the different types of action that not only co-occur with this event but also precede and follow it. Moreover, participants themselves attend to the distinctiveness and salience of such segmental phenomena; for example they distinguish an **assessment segment** from events that precede it, and treat it as a place for heightened mutual orientation and action (a phenomenon to be explored in detail later in this chapter).

  (ii) In addition to using phenomena that can be neatly segmented in the stream of speech, such as assessment adjectives, participants can also display their involvement in an assessment through nonsegmental phenomena such as intonation, and also through recognizable nonvocal displays (M. H. Goodwin 1980b). Indeed it sometimes becomes quite difficult to precisely delimit the boundaries of an assessment.[3] As a function of language (in the Prague sense of that word) rather than a specific act, the activity of assessment is not limited to word- or syntactic-level objects, but rather, like prosody in an utterance, runs over syntactic units. In this sense it acts much like intonation (which is indeed one principal resource for displaying evaluation)[4] *vis-à-vis* segmental phonology.[5] A display showing a party's involvement in an assessment can be called an **assessment signal**. **Assessment segments** constitute a particular subset of **assessment signals**. It is however quite relevant to distinguish **assessment segments** from the larger class of **assessment signals** since they have the special, and quite useful, property of being precisely delimited in the stream of speech.

(iii) The term "assessment" can also be used to designate a particular type of speech act. This sense of the term differs from the first two in that emphasis is placed on an action being performed by an actor, rather than on the speech signal used to embody that action, or the particular place where it occurs in the stream of speech. An assessment in this sense of the term can be called an **assessment action**. Several issues relevant to the analysis of assessments on this level of organization can be briefly noted. First, while most analysis of speech acts has focused on actions embodied by complete sentences or turns, assessments constitute a type of speech act that can occur **in the midst of an utterance**. Subsequent analysis in this chapter will investigate some of the consequences of this. Second, a crucial feature of assessment actions is the way in which they involve an actor taking up a position toward the phenomena being assessed. For example, in assessing something as "beautiful" a party publicly commits him- or herself to a particular evaluation of what he or she has witnessed. By virtue of the public character of this display, others can judge the competence of the assessor to properly evaluate the events they encounter (such a process is clearly central to the interactive organization of culture), and assessors can be held responsible for the positions they state. Third, insofar as assessments make visible an agent evaluating an event in his or her phenomenal world, they display that agent's **experience** of the event, including his or her affective involvement in the referent being assessed. **Affect displays** are not only pervasive in the organization of assessments, but also quite central to their organization. Moreover, public structures such as this which display the experience of one participant provide resources for the interactive organization of **co-experience**, a process that can be accomplished and negotiated in fine detail within assessments.

(iv) Assessment actions are produced by single individuals. However (as will be investigated in some detail in this chapter), assessments can be organized as an interactive activity that not only includes multiple participants, but also encompasses types of action that are not themselves assessments. This can be called an **assessment activity**. Within this activity

individuals not only produce **assessment actions** of their own but also
monitor the assessment-relevant actions of others (M. H. Goodwin
1980b), and indeed dynamically modify their own behavior in terms of
both what they see others are doing, and the recognizable structure of the
emerging assessment activity itself (a topic to be explored in detail later in
this chapter).

(v) Finally the word **assessable** will be used to refer to the entity being
     evaluated by an assessment.

In subsequent analysis the context in which the word "assessment" is
being used will usually indicate which of the several senses of the term
noted above is relevant at that point. Therefore these distinctions will not
be marked in the text unless necessary.

3   Assessments that precede assessables

What consequences does the fact that a speaker doesn't just describe
something, but also does an assessment of it, have for how that talk is to be
heard and dealt with by recipients? To start to investigate this issue we will
look at example (1) in some detail. For completeness a full transcript of
this sequence is given below. However, to make the presentation of the
analysis as clear as possible, simplified extracts from this transcript will
then be used to illustrate specific phenomena.

(1) Paul:	Tell y- Tell Debbie about the dog on the
	((smile intonation begins)) golf course t'day.
Eileen:	°eh hnh┌hnh ha has!┌ha!
Paul:	└hih hih └Heh Heh! *hh hh
Eileen:	*h Paul en I got ta the first **green**,
	(0.6)
Eileen:	*hh An this beautiful, *((swallow))*
Paul:	I┌rish Setter. *((reverently))*
Eileen:	└ Irish Setter
Debbie:	Ah:::,
Eileen:	Came tear┌in up on ta the first=
Paul	└°Oh it was beautiful
Eileen:	=**gree**(h)n an tried ta steal Pau(h)l's
	go(h)lf ball. *hh
Paul:	Eh **hnh** hnh.
Eileen:	*hheh! *hh

3.1   Using an assessment to secure recipient co-participation

Returning to the question of how a speaker's assessment might be
consequential for her recipients' action, it can be noted that in (1) just after
the noun phrase containing the assessment, one of Eileen's recipients,
Debbie, responds to what has just been said with an elaborated "Ah:::."

```
(1) Eileen:      *hh An this beautiful, (0.2) Irish Setter.
 →  Debbie:      Ah:::,
    Eileen:      Came tearin up on ta the first gree(h)n an tried ta steal
                 Pau(h)l's go(h)lf ball. *hh
```

By placing an assessment in her talk, the speaker secures an immediate subsequent assessment from a recipient. Moreover, through the way in which she pronounces her "Ah:::'" Debbie co-participates in the **evaluative loading** of Eileen's talk, and indeed matches the affect display contained in Eileen's assessment with a reciprocal affect display. The talk marked with the assessment is thus not treated simply as a description, but rather as something that can be responded to, and participated in, in a special way.

Further insight into what this might mean from an organizational point of view can be gained by examining the sequential structure of this talk in more detail. It can be noted that the recipient's action does not occur at the end of the speaker's current turn-constructional unit, the characteristic place for recipient response, but rather at a point where her current sentence has recognizably not reached completion. Structurally, the assessments of both the speaker and the recipient are placed in the **midst** of a turn-constructional unit.[6]

3.2 Differential treatment of talk as it emerges and when it reaches completion

The issue arises as to what relevance such sequential placement has for the organization of action within the turn. For example, does access to multiple places to operate on the same strip of talk provide participants with resources for the organization of their action that they would not otherwise have, and if so how do they make use of these resources? One way to investigate this issue is to look at how this talk is treated when it does eventually come to completion. Looking again at the data, it can be seen that at its completion Eileen's talk is not dealt with as an assessable but rather as something to be responded to with laughter. Moreover, such treatment of this talk was in fact projected for it before it began (arrows mark laughter in the preface, climax, and response sequences):

```
(1) Paul:        Tell y– Tell Debbie about the dog on the
                 ((smile intonation begins)) golf course t'day.
 →  Eileen:      °eh hnh ┌hnh ha has! ┌ha!
 →  Paul:               └hih hih    └Heh Heh! *hh hh
    Eileen:      *h Paul en I got ta the first green,
                         (0.6)
    Eileen:      *hh An this beautiful, (0.2) Irish Setter
    Debbie:      Ah:::,
    Eileen:      Came tearin up on ta the first gree(h)n
 →               an tried ta steal Pau(h)l's go(h)lf ball. *hh
```

→ Paul: Eh hnh hnh.
→ Eileen: *hheh! *hh

Components of this sentence are thus dealt with in one way as it emerges through time, while the sentence as a whole is treated in a different fashion when it reaches completion. Schegloff (1980) has argued that one systematic issue posed for recipients of extended sequences of talk is whether to operate on a current piece of talk in its own right or treat it as a preliminary to something else. Here we find the participants able to deal with a single piece of talk in both ways. By marking the description of the dog as an assessable, the speaker was able to extract the description from its embedded position within the story as a whole for independent treatment on its own terms. However, in that that description occurred at a point where the speaker's sentence was recognizably incomplete, the not-yet-actualized tying of this talk to relevant further talk is also an operative feature of its structure, with the effect that the larger sentence remains something to be returned to after the assessment activity has been brought to completion. Within this single utterance the participants are thus able to perform a range of different interactive activities, and deal with the talk that it contains in distinctive, separable ways.

3.3   Pre-positioned assessment adjectives as guides for hearers

Let us now examine in more detail the interactive organization of the noun phrase itself, and the way in which its components might be attended to as it emerges through time. It can be observed that within the noun phrase the speaker's assessment term occcurs in a particular position relative to the object being assessed, i.e. it occurs before that object. Thus **by the time the object itself emerges the recipients have been alerted to hear it in a particular way**. The issue arises as to whether recipients do in fact track the emerging structure of a noun phrase on this level of detail. Is it the case that at the completion of the word "beautiful" a recipient will deal with the next words to be spoken in a different way than she would have before hearing this term? Features of these data not yet examined provide some evidence that indeed recipients do deal with the interactive import of emerging talk on this level of detail. Just after saying "beautiful", the speaker hesitates. Paul, the party who experienced with the teller the events being described, appears to interpret this hesitation as the beginning of a word search; just after it he provides the projected next item in the speaker's talk, the words "Irish setter," beginning an instant before the speaker herself says this. However, Paul does not simply speak these words; rather through his actions while speaking he makes visible an **alignment toward them** that is congruent with the assessment just made by the speaker. His talk is produced in a lowered "reverent" tone and while speaking Paul performs a prototypical nonvocal assessment marker, a lateral headshake.[7] Indeed this action is escalated during Debbie's receipt of the assessment when he closes his eyes and performs an even larger headshake over her "Ah:::,":

(1) Eileen: An this beautiful, (0.2)⌐Irish Setter.

     Paul: └Irish Setter ┐ ((*reverently*))

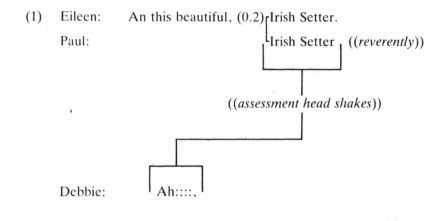

((*assessment head shakes*))

     Debbie: ⌐Ah::::,┐

Thus in the very next moment after Eileen says "beautiful," Paul treats as an assessable what is about to be described in the still incomplete noun phrase. Moreover this marks a definite change in his alignment to that phenomenon. When, in asking Eileen to tell the story, he first made reference to "the dog," he did not orient himself to it as an assessable.

What happens here is also relevant to the analysis of affect as an interactive phenomenon. It was noted earlier that Debbie reciprocated the affect display made available by Eileen's assessment. We now find that Paul does this as well. Eileen's assessment thus leads to a sequence of action in which three separate parties co-participate in the experience offered by the assessment through an exchange of affect displays. These data also demonstrate how evaluative loading is not restricted to specific segments within the stream of speech, but instead can accrue to a sequence of rather heterogeneous phenomena (for example the noun "Irish Setter" and the nonlexical "Ah:::") and can even bridge actions performed by separate speakers (i.e. Paul's headshake encompasses not only the joint production of "Irish Setter" but also Debbie's subsequent "Ah:::").[8] In brief, while on the one hand assessments constitute a mode of interaction that can occur within utterances, indeed within subcomponents of utterances, on the other hand they also provide an example of an activity structure that can seamlessly span multiple utterances, and even utterances by different speakers.

Sequence (3) provides further information about how the activity of assessing what is being said might provide organization for the interaction of participants within relevant descriptive units, such as the utterance manifestations of noun phrases. Here, even though the original description of the ice cream is responded to as an assessable (lines 1 and 2), when the speaker, after describing the machine used to make it, returns to the ice cream itself in line 8, the recipient does not display any heightened alignment to it. The speaker then interrupts the noun phrase in progress before it has reached a recognizable completion and redoes it, only this time placing the word "homemade" before the type of ice cream. Just after this word, over the second production of "peach," the recipient begins to treat the talk in progress as an assessable:

```
(3) 1 Debbie:      Oh we had homemade ice cream today.
    2 Eileen:      Ah::
    3 Debbie:            ⌈They had big– (0.4) We– I don'
    4              know what they're like.=I never saw 'em
    5              before. But'you'put'ice'and'salt'
    6              around'them?=And'there's a'little'can'
    7              in'the'middle'and'you'just'pert– We had
    8              pea:ch? Homemade peach, en ⌈strawberry.
    9 Eileen:                     ↑              ⌊Ahoh:,
```

((Eileen begins
assessment headshake))

The second version of "peach" (line 8) is treated by the recipient in a way that the first wasn't, and this change in alignment appears to be in response to the details of the way in which the speaker organizes her emerging description. First, by interrupting that talk before it has reached a point of recognizable completion, the speaker shows the recipient that for some reason it is no longer appropriate for that talk to continue moving towards completion. What the speaker does next, recycle "pea:ch?:" as "Homemade Peach," in part by virtue of its status as a repair of the talk just marked as flawed, provides some information about what she found to be problematic with the earlier talk. Insofar as the second version differs from the first primarily through the addition of the word "homemade," that term is marked as in some sense essential for proper understanding of the description in progress. However, her recipient has already been told in line 1 that the ice cream was homemade. Thus the speaker is not telling her recipient something new but instead informing her that something that she already knows has not yet been taken proper account of. By taking up the same alignment to this new version of the description that she gave to the first production in "homemade," the speaker attends to the repair as having precisely this import.

In brief it would appear that the problem being remedied with the repair lies not so much in the talk itself as in the way in which the recipient is visibly dealing with it. Moreover, the speaker is able not only to see this problem but to initiate action leading to a remedy of it while the description itself is still in progress. Such events enable us to see in greater detail some of the ways in which concurrent operations on talk are sustained and shown to be relevant through active processes of interaction between speaker and recipient as the talk is being spoken.

4   Post-positioned assessments

In the data so far examined the assessment term and the phenomenon being assessed have been packaged together within a single unit, for example a single noun phrase. It is, however, possible to perform these activities separately. For example, in (4), "asparagus pie" is introduced in a first sentence and then it is assessed in a second:[9]

> (4) Dianne: **Jeff** made en asparagus pie
>   it wz s::**so: goo:**d.

Here the assessment occurs after the assessable has been made available[10] and is the only activity done in the speaker's second sentence. The ability to perform assessments in this fashion is useful to participants in a number of different ways. For example, with such a structure participants are able to assess phenomena that would not fit neatly within a single unit. In (5), the speaker has provided an extended description of a movie she has seen:

> (5) Hyla: A:n then they go t'this country club fer a party
>   en the gu:y, *hh u::m. (0.2)
>   en they kick him out becuz they find out eez **Jewi:**sh,
> →   *hh an it's j's r:rilly s:::sa::d,

How are actions such as these perceived by their recipients? What consequences does the way in which a speaker's action is built have for a recipient's participation it it?

4.1   Post-positioned assessments as techniques for displaying closure

A first observation that can be made about such post-positioned assessments is that by moving to the assessment the speaker shows that though her talk is continuing, a marked structural change has occurred in it. Looking again at (5), it can be observed that when the speaker begins the assessment she is no longer describing events (here incidents in the movie), but instead commenting on the description already given:

```
(5) Hyla:      Jewi:sh, *hh an it;s=
  →            =j's r:ril ly s:::s a : : d,
    Nancy:                 Guy that sounds so goo::d?
    Hyla:      =En ao I mean it jist (.) a f:fantastic
               moo-oh en then the one thet's bigotted,
               *hhh she's married tih this guy who's,
```

Such a shift from **description to assessment of described events** in fact constitutes one of the characteristic ways that speakers begin to exit from a story. Here Hyla does not end her story but instead begins to tell Nancy more about what happened in the movie. However, the way in which she resumes the telling in fact supports the possibility that participants do attend to assessments as marking a move toward closure. After Nancy produces her own assessment, Hyla does not, as she had after earlier continuers and brief assessments, produce a next event in the story. Instead she follows the recipient's assessment with another one of her own. Hyla then interrupts this assessment before it reaches completion and marks her return to the description of the movie with a misplacement marker, "*oh.*"[11] Thus the resumption of the telling is shown to be a misplaced activity, rather than one that would follow unproblematically from the assessment activity then being engaged in.

5   Performing an assessment as a structured interactive activity

Looking now at the structure of the sentences used to construct post-positioned assessments in (4) and (5), it can be noted that despite differences in the words used a similar format is found in both assessments:

(4)   It wz s::**so**: **goo**:d.
(5)   an it's r:rilly s:::sa::d,
       [it] + [copula] + [adverbial intensifier] + [assessment term]

A first observation that can be made about this format is that it seems to reflect a division of activity within the utterance, with the first part of the sentence being occupied with referencing the assessable, and the second, specifically the material after the verb, with the activity of assessment itself. Moreover, the way in which each utterance is spoken is consistent with such a possibility. In both cases the speech quality of the assessment term itself is heightened through noticeable lengthening of sounds within it. Such enhancement of the talk is absent from the first part of the utterance but begins to emerge at the beginning of the adverbial intensifier, which in both cases receives additional stress in addition to the lengthening of sounds within it. In brief, both the semantic organization of these sentences and the way in which they are spoken seem to reveal a movement toward heightened participation in the activity of assessing by the speaker as the sentence unfolds.

Looking at these data from a slightly different perspective, it can also be noted that the speaker's heightened participation in this activity of assessment begins before the assessment term itself, with the intensifier.[12] Earlier it was seen that as soon as the assessment adjective occurs its recipients could begin to treat the talk to follow as an assessment. This raises the possibility that by attending to the pre-positioned intensifier, recipients of sentences of the type now being examined might be able to align themselves to the emerging talk as an assessment before the assessment term itself is actually produced. Indeed, when the responses made by the recipients of these utterances are examined, it is found that in both cases the recipient starts to produce an assessment of her own just as the intensifier comes to completion:

(4) Dianne: **Jeff** made en asparagus pie
            it wz s : :so⌐: **goo**:d.
→   Clacia: ⌊I love it.

(5) Hyla: an it's j's r:ril⌐ly s : : :s a : : d,
→   Nancy: ⌊Guy that sounds so goo ::**d**?

Thus at the point where the speaker actually produces her assessment term, her recipient is simultaneously providing her own assessment of the same material. Such activity has a number of consequences for the present analysis. First, it provides a clear demonstration of how the production of an assessment can constitute a social activity involving the collaborative action of multiple participants. Second, the placement of the recipient's action supports the possibility that she is tracking in rather fine detail both the emerging structure of the speaker's sentence and the activity that the speaker is progressively entering. It would thus appear that subcomponents of a speaker's utterance, such as the intensifier, as well as the details of its sound production, contribute to the interactive organization of the actions of speaker and hearer in the activity they are jointly engaged in. In this sense the emerging structure of the speaker's utterance, and the details of the way in which it is spoken, constitute one aspect of the context that recipients are actively attending to within the turn as consequential for the organization of their own actions. Moreover, that context, and the utterance itself, are intrinsically dynamic, and are attended to as such by participants. By making projections about the future course of an utterance, these recipients demonstrate that they are not dealing with it as a monolithic whole. Instead they treat the utterance as a process that emerges through time, and that carries with it an expanding horizon of projective possibilities that are relevant to how the recipient can respond to the utterance while it is still being spoken.[13]

Listening to talk thus involves constructing a continuously changing horizon of projected possibilities for what the unfolding talk might become. Moreover, making such projections is not simply an individual cognitive process, but a relevant component of the visible actions that a recipient is engaged in. In these data recipients project what is about to happen in order to be able to perform an appropriate reciprocal action at a particular moment in time. If recipients were not engaged in such projection, coordinated action of the type found in these data might not be possible. In brief, within interactive activities, cognitive operations can be analyzed as processes embedded within particular modes of social practice.

5.1   Extended overlap

The assessments produced by recipients in these data take the form of complete substantial sentences in their own right. In that they are placed not after a speaker's action has come to completion but **while** a speaker's assessment is also in progress, a state of extended simultaneous talk by different participants results (i.e. in length and structure something more than overlap of ongoing talk by continuers or brief assessment tokens such as "oh wow"). This is not, however, treated as a situation requiring a remedy;[14] for example, neither party's talk contains restarts, hitches, or other perturbations, or indeed any displays that problems exist with the current state of talk. Moreover, if the analysis developed above is correct, this simultaneous talk is not the result of an accidental failure to achieve proper coordination but rather something that the participants have systematically achieved through close attention to the emerging structure of the talk and activity in progess. What happens here thus provides further support for the possibility that assessments do indeed constitute ways of analyzing and operating on talk that can be performed while that talk is still in progress. Indeed it appears that constraints which elsewhere exert quite powerful influence on the sequential organization of talk, for example an orientation to one, but only one, party speaking at a time, can be relaxed for assessments. It would thus appear that in a number of different ways the activity of assessing something provides participants with resources for performing concurrent operations on talk that has not yet come to completion.

5.2   Differential access as an organizing feature of concurrent assessments

Though the talk of both the speaker and the recipient in (4) and (5) is assessing the same material, each party in fact says rather different things. Is such variation simply haphazard or does it reveal further aspects of the phenomena the participants are orienting themselves to as relevant for the organization of their activity? Looking more carefully at precisely what is said, it can be noted that in its details the talk of each party attends to the access each has to the phenomena being assessed. For example, Hyla with her initial "it's" makes reference to an actual movie she has seen, and she assesses it in unequivocal terms. Nancy, however, by saying "that sounds so: goo::d?" attends to what she is assessing as being available only through Hyla's current description of it. Similarly in (4), Dianne, who depicts herself as having directly experienced in the past the pie she is now describing, makes reference to that specific pie. However, Clacia, by putting her assessment in the present tense, deals not with the specifics of that particular pie, but rather with it as a class of phenomena that the pie currently being described instances. A moment later, after Dianne has described the pie in more detail, Clacia says "Oh: *Go:d* that'd be fantastic." Here, by constructing her assessment in conditional tense, she again makes visible in her talk the limited access[15] she has to the phenomena she is assessing. Thus one of the reasons that the assessments of the separate participants differ from each other is that each has different access to and experience of the event being assessed. This feature provides organization for a range of phenomena implicated in the construction of each utterance, such as the choice of particular words and verb tenses. By constructing their assessments in this fashion participants also attend in detail to how they have been organized relative to each other by the telling in progress. For example, the different positions of describer and describee are shown to remain relevant even when both are assessing in a similar fashion the events which have been described. In brief, despite their apparent simplicity, assessments show a view of the assessable as something perceived by an actor who both takes up a particular alignment to it and sees the assessable from a particular perspective, one that may be quite different from that of a co-participant who is simultaneously assessing the same event.

5.3   Making congruent understanding visible

Though the talk of the separate parties shows that each is viewing the assessable from a different perspective, in other ways the assessments produced by each seem to have an underlying similarity. For example, in (4) both the speaker and the recipient assess asparagus pie positively. Thus with their assessments the participants are able to display to each other that they evaluate the phenomena being assessed in a similar way. Moreover, by virtue of the way in which each assessment takes into account the distinctive position of the party making it, these similar evaluations are shown to result from independent appraisals of the phenomena being assessed. In essence, with their assessments the participants show each other that, on this issue at least, their minds are together; they evaluate the phenomena being discussed in a similar way.

Assessments reveal not just neutral objects in the world, but an alignment taken up toward phenomena by a particular actor. Furthermore, this alignment can be of some moment in revealing such significant attributes of the actor as his or her taste and the way in which he or she evaluates the phenomena he or she perceives. It is therefore not surprising that displaying congruent understanding can be an issue of some importance to the participants.[16] Further support for active attention to such an issue is found when a visual record of the actions of the participants in (4) is examined. As Clacia produces her assessment she nods toward Dianne, as shown in the diagram in (4).

(4) Dianne: **Jeff** made en asparagus pie
                 it was s : : so ⌈: **goo:d.**
       Clacia: I love   it.
                            ⌊_____⌋   ⌊__⌋
                               ┬   ┬
                            ((nod   nod))

With her nods, Clacia proposes that the talk she is producing, and the position taken up through that talk, is in agreement with Dianne's. Indeed, taken as a whole the actions she performs here provide a strong display of agreement. First, with the content of her utterance she states a view of the assessable that is compatible with Dianne's. Second, with her nods she marks that talk nonvocally as an **agreement**. Third, she performs this action not after hearing Dianne's assessment but at the very moment it is being spoken. It is of course true that the talk so far produced provides materials (for example the intensifier) that strongly suggest, and perhaps actually project, a favorable assessment. Nevertheless at the point where Clacia acts, Dianne has not officially stated a position. By placing her talk where she does, Clacia argues that her way of viewing the assessable is so attuned to Dianne's that she is prepared to both commit herself to a position and categorize that position as an agreement without actually hearing Dianne's.[17] Goffman (1959: 87–8) has observed that

There seems to be a general feeling that most real and solid things in life are ones whose description individuals independently agree upon. We tend to feel that if two participants in an event decide to be as honest as they can in recounting it, then the stands they take will be acceptably similar even though they do not consult one another prior to their presentation.

In sum, with the content of her talk, nonvocal displays about it, and its sequential placement, Clacia argues strongly that her view of the assessable is congruent with Dianne's.

We are suggesting that recipients produce concurrent assessments by making projections about events which have not yet occurred. If this is indeed the case, then it would be expected that on some occasions the projections made by recipients would turn out to be inaccurate. Rather than providing evidence against the position being argued in this chapter, such an event would constitute strong evidence that recipients are in fact engaged in the activity of anticipating future events on the basis of the limited information currently available to them. Example (6) provides an illustration of how a recipient's projection of an emerging assessment can be erroneous, with the effect that the concurrent appreciation being displayed by the recipient is quite inappropriate to what the speaker turns out to in fact be saying:

```
(6)  1    Emma:    *hh I: MA:DE ME A DAHLING
     2             DRESS tih WEAR dih the
     3             DESERT. God I go to the
     4             p-purti es:        [
     5    Nancy:                  ]       Didju ::h?
     6             (0.2)
     7             p-print it's almos'like s:ilk
     8             but it' s euh*hh h<
     9    Nancy:         [°Mm:,  [°Mm]hm
    10             (.)
    11    Emma:    u evry color' n it's rea:l tiny.=
    12    Emma:    =i t's uh kinda psy che delic but it's
    13    Nancy:     [°Oooo:::::::::    ]    [         ]
    14    Emma:    -tiny it I mean ih-u- ih-it
    15    Nancy:          [°Mm: hm?    ]
    16    Emma::   u-Psychedelic isn the word
    17             but ih has all the colors 'n
    18             God I went'n got blue: sho:es
    19             tih go w  it °hhhh  En yihknow-
    20    Nancy:         [  °Ahhh::!:
    21    Emma:    =wz so  ho:t there we: w'r =
    22 → Nancy:          [°A h : : : : : :      ]
    23    Emma:    jist in shorts=I didn' ev'n stay
    24             fuh the dinner et theay uh we
    25             w'r et the Indian Wo:rld.
    26             (.)
    27    Nancy:   *t oh :.
    28    Emma:          [*hh]h En I wouldn' ev'n
    29             stay fer the dinner it wz so
    30             da:mn hot I seh gotta get
    31             the heck outta here it wz
    32             ji s so uncomfterb le,
    33    Nancy:     [°O h : : : : :.    ]
```

In the beginning of this sequence Emma describes a "DAHLING DRESS" that she has made and Nancy replies to her description with concurrent assessments in lines 5, 13 and 20. In lines 19 and 21 Emma starts to move toward a recognizable assessment, following "was" with the intensifier "so." Right after this happens, Nancy in line 22 starts to co-participate in the assessment by producing an elaborated, appreciative "A h : : : : : :." The positive affect displayed by Nancy is quite congruent with the favorable way that the dress has been described in the sequence until this point. However, it turns out that Emma is now moving her talk to a **negative** description of the weather on her trip, i.e. it "wz so **ho:t there**" that she couldn't wear the dress and didn't even stay for dinner.

By relying on cues of the type being analyzed in the present chapter, Nancy has attempted to align herself to an assessment before it is actually produced, but the talk has progressed in ways quite incompatible with her projection of it, with the effect that she is responding inappropriately to what Emma is saying. Such data provide a strong demonstration of how projecting what another is about to say – so as to concurrently co-participate in it – constitutes a contingent accomplishment. Fortunately the emerging structure of interaction provides resources for moving past and attempting to recover from such a *faux pas*, and in line 33 we find Nancy once again producing a concurrent assessment to Emma's description of the weather, only this time her response is quite appropriate.

Returning now to example (4), we find that Dianne also performs a number of relevant nonvocal actions. As she produces the assessment term she lowers her head into a nod while simultaneously lifting her brows into a marked eyebrow flash. These actions are preceded by movement of her head and upper body in a way that demonstrates heightened orientation toward the recipient over the intensifier, as shown in (4).

(4) Dianne: **Jeff** made en asparagus pie

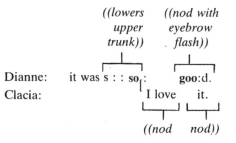

Dianne's nonvocal behavior like her talk seems to display a progression toward heightened involvement in the assessment as her utterance unfolds.[18] These actions become most intense over the assessment term itself and indeed at this point in the talk quite a range of both vocal and nonvocal action is occurring. The ensemble of things done over the assessment does not, however, seem a collection of separate actions, but rather integrated elements of a single interactive activity of assessment.

Moreover, the visible behavior of the speaker, as well as the unfolding structure of her talk and the recipient's participation in that talk, seem to demonstrate systematic movement toward this point through time. In essence one seems to find here an **organized activity** that participants recognize and systematically bring to a visible apex or climax.

5.4   Bringing assessment activity to a close

We will now look at some of the ways in which movement away from the apex of activity might be accomplished. One way to approach this issue is to ask "What can participants do next?" Some actions within conversation have the property of being nonrepeatable (see for example the analysis of summons–answer sequences in Schegloff 1968), i.e. once they have been validly performed they cannot be immediately redone. Assessments, however, are repeatable. Moreover, while some repeatable actions are used to operate progressively on new material, for example a series of questions in a medical interview, so that each instance of a similar action actually deals with separate phenomena, a participant can make continuing assessments of the same assessable. In (4), just after the assessment produced concurrently with Dianne's, Clacia repeats that assessment:

> (4) Dianne: **Jeff** made en asparagus pie
>   it wz s::**so**⌈: **goo**:d.
> → Clacia: ⌊I love it. °Yeah I love tha:t.

However during this second assessment she acts quite differently than she had during the first. Thus the subsequent assessment is spoken with markedly lowered volume (this is indicated in the transcript by the degree sign before it). Moreover, while speaking Clacia actually withdraws from her co-participant, as shown in (4).

> (4) Dianne: **Jeff** made en asparagus pie
>   it was s : : **so**⌈: **goo**:d.
>   Clacia: ⌊I love it.   °Yeah I love that.
>   ↑
>   ((*Clacia starts to
>   withdraw gaze*))

Thus, while the initial concurrent assessment was produced within a state of heightened orientation toward her co-participant and the talk in progress, this second assessment is done while Clacia is displaying diminished participation in the activity, and indeed seems to be withdrawing from it.

It is thus found that **a single assessment activity can encompass a range of different types of participation**. The sequencing of participation in these data – collaborative orientation toward the emerging of the assessment, elaborated participation in it as it is actually produced, and finally a trailing off of involvement in it – is consistent with the possibility that what is occurring here are successive stages of a single natural activity that emerges, comes to a climax, and is then withdrawn from.

5.5   Assessments as resources for closing topics

Instead of just analyzing these different participation structures solely as successive stages of an unfolding activity, it is also useful to examine in more detail how the possibility of investing assessments with different kinds of participation might provide participants with resources for the organization of their activity. For example, assessments are one of the characteristic activities used to exit from larger sequential units in talk such as stories and topics. Indeed one frequently finds strings of assessments at such places. When one examines precisely how such assessments are spoken, it is found that frequently they are operating not only to exit from what was being talked about in the story, but that in addition the different participation possibilities provided by assessments are systematically being used to bring the heightened mutual orientation that such a focused activity has engendered to a close. A simple example is found shortly after the sequence analyzed in (4). In the intervening talk Dianne has described in greater detail the asparagus pie that Jeff made, as shown in (7).

(7) Dianne: En then jus' (cut-up) the broc- 'r
the **aspa**ragus coming

((*assessment
headshakes*))

((*withdraws gaze
from Clacia*))
↓
out in spokes.= °It wz **so g**ood.

As Dianne moves from a description of the pie to an assessment of it, she noticeably reduces the volume of her talk while simultaneously withdrawing her gaze from Clacia. Thus she has not only moved into a different kind of talk (e.g. from description to assessment) but also changed the nature of her involvement in that talk and the structure of her orientation to her co-participant. Despite the apparent simplicity of what Dianne has done, the changes produced are in fact rather intricate. Thus some of what happens – the move from description to assessment, the reduction in volume and the withdrawal of gaze from recipient – seems to clearly indicate that she is proposing topic closure. However, even as she does this she is displaying heightened involvement in the substance of her talk. The assessment itself, with its "savoring" voice quality (achieved in part through the same lowering of volume that might otherwise indicate move toward closure of the sequence), and the actions of her body during it, such as the assessment headshakes, all display elaborated appreciation of what she has been talking about. In essence the actions Dianne performs seem **both to foreshadow topic closure and to show heightened involvement in the topic**.

At first glance such a combination might appear inconsistent or even contradictory. However, to see this mixture of phenomena in such a way is to implicitly assume that topics run out only because participants lose interest in them. If a topic has in fact engrossed the attention of those talking, this would be a very poor way to end it. On the other hand, one would not want to talk about that topic forever. Thus one might want to look for ways of dealing with talk in progress that show heightened appreciation of it without however proposing that others need continue talking about it forever. Dianne's assessment has precisely these properties. She is able to show her co-participant (for example with her gaze withdrawal) that she is not awaiting further talk from her, while simultaneously appreciating what has just been said. Indeed one of the reasons why assessments might be used so extensively to close stories and topics is that they provide this **mixture of participation possibilities** for organizing the interaction then in progress. Such **activity-occupied withdrawal** is in fact one of the characteristic ways in which participants close down a range of activities within conversation (see C. Goodwin 1981: 106–8).

Some demonstration that the participants themselves might analyze an assessment such as Dianne's as including an ensemble of activity of the type just described is provided by the talk Clacia produces next. In its productional features this talk responds to the various elements of Dianne's talk, while ratifying the change in participation status she has proposed. First, as Clacia begins to speak she too withdraws her gaze from her co-participant. Second, her talk is produced with not simply lowered volume but drastically reduced volume (indicated in the transcript in [7] below by the two degree signs before it.) The talk itself is, however, a marked upgrade of the assessment Dianne just made, as shown in (7).

The exchange of affect provided by the exchange of assessments gives the withdrawal the intimacy of a parting touch in which the character of the apparent **referent** of the assessment becomes far less important than the shared affect and co-experience the participants display to each other. In these data the speaker and her recipient, through the details of the ways in which they performed their assessments, have moved away from the substance of the topic in progress while simultaneously showing their ongoing appreciation of it. At the same time they have dismantled the facing formation that had been sustained through that talk. Insofar as no new topic is yet on the floor the state of disengagement which has thus

(7) Dianne: En then jus' (cut-up) the broc– 'r
the **aspa**ragus coming

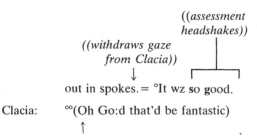

been collaboratively entered through this process of phased withdrawal[19] is quite appropriate to their current actions.

Rather than looking at the talk, intonation, and body movement that occur in these data as different channels of behavior to be analyzed separately, it seems more profitable to conceptualize what is happening as a single **interactive activity** of assessment that the participants collaboratively recognize and bring to a visible climax or peak and then withdraw from. Being able to work together to come to such a peak is precisely why it is relevant for a recipient to be able to **project** what is about to happen next.

In brief, instead of taking any single element of this process – language, nonverbal behavior, participants, type of 'speech action' in progress, etc. – as the primary object of interest, it seems more appropriate to focus on an **interactive activity structure** which the participants collaboratively accomplish by deploying as resources talk, intonation, body movement, etc.

Several features of such an activity structure deserve further comment. First, in a manner quite consistent with Garfinkel's analysis of the "documentary method of interpretation" (Garfinkel 1967: 78; see also Heritage 1984a: 84–97), participants use their ability to recognize an underlying pattern – the activity of assessment – as a resource for the further accomplishment of that very same activity. Thus a recipient sees the intensifier as evidence for a larger pattern that is not yet complete (an assessment utterance), and on the basis of such analysis produces behavior (her own concurrent assessment) that further elaborates and accomplishes the guessed-at activity.

Second, the recipient's behavior provides visible evidence for how she has analyzed the talk and other events in progress. Such analysis is not, however, neutral – for example, simple recognition of some "intention" that a speaker has; it is rather an aspect of embedded praxis, a way of helping to accomplish the very same activity that is being analyzed. Moreover, this analysis encompasses not only what a speaker has already done but also what is about to happen. By virtue of the way it is embedded within an ongoing sequence of interaction, the process of analysis that a recipient is engaged in has prospective as well as retrospective components.

Third, time is an integral feature of the organization of an activity; the activity emerges and is shaped through a dynamic process of interaction. Indeed, one of the strong contributions that study of human interaction can make to general social theory is the way in which it permits, and indeed requires, the analysis of social organization as a dynamic process.

Fourth, an activity knits an array of heterogeneous phenomena – syntactic position, intonation, body movement, displays of agreement, differential access to a world beyond the activity, etc. – into a coherent course of collaborative action. By looking at how strips of talk are embedded within activities, it becomes possible to see how diverse phenomena within the utterance – the placement of intensifiers, changes in intonation and volume, etc. – are attended to by participants in a way that is relevant to the tasks at hand. The activity itself, and the articulation of the interaction through which it is accomplished, constitute a self-explicating system of meaning and relevance. This is not surprising. In order to achieve coordinated action participants must display to each other the intelligibility of the events they are engaged in, including what activities are in progress and what they expect to happen next (Garfinkel 1967; Heritage 1984a; Kendon 1990, this volume).

The data examined here have enabled us to investigate a range of issues relevant to how assessments are organized as an activity within the turn at talk. One of the very interesting things about assessments is the way in which they integrate a range of phenomena occurring within the turn that are frequently studied quite separately. Insofar as assessments are achieved through the collaborative action of multiple participants, they provide an elementary example of social organization within the boundaries of the turn. At the same time they constitute a key locus for the display and achievement of congruent understanding, and thus are quite relevant to the study of cognition as a practical, everyday activity. In addition they provide an example of how affect and the display of emotion are organized as interactive phenomena. In accomplishing this activity participants may pay close attention to what other participants are doing, the details of what is happening in the stream of speech, and the recognizable structure of the activity itself. The study of assessments thus permits analysis in an integrated fashion of a range of phenomena relevant to the organization of language, culture, cognition, and emotion in the midst of actual interaction.

6   Invoking larger activities within the turn

Analysis has so far focused on the organization of activities that emerge, run their course, and terminate within the boundaries of the turn itself. However, events within the turn are both informed by, and consequential for, larger activities that extend far beyond its scope. We will now briefly investigate some aspects of this process by focusing on events that occur within a gossip-dispute activity called "he-said-she-said." The exchanges that will be examined are from the talk of a group of urban black pre-adolescent girls who were recorded as they played with each other on the street in front of their houses.

One of the speech activities that the girls engage in is a gossip-dispute that they call **he-said-she-said**. In the confrontation stage of this activity (analyzed in more detail in M. H. Goodwin 1980a, 1990), one girl uses a highly structured accusation statement to charge another with having talked about her behind her back. Insofar as these disputes center on the offense of talking about someone in their absence, the offended party is not present when the offense is committed. They must therefore learn about it from some third party.

The third party, though not a direct participant in the confrontation, in fact occupies a crucial position in the structure of this activity. By going to someone and telling them that someone else has been talking about them, such a third party can promote a confrontation. Indeed the girls themselves sometimes call this activity **instigating**. The activity of reporting to a recipient what was said about her in her absence thus constitutes an important preliminary stage to confrontation. It is the point where the absent party's talk becomes socially recognizable as an actionable offense.

Informing the offended party of what was done to her is typically accomplished through use of structured descriptions of past events or "stories" (Sacks 1974). We will now investigate one instigating session, focusing on the way in which assessments and evaluations are used both to formulate the character of relevant participants and to elicit a public commitment to initiate a confrontation in the future. These data will give us an opportunity both to look at how a framework of events extending well beyond a particular turn can be constituted within it and to investigate phenomena such as the negotiation of congruent understanding and shared assessments within more complex, multi-party participation frameworks.[20]

6.1   Instigating

The talk to be examined occurred when three girls, Pam, Florence, and Maria, were sitting on Maria's steps. After Pam alludes to something involving Maria and Terry (who is absent), Maria asks "**Isn't Terry mad** at

me or **s:omp'm.**" Since the data to be examined are quite complex, we will briefly outline what happens in the sequence before presenting the data.

After Maria raises the question of Terry being mad at her Florence says that Terry is always mad at somebody. Pam and Maria then collaboratively recall a series of related incidents involving Terry's treatment of Maria that occurred at school. Pam tells Maria that Terry has said that she was "acting stupid," and they both recall incidents in which Terry refused to add Maria's name to a bathroom pass. Pam portrays herself as having acted to defend Maria in such encounters, for example snatching the bathroom pass from Terry. Eventually Maria says about Terry, "I'm a tell her about herself **today.**"
Throughout all of this Florence has been talking about Terry's character in more general terms, e.g. "Terry **always** say something. When you **jump** in her **face** she gonna de**ny** it." The first sequence closes with Pam suggesting that Maria "should say it in front of her face."
A second sequence occurs 45 seconds later, after Maria has left. Pam now talks about things that Terry said about Florence (**"Flor**ence, Florence need to **go** somewhere") to which Florence replies "Well you **tell** her to **come** say it in front of my face. And I'll put **her** somewhere."
This is followed by considerable further talk between Pam and Florence about Terry which is not reproduced here.

This brief overview in no way captures the subtlety and intricacy of this talk. However, we hope that it will make the sequence itself more accessible to the reader.

```
(8)  ((Pam (12), Florence (13), and Maria (12) are sitting on Maria's Steps.))
      1 Pam:     How- how- h- um, uh h- h- how about me
      2           and Maria, *h and all them um, and
      3           Terry, *h ⌈and all them-
      4 Maria:            ⌊Isn't Terry mad at me
      5           or s:omp' m,
      6                (0.4)
      7 Pam:     I'on' kn/ /ow.
      8 Flo:     Terry~always~mad~at somebody.
      9           °I⌈'on' care.
     10 Maria:    ⌊Cuz- cuz cuz I wouldn't, cu:z she
     11           ain't put my name on that paper.
     12 Pam:     I know cuz⌈OH yeah. Oh yeah.
     13 Flo:               ⌊An next she,
     14                (0.2)
     15 Flo:     ⌈talk~bout~people.
     16 Pam:     ⌊that- (0.8) if that girl wasn't
     17           there-You know that girl that always
     18           makes those funny jokes, 'h Sh'aid if
     19           that girl wasn't there you wouldn't be
     20           actin, (0.4) a:ll stupid like that.
     21           °Sh-
     22 Maria:   ⌊But was I actin stupid w⌈ith them?
     23 Pam:                               ⌊ Nope, no,=And
```

```
24              she- and she said that you sai:d, that,
25              "Ah: go tuh-" (0.5) somp' m like ┌tha:t.
26 Maria:                                       └°No I
27              didn't.
28 Pam:         She's- an uh- somp'm like that. She's-
29 Flo:         Te┌rry always say somp'm.=When you=
30 Pam:           └She-
31 Flo:         =jump in her face she gonna deny it.
32 Pam:         Yah:p Y┌ahp.=An she said, *h An-
33 Maria:              └°Right on.
34 Pam:         and she said, hh that you wouldn't be
35              actin like that aroun- around people.
36 Maria:       So: she wouldn' be actin like that wi'
37              that other girl.=She the one picked me
38              to sit wi'them.=*h She said ┌"Maria you
39 Pam:                                      └Y:ahp.
40 Maria:       sit with her, *h and I'll sit with her,
41              *h an Pam an- an Pam an-
42              an an ┌Sharon sit together."
43 Flo:               └SHE TELLIN Y' ALL WHERE TA SIT
44              AT?
45                  (0.2)
46 Pam:         An so we sat together, An s- and s- and
47              so Maria was ju:st s:ittin right
48              there.-An the girl, an- an- the girl:
49              next to her? *h and the girl kept on
50              getting back up. *h Ask the teacher
51              can she go t'the bathroom. An Maria
52              say she don' wanna go t' the bathroom
53              w'her. An m- And Maria w'just sittin
54              up ther actin- actin:, ac- ac- actin
55              sensible. An she up- and she up there
56              talking bout, and she- I said, I s' d I
57              s'd I s'd "This is how I'm- I'm gonna
58              put Maria na:me down here." Cu- m- m-
59              Cuz she had made a pa:ss you know. *h
60              She had made a pa:ss.
61                  (0.2)
62 Pam:         ┌For all us to go down to the bathroom.
63 Flo:         └Y'all go down t'the bathroom?
64 Pam:         For ALLA- yeah- yeah. Yeah. For u:m, (0.4)
65              for- for alla us- t'go to the
66              bathroom.= I s'd- I s'd "How: co:me you
67              ain't put Maria name down here. *h So
68              she said, she said "That other girl
69              called 'er so, she no:t wi:th u:s, so,"
70              That's what she said too. (0.2) So I
71              said, s- so I snatched the paper
```

72		wi'her. I said wh- when we were playin
73		wi'that paper?
74	Maria:	I'm a I'm a tell her about herself
75		toda_ry. Well,
76	Pam:	⌐Huh? huh remember when we're
77		snatching that ⌐paper.
78	Flo:	⌐An she gonna tell you
79		another story **anyway**. / / (Are you gonna
80		talk to her today?)
81	Pam:	But she ain't even put your **na**me down
82		there. I just put it **down** there. Me
83		and Sharon put it down.= An I said, and
84		she said "Gimme-that-paper.=I don't
85		wanna have her **na**me **d**own here." I s- I
86		s- I s- I said "She woulda allowed **you**
87		name (if you star:ted)."
88		(1.0)
89	Maria:	I said "Terry °how come you ain't put my
90		name."
91	Flo:	Here go P_ram, "uh uh uh well-"
92	Maria:	⌐"You put that other girl (name down)
93		didn't you. I thought **you** was gonna
94		have- owl: a hall pass with that other
95		girl." That's °what Terry said. I said
96		(What's~her~problem.) "OO:r'mind me a-
97		you old b:aldheaded Terry."
98	Pam:	**I** should say it in fronta her **f**ace.
99		(0.8) Bal: head.
100	Flo:	Hey member when what we did th(h)e
101		o(h)ther ti(**h**)me.

((The following occurs 45 seconds later, after Maria has gone inside.))

102	Pam:	She shouldn't be **wr**itin things, about
103		me. (0.5) an so- An so- so she said
104		"**Flor**ence, Florence need ta **go**
105		somewhere."
106		(1.0)
107	Flo:	Well you **t**ell her to **c**ome say it in
108		front of my fa:ce. (0.6) and **I'll put**
109		**her** somewhere. (3.8) An Florence
110		ain't got nuttin t'do with **what**.
111	Pam:	**Write**- um doin um, ⌐that- that thing.
112	Flo:	⌐What do y' **all** got
113		ta do with it.
114	Pam:	Because because um, **I** don't know what
115		we got to do with it. Bu_rt she said-
116	Flo:	⌐W'll **she**

```
117                    don't know what she talkin bout.
118  Pam:             But- but she- but we di:d have somp' m
119                    to do because we was ma:d at her.
120                    Because we didn't like her no more.
121                    (0.6) And that's why, (0.6) Somebody
122                    the one ┌that use-
123  Flo:                     └So, she got anything t'say she
124                    come say it in front of my face. (1.0)
125                    I better not see Terry today. (2.5) I
126                    ain' n gonna say- I'm~a~say "Terry what
127                    you say about m┌e." She gonna say "I ain't
128  Pam:                            └((whiny))(Nyang)
129  Flo:             =say nuttin."
```

In this talk Pam tells both Maria and Florence about offensive actions
that Terry has committed against them, and both Maria ("I'm a I'm a tell
her about herself to**day**," lines 74–5) and Florence ("Well you **t**ell her to
come say it in front of my fa:ce. (0.6) And **I**'ll **put her** somewhere," lines
107–9) state that they will confront Terry. Such a process has a clear
relevance to specific future activities, such as the initiation of a he-said-she-
said confrontation. Indeed, when Maria later fails to confront Terry,
others use her actions in the present exchange to talk about the way in
which she had promised to tell Terry off but then did nothing.

(9) Pam: Yeah and Maria all the time talking
              bout she was gonna tell whatshername off.
              And she ain't do it.

Alignments taken up in the midst of an exchange such as this can thus be
interpreted as public commitments to undertake future action for which
parties may be held responsible by others.

Assessments are central to the organization of this process. In her stories
Pam uses evaluations to portray her own character, as well as that of her
addressed recipient and the absent party who offended that recipient, in
ways that are relevant to the activities currently in progress. Thus in lines
53–5. Maria is depicted as just "sittin up there actin actin:, ac- ac- actin
sensible," while Terry in line 20 is reported to have said that Maria was
"actin, (0.4) a:ll **stu**pid like that." By portraying Maria in a positive fashion
and Terry in a negative one, Pam makes implicit assertions about her own
alignment, and indeed the processes of evaluation found in this sequence
go beyond explicit assessment terms to include reports of **actions** displaying
a party's alignment for or against different protagonists. For example, in
lines 57–67 Pam describes herself as confronting Terry for not having
included Maria's name on the bathroom pass.

Providing evaluation through action descriptions is quite consequential
for the process of eliciting from a recipient a promise to confront the

offender in the future. On the one hand pejorative actions performed by the absent party can be interpreted as explicit offenses against a current recipient. On the other hand a speaker's description of her own actions in response to such offenses, i.e. confronting the offender, can provide a recipient with a guide for how she should act toward that party. Thus Maria's statement that she will confront Terry (lines 74–5) occurs right after Pam has described both how she confronted Terry in the past in defense of Maria, and a response to that action by Terry that included further attacks on Maria. Reports of actions in the past can thus lead to commitments to perform relevant answers to them in the future.

The narratives used to do instigating contain extensive reported speech (Vološinov 1973) as speakers animate (Goffman 1974: 516–44) the characters in their talk. One consequence of this is that a current participant, who was absent when the things said about her were reported to have been said, can now answer those charges. Thus after Pam in lines 23–5 cites Terry as having said that Maria said to Terry "'**Ah:** go tuh-' (0.5) somp'm like tha:t," Maria replies with a denial to this charge "'°No I didn't" (see also lines 36–42, in which Maria counters charges purportedly made by Terry by animating her version of what Terry said in the past). Current participants are thus able to address actions attributed to absent parties at another time, and reconstitute the actions of such figures in the talk of the moment. The present encounter now encompasses a dialogue between participants and events in the present, and those from previous encounters, as a present participant answers charges made by someone who currently exists only as a cited figure in the talk of another speaker.

No simple reporting of past events is at issue here; rather the incidents being recounted from the past are being constituted and shaped within the interaction of the moment in terms of the interests and projects of current participants. Indeed the constitutive elements of this process are vividly illustrated by the way in which participants in an instigating session will not only cite past events but also project the events that will occur in future encounters. Thus in lines 125–9 Florence not only says what she will tell Terry when she confronts her, but also how Terry will answer her.[21] We can thus see how participants within the talk of the moment can invoke and shape events from the past in ways that have import for future encounters. Crucial to this process is the way in which cited figures and actions are evaluated in the present. The actions of cited figures, and the responses of present participants to them, are part of the process through which coalitions and alliances are forged among the girls. The events that are occurring here thus have political consequences for the social organization of the girls' group as well.

It was noted earlier that in building their talk one of the things that participants pay close attention to is the differential access they have to the events being talked about. The present data permits further investigation of this process. Initially Pam has two recipients, Maria and Florence. However, her talk does not involve each of them in the same way. Maria is one of the principal protagonists in Pam's stories but Florence never appears as a character. Moreover, the incidents Pam describes – offenses committed by Terry against Maria – have a relevance to the party being talked about that they do not have for others. Maria and Florence are thus implicated in the field of action created by the talk in very different ways, and indeed each attends to such positioning in the talk that they produce. Thus Maria addresses the particulars of the charges raised in Pam's talk, openly denying some (e.g. "°No I didn't" in lines 26–7), inviting Pam to dispute Terry's negative assessments of her ("But was I actin stupid with them?" in line 22), providing her own version of the events under discussion ("**She** the one picked **me** to **sit** wi'them.=*h She said 'Maria you sit with her, *h and I'll sit with her, and Pam and Sharon sit together'," lines 37–42), etc. Florence, however, never deals with the particulars of what is being talked about, or threatens to comfront Terry, but instead uses present tense to formulate Terry's negative character in general rather than specific terms. For example:

- "Terry~**always**~mad~at somebody." (line 8)
- "Terry **always** say somp'm.=When you-**jump** in her **face** she gonna **deny** it." (lines 29–31)
- "An she gonna tell you another story **anyway**." (lines 78–9)

Though Maria and Florence are both audience to the stories that Pam tells, their talk systematically differs. On the one hand Maria has access to the events being talked about that Florence lacks; she can, for example, answer Terry's charges with her own version of the incidents at issue. On the other hand these events have differential relevance to the current situation of each participant; while Maria's character has been called into question Florence's has not. Maria, unlike Florence, thus has both motivation and standing to answer the charges raised by Terry. From a slightly different perspective, the structures used by Terry provide a creative solution to the problem she faces of talking into the event that is currently on the floor, helping to constitute it in the talk of the moment, despite the fact that this event does not involve her in the way that it does the others present. In brief, the talk of the moment creates a field of relevance that implicates those present in a variety of different ways, and this has consequences for the detailed organization of the action that each party produces.

A short time later Maria leaves and Pam changes the structure of her stories so that Florence (rather than Maria) becomes the character that Terry is saying things about (e.g. "And so she said '**Flor**ence, Florence need ta **go** somewhere.' " lines 103–5). At this point, instead of talking about Terry's character in general terms, Florence responds in the way that

Maria had earlier, for example threatening to confront Terry (e.g. lines 107–9, lines 123–9). Such events shed light on a number of different aspects of the ties between talk and context. First they provide some demonstration of how changes in recipients can lead to related changes in the character structure of the narrative events in progress at the moment. Second, as characters change, the responses of recipients located (or not located) as characters also change. Recipients are not simply listening to the talk but dealing with it in terms of how they are positioned by it. Finally, in these data the incidents being described, the characters involved in those incidents, and the responses that recipients make, all have implications for events beyond the current exchange. The internal organization of the story can elicit particular types of responses from current recipients (e.g. statements that they will confront the party who talked about them). On the one hand such a process of instigating can lead to a confrontation. On the other hand, if someone who has said that she will confront the party who offended her does not do so, she can be held accountable for failing to perform that move. Though this larger activity extends beyond the immediate encounter, it is shaped, constituted, and negotiated within the current talk.

7   Conclusion

Assessments provide an example of a small activity system that can emerge, develop, and die within the boundaries of a single turn, while also having the potential to extend over multiple turns, and to bound units considerably larger than the turn. Assessments also provide participants with resources for displaying evaluations of events and people in ways that are relevant to larger projects that they are engaged in. Of crucial importance to the present chapter is the way in which this activity provides participants with resources for both accomplishing social organization within the turn, and negotiating and displaying congruent understanding of the events they are dealing with.

The activity of performing an assessment is intrinsically social in that it can provide for the collaborative, but differentiated, participation of multiple actors. This has a number of consequences. First it provides further demonstration of how the turn, and events occurring within it, are intrinsically interactive (C. Goodwin 1981). Second, the presence of such coordinated action poses the question of how participants are able to accomplish it. Attempting to answer that question has enabled us to look in some detail at phenomena that participants are not only attending to, but actively using as a constitutive feature of the events they are engaged in within the turn. One aspect of what participants orient themselves to in performing assessments is the unfolding properties of the activity itself. As a coherent activity, assessments have a recognizable structure, including

(1) a peak of involvement that is preceded by (2) visible precursors of that peak that participants can utilize to coordinate their arrival at the peak, and (3) procedures for withdrawing from this state of heightened mutual involvement. The presence of such an activity structure has consequences for the way in which participants deal with the talk that is occurring within the turn. In order to co-participate in an appropriate fashion at an appropriate moment, recipients track in fine detail the unfolding structure of the speaker's utterance, paying close attention to not only the projective possibilities made available by its emerging syntactic structure (e.g. the type of unit that is **about** to occur), but also the precise way in which it is spoken (e.g. lengthening of sounds within words and intonation changes). The detailed organization of the talk occurring within a turn thus constitutes a most important aspect of the context that participants are attending to, both to make sense out of what is happening at the moment, and as a resource for the organization of their subsequent action. The study of activities such as assessments thus provides one way of analyzing talk and context as dynamic, interrelated phenomena.

From a slightly different perspective the activity of performing assessments constitutes one of the key places where participants negotiate and display to each other a congruent view of the events that they encounter in their phenomenal world. It is thus a central locus for the study of the "shared understandings" that lie at the heart of the anthropological analysis of culture.[22] Indeed it permits the analysis of such shared understandings on two very different levels: (1) the procedures participants use to coordinate their perspectives with each other; (2) the products of those procedures, i.e. particular agreements (or disagreements) about how specific events should be interpreted and evaluated. In the past many ethnographies have focused largely on the second of these levels (i.e. "the people of X culture believe Y"). However, particular interpretations of events in the world may be far less important than the structures used to accomplish such congruent interpretations as a social activity in the first place. Paying close attention to what participants actually say, and focusing analysis on the underlying structures and procedures they employ to accomplish the events they are engaged in, is quite consistent with Goodenough's (1965) call for methods of analyzing culture that increase the rigor of ethnographic description.

Finally, it is interesting to speculate about what import the phenomena being examined here might have for broader issues. We will therefore briefly consider how the interactive organization of assessment activity might be relevant to the study of the way in which language and culture are acquired.

Assessments provide for the possibility of collaborative participation in an emerging utterance. Moreover, someone can display appropriate participation without producing a complete syntactic sentence. Recipients' concurrent assessments frequently consist of sounds such as "mhm::" whose main function seems to be the carrying of an appropriate intonation contour, which can in fact be both quite elaborated and shaped in fine detail to fit the utterance it is responding to (C. Goodwin 1986). Even very young children are capable of producing such intonation contours and of tying them to the intonation contours of the speech being directed to them. For example, the Nova film *Benjamin* contains a sequence in which a mother swings a two-month-old child in her arms while counting "one two three:::." Immediately after the mother stops speaking the child responds with a cry that replicates the distinctive intonation pattern found in the mother's "three:::." More generally, Keenan (1983) has noted the importance of children matching the sounds of others in language development.

Assessments provide an opportunity for a child to produce such behavior in a rich linguistic environment that is both socially organized and highly structured. The way in which the behavior of the child in this activity is tied in detail to the behavior of others creates a framework within which the child's behavior can be guided through ongoing feedback as the utterance emerges. Moreover, as analysis in this chapter has demonstrated, producing concurrent assessments at appropriate moments requires that one pay close attention to emerging structure in the stream of speech (and again some of this structure, such as intonation patterns and the lengthening of sounds, can be recognized even before the child can understand the syntactic and semantic structure of the sentence). The child is thus placed in a situation where first, noting relevant distinctions in the stream of speech is consequential for its own behavior, and second, the child's developing perception can be guided by feedback from "experts" who are participating on a moment-by-moment basis in the very same activity structure that encompasses the child. Furthermore, the possibilities for creative learning within the structure provided by assessments are not restricted to the infant. As analysis in this chapter of phenomena such as congruent understanding demonstrates, producing assessments poses the task of coordinating one's perception and evaluation of the phenomena one encounters with that of co-participants throughout life. In addition, as the girls' instigating demonstrated, this basic process can be turned to the service of other social projects, such as forging coalitions and alliances. Vygotsky and his followers have stressed the importance of both social phenomena and activity structures in the development of the child (see for example Wertsch 1981, 1985a, 1985b). Though they use the term "activity" in a more technical sense than we are using it here, structures of the type being analyzed here seem quite relevant to the issues they raise about frameworks embedded in practical activities that make possible the social and linguistic development of the child. The activity structure provided by assessments might thus constitute a fruitful locus for investigating the development of language and culture within a framework of dynamic social action.

In brief, despite their apparent simplicity, assessments provide an arena within which language structure, cognition, affect, and social coordination can be investigated in fine detail as integrated components of a single process. Because of this they have a clear relevance to larger issues posed in the analysis of language, culture, and social organization.

Acknowledgments

We are very deeply indebted to Alessandro Duranti, William Hanks, Gail Jefferson, and Emanuel Schegloff for insightful comments and suggestions. A preliminary report on the first section of this chapter appeared in 1987 in *IPrA Papers in Pragmatics* 1 (1): 1–54.

Notes

1 For more detailed analysis of the data and the means used to obtain it see C. Goodwin (1981) and M. H. Goodwin (1990).
2 For other relevant analysis of how assessments are organized within conversation see C. Goodwin (1986), M. H. Goodwin (1980b), C. Goodwin and M. H. Goodwin (1987) and Pomerantz (1978, 1984).
3 Frequently the left boundary of an assessment is especially difficult to delimit precisely. Later in this chapter we will investigate how participants interpret the intensifiers, etc., that precede assessment segments as the beginning of involvement in the activity of assessment. In other work we are currently investigating how prior talk can "seed" a subsequent assessment by foreshadowing an evaluation that is about to occur.
4 With respect to the close ties between evaluation and intonation, note that Pike, in his seminal study of English intonation (Pike 1945), argued that the principal function of intonation was to show the attitude of the speaker toward what he or she was saying. While such a view of the function of intonation is clearly inadequate as a general analysis of the work that intonation does, it does capture and highlight the way in which intonation can tie together phenomena being talked about with the speaker's alignment to, and experience of, those phenomena. Such analysis of the way in which intonation can display the speaker's evaluation of the talk being produced is most relevant to the structure and organization of assessment actions.
5 In his analysis of narrative, Labov (1972) classifies **evaluation** as one distinct element of narrative structure, but also notes that unlike other features of narrative which occur at specific places within the overall structure of a narrative (for example the coda occurs at the end), evaluation can pervade the

narrative. Such analysis supports the argument about the distribution of assessment signals that is being made here.

6 For more detailed analysis of how assessments contrast with continuers in terms of their precise placement relative to the talk of another see C. Goodwin (1986).

7 For more detailed analysis of the way in which such a headshake is used as an assessment marker, see M. H. Goodwin (1980b).

8 For other analysis of actions spanning multiple speakers see Ochs, Schieffelin, and Platt (1979).

9 Constructions such as this, in which an entity is introduced in a first structure, and then commented on in a second, have been the subject of extensive analysis from a number of different perspectives. Thus linguists have studied such structures both in terms of syntactic processes such as left dislocation (Gundel 1975, Ross 1967), and in terms of how topics, and comments on these topics, are organized with respect to the contrast between "given" and "new" information (Chafe 1976, Li and Thompson 1976). More recently students of discourse (Duranti and Ochs 1979; Ochs and Schieffelin 1983a, 1983b) have begun to investigate their pragmatic organization, focusing on phenomena such as how the "Referent + Proposition" structure can be used to organize and focus a recipient's attention, and the way in which such structures might be fruitfully investigated as **discourses** (i.e. sequences of communicative acts) rather than as single syntactically bound units (Ochs and Schieffelin 1983a). Such a pragmatic focus is quite consistent with the analysis developed here. It should however be noted that treating assessments as utterances whose primary function is to provide "new" information does not seem to be the most appropriate way to conceptualize what they are doing. Thus, as will be seen later in this chapter, in many cases the recipient collaborates in the assessment, operating on it even before the speaker has explicitly stated her position. Instead of simply marking new information, such a structure invokes a framework of heightened mutual focus on, and co-participation in, the talk containing the assessment. Though the current analysis emphasizes the organization of participation structures, rather than the transfer of information, it seems quite compatible with the emphasis in previous analysis on foregrounding the material in the comment or proposition. The present data thus provide an opportunity to expand the dimensions and frames of reference that have so far been employed to study structures of this type. On a more general level, we think that it is quite important that study of the functional organization of linguistic and discourse structure not be restricted to issues of information management, but also include the multifaceted activities and participation structures that are invoked through talk.

10 Where the assessment occurs in the stream of speech relative to the assessable is marked in the fine detail within these utterances. Thus in (1), in which the assessment preceded the assessable, the clause containing the assessment was introduced with "this" (i.e. "this beautiful Irish Setter") which established its upcoming referent as an available object for commentary, while in (4) the anaphoric term "it" presupposes the prior establishment of the referent as available within the discourse.

11 See Heritage (1984b) for more detailed analysis of how the particle "oh" functions within interaction.

12 The intensifier is clearly part of the **assessment activity** and it would be wrong to suggest that the assessment does not begin until the adjective explicitly states an evaluation. It is however quite useful to distinguish the intensifier from the assessment adjective in order to demonstrate how participants collaboratively work toward achieving heightened mutual focus over the assessment adjective. The distinctions made at the beginning of the chapter between **assessment segments** and **assessment activity** were drawn precisely to deal with situations such as this. The intensifier is an **assessment segment** in its own right, but one that can be clearly distinguished from the **assessment adjective** that follows it.

13 For other analyses of how the way in which recipient projections about the future course of a sentence are relevant to the organization of the recipient's interaction with the speaker see Jefferson (1973) and Sacks, Schegloff, and Jefferson (1974). For analysis of how deictic terms dynamically modify emerging context as an utterance unfolds see Hanks (1986).

14 For analysis of how participants can negotiate speakership within overlap see Jefferson (1973) and Schegloff (1987).

15 For other analyses of how the structure of talk displays the type of knowledge that a speaker has of the event being talked about see M. H. Goodwin (1980b) and Pomerantz (1980). For extensive analysis of how access is relevant to the organization of talk, and deictic systems in particular, see Hanks (1990, this volume).

16 For other analysis of displaying congruent understanding see C. Goodwin (1981: 114–16) and Jefferson (1983).

17 It may be noted that the placement of this strong agreement is almost the mirror image of one of the ways in which impending disagreement is displayed sequentially. Pomerantz (1984) describes how recipients prepared to disagree frequently delay a response to what has just been said.

18 In that the recipient's nods begin after the speaker's body displays heightened orientation toward her over the intensifier, one might be tempted to argue that the nods are solicited or at least triggered by the body movements the speaker has just made. However, it seems more accurate to say that the recipient is responding to the emerging activity of assessment, something visible in a range of different ways, e.g. the intensifier itself, its placement in the talk so far produced, the way in which it is articulated, the visible actions of the speaker's body relevant to it, etc. Arbitrarily segregating interactive events in terms of whether they are produced vocally or nonvocally seems neither helpful analytically nor to accurately reflect what the participants are doing.

19 For more extended analysis of the organization of engagement displays and entry into disengagement see C. Goodwin (1981: Ch. 3).

20 See M. H. Goodwin (1982) for more detailed analysis of instigating.

21 For more detailed analysis of how such "future stories" provide insight into the underlying cultural models being used by participants to construct events such as he-said-she-said confrontations see M. H. Goodwin (1982).

22 Ethnomethodology (Garfinkel 1967), with its emphasis on analysis of the procedures participants utilize to reflexively constitute and understand the events they are engaged in, has great relevance for the issues being dealt with here, and indeed the analysis of culture in general. For an interesting discussion of such issues, and of ethnomethodology in general, see Heritage (1984a).

References

Atkinson, J. Maxwell, and John Heritage (eds.). 1984. *Structures of Social Action*. Cambridge: Cambridge University Press.

Chafe, Wallace L. 1976. Givenness, Contrastiveness, Definiteness, Subjects, Topics and Point of View, in *Subject and Topic*, ed. C. Li. New York: Academic Press.

Duranti, Alessandro, and Elinor Ochs. 1979. Left-Dislocation in Italian Conversation, in *Syntax and Semantics. Vol. 12; Discourse and Syntax*, ed. Talmy Givon. New York: Academic Press.

Garfinkle, Harold. 1967. *Studies in Ethnomethodology*. Englewood Cliffs, N.J.: Prentice – Hall.

Goffman, Erving. 1959. *The Presentation of Self in Everyday Life*. Garden City, NY: Doubleday.

 1963. *Behavior in Public Places: Notes on the Social Organization of Gathering*. New York: Free Press.

 1964. The Neglected Situation. *American Anthropologist* 66 (6) Pt. II: 133–6.

 1974. *Frame Analysis: An Essay on the Organization of Experience*. New York: Harper and Row.

 1981. *Forms of Talk*. Philadelphia: University of Pennsylvania Press.

Goodenough, Ward H. 1965. Rethinking "Status" and "Role": Toward a General Model of the Cultural Organization of Social Relationships, in *The Relevance of Models for Social Anthropology*, ed. Michael Banton, pp. 1–24. London: Tavistock.

Goodwin, Charles. 1981. *Conversational Organization: Interaction Between Speakers and Hearers*. New York: Academic Press.

 1986. Between and Within: Alternative Treatments of Continuers and Assessments. *Human Studies* 9: 205–17.

Goodwin, Charles, and Marjorie Harness Goodwin. 1987. Concurrent Operations on Talk: Notes on the Interactive Organization of Assessments. *IPrA Papers in Pragmatics* 1 (1): 1–52.

Goodwin, Marjorie Harness. 1980a. He-Said-She-Said: Formal Cultural Procedures for the Construction of a Gossip Dispute Activity. *American Ethnologist* 7: 674–95.

 1980b. Processes of Mutual Monitoring Implicated in the Production of Description Sequences. *Sociological Inquiry* 50: 303–17.

 1982. 'Instigating': Storytelling as a Social Process. *American Ethnologist* 9: 799–819.

 1990. *He-Said-She-Said: Talk as Social Organization among Black Children*. Bloomington: Indiana University Press.

Gumperz, John J. 1982. *Discourse Strategies*. Cambridge: Cambridge University Press.

Gundel, J. 1975. Left Dislocation and the Role of Topic–Comment Structure in Linguistic Theory. *Ohio State Working Papers in Linguistics* 18: 72–132.

Hanks, William F. 1986. The Interactive Structure of Indexical Reference. Paper presented at the invited session on Rethinking Context at the 1986 Annual Meeting of the American Anthropological Association.

 1990. *Referential Practice: Language and Lived Space among the Maya*. Chicago: University of Chicago Press.

Heath, Christian. 1986. *Body Movement and Speech in Medical Interaction*. Cambridge: Cambridge University Press.

Heritage, John. 1984a. *Garfinkel and Ethnomethodology*. Cambridge: Polity Press.
  1984b. A Change-of-State Token and Aspects of its Sequential Placement, in *Structures of Social Action*, ed. J. Maxwell Atkinson and John Heritage, pp. 299–345. Cambridge: Cambridge University Press.
Heritage, John, and J. Maxwell Atkinson. 1984. Introduction, in *Structures of Social Action*, ed. J. Maxwell Atkinson and John Heritage, pp. 1–16. Cambridge: Cambridge University Press.
Jefferson, Gail. 1973. A Case of Precision Timing in Ordinary Conversation: Overlapped Tag-Positioned Address Terms in Closing Sequences. *Semiotica* 9: 47–96.
  1983. Caveat Speaker: Preliminary Notes on Recipient Topic–Shift Implicature. *Tilburg Papers in Language and Literature* 30.
Keenan, Elinor Ochs. 1983. Making It Last: Repetition in Children's Discourse, in *Acquiring Conversational Competence*, ed. Elinor Ochs and Bambi B. Schieffelin, pp. 26–39. Boston: Routledge and Kegan Paul.
Kendon, Adam. 1990. *Conducting Interaction: Patterns of Behaviour in Focused Encounters*. Cambridge: Cambridge University Press.
Labov, William. 1972. The Transformation of Experience in Narrative Syntax, in *Language in the Inner City: Studies in the Black English Vernacular*, pp. 354–96. Philadelphia: University of Pennsylvania Press.
Li, Charles, and S. Thompson. 1976. Subject and Topic: A New Typology of Language, in *Subject and Topic*, ed. Charles Li. New York: Academic Press.
Ochs, Elinor, and Bambi B. Schieffelin. 1983a. Foregrounding Referents: A Reconsideration of Left Dislocation in Discourse, in *Acquiring Conversational Competence*, ed. Elinor Ochs and Bambi B. Schieffelin, pp. 158–74. Boston: Routledge and Kegan Paul.
  1983b. Topic as a Discourse Notion: A Study of Topic in the Conversations of Children and Adults, in *Acquiring Conversational Competence*, ed. Elinor Ochs and Bambi B. Schieffelin, pp. 66–113. Boston: Routledge and Kegan Paul.
Ochs, Elinor, Bambi Schieffelin, and Martha Platt. 1979. Propositions across Utterances and Speakers, in *Developmental Pragmatics*, ed. Elinor Ochs and Bambi Schieffelin, pp. 251–68. New York: Academic Press.
Pike, Kenneth L. 1945. *The Intonation of American English*. Ann Arbor: University of Michigan Press.
Pomerantz, Anita. 1978. Compliment Responses: Notes on the Co-operation of Multiple Constraints, in *Studies in the Organization of Conversational Interaction*, ed. Jim Schenkein, pp. 79–112. New York: Academic Press.
  1980. Telling My Side: "Limited Access" as a "Fishing" Device. *Sociological Inquiry* 50: 186–98.
  1984. Agreeing and Disagreeing with Assessments: Some Features of Preferred/ Dispreferred Turn Shapes, in *Structures of Social Action*, ed. J. Maxwell Atkinson and John Heritage, pp. 57–101. Cambridge: Cambridge University Press.
Ross, J. 1967. Constraints on Variables in Syntax. Ph.D. dissertation, MIT, Cambridge, Mass.
Sacks, Harvey. 1963. Sociological Description. *Berkeley Journal of Sociology* 8: 1–16.
  1974. An Analysis of the Course of a Joke's Telling in Conversation, in *Explorations in the Ethnography of Speaking*, ed. Richard Bauman and Joel Sherzer, pp. 337–53. Cambridge: Cambridge University Press.

Sacks, Harvey, Emanuel A. Schegloff, and Gail Jefferson. 1974. A Simplest Systematics for the Organization of Turn-Taking for Conversation. *Language* 50: 696–735.

Schegloff, Emanuel A. 1968. Sequencing in Conversational Openings. *American Anthropologist* 70: 1075–95.

1980. Preliminaries to Preliminaries: "Can I Ask You a Question." *Sociological Inquiry* 50: 104–52.

1986a. On the Organization of Sequences as a Source of "Coherence" in Talk-in-Interaction. Prepared for discussion at SRCD conference on Development of Conversational Coherence, University of New Orleans, May 7–10, 1986.

1986b. The Routine as Achievement. *Human Studies* 9: 111–51.

1987. Recycled Turn Beginnings: A Precise Repair Mechanism in Conversation's Turn-Taking Organisation, in *Talk and Social Organisation*, ed. Graham Button and John R. E. Lee, pp. 70–85. Clevedon, England: Multilingual Matters.

1988. Presequences and Indirection: Applying Speech Act Theory to Ordinary Conversation. *Journal of Pragmatics* 12: 55–62.

Vološinov, Valentin Nikolaevic. 1973. *Marxism and the Philosophy of Language*, trans. Ladislav Matejka and I. R. Titunik. New York: Seminar Press. (First published 1929 and 1930.)

Wertsch, James V. (ed.). 1981. *The Concept of Activity in Soviet Psychology*. Armonk NY: M. E. Sharpe

(ed.). 1985a. *Culture, Communication, and Cognition: Vygotskian Perspectives*. Cambridge: Cambridge University Press.

1985b. *Vygotsky and the Social Formation of Mind*. Cambridge Mass.: Harvard University Press.

7   In another context

EMANUEL A. SCHEGLOFF

Editors' introduction

Emanuel A. Schegloff is Professor of Sociology at the University of California in Los Angeles. He received his doctorate in Sociology from Berkeley. Most of Schegloff's research has been devoted to the analysis of conversation, a field of research that originated in the 1960s through intense collaboration between Harvey Sacks, Schegloff, and Gail Jefferson.

Conversation analysis differs from most other fields that take talk as their primary subject matter in that it uses as its point of departure not linguistics but rather a deep interest in elementary properties of social action. Influenced by Harold Garfinkel's **ethnomethodology**, early work in conversation analysis approached talk in interaction as a perspicuous site for investigating how human social organization was dynamically accomplished by participants within the indigenous settings where they lived their lives. In order to sustain and elaborate the events they are engaged in, participants must display to each other their ongoing understanding of those events while simultaneously interpreting in a relevant fashion the actions of others. When the analysis of talk was approached from such a perspective, it was found that in order to understand utterances (and other forms of action) in a relevant fashion, parties engaged in conversation do not approach a strip of talk as an isolated object but instead interpret whatever is being said by tying it to the **context** within which it occurs. For example, a bit of talk cannot be recognized as an **answer** by looking at it in isolation. Instead it must be seen as responsive to a particular type of prior action, e.g. a **question**. A key aspect of context is thus the **sequence** of talk within which a particular utterance is lodged (hence the strong interest of conversation analysts in **sequential organization**).

Many of these themes were elaborated in Schegloff's first major publication, "Sequencing in Conversational Openings" which appeared in *American Anthropologist* in 1968. One of the issues addressed by Schegloff in this article is specification of what in fact constitutes a sequence. Clearly the mere fact that two events occur in close proximity to each other does not establish that participants treat these events as a sequence of actions tied to each other. Schegloff proposed that a defining characteristic of true sequences is the property of **conditional relevance**: a first action creates a slot for an appropriate next action such that even the **absence** of that action can be perceived as a relevant and noticeable event (consider for example a student's silence after a teacher's question, or someone who says nothing in response to a greeting). The power of sequential organization as a contextual resource for interpretation is thus so strong that even things which fail to happen become relevant events for participants. Notions such as conditional relevance integrate interpretive issues with analysis of the ongoing production of social action. Producing a sequence of responsive action, such as an exchange of greetings, not only requires that participants engage in appropriate interpretation, but is itself an elementary example of coordinated social action.

In subsequent research Schegloff has described and analyzed a range of different types of conversational phenomena. His work includes elaborate and detailed analysis of how participants coordinate entry into interaction (Schegloff 1968, 1979, 1986) and, in collaboration with Harvey Sacks, how they exit from interaction (Schegloff and Sacks 1973). A key constitutive feature of conversation is the exchange of turns at talk. Sacks, Schegloff, and Jefferson (1974) have provided a classic analysis of this process, one that ties the accomplishment of elementary social organization to the detailed shaping of units of talk. While most students of language dismiss phenomena such as hesitations and restarts as "performance errors" that obscure ideal linguistic form, Schegloff notes that conversation is a "self-righting mechanism" with its own indigenous mechanisms for repairing the troubles it systematically encounters as a real-world phenomenon; he has provided extensive analysis of how repair is organized as a social and interactive phenomenon (for example Schegloff, Jefferson, and Sacks 1977). Conversation permits detailed analysis of how participants employ general, abstract procedures to build the local particulars of the events they are engaged in. One key aspect of this process is **recipient design**, the multiplicity of ways in which participants take into account the particulars of who they are talking to, and the events they are engaged in, in the organization of their action. Schegloff's (1972) analysis of "formulating place" provides a classic illustration of this process.

In his chapter in the present volume, Schegloff begins by addressing a number of theoretical and methodological issues posed in the investigation of context. He argues strongly that an analyst is not free to invoke whatever variables he or she feels appropriate as dimensions of context, no matter how strongly grounded in traditional social theory – e.g. class, gender, etc. – but instead must demonstrate in the events being examined that the participants themselves are organizing their behavior in terms of the features being described by the analyst. He then uses a specific storytelling episode to demonstrate how sequential organization provides multiple levels of context for the organization of participants' action. In a previous analysis of part of this same sequence, C. Goodwin (1987) investigated how an utterance specifically designed to be a single-party, context-free event was in fact contextually shaped through a process of collaborative interaction. Schegloff now reanalyzes this same event by placing it within a much larger sequence than Goodwin looked at, an entire storytelling episode. Schegloff finds that this larger sequence is in fact consequential in detail for the organization of the event that Goodwin examined. However, Schegloff notes that his current analysis in no way undercuts Goodwin's earlier analysis. Instead multiple levels of sequential context mutually reinforce each other as they provide alternative types of organization for the local production of action. In the course of his analysis, Schegloff also provides an extended demonstration of how one of the speech events recurrently examined in this volume – storytelling – is studied within conversation analysis.

References

Goodwin, Charles. 1987. Unilateral Departure, in *Talk and Social Organisation*, ed. G. Button and J. R. E. Lee, pp. 206–16. Clevedon, England: Multilingual Matters.

Sacks, Harvey, Emanuel A. Schegloff, and Gail Jefferson. 1974. A Simplest Systematics for the Organization of Turn-Taking for Conversation. *Language* 50: 696–735.

Schegloff, Emanuel A. 1968. Sequencing in Conversational Openings. *American Anthropologist* 70: 1075–95.

1972. Notes on a Conversational Practice: Formulating Place, in *Studies in Social Interaction*, ed. D. Sudnow, pp. 75–119. New York: Free Press.

1979. Identification and Recognition in Telephone Conversation Openings, in *Everyday Language*, ed. G. Psathas, pp. 23–78. New York: Erlbaum.

1986. The Routine as Achievement. *Human Studies* 9: 111–51.

Schegloff, Emanuel A., Gail Jefferson, and Harvey Sacks. 1977. The Preference for Self-Correction in the Organization of Repair in Conversation. *Language* 53: 361–82.

Schegloff, Emanuel A., and Harvey Sacks. 1973. Opening Up Closings. *Semiotica* 8: 289–327.

In another context

1   Introduction

Invocations of the relevance of context, in both everyday vernacular and in scholarly or scientific discourse, have commonly been characterized by certain features.

First, omission of what is claimed to be appropriate context is treated as having distorted the sense of what has been (as we say in ordinary discourse) "taken out of context." Putting something "in context," accordingly, is treated as transforming, and correcting, our understanding.

Secondly, the project of putting something in proper context ordinarily has commonly treated that context as reasonably well understood by the one undertaking the project, though possibly in need of explication for others. The focus of analysis is on what is being put in context. The context itself is not so much subjected to analysis or review as it is "invoked"; in being relied on, our understanding of it is treated as reliable. What is being advanced is our understanding of the contexted object, rather than our understanding of the context itself.[1]

Such a stance has been not only understandable, but warranted and salutary when confronting certain contemporary modes of inquiry on language, discourse, and other forms of conduct in interaction. It has been especially pertinent in confronting styles of research which do not even address themselves to actual occurrences, but to invented or idealized versions of supposedly actually occurring types of events – as in certain formal approaches to language, speech act theory, and other undertakings in pragmatics. Such modes of research commonly address their targets of inquiry – whether sentences or actions or stories – as if they were intrinsically autonomous objects, that is, objects designed to have integrity and coherence which are entirely "internal" to the object itself. In doing so, they systematically obscure the possibility that their objects of inquiry are designed not for splendid and isolated independence, but for coherence and integrity as part and parcel of the environment or context in which, and for which, they were produced by its participants. In response to such modes of analysis, it has seemed quite important to make clear how different a picture of the object of analysis emerges if one reengages it – sentence, story, gesture, and the like – to its context, and then reconfigures our understanding of its structure and character.[2]

In such polemical contexts (i.e. ones in which another stance is being challenged), it is important to underscore the "transformative" potential of context, and the robustness of our invocation of the context as already understood can be strategic. But the general thrust of the present chapter is to suggest that this stance should itself be context-sensitive.

Because any demarcation of a segment of an actually occurring interaction or occasion of language use as an object of analysis will necessarily leave some portion or aspect(s) of it unincluded, there will always and inescapably be something which can be claimed to be context for what has been focused on. Especially when what has been selected out for attention is a relatively small bit of the stream of events in which it occurred, it can appear vulnerable to the same concerns for context described above, and the argument can be (and has been) made that proper understanding of the object of inquiry is forfeit if its context is not taken into account.

It is on this point that the present chapter aims to sound a note of caution. That caution is that when confronting prior analyses which have themselves been empirically based and have been sensitive to the details of a particular occasion, the transformative thrust of invocations of context may be substantially mitigated, and insistence on it can be misplaced and misleading.

In what follows, I want to make explicit two quite simple points: (1) that "putting something in context" **can** take (and perhaps increasingly **should** take) the proposed **context** as the "news" and as the object of analysis (rather than as the "given" relative to the object of analysis); and (2) that putting something in context may **not** necessarily transform the proper understanding of what has been so "contextualized." The support of these points requires first some clarity about what will be intended by the term "context."

The concern with "context" in the social and human sciences, especially with respect to interaction and discourse, is commonly understood to be addressed to two **types** of context – what can be called "external" or "distal" on the one hand, and "intra-interactional" or "discourse" or "proximate" on the other. Under the former rubric may be grouped aspects of social life long central to the social sciences – the class, ethnic, and gender composition of an interaction, each of these understood either as a distinctive source of ordering of and constraint on social life, or as an embodiment of more general properties such as "power" (in various of the senses in which that term is used). Here as well are found the various institutional matrices within which interaction occurs (the legal order, economic or market order, etc.) as well as its ecological, regional, national, and cultural settings, all of which may be taken as "shaping" what goes on under their auspices or in arenas of social life on which they have a bearing.

By the second type of context we can understand the sort of occasion or genre of interaction which participants, by their conduct, make some episode be an instance of, the sorts of sequences of talk or courses of conduct in which particular events may occur (stories, request sequences, etc.), the capacity in which participants act relative to the episode in progress (e.g. as the initiator of a conversation or a topic, or its recipient), etc.

Now clearly, these two types need not constitute disjunct, or non-overlapping, sets. "Buyer" and "seller" can refer both to the "objective statuses" of participants in an interaction in a marketplace, and to the relevant "capacities" in which they engage one another in a particular spate of talk. But as that very example may suggest, although "external" and "intra-interactional" contexts **need not** be disjunct, their relationship can be problematic, and must be **taken as problematic** for the purposes of disciplined analysis.

A number of difficulties can be (and have been) raised concerning the invocation by academic analysts of contexts of the first type in addressing data of social interaction.

(1) As various writers have shown, the range of "objective" identities of participants in interaction is virtually infinite, and so also are the aspects of the situations in which some interaction might be described to be occurring. The sheer correctness of some description of a possible invocation of context, e.g. that an interaction took place in a hospital or in a courtroom, is equivocal in its import; for we know that not everything that goes on in a courtroom has anything to do with the law, and we know as well that endless numbers of other descriptions would also be "correct" (e.g. that it was in a north-facing room). The issue then becomes, **which** of the possible characterizations of context (whether of setting or of participants) can be shown to be **relevant**. Relevant to whom?

If one is concerned with understanding what something in interaction was for its participants, then we must establish what sense of context was relevant **to those participants**, and at the moment at which what we are trying to understand occurred. And we must seek to ground that claim in the conduct of the participants; they show (to one another in the first place, but to us students as a by-product) what they take their relevant context and identities to be. This is so precisely because their grasp of the setting supplies the basis for each next increment of their conduct, either further confirming and constituting a setting along certain lines or moving to reshape it. They may well embody for one another the relevance of "courtroom" or "hospital" or "marketplace" as the setting, and of personal identities related to these settings – judge and defendant, doctor and colleague doctor, merchant and customer; that is why "external" and "intra-interactional" are not mutually exclusive sets of contexts. But it is only by a display of relevance that the former becomes the latter.

Showing that some orientation to context is demonstrably relevant to the participants is important, as well, in order to ensure that what informs the analysis is what is relevant to **the participants in its target event**, and not what is relevant in the first instance to its academic analysts by virtue of the set of analytic and theoretical commitments which they bring to their work.

(2) Not all aspects of setting or of capacity in which persons are acting are consequential for all aspects of what they say or do. That two interactants are relevantly doctors talking in a medical setting, and about medical matters, is not necessarily consequential for the way in which they deploy hand gestures which occur in the course of their talk or the way in which they refer to a prospective fourth for their golfing outing on Wednesday. So, even if one can show that, of the descriptions of the settings and persons which **could** be invoked, some particular ones **are** relevant to the participants in the interaction, it remains to be shown that they are **procedurally consequential** for the particular aspect of the talk or other conduct which is the focus of analysis – that is, that there is a consequential tie (again, for the **participants**) between the setting and interactional identities so understood and a particular facet of their conduct.

There are other problems to be faced in bringing "external" formulations of context to bear on interactional conduct which cannot be detailed here. For now, two points which follow from the preceding discussion will have to suffice.

The first might be termed the "paradox of proximateness" (Schegloff, 1991), and it concerns the need for showing some "external" aspect of setting or role to be relevant to the participants and displayed in particular details of their conduct. If the analyst **can** show with explicit analysis that the participants take themselves to be relevantly "doctors" and relevantly "in the hospital" or "in intensive care," then it is their so taking themselves and "marking the setting" by so conducting themselves which is germane to the analysis of their conduct, and not their "objective status" of being in such a setting. If, on the other hand, the analyst **cannot** show from the details of their conduct that they take themselves to be relevantly in such a setting and acting in such capacities, then the analyst's invocation of the objective correctness of so describing them is rendered equivocal in the ways mentioned earlier -- there are indefinitely many such objective characterizations which could also be shown to be "true."

The paradox, then, is this: if some "external" context can be shown to be proximately (or intra-interactionally) relevant to the participants, then its external status is rendered beside the point; and if it cannot be so shown, then its external status is rendered equivocal.

The second point which is suggested by the preceding discussion is this. If there are indefinitely many potentially relevant aspects of context and of personal or categorical identity which could have a bearing on some facet of, or occurrence in, interaction, and if the analyst must be concerned with what is relevant to the parties at the moment at which what is being analyzed occurred, and is procedurally consequential for what is being analyzed, then **the search for context properly begins with the talk or other conduct being analyzed**. That talk or conduct, or what immediately surrounds it, may be understood as displaying which out of that potential infinity of contexts and identities should be treated as relevant and consequential (both by co-participants and by professional analysts).

Thus, for example, the use of technical medical terminology by interactional participants (e.g. terminology such as "cellulitis," "group A strep," "bacteremia," etc., as in Cicourel 1987, this volume) anchors **within the interaction** the relevance for the participants of the medical cast of the setting and of the participants (even for ones for whom it is not in fact correct), and invokes it **within the interaction;** it need not be independently invoked by the analyst on extrinsic ethnographic grounds.[3]

Curiously, then, it seems at least as appropriate, and perhaps more so, to speak of talk or other conduct invoking its contexts than it is to speak of context impacting on talk or other conduct.

These analytic constraints on the invocation of "external" formulations of context are not impossible to meet (cf., for example, Heritage and Greatbatch 1989 for one line of solution). But, in view of these considerations and the paradox of proximateness, it seems increasingly useful to focus, at least in the near term, on the so-called intra-interactional or proximate contexts for talk and conduct. The problems which have been discussed are either mitigated, or simply do not arise in the same fashion, in the case of this sense of context. This is because these contexts tend to be formulated in the first instance by virtue of the observable conduct of the participants, and problems of showing relevance to the participants thus do not arise. Perhaps one product of sustained study of the organization of interaction will be analytic resources for new ways of warranting the analytic incorporation of aspects of setting or identity which we may feel to be relevant to interaction, but at present have no way of showing in an analytically warrantable way.

One consequence of the considerations which have been reviewed so far concerns the sense or type of context which will be central to the analysis to follow, given its main themes. These themes are to show that preoccupations with context may/should focus on its **analysis** and not only its invocation,[4] and that such analysis may add to our understanding **of the context** without necessarily transforming our understanding of what occurred **in** that context. For these themes, intra-interactional or discourse senses of context are central, and provide a strategic focus for disciplined inquiry at the present time.

2   Thematic

There are various aspects of conduct which appear to us (both as ordinary members of cultures and as professional students of them) to be immensely consequential and meaningful, but which can, on occasion, challenge our capacity to specify their consequentiality. One aspect of conduct for which this may sometimes be the case is context.

Given that context can be taken to refer to anything outside the boundaries of a unit of analysis, it is hard to contest the principle of the "decisive relevance of context." Quite often, putting an utterance or a fragment of an interaction in some version of "its context" (e.g. the preceding talk, or a description or picture of the physical setting, or a formulation of the dramatic moment in a developing line of action at which it occurs) will engender the sense, "Ohhh, so **that's** what it was about/ doing!" But, if pressed, we may be unable to specify exactly how that packaging of context has interacted with the original object of attention, and with our perceptual and analytic apparatus, to transform our "grasp" of its import. We may be unable to access and explicate the "how," – both in the sense of the **substance** of the change in our understanding and in the sense of the **mechanism** of that change.

Is it that there are respects in which, commonsense experience to the contrary notwithstanding, context is **not** actually consequential (except if imparted bizarre realizations)? Or is it that we do not yet know enough to get at the mechanisms involved and their consequences?

This experience of an unexplicatable, and therefore analytically infertile, "aha" when some bit of talk is supplied its context coexists with another, in some ways contrary, tendency.

One corollary which has seemed to go with the principle of the decisive relevance of context has been the expectation of a revelatory or transformational significance of context for analysis. If one begins with the premise that the prototypical occurrences of talk in interaction cannot be properly understood, described or analyzed without reference to context, then showing something to be relevant context which had not previously been included in the description or analysis might be expected to yield a transformation in our understanding – an analytic revelation of sorts. Indeed, one pay-off regularly claimed by new analyses which claim to demonstrate previously unappreciated "contexts" is the revision, if not transformation, in our understanding which has been made possible.

As suggested earlier, one of the points of the present chapter is to show that this need not be the case. Previous accounts of a phenomenon or an event need not be shown to be wrong in order to warrant the value of the contribution of showing previously undescribed context(s) in which they occur. If well crafted and grounded in careful and detailed empirical analysis, they may survive robust even as layers of context in which they are embedded are subsequently explicated. I want not merely to claim this point, but to exemplify it.

I take as a point of departure an utterance in a course of action of leavetaking from a cluster of persons engaged in conversation. This utterance ("Need some more ice") has been taken up by C. Goodwin (1987) as one which appears to apotheosize something detached from context (like Goffman's "self-talk," 1978). But Goodwin shows that this very appearance is a context-sensitive interactional achievement, one which the several participants collaborate to achieve as a "unilateral departure." One point of Goodwin's paper, thus, appears to dot the "i" on the "contextualist" stance: even an utterance **specifically designed to be context-free** must be understood as context-oriented, even context-dependent.

I will try to show that the utterance concerned occurs in a demonstrable sequential context in addition to the elements of context incorporated into Goodwin's account, and at a strategic point in that sequential context. The **type** of context involved here, then, is the intra-interactional context constituted by a course of action, here especially as embodied in turns and sequences of talk. I will conclude that reexamining the target occurrence in its sequence-organizational context – though it may produce an "aha" sensation – leaves Goodwin's analysis of it essentially intact.

I hope thereby to establish as a useful kind of find or result a factual addition of relevant contextedness which does not, however, transform our understanding of the import of what has been shown to be so contexted.

3   Background[5]

The "departure" which is the focus of Goodwin's account and of the present chapter is that of Phyllis, a guest at a backyard picnic, from a grouping which has included her husband, Mike; the host, Curt; and Gary, the husband of Curt's cousin Carney (who is an intermittent participant in this grouping).[6] The episode of talk involved can be said to have begun with an inquiry by Curt to Mike about the automobile races which the latter had attended the previous evening (this portion appears in the Appendix 1: 001–34, and is treated in Schegloff 1987b). A bit into the ensuing talk, Mike's wife Phyllis launches him into a storytelling episode which is not entirely uneventful (this portion appears in Appendix 1: 035–126 and is treated in C. Goodwin 1986), and then, a few minutes after the story has ended, Phyllis leaves the table, at the arrow in the transcript fragment which follows.

250	Curt:	Keegan usetuh race uhr uh- er ih was um, (0.4)
251		usetuh run um,
252		(2.7)
253	Curt:	Oh:: shit.
254		(0.4)
255	Curt:	Uhm,
256		(0.4)
257	Curt:	Fisher's car.
258	Mike:	Three en ⌈na ⌈quarter?
259	Curt:	⌊Thr⌊ee enna quarter.
260 →	Phyl:	°Need some more i ⌈ce.
261	Mike:	⌊Yeh,
262		(1.0)
263	Curt:	(When I) wz foolin around.

This last occurrence is treated by Goodwin (1987) under the title "Unilateral Departure," a term employed because, as noted earlier, Phyllis' departure is brought off without apparent notice by, or involvement with, any of the others in the interactional huddle. Goodwin provides a subtly observed account of the components of Phyllis' leavetaking, one which provides for its design by Phyllis not-to-be-noticed, and of the conduct of the others, whose noticing is designed not to be noticed. The "unilateral departure" is thus shown to be an entirely interactional accomplishment.

Part of its "unilaterality" is that the components out of which Phyllis' departure is assembled, including her departure utterance, do not display any apparent sequential relationship to the talk into which they are interpolated, nor is any talk by others directed to it. It seems entirely a self-contained sequential bubble in its interactive environment, and its components are built to display only an internal ordering as the parts of a sustained, "private" course of action – going to get some more ice for her drink. Goodwin accordingly examines the departure within a relatively small stretch of tape and transcript (Appendix 1: 250–64), for the action involved thus appears to be disengaged from even that immediate context.

In the present chapter, Phyllis' departure from the table is situated within a larger stretch of talk, which provides a different order of sequential context in which it is embedded.[7] One goal, again, is to show that "putting something in context" may sometimes **not** transform a previously developed account and understanding of it. If it has been carefully and empirically described, we may add to the account, enrich it, but not subvert what had been understood about the phenomenon addressed in the more proximate context.

Another goal of this analysis is to provide an account of another form or shape of extended or expanded sequence, to add to a number of such accounts already in the literature (e.g. Jefferson and Lee 1981; Jefferson and Schenkein 1977; Schegloff 1980: 117–20, 128–31; 1988a: 118–31; 1990). In the present case we will be dealing with what currently appears to be to be the main type of structured sequence other than ones based on adjacency pairs – namely, **storytelling sequences**.

The very term used to characterize these sequences should serve to underscore the contrast with "stories" *per se*; more is involved here than "stories" or "narratives" themselves. Whatever sort of "discourse unit" stories may turn out to be (as treated by, among others, cognitive scientists, folklorists, linguists, and literary theorists), as naturally occurring events in conversation (and perhaps in **most** forms of talk-in-interaction) stories appear as parts of larger sequentially organized spates of talk – **storytelling sequences**. Examining stories within their sequential context permits the explication of how stories are articulated with what has preceded them, how that relationship to what has preceded enters into the constitution of the story itself, how the passage from the story to what follows it is managed, and how the exigencies of **that** transition enter into the shaping of the story, and (as it happens) into the initiation of the story as well (for such a treatment of an extended sequence in which storytelling is implicated, see M. Goodwin 1982). The contingencies of initiating and closing the telling of stories have supplied one major focus of past work on storytelling in conversation.

I propose to examine the materials being addressed in the present exercise by drawing primarily on two major prior accounts of storytelling in conversation by two different authors (Sacks 1974, Jefferson 1978), to see how they can be brought to bear on this fragment, which is on the surface quite different from the materials examined in either of these prior accounts.[8] I will begin by reviewing briefly some of the main points developed in the papers by Sacks and Jefferson. Because these points will subsequently be brought to bear on the episode which is the concern of the present chapter – which **is** an episode of storytelling – I will not separately exemplify these points with data displays.[9]

3.1 Background analyses

Sacks (1974) parsed storytelling sequences into three main components (each subject to elaboration, expansion, etc.): the **preface sequence**, the

telling sequence, and the **response sequence**. The focus here will be on the first and third, and predominantly the latter.

Story **prefaces** address a number of issues posed by the project of telling a story in conversation. This is not the place for a full discussion, but several of these issues may be mentioned. One is establishing that what the teller means to tell is not already known to the intended audience. The common incorporation in the preface of mentions of the source of the story, of when it occurred, and of some characterization of the "type" of story ("funny," "awful," etc.) can allow recipients to assess whether they have heard it, and to stop the telling by virtue of this, if they choose. Some of these components of preface turns, most notably the characterization of the story, can also provide recipients with an interpretive key or context by reference to which the story may be monitored and understood step by step in the course of its telling, and by reference to which recipients may recognize the story's possible completion.

The last of these uses of an interpretive key is relevant because of the special management of turn-taking contingencies during storytelling. Telling a story requires a substantial withholding by others of the initiation of full turns of their own at points at which such full turns would otherwise be options – that is, at the possible ends of "turn-constructional units" such as clauses or sentences. Prefaces, when taken up approximately, occasion a shift by the participants to a somewhat different mode of organizing turns: story recipients largely suspend using possible completion of clauses and sentences as licenses to talk, thus allowing the teller to build an extended turn; and if they do talk, interpolations generally are fitted to the telling of the story in restricted and describable ways. This modification of the operation of turn-taking shifts has as its proper end point the completion of the story, at which the otherwise prevailing, turn-by-turn mode of turn-taking organization (Sacks, Schegloff, and Jefferson 1974) is resumed. Hence the strategic importance of a proper grasp by recipients that the story has come to possible completion, and hence the importance of resources which arm the recipients for such a recognition, resources provided both in the preface and in the design of the story itself. Jefferson's account of story initiation (1978) focuses on the ways in which non-preface starts of storytelling episodes (a) reveal the "triggers" which occasion their telling – that occurrence in the ongoing interaction by virtue of which the story has "come up," and (b) manage the introduction of the story into turn-by-turn talk while displaying the basis in the prior talk for the story's telling.

Preface sequences can themselves be implemented by an organized sequence type, the adjacency pair, with all the sequential contingencies such units embody. Thus, Sacks proposed that story prefaces can be done through offers-to-tell, offers which then may make acceptance/rejection relevant as responses. In the episode which furnishes the materials for the present exercise, the preface is implemented not by an offer (or a request), but by an informing/announcement of sorts, "Mike says there was a big fight . . .," which makes a different set of response types, e.g. news receipts or uptakes, relevant next.[10]

The **telling sequence** is in many ways the most distinctive component of storytelling sequences, but the concerns of this chapter will involve little preoccupation with it. Let me note, however, that one consideration which entered centrally into Sacks' material and analysis shows up in the telling sequence of the present episode as well. Sacks noted (1974: 344):

In contrast with the organization of the preface sequence, place for the talk of recipients within the course of the telling sequence need not be provided by the teller . . . If recipients choose to talk within the telling sequence, they may have to do their talking interruptively.

In the data which Sacks addressed, such an interruption occurs shortly after the start of the telling, and takes the form of a questioning or challenging or heckling of the telling which is in progress. In the present data, the telling is interrupted before its first sentence is brought to completion,[11] and also for a heckle or challenge.

Response sequences provide for displays of understanding by a storytelling's recipients that the story is over, making relevant a resumption of turn-by-turn talk, as well as appropriate appreciations of the upshot or point of the story (Sacks 1973: 137–8). Story response should provide evidence that the story can generate "topically coherent subsequent talk" (Jefferson 1978: 228), thereby proposing "the appropriateness of its having been told" (*ibid.*).

Jefferson displays various exemplars of story increments added by tellers to their stories when appropriate story responses are not initially forthcoming. Most of these involve relatively brief increments, which either succeed in generating further talk, or are followed by further rounds of such increments. The present analysis will be concerned largely with problems of story completion, response, and generating further talk, and the ways in which such contingencies can provide for substantial expansion of what should properly be considered the full storytelling sequence.

3.2   Background talk

As noted, the parties to this conversational cluster have begun talking about the automobile races the previous evening and, more generally, which drivers are competing and in which cars. Into this discussion, Phyllis recruits her husband Mike to tell a story with the story preface, "Mike sz there was a big fight down there last night." A moment later Mike begins the telling of the story only to be almost immediately confronted by the interruption mentioned above, an interruption which raises an alternative

interpretation of the sorts of events he is apparently beginning to recount –
an interpretation of them not as events in a serious big fight but as a kind of
routinized mock violence. This alternative interpretive set toward the
story's events comes to be developed by all the members of the audience,
but is instigated and developed primarily by Gary and Phyllis (Appendix 1:
047–64). Mike contests this incursion into the story and eventually resumes
the telling (Appendix 1: 065), but now under auspices which are equivocal
as between a story of impending serious violence and one of pretense.

C. Goodwin (1986) follows the telling of the story to the point at which
the competing – non-serious – interpretation of it is used by Gary to treat
the story as effectively over, a treatment embodied (a) in his summary
assessment ("All show") after the canonic elements of "pretend violence"
have been reported (e.g. throwing helmets down; Appendix 1: 055,
090–1); (b) in his request for a beer; and (c) in the joining in by Carney's
remark that she is reminded of TV wrestlers (Appendix 1: 098–111).

Mike however does not treat this as the end of the story. Initially
(Appendix 1: 101, 103), he persists in trying to continue the telling in which
he was engaged at the point of interruption. Then, after he addresses
himself to denying the assessment with which Gary treats the story as over
(Appendix 1: 106, 108, 113, 115), his continuation ("he made his first
mistake . . .," Appendix 1: 117–24) itself suggests closure–relevance in its
apparent move to summarize the upshot of the incident he has been telling
about.

That Curt may be sensitive to the possible closure-relevance of this talk
is suggested by his joining into a collaborative completion of the observation with Mike (Appendix 1: 121),

```
116 Curt:     Well, h ⌈e deserved it. ⌉
117 Mike:            ⌊But yihknow eh-⌋ uh-he made iz first
118            mistake number one by messin with Keegan
119            because a'pits'r fulla Keegans en when there
120            is ⌈n't a Keegan there ere's a'Fra ⌈:nks,
121 Curt:       ⌊°Mmhm,                        ⌊There's a'Fra:nks,
```

a move noted by C. Goodwin (1986: 288) as evidence of his (i.e. Curt's)
knowledgeability in the domain in which the story is set. In the present
context it is relevant to note as well that it moves to provide a collaborative
(co-)completion of Mike's utterance, a kind of action well suited to
showing understanding (Sacks, in press [Fall, 1965:1; Fall, 1968:5]; Lerner
1987) – at a place (i.e. just after possible story completion) at which
displays of understanding are of heightened sequential relevance (Sacks
1973: 137–8; 1974; Schegloff 1984 [1976]: 44).

There are, then, different stands taken up by different parties on the
possible completion of the story at this point.[12] It may be remarked,

however, that it is in any case not the end of the **storytelling sequence**
within which the story proper is recounted.

4   Further developments

If we track the trajectory of the interaction further, we can try to describe
the actual subsequent course of this storytelling episode to its resolution.
To anticipate: what we find first is an insistent completion by Mike of "his
story" with another collaboration by Curt in its achievement. There follows
a succession of efforts to resume turn-by-turn talk which has the story as its
source, efforts which fail, and end up by leaving the talk just where it had
been at the story's start. The following pages explicate this interactional
trajectory.

4.1   Completing the telling

After the jointly ended utterance by Curt and Mike already examined
above, there is at first a kind of collective withholding of participation: a
throat-clearing by Curt (125), 0.8 seconds of silence (126), a cough by Mike
(127).

```
119                 because a'pits'r fulla Keegans en when there
120.                is ┌n't a Keegan there ere's a'Fra ┌:nks,
121    Curt:          └°Mmhm,                          └There's a'Fra:nks,
122    Mike:       ┌(     )=
123    Curt:       └(I kno┌w.)
124    Mike:             =└Because they'relatedjih kno:┌w?
125    Curt:                                           └((clears throat))
126    Mike:       (0.8)
127    Mike:       ((cou┌gh))
128    Curt:            └Oh that's (screwy at-)
129                 (0.2)
130    Mike:       So it ended up thet-
131                 (0.2)
132    Mike:       d┌e t    u h : .┐
133    Curt:        └Dat see dat re┘minds me of,┌ we   wz o::,┐
134    Mike:                                    └He wz up on┘ the.::
135                 (0.1)
136    Mike:       trailer hh, er up ┌on the back of iz pickup truck=
137    Carney:                       └Gary:
138    Mike:       =with a, (0.4) with a ja┌:ck.
139    Gary:                               └(              cups.)
140    Curt:       Who DeWa:ld?
141    Mike:       DeWa:ld. Ye(h)ah
142                 (0.2)
```

What follows are two competing stances on where the telling episode is, and how it should develop.

Curt appears to treat the telling as over, and continues to produce forms of talk appropriate for a story recipient upon story completion. First, he provides a sort of assessment (128): "Oh that's screwy at-."[13] Then (133) he offers a possible "second story" (Sacks, in press [Fall, 1968: 1]; Ryave 1978): second (or "follow-up") stories serve as appropriate responses by hearers by revealing what the hearer took the story to be about, for this is displayed in the follow-up story they come to tell. Here, a story told by Curt as prompted by what he has just heard can display what Mike's story reminds Curt of, a telling which will display aspects of his understanding of the story which has just been told: "Dat see dat reminds me of, we wz o::,." Of course, to launch a second story is to take the stance (and thereby claim the understanding) that the prior story is over.

In between these continuation tacks of Curt's (130, 132, 134, 136), Mike takes up a different line: a move to return to the story to give its completion ("So it ended up . . ."):

So it ended up thet- (0.2) det uh: . . . he wz up on the.::
(0.1) trailer hh, er up on the back of iz pickup truck with a, (0.4) with a ja:ck.

Curt's effort to launch a second story and Mike's effort to return to a completion of the first story collide in an overlap – from which Curt withdraws (133–4), yielding to Mike's resumption of a story claimably still in progress. This collision and resolution are by no means straightforward, however. Mike starts up after Curt has already shown himself ready to move on to a new unit of talk (128–30). Curt starts his launching of a second story after Mike has already shown himself committed to returning to his story for its final chapter (130–3). Mike presses the completion of the story after having already heard that Curt is beginning a second story (133–4). The outcome of this last convergence is a full-fledged competitive overlap, from which Mike's story completion emerges "victorious" – that is, with first access to the floor. But there are consequences.

It may be remarked about this competition and its resolution that the "loser" (Curt) makes subsequent efforts at what he tries here (at lines 146, 168), and eventually succeeds. And that the "winner" (Mike), in winning the resumption of his story, appears to substantially foreshorten it.[14]

Now this increment of talk by Mike is not only announced in advance (130) to be the end of the story; its status as ending is displayed in another way as well.[15] At the very beginning of this whole storytelling episode, Mike takes up a "telling" posture or position (chin resting on hand, with elbow planted on table) at just the point at which the telling proper initially gets underway (Appendix 1: 045): "Evidently Keegan musta bumped im. . ." When Gary and Phyllis join forces to subvert the initial auspices under which the story is being told, Mike breaks out of this position (at his second response to Gary's intervention [Appendix 1: 052], "I don't kno:w") and spins around toward Gary (as Gary is saying "they-spun aroun th' tra:ck"). When he resumes the telling (Appendix 1: 065–6) – with "This: De Wa::ld spun ou:t" – he assumes a modified form of the same telling position, which he thereafter sustains (except for excursions of hand gestures, which however return to the same "home" position) until the end of this "So it ended up . . ." utterance. At its end (138), in "with a ja:ck," he breaks the posture and picks up his beer can.[16]

This increment of telling is thus marked in various ways as Mike's ending for the story, one which seems designed to embody **his** version of its key incident – that is, as a dramatic and truly violent one.

Several responses from others collaborate in marking uptake of this increment as a possible end of the story proper.

```
133   Curt:     [Dat see dat re]minds me of, ⌈we   wz o::,  ⌉
134   Mike:                                  ⌊He wz up on⌋ the.::
135             (0.1)
136   Mike:     trailer hh, er up ⌈on the back of iz pickup truck=
137   Carney:                     ⌊Gary:
138   Mike:     =with a, (0.4) with a ja ⌈ck.
139   Gary:                              ⌊(              cups.)
140   Curt:     Who DeWa:ld?
141   Mike:     DeWa:ld. ⁻Ye(h)ah
142             (0.2)⁻
143   Curt:     Try(h) ina keep (h)evry ⌈body keep f'm ⌉ g(hh)et-=
144   Mike:                             ⌊body  ba:ck  .⌋
145   Mike:     =k(hh)eep imse(h)lf fm gettin iz ass beat.
```

First, Curt. At possible story completion, it is relevant for recipient(s) to display an understanding **that** the story is over and what its upshot or point was (Sacks 1973, 1974). If understanding problems remain, this is a place where they may be raised (Schegloff 1984[1976]: 45–6). Then note, first, that Curt (140) checks his understanding that this last story increment refers to DeWald ("Who, DeWald?").[17] Then he offers his understanding of the import of the last increment (143), which he formats again as a collaboration with Mike's telling (as he had done at the prior point which he had understood as possible story completion, 121). This is produced as an understanding which is collaborative not only in its grammatical format, but in its casting of the scene (as Mike had) as one of potentially serious violence as well. Mike intervenes into the course of this proffered understanding to establish forcefully again the threat of real bodily harm which DeWald faced, both confirming and correcting Curt's collaboration (144–5).

A second evidence that Mike has been recognized as doing story completion is that Carney departs from the conversational cluster at just this point.

But showing understanding that the story is over and showing understanding of the story's import are not the only sequential contingencies prompted by story completion. Jefferson (1978) has shown that participants (a) can be oriented to the resumption of turn-by-turn talk from the state of partial suspension which storytelling will have involved, and (b) can be oriented to showing that the story is implicative for further talk, can generate further talk, and hence was appropriately told in the present context.

Some forms of talk after a story's possible completion can satisfy several of these constraints at once. Telling a second story can show understanding that the prior story is possibly complete; can by the choice and manner of telling the follow-up story display an understanding of the prior story as an assessment of it (as sad, funny, tragic, etc.); can demonstrate the generative force of the prior story in its capacity to motivate a next story, etc. Other forms of talk may do these jobs as well – on-topic talk derived from the point of the story or the characters (or other elements) in the story, for example. Given the methodically accountable features of Mike's talk as a designed ending of the story, and the recognition/ratification of that completion by Mike and Carney, we can focus on how the story's sequelae satisfy these relevant contingencies.

Before doing so, however, it may be useful to recall the circumstances under which this story came to be told. Curt had proffered as a topic (Appendix 1: 001) the races which Mike had attended the previous evening. Initially Phyllis does not talk in this sequence, but after several exchanges she enters (Appendix 1: 015), with an utterance designed at least in part to "do 'boring'" (apparently targetted at the report of the same fellow winning all the time, which it directly follows; cf. Schegloff 1987b: 109–10).

When the talk comes to be preoccupied with which drivers are in competition and what cars they are driving (or, as they say, "running"), Phyllis intervenes with "Mike siz there wz a big fight down there las' night," as if to rescue the conversation from the boredom with which she has already displayed herself to regard the races and this talk of them to something possibly more exciting (a "big fight"), even if it is a story which she has heard before (and even if, as Goodwin [1986: 293] shows, the whole domain of talk, and manner of talking, is for men and not for women). And now the issue is, on completion of the story, whether it can generate further talk, including (eventually) a return to turn-by-turn talk.

4.2   After the telling

Directly on completion of Mike's version of the upshot of the proper understanding of his story's completion, Curt and Phyllis simultaneously start possible sequelae (146–7).

```
145  Mike:      =k(hh)eep imse(h)lf fm gettin iz ass beat.
146  Curt:      ⌈We:ll      ⌈you w-
147  Phyl:      ⌊Mike said ⌊'e usetuh:⌋::=
148  (Carney):  =⌈° (Oh).
149  Phyl:      =⌊race go⌈carts en 'e got barred f'm the go-=
150  Mike:              ⌊He use-
151  Phyl:      =cart track be ⌈cuz he ra:n little ⌈kids (h)off=
152  Mike:                     ⌊over  in Tiffen. ⌋
153  Phyl:      =the tr(h) a⌈ck,
154  Curt:                  ⌊hh ⌈hhhhhh ⌉
155  Mike:                      ⌊That's a-⌋ that's a fact.=
156  Phyl:      = ⌈·hhh
157  Mike:      = ⌊'n-
158  Mike:      D⌈eWa:ld is a  big burly ((silent)) basterd=
159  Curt:       ⌊Jeezuz.
                                ⌈
160  Phyl:                      ⌊·hhhh hhehhhhhhehheh,
161  Mike:      =⌈jihknow.
162  Curt:      =⌊Mmhm,
163  Phyl:      hh⌈hheh
164  Mike:        ⌊En that's a fact he got barred from runnin go
165             carts o⌈ver in Tiffen because he usetuh run the=
166  Phyl:              ⌊°ohhh
167  Mike:      =little kids off the track.=
168  Curt:      =Well you remember when McKuen did that,
169             (0.2)
170  Mike:      ⌈Yeh.
171  Curt:      ⌊Lo:ng time ago it reminds me when you were tellin
172             about, DeWald en uh s:sittin up there'n, pst!
173             (3.7)
```

Curt begins (146) with "We:ll you w-," an utterance which on a subsequent repetition (line 168) will be revealed to be the start of "Well you remember when . . .," the "w" being the first formant of the "r" sound. Enough of this utterance start comes out to suggest that Curt is trying again the post-story-completion tack he has tried before (line 133), "dat reminds me of . . ." On that try, Curt found himself in overlap with Mike's effort to produce a story completion. On this try, he finds himself in overlap with Phyllis, who is launching a follow-up story of her own. Once again, Curt yields to his partner in overlap.

Phyllis' follow-up topicalizes one of the characters in the prior story, DeWald, the character on whom the story had ended, its villain, and, drawing again on Mike as story source, she tells a further story of his villainy. For brevity, we will omit here an explication of the ways in which Mike enters recurrent claims to this story (which, after all, was attributed to him) in the course of its telling, and then (164–7) reprises that telling on its completion by Phyllis.[18]

Suffice it to note that directly on completion of Mike's reprise of the story, Curt returns (line 168) with yet another effort to tell his second story. The second story he has to tell is a follow-up **not** to Phyllis' sequel, but to Mike's initial story. Curt shows this first by using the identical words in launching this telling as he had used in launching the last try, including the turn-initial marker "well" ("Well you remember . . ."). Secondly, Curt shows this (171–2) by explicating the source of his second story: ". . . it reminds me when you were tellin about, DeWald en uh s:sittin up there'n," (and note that the "it reminds me" echoes the first try at this "being reminded" – "see dat reminds me of . . ." at line 133).

Note then, first, that this deprives Phyllis' sequel of its capacity to serve as a link in a progressive movement of the talk away from the initial story in the episode. In being another "next" to the **first** story, Curt sequentially deletes Phyllis' contribution to generating a further line of talk and, in effect, replaces it with his own. Note, secondly, that in this regard his own contribution is a dismal failure. To its first part, Mike replies minimally (and after a gap), "Yeh" (170). After its continuation and source-citation, there is nothing. In the 3.7 seconds of silence (an exceptionally long silence in conversation) there is alarming evidence of the failure of Mike's story to be returned to turn-by-turn talk, or indeed, to engender any further talk of any kind.

Into this conversational vacuum leaps Gary, the remaining recipient of Mike's story, with a resource of the same sort as was drawn on by Phyllis. Phyllis' sequel had drawn on one of the characters in the original story, DeWald; Gary draws on the other, Keegan.

```
173                    (3.7)
174    Gary:           'N Keegans aren't (always) very big are they?
175                    (0.4)
176    Curt:           No. They're a ll thin.
177    Mike:                       [They're not] they're not
178                    to o bi:g but-
179    Gary:               [° ('T's right if) they're all Keegans like the
180                    ones around Greensprings they're all kind'v,
181                    [ 'bout   five   five,   five   si x,
182    Mike:           [They're all from around Greensprin gs.
183    Curt:                                              Ye h,
184    Mike:                                                [Yeah.
185    Mike:           They're the ones, mm- hmh-hmh-hmh-hmh- -hmh
186    Gary:                               [O:h.            [hhOh my
187                    Go::d that's a, topnotch society over the:re,
```

```
188   Curt:      eh heh heh
189   Mike:      ((sniff // sniff))
190   Gary:      eh-heh-heh eh(h) livi⌈n aroun Bidwell en=
191   Mike:                          ⌊Yea:h,
192   Gary:      =Greensprings (with th(h) e ⌈be(h)st) · hhh hh
193   Mike:                                  ⌊We:ll,
194   Gary:      They got nice ca:rs th.
195   (    ):    ° (Yeh)
196              (3.0)
197   Gary:      ((clears throat))
198              (0.5)
199   Gary:      Fraid tih g- (0.2) ((swallow)) go down there after
200              da:rk, specially walking. hh
201              (0.6)                          .
202   Curt:      ((ve)) Ahhhhhhh
203              (1.7)
204   Curt:      Well Doug isn't too bad a gu:y,
205   Mike:      No.
206   Mike:      His bro⌈ther's a   ⌉ n-=
207   Curt:            ⌊He usetuh,⌋
208   Mike:      =(Yeh) brother's a pretty nice guy I
209              ⌈spoze probly the younger kids thet'r raisin hell=
210   Curt:      ⌊I::-
211   Mike:      =over there,
212              (0.5)
213   Curt       I kn⌈ow.I d- ⌉ I know Dou:g=
214   Gary:         ⌊No: they-⌋
215   Curt:      =⌈en he isn't,
                 ⌊
```

Although in many ways a disaster, Gary's efforts are precisely attuned to the sequential demands of the interaction. In his drawing on Keegan as a topical resource for follow-up, he retrieves the relevance of Phyllis' follow-up as well, for his question "Keegans aren't (always) very big are they?" seems to draw not only on the initial story but on a component of Mike's reprise of Phyllis' sequel (line 158), "DeWa:ld is a big burly basterd."

Although sequentially successful in temporarily restoring turn-by-turn talk, Gary's sequel is an interactional disaster. His ignorance is revealed at virtually every point (cf. C. Goodwin 1986: 289–93 on Gary's lack of knowledge in this area) – on the size of the Keegans, on where they come from, in the negative assessment of the Keegans (186–7, 199–200), which is rejected by Mike and Curt.[19] From these rebuffs Gary escapes into a story about twins who live in the same area – but are not Keegans, a story told very haltingly, with many hesitations and little uptake from its audience, a story implicating possible adultery (the theme from which the earlier discussion of the races has tried to free itself), and in various other ways infelicitous. It gets token laughs from Mike and Curt.

```
213  Curt:      I kn ow. I d-     I know Dou:g-
214  Gary:         No: they-
215  Curt:      = en he isn't,
216  (    ):       C'mon over here en git  (                    )
217  Gary:                                   There's twins thet-
218             (0.8)
219  Gary:      twins thet live over there, they're younger (yuh) –
220             (prolly) twunny three twunny four years old,
221             (1.2)
222  Gary:      Round Carney's age'n,
223             (1.3)
224  Gary:      They work over et the pla:nt. · (          )
225             (2.0)
226  Gary:      The khhh, th(h)e(h)e wuh- The o:ne:: t'win's wife
227             come right'n the plant one night'n wanna know
228             who in the hell the girl was thet'er husbin
229             wz spe nnin the   night with evry night after work.=
230  Curt:       hmh   hmh-hmh
231  Gary:      =mh- heh
232  Curt:           nhh hn hhuh hu h huh
233  Gary:                         heh heh
234  Mike:                         Hhmmm.
235  Curt:      (She          )?
236  Curt:      hu:h  hu:h huh-huh
237  Gary:           (She                    I don'know what=
238  Curt:                                   huhh
239  Gary:      =she wannit with it),
240             (1.0)
241  Gary:      Ahhhhh!
242             (2.0)
243  Pam:       You all will have tuh  carry on without us fer a=20
244  Gary:                             Went home after work from
245             then on I guess,
246  Pam:       =minute.
247  Mike:      Mhhhhmmhhmmmmm
248  Curt:      he::h heh heh heh-eh heh
249  Mike:      ·hheh hh
250  Curt:      Keegan usetuh race uhr uh- er ih was um, (0.4)
251             usetuh run um,
252             (2.7)
253  Curt:      Oh:: shit.
254             (0.4)
255  Curt:      Uhm,
256             (0.4)
257  Curt:      Fisher's car.
```

Although this story is problematic in various ways, it **is** followed by
turn-by-turn talk, talk which it engenders by having keyed on Keegan.

However, the turn-by-turn talk which it sets off (250ff.) is a return precisely to the talk out of which Phyllis had drawn the conversation by "staging" Mike's story about the fight – who is driving what car (Appendix 1: 017–34).

That the talk has come full circle is most exquisitely represented in a small detail – Curt's shift (250–1) from the phrase "usetuh race" to the phrase "usetuh run." To show how this is consequential, a brief digression will be necessary to make clear how choice of terms can be seen to matter to this talk occasion.

In his treatment of the "big fight" storytelling episode and talk of the races more generally, C. Goodwin (1986: 290–3) showed that talking with expertise in this domain is embodied in part in the selection of the words which implement the talk. And he showed as well that Gary is, in general, incompetent in this area, and tries to imitate the others. Thus, in the talk just preceding Phyllis' launching of Mike's story, Curt and Mike use three terms for the activities of the drivers at the races: going/being out there (e.g. line 018–20, "Keegan's out there"), doin' real good (e.g. line 026–7, "M'Gilton's doin real good"), and runnin (e.g. line 030, "Oxfrey runnin"). When Curt and Mike have just spoken of some drivers as being "**out there,**" Gary introduces his relative into the discussion (line 025) with "My brother in law's **out there**"; when they have switched to "**runnin**," Gary makes his next try to introduce his brother-in-law into the talk (line 032) as "Hawkins is **runnin**." And this utterance, and its interruption by Mike (line 033–4) with "Oxfrey's **runnin** the same car 'e run last year," are what immediately precede Phyllis' "Mike siz there wz a big fight. . ."

That is, just preceding the story, the talk was about activity at the race track; it was being formulated in terms of **runnin** cars; and the use of this term was understood by Gary as sufficiently relevant as to modify his talk to incorporate it.

Let us now return to the end of Gary's follow-up story about the twins and to Curt's reversion to talk about drivers and their cars. Having begun (250) "Keegan usetuh race . . .," Curt self-interrupts as he begins a search for the name of the car's owner, but in the course of the search he reverts to the choice of terminology which had been in effect earlier, "usetuh run uhm." However subtle, the choice of this implementing lexical item betokens quite clearly that the talk has returned to the state from which it departed with "Mike siz there wz a big fight . . . las' night."

It is at this juncture, with this evidence that her effort to launch a diversion from this topic (with the "big fight" story) some 4¼ minutes earlier has failed to sustain itself, that Phyllis undertakes the "unilateral departure" which Goodwin has so delicately described.

Although the departure itself is built to be detached from the surrounding sequential and interactional organization, if we ask "why that now" (Schegloff and Sacks 1973: 299) at a somewhat grosser level of sequential organization,[21] we can locate this departure at the point at which an interactional project or undertaking has shown itself to have failed. It is so located by reference to a determinately shaped sequential structure, built on the underlying armature not of adjacency pairs but of storytelling sequences, located at a place where a sequence-organizational contingency of storytelling sequences has shown itself to have not been met.

Virtually **nothing** in Goodwin's account of "unilateral departure," or of **this** unilateral departure, needs to be changed by virtue of this sequence-organizational contextual account. Perhaps only a small twist would be appropriate.

Goodwin writes near the end of his account (1987: 213) that Phyllis' departure runs the risk of casting aspersions on the conduct of the conversational cluster which she is leaving:

> . . . such a noticeable action may have the effect of focusing attention on the fact that those she is with are not providing for her inclusion in their talk, i.e., her departure from the cluster could be seen as responsive to the way that she is being treated by the others in the cluster. The talk that she produces while leaving undercuts such a possibility by providing not simply an account for the departure but *the* official account for why she is leaving.

The twist one might add is that perhaps her departure is indeed to be understood as a response to developments in the talk of her cluster. The talk which she produces while leaving provides a cover – exquisitely constructed and built into a whole course of action, as Goodwin shows – but nonetheless a cover, whose viability requires just that studied disattention which Goodwin documents.

So, there **is** a determinate interactional project being sustained through this talk. It **is** embodied in describable practices of talking. The target occurrence **is** situated at a strategic juncture in that course of action. Specifically, there is an expanded storytelling sequence being sustained in this segment of interaction; its participants are engaged in trying to bring it to a satisfactory conclusion; the departure is situated at the moment when the sequential aftermaths of the storytelling come to an end. In disengaging her departure from the ongoing activities of the interactional episode which she is leaving, it is precisely the relevance of these activities and this juncture in them for her leaving which may be being masked by Phyllis. But the consequence of all this need not be, and here is not, a transformation of the previous analysis of the departure. Sometimes a context is just a context.

5   Closing

At its worst, "context" is deployed as a merely polemical, critical tool. In this usage, it is roughly equivalent to "what I noticed about your topic that you didn't write about." With that club, I can relativize what you have to say by reference to what I have noticed or know about or care about, potentially diminish or obliterate what you have offered and put what I have offered center stage. This is partially facetious, but only partially.

On the one hand, the notion of "context" can be understood as a kind of formal orientation of practical actors – participants in the scenes of their everyday lives. Sacks once referred to members' (i.e. persons') orientation to the "in-principle settinged character" of everyday life, including talk. That is, talk and other ordinary conduct are informed by a principled orientation to the setting-specificity of their undertakings.

On the other hand, in any particular scene, on any particular occasion, moment-by-moment, this formal orientation is "filled in" by particulars, is implemented or realized in particular contextual orientations. Our access to these particular contextual orientations as social science analysts is, in principle, the same as those of real-world co-participants: they (the orientations) infiltrate and permeate and enter constitutively into the talk and other conduct of each participant, and are thereby made accessible to others for uptake.

To be sure, the resources which an academic analyst brings to their recognition may be different in various respects from those available to co-participants. For this there is no remedy. (But we should bear in mind that the disparity involves for the analyst not only deficits but also potential virtues – such as freedom from participant blindspots, either those cultivated by the history of a relationship, or by cultural induction of studied disattention). Surely there is no appropriate remedy in freeing the analysis of context from the constraint that it be subject **in the first instance** to contingencies that the parties seem oriented to, not to ones which preoccupy academic or political commitments.

"Demonstrable relevance to the participants" continues to seem the most compelling warrant for claims on behalf of context. Any prospective context which can be so warranted – including the ones of both classical and contemporary social theory – earns its way into the arena of analysis. Otherwise, its status remains profoundly equivocal. Because the evidence of relevance of any order or type of context will be found "on the scene" so to speak – **in** the talk and conduct – there is reason to believe that interest in **all** sorts of context will be well served by enhancing our understanding of the immediate or proximate contexts in which all conduct is situated.

The upshot is that "rethinking context" is not a task for single convention sessions or special volumes alone. If "context" is **in** the conduct itself, if it **is** in a sense the conduct itself, then rethinking context is the omnipresent job of analysis.

Appendix 1

```
001  Curt:       (W—) how wz the races las'night.
002              (0.8)
003  (    ):     (Ha-[ uh )  ]=
004  Curt:          [Who w'n] [ th'feature. ]
005  Mike:                   =[ Al won,    ]
006              (0.3)
007  Curt:       [(Who) ]-
008  Mike:       [ Al.  ]=
009  Curt:       =Al did?
010              (0.4)
011  Curt:       Dz he go out there pretty regular?
012              (1.5)
013  Mike:       Generally evry Saturdee.
014              (1.2)
015  Phyllis:    He wins js about evry Saturday too.
016  Curt:       He- he's about the only regular <he's about the
017              only good regular out there'z, Keegan still go out?
018  Mike:       Keegan's,
019              (0.2)
020  Mike:       out there he's,
021  Mike:       He run,
022              (0.5)
023  Mike:       E:[ r  he's  uh::         ]
024  Gary:         [Wuhyih mean my:,
025  Gary:       My [ brother in law's out there,        ]
026  Mike:          [doin  real  good  this  year'n] M'Gilton's doing
027              real good thi[s year,
028  Curt:                    [M'Gilton still there?=
029  Gary:       =hh Hawki[ns,
030  Curt:                [Oxfrey runnin-I heard Oxfrey gotta new
031              ca:r.
032  Gary:       Hawkins is ru[nnin.
033  Mike:                    [Oxfrey's runnin the same car 'e run
034              last year,=
035  Phyl:       =Mike siz there wz a big fight down there las' night,
036  Curt:       Oh rilly?
037              (0.5)
038  Phyl:       With Keegan en, what. Paul [DeWa::ld?        ]
039  Mike:                                  [Paul deWal]d. Guy out of,=
040  Curt:       =DeWa:ld yeah I[ (°know ] 'm.)=
041  Mike:                      [Tiffen. ]
042  Mike:       =D'you know him?
043  Curt:       ·Uhhuh=I know who 'e i:s,
```

```
044                     (1.8)
045     Mike      Evidently Keegan musta bumped im in the,
046                     (0.6)
047     Gary:     W'wz it la:st week sumpn like th't
048               ha pp'n too?
                     [
049     Mike:         Ohno:, thi s:
                              [
050     Gary:                Somebody bumped somebody else'n
051               they- spun    aroun th'tra: ck
                  [            [           [
052     Mike:     I don't know.        Oh that wz::uh
053               a 'week be fore last in the late models
                            [
054     Phyl:              (Yeh they'd be doin'it) en den ney go
055               down'n ney thrrow their hhelmets off'n nen n(h)ey
056               l:lo ok-et each  othe r.
                  [               [   [
057     Mike:     But,             this  =
                                       ]
058     Curt:                            =Ye::h hh heh heh
                                                  [
059     Phyl:                                     · ehhehhhhh
                                                  [
060     Mike:                                     This:: uh:::.
061     Gary:     (They kno:w)              //      ),
062     Phyl:     ehh heh!
                  [
063     Curt:     Liddle high school ki ds,=
                                      [     [
064     Gary:                        (No   matter what  ju:re)
                                           [           [
065     Mike:                         = This,          DeWa::ld
066               spun ou:t. 'n he waited.
067                     (0.5)
068     Mike:     Al come around'n passed im Al wz leadin the
069               Feature,
070                     (0.5)
071     Mike:     en then the sekint- place guy,
072                     (0.8)
073     Mike:     en nen Keegan. En boy when Keeg'n come around he
074               come right up into im tried tuh put im imtuh
075               th'wa:ll.
076     Curt:     Yeh?
077     Mike:     'n 'e tried it about four differn times finally
078               Keegan rapped im a good one in the a:ss'n then
079               th-b- DeWald wen o:ff.
080                     (0.5)
081     Curt:     Mm
                  [
082     Mike:     But in ne meantime it'd cost Keegan three
083               spo:ts'nnuh feature.
084     Curt:     Yeah?
085     Mike:     So, boy when Keeg'n come in he-yihknow how he's
086               gotta temper anyway, he js::: ·wa:::::::h
087               sc reamed iz damn e:ngine yihknow,
                  [
088     Curt:     Mm
089                     (0.5)
090     Mike:     settin there en 'e takes iz helmet off'n clunk it
091               goes on top a' the car he gets out'n goes up t'the
```

```
092              trailer 'n gets a °god damn iron ba:r? .hhh rraps
093              that trailer en away he starts t'go en evrybuddy
094              seh hey you don't need dat y'know, seh ye:h yer
095              righ'n 'e throws ┌that son'vabitch down- .hhhhhhh
096   Curt:                      └·Mm hm hm
097   Mike:     So they all ┌go dow┌n
098   Gary:                 └A:ll   └All show.
099              (0.2)
100   Carney:   Yeah, th┌ey all, =
101   Mike:             └They all-
102   Gary:     =hn-┌-hn!
103   Mike:         └They all go down th┌ere,=
104   Gary:                             └·Gimme a
105              ┌beer Curt,
106   Mike:     └-N┌o some  somebuddy so:mebuddy,    ┐
107   Carney:      └It reminds me of those wrestl(h) ┘ ers..hhh
108   Mike:     So:me┌body ra:pped=
109   Carney:        └hhh(h) on t(h)elevi┌sion. ° (      ).
110   Gary:                       = └Bartender  how   about   a
111              beer. While yer settin ┌there.
112   Carney:                           └·(        ).
113   Mike:     So:mebuddy rapped uh:.
114   Curt:     ·((clears throat))
115   Mike:     DeWald'nna mouth.
116   Curt:     Well, h┌e deserved it.        ┐
117   Mike:            └But yihknow eh-┘ uh-he made iz first
118              mistake number one by messin with Keegan
119              because a'pits'r fulla Keegans en when there
120              is┌n't a Keegan there ere's a'Fra:nks,
121   Curt:       └°Mmhm,                    └There's a'Fra:nks,
122   Mike:     (      )=
123   Curt:     └(I kno┌w.)
124   Mike:            =└Because they'relatedjih kno┌w?
125   Curt:                                         └((clears throat))
126              (0.8)
127   Mike:     ((cou┌gh))
128   Curt:          └Oh that's (screwy at-)
129              (0.2)
130   Mike:     So it ended up thet-
131              (0.2)
132   Mike:     d┌e t    u h : .        ┐
133   Curt:      └Dat see dat re┘minds me of, ┌we   wz o::, ┐
134   Mike:                                   └He wz up on┘the.::
135              (0.1)
136   Mike:     trailer hh, er up ┌on the back of iz pickup truck=
137   Carney:                     └Gary:
138   Mike:     =with a, (0.4) with a ja┌:ck.
139   Gary:                             └(              cups.)
```

```
140   Curt:      Who DeWa:ld?
141   Mike:      DeWa:ld. Ye(h)ah
142              (0.2)
143   Curt:      Try(h)ina keep (h)evry┌body keep f'm ┐g(hh)et-=
144   Mike:                            └body  ba:ck . ┘
145   Mike:      =k(hh)eep imse(h)lf fm gettin iz ass beat.
146   Curt:      ┌ We:ll  ┌ you w-          ┐
147   Phyl:      └Mike said└ 'e usetuh:┘::=
148  (Carney):   = ┌° (Oh).
149   Phyl:      = └race go┌carts en 'e got barred f'm the go-=
150   Mike:                └He use-
151   Phyl:      =cart track be┌cuz he ra:n little ┌kids (h)off=
152   Mike:                    └over  in  Tiffen. ┘
153   Phyl:      =the tr(h) a┌ck,
154   Curt:                  └hh┌ hhhhhh    ┐
155   Mike:                     └That's a=┘ that's a fact.=
156   Phyl:      =┌·hhh
157   Mike:      =└'n-
158   Mike:      D┌eWa:ld is a┌ big burly  ((silent)) basterd=
159   Curt:       └Jeezuz.    │
160   Phyl:                   └.hhhh hhehhhhhhehheh,
161   Mike:      = ┌jihknow,
162   Curt:      = └Mmhm,
163   Phyl:      hh┌hheh
164   Mike:        └En that's a fact he got barred from runnin go
165              carts o┌ver in Tiffen because he usetuh run the=
166   Phyl:             └.ohhh
167   Mike:      =little kids off the track.=
168   Curt:      =Well you remember when McKuen did that,
169              (0.2)
170   Mike:      ┌Yeh.
171   Curt:      └Lo:ng time ago it reminds me when you were tellin
172              about, DeWald en uh s:sittin up there'n, pst!
173              (3.7)
174   Gary:      'N Keegans aren't (always) very big are they?
175              (0.4)
176   Curt:      No. They're a┌ll  thin.         ┐
177   Mike:                   └They're not┘ they're not
178              to┌o bi:g but-
179   Gary:        └° ('T's right if) they're all Keegans like the
180              ones around Greensprings they're all kind'v,
181              ┌ 'bout    five    five,    five si┌x,
182   Mike:      └They're all from around Greensprin└gs.
183   Curt:                                         └Ye┌h,
184   Mike:                                            └Yeah.
185   Mike:      They're the ones, mm-┌hmh-hmh-hmh-hmh-┌hmh
186   Gary:                           └O:h.            └hhOh my
187              Go::d that's a, topnotch society over the:re,
```

```
188   Curt:      eh heh heh
189   Mike:      ((sniff // sniff))
190   Gary:      eh-heh-heh eh(h) livi┌n aroun Bidwell en=
191   Mike:                           └Yea:h,
192   Gary:      =Greensprings (with th(h) e ┌be(h)st) ·hhh hh
193   Mike:        ·                          └We:ll,
194   Gary:      They got nice ca:rs th.
195   (    ):    ° (Yeh)
196              (3.0)
197   Gary:      ((clears throat))
198              (0.5)
199   Gary:      Fraid tih g- (0.2) ((swallow)) go down there after
200              da:rk, specially walking. hh
201              (0.6)
202   Curt:      ((vl)) Ahhhhhhh
203              (1.7)
204   Curt:      Well Doug isn't too bad a gu:y,
205   Mike:      No.
206   Mike:      His bro┌ther's a    ┌n-=
207   Curt:             └He usetuh,┘
208   Mike:      =(Yeh) brother's a pretty nice guy I
209              ┌spoze probly the younger kids thet'r raisin hell=
210   Curt:      └I::-
211   Mike:      =over there,
212              (0.5)
213   Curt:      I kn┌ow. I d-  ┐    I know Dou:g=
214   Gary:          └No: they-┘
215   Curt:      =┌en he isn't,
216   (    ):     └C'mon over here en git  ┌(                    )
217   Gary:                                └There's twins thet-
218              (0.8)
219   Gary:      twins thet live over there, they're younger (yuh)-
220              (prolly) twunny three twunny four years old,
221              (1.2)
222   Gary:      Round Carney's age'n,
223              (1.3)
224   Gary:      They work over et the pla:nt. ·(              )
225              (2.0)
226   Gary:      The khhh, th(h)e(h)e wuh- The o:ne:: t'win's wife
227              come  right'n  the  plant  one  night'n  wanna  know
228            · who in the hell the girl was thet'er husbin
229              ┌wz spe┌nnin the ┌night with evry night after work.=
230   Curt:      └hmh   └hmh-hmn┘
231   Gary:      =mh-┌-heh
232   Curt:          │ nhh hn hhuh hu h huh
233   Gary:          │                  ┌heh heh
234   Mike:          │                  └Hhmmm.
```

```
235   Curt:    (She                    )?
236   Curt:    hu:h ⌈ hu:h huh-huh
237   Gary:         ⌊ (She                        ⌈I don'know what=
238   Curt:                                       ⌊huhh
239   Gary:    =she wannit with it),
240            (1.0)
241   Gary:    Ahhhhh!
242            (2.0)
243   Pam:     You all will have tuh ⌈carry on without us fer a=
244   Gary:                          ⌊Went home after work from
245            then on I guess,
246   Pam:     =minute.
247   Mike:    Mhhhhmmhhmmmmmm
248   Curt:    he::h heh heh heh-eh heh
249   Mike:    °hheh hh
250   Curt:    Keegan usetuh race uhr uh- er er ih was um,   (0.4)
251            usetuh run um,
252            (2.7)
253   Curt:    Oh:: shit.
254            (0.4)
255   Curt:    Uhm,
256            (0.4)
257   Curt:    Fisher's car.
258   Mike:    Three en ⌈na  quarter?
259   Curt:             ⌊Thr⌈ee enna quarter.
260   Phyl:               ⌊°Need some more i⌈ce.
261   Mike:                                 ⌊Yeh,
262            (1.0)
263   Curt:    (When I) wz foolin around.
264   Gary:    I usetuh go over there with my cousin. . .
```

Appendix 2

A brief guide to a few of the conventions employed in the transcripts may help the reader in what appears a more forbidding undertaking than it actually is. Some effort is made to have the spelling of the words roughly indicate the manner of their production, and there is often, therefore, a departure from normal spelling. Otherwise:

→   Arrows in the margin indicate the lines of the transcript relevant to the point being made in the text.

( )   Empty parentheses indicate talk too obscure to transcribe. Letters inside such parentheses indicate the transcriber's best try at what is being said.

[ ]   Elongated square brackets indicate overlapping talk; the left-hand bracket marks the beginning of the overlap, the right-hand bracket marks the end.

((points))   Words in double parentheses indicate comments about the talk, not transcriptions of it.

(0.8)   Numbers in parentheses indicate periods of silence, in tenths of a second.

:::   Colons indicate a lengthening of the sound just preceding them, proportional to the number of colons.

-    A hyphen indicates an abrupt cut-off or self-interruptions of the sound in progress indicated by the preceding letter(s).

He says   Underlining indicates stress or emphasis.
°   A degree sign indicates "very quiet."

A fuller glossary of notational conventions can be found in Sacks *et al.* 1974, and in Atkinson and Heritage 1984: ix–xvii.

Acknowledgements

The empirical portions of this chapter have developed in the context of my courses at UCLA over the last dozen years or so. My appreciation goes to cohorts of students for helping to prompt some of what is presented here, and to Charles and Marjorie Harness Goodwin for making available data which they collected, and on which they themselves work, for the benefit of poaching colleagues. For the less empirical portions of the chapter, I have drawn on two previous efforts to deal with the proper treatment of "context" in studies of talk-in-interaction (Schegloff 1987a, 1990). Throughout, I have drawn on the sympathetic and critical readings of Chuck Goodwin and Sandro Duranti, whose suggestions regarding both substance and style have been very helpful indeed.

Notes

1 One basis for this is suggested in Note 4 below.
2 The thrust of the intellectual stance I have in mind here is represented by undertakings such as those (to cite only a few of the major earlier works) of Gumperz and Hymes in anthropology (both together, e.g. 1964 and 1972, and separately, e.g., the interactional sociolinguistics of Gumperz 1971, 1982, and the ethnography of communication of Hymes 1974); Labov (1972) (and **especially 1970) in linguistics; and Garfinkel (1967), Goffman (1964) (among**

others), and Cicourel (1978) in sociology. See also the early collection edited by Giglioli (1972) and the recent one edited by Baugh and Sherzer (1984). Much of the subsequent work on language and conduct in context locates itself in one of these traditions.

3 Ethnographic research may, of course, have been necessary to enable the analyst to recognize the sense and import of such terms as display the relevance of some aspect of context, or to recognize that seemingly ordinary words have such an import. But the relevance of whatever has been learned through fieldwork (or in any other manner) must be warranted as relevant to the participants by reference to details of the conduct of the interaction.

4 Now that we have incorporated the distinction between the participants' view of context and the analyst's, we can entertain a conjecture about one basis for the tendency to invoke rather than explore context. "Context" can appear to be a "horizonal" phenomenon. That is, like the horizon or like peripheral vision, it by definition eludes direct examination; when examined directly, it is no longer peripheral.

However, this is the case only for what context is for **analysts**. What is demonstrably context for the participants in some interaction does not have **its** peripheral or horizonal status changed by being made the focus of direct examination by analysts. Here again we are brought up against the centrality of **establishing** with evidence that something serves as context **for the participants** in the event being studied.

5 Another of my goals in this chapter is to contribute another increment to what has become an entirely unplanned but progressive examination of a longish stretch of talk from an episode of interaction videotaped some fifteen years ago by Charles and Marjorie Goodwin. The past papers in which portions of this stretch of conversation are examined are C. Goodwin (1986, 1987) and Schegloff (1987; 1988: 8–9). Although not designed as a sustained treatment or otherwise coordinated, these papers may be read as partially converging accounts, in some (although variable) detail, of a substantial episode of talk. Closure is far from having been reached. A full transcript of this episode appears as Appendix 1 to this chapter. Some notational conventions are explained in Appendix 2.

6 This identification of the participants is itself subject to the considerations of relevance and consequentiality raised earlier in this chapter, and is warranted by various events which occur in the episode to be examined, which will be discussed in due course. To anticipate, at least briefly, here:

The relevance of the characterization of Phyllis as Mike's wife is provided by her action (Appendix 1: 035) in prompting and staging his telling of a story which she reports him to have earlier told to her. It is the course and aftermath of this story with which the segment of interaction examined here is preoccupied. The tie between Carney and Gary is displayed by their physical positioning throughout the episode (Carney has sat on, and fallen from, Gary's lap, and stands by him throughout the segment considered in the text), and is made possibly consequential by the introduction by Gary of a competing cover interpretation of the story in question, an interpretation with which Carney publicly affiliates (*vis-à-vis* the story's teller, Mike) in the course of the talk (Appendix 1: 107–9).

To the degree that these warrants cannot be more formally developed here because of considerations of space, an element of informality remains in the overall account. I have offered rudimentary indications of the lines along which these characterizations might be warranted in order to ground the claim that they have not been casually introduced and that such warrants are possible.

7 This involves filling in some analysis for portions of this extended episode which have not yet been treated in print in any of the papers previously cited.

8 This, then, is yet another of this chapter's goals – to employ some analytic resources from "the literature" on data somewhat different from those for which they were introduced in order to see how they work . . . and how they can be made to work.

Readers of analyses of conversational material sometimes marvel at how the author has found bits of data which "seem to fit the argument so perfectly" – apparently not entertaining very seriously that the analysis was built to accommodate the data, rather than data being sought out to fit an analysis constructed independently of it. But frequently students and colleagues seek to apply the terms of analysis to other data, data in their own experience, and are unclear about the proper analytic articulation of existing analytic resources and initially apparently divergent data. Perhaps the present analysis can help to see how the analytic thrust of past work can be extracted and found to inform data (and even practices) different from those analyzed by the authors of the prior work.

9 Although I am not proposing here any substantial revision in the accounts of storytelling sequences by Sacks and Jefferson, I am not simply invoking them in the manner attributed to others at the outset of this chapter. On the one hand, in undertaking to employ those resources for the empirical analysis and explication of a stretch of interaction to which they might not initially appear relevant, the present exercise is engaged in a detailed **analysis** of the empirical data as embodying the phenomenon at issue, and not a broad subsumption of the data under some analytic category or rubric. On the other hand, our understanding of the sort of data which these past analyses can illuminate can potentially be expanded, although the text of the chapter does not address itself to this theme explicitly for lack of space.

10 And, as it happens, occurrent; see Appendix 1: 036.

11 Appendix 1: 045, "Evidently Keegan musta bumped im in the (0.6)." Note that this is an interruption even though the teller is momentarily silent in a pause because, among other features of the talk, a unit of turn construction is in progress but is not possibly complete.

12 Goodwin's analysis stops at this point for it marks the end of the portion of the storytelling most relevant to his analytic theme – audience differentiation and its bearing on the telling.

13 Recall that Gary's earlier treatment of the story as over was done by offering an assessment (098).

14 This foreshortening can be seen in several of its features.

 (a) The return to the story does not resume at the point where the telling proper had previously been abandoned. The point of abandonment had been (Appendix 1: 097, 103), "So they all go down (there) . . ." The resumption is (134–7) "He wz up on the trailer . . ."

(b) "Trailer" is immediately self-corrected to "pickup truck" (136). It may be noted that the character "Keegan" is "associated with" the trailer, and it was Keegan at the trailer that was the scenario (Appendix 1: 085–95) immediately preceding the interrupted continuation "They all go down . . ." The reference to "trailer" thus appears to be a perseverance from where the story had been abandoned. The shift to "pickup truck" from "trailer" (and to "jack" from "goddamn iron ba:r," lines 092, 138) marks a jump forward in the action. That Curt has "tracked" this foreshortening he shows by proffering his understanding (140–41) that the "he" being talked of now is "De Wald" and not Keegan.

(c) The phrase "So it ended up thet- . . ." may itself serve as a marker of omission (a suggestion which I owe to Chuck Goodwin).

15 Perhaps it would be useful to make explicit what is otherwise implicit here and elsewhere in the analysis. Although it may be "obvious" to the reader that this is the "end of the story," the task of analysis remains to specify what is done in the talk, or how the talk is done, that **makes it** "the end," and makes it "obvious" (**if** it is obvious – to the participants, that is). So also is it relevant to make analytically explicit what it is about the ensuing talk of the co-participants that shows them to grasp that the story is over, for it is that which will display that grasp to one another as well, and thereby allow the teller to act accordingly.

16 Treatments of posture as marking aspects of the organization of talk and other conduct in interaction (for example, serving as a "frame") may be found, *inter alia*, in Scheflen 1964 and 1973, in various writings in Kendon 1977, and in his contribution to the present volume, and various writings of C. Goodwin, e.g. 1984.

17 Two further observations may usefully complement the text at this point.
First, that Curt produces any responsive utterance at all here can be understood in part as prompted by Mike's continuing to look at him after bringing his talk to completion (cf. C. Goodwin 1981: 108–9).
Second, in the data considered in Schegloff 1984[1976], where possible story completion is also followed by an apparent addressing of an issue of understanding, the final segment of the telling had also been explicitly marked or announced: "It come down to this."

18 Cf. Schegloff (1988b: 8–9) for a brief account.

19 And recall that earlier (line 017) Keegan was the first exception to the assertion that A1 was "the only good regular."

20 This utterance of Pam's does not appear germane to the interaction being described in the text, a possibility raised by Sandro Duranti.

21 Grosser, that is, than the observation (C. Goodwin 1987: 207) that she begins her utterance "Need some more ice" while two others are talking and with no claim on their attention, etc.

References

Atkinson, J. Maxwell, and John C. Heritage (eds.). 1984. *Structures of Social Action*. Cambridge: Cambridge University Press.

Baugh, John, and Joel Sherzer (eds.). 1984. *Language in Use: Readings in Sociolinguistics*. Englewood Cliffs, NJ: Prentice–Hall.

Cicourel, Aaron. 1978. Language and society: Cognitive, Cultural and Linguistic Aspects of Language Use. *Sozialwissenschaftliche Annalen* 2: 25–58.

1987. The Interpenetration of Communicative Contexts: examples from Medical Encounters. *Social Psychology Quarterly* 50(2): 217–26.

Garfinkel, Harold. 1967. *Studies in Ethnomethodology*. Englewood Cliffs, NJ: Prentice–Hall.

Giglioli, Pier Paolo (ed.). 1972. *Language and Social Context*. Harmondsworth: Penguin Books.

Goffman, Erving. 1964. The Neglected Situation. *American Anthropologist* 66(6): 133–6.

1978. Response Cries. *Language* 54: 787–815.

Goodwin, Charles. 1981. *Conversational Organization: Interaction Between Speakers and Hearers*. New York: Academic Press.

1984. Notes on Story Structure and the organization of participation, in Atkinson and Heritage 1984, pp. 225–46.

1986. Audience Diversity, Participation and Interpretation. *Text* 6(3):283–316.

1987. Unilateral Departure, in *Talk and Social Organization*, ed. Graham Button and John R. E. Lee, pp. 206–16. Clevedon, England: Multilingual Matters.

Goodwin, Marjorie Harness. 1982. 'Instigating': Storytelling as Social Process. *American Ethnologist* 9(4): 799–819.

Gumperz, John, 1971. *Language in Social Groups*. Stanford: Stanford University Press.

1982. *Discourse Strategies*. Cambridge: Cambridge University Press.

Gumperz, John, and Dell Hymes (eds.). 1964. The Ethnography of Communication. *American Anthropologist* 66(6), Pt. II.

1972. *Directions in Sociolinguistics*. New York: Holt, Rinehart and Winston.

Heritage, John. 1984. *Garfinkel and Ethnomethodology*. Cambridge: Polity Press.

Heritage, John, and David Greatbatch. 1989. On the Institutional Character of Institutional Talk: The Case of News Interviews, *Discourse in Professional and Everyday Culture*, ed. P. A. Forstorp, pp. 47–98. Linkoping Studies in Communication, University of Linkoping, Sweden. [A shortened version to appear in *Talk and Social Structure* ed. Deirdre Boden and Don H. Zimmerman. Cambridge: Polity Press.]

Hymes, Dell. 1974. *Foundations of Sociolinguistics: An Ethnographic Approach*. Philadelphia: University of Pennsylvania Press.

Jefferson, Gail. 1978. Sequential Aspects of Storytelling in Conversation, in *Studies in the Organization of Conversational Interaction*, ed. Jim Schenkein, pp. 219–48. New York: Academic Press.

Jefferson, Gail, and John R. E. Lee. 1981. The Rejection of Advice: Managing the Problematic Convergence of a 'Troubles-Telling' and a 'Service Encounter'. *Journal of Pragmatics* 5:399–422.

Jefferson, Gail, and Jim Schenkein. 1977. Some Sequential Negotiations in Conversation: Unexpanded and Expanded Versions of Projected Action Sequences. *Sociology* 11: 87–103.

Kendon, Adam. 1977. *Studies in the Behavior of Social Interaction*. Bloomington: Indiana University Press.

Labov, William. 1970. The Study of Language in its Social Context. *Studium Generale* 23: 66–84.

1972. *Sociolinguistic Patterns*. Philadelphia: University of Pennsylvania Press.

Lerner, Gene H. 1987. *Collaborative Turn Sequences: Sentence Construction and Social Action*. Ph. D. dissertation, University of California, Irvine.

Levinson, Stephen C. 1983. *Pragmatics*. Cambridge: Cambridge University Press.

Ryave, Alan L. 1978. On the Achievement of a Series of Stories, in *Studies in the Organization of Conversational Interaction*, ed. Jim Schenkein, pp. 113–32. New York: Academic Press.

Sacks, Harvey. 1973. On Some Puns with Some Intimations, in *Sociolinguistics: Current Trends and Prospects*, 23rd Annual Round Table Monograph Series on Languages and Linguistics, ed. Roger W. Shuy, pp. 135–44. Washington, DC: Georgetown University Press.

1974. An Analysis of the Course of a Joke's Telling in Conversation, in *Explorations in the Ethnography of Speaking*, ed. Richard Bauman and Joel Sherzer, pp. 357–53. Cambridge: Cambridge University Press.

1987. On the Preferences for Agreement and Contiguity in Sequences in Conversation, in *Talk and Social Organization*, ed. Graham Button and John R. E. Lee, pp. 54–69. Clevedon, England: Multilingual Matters.

In press [1964–1972]. *Lectures on Conversation*. Oxford: Basil Blackwell.

Sacks, Harvey, Emanuel A. Schegloff, and Gail Jefferson. 1974. A Simplest Systematics for the Organization of Turn-Taking for Conversation. *Language* 50 (4): 696–735.

Scheflen, Albert E. 1964. The Significance of Posture in Communication Systems. *Psychiatry* 27: 316–21.

1973. *Communicational Structure: Analysis of a Psychotherapy Transaction*. Bloomington: Indiana University Press.

Schegloff, Emanuel A. 1980. Preliminaries to Preliminaries: 'Can I Ask You a Question?' *Sociological Inquiry* 50:104–52.

1984[1976]. On Some Questions and Ambiguities in Conversation, in Atkinson and Heritage 1984, pp. 28–52.

1987a. Between Macro and Micro: Contexts and Other Connections, in *The Micro–Macro Link*, ed. Jeffrey Alexander, pp. 207–34. Berkeley: University of California Press.

1987b. Analyzing Single Episodes of Interaction: An Exercise in Conversation Analysis. *Social Psychology Quarterly* 50(2): 101–14.

1988a. Goffman and the Analysis of Conversation, in *Erving Goffman: Exploring the Interaction Order*, ed. Paul Drew and Anthony Wootton, pp. 89–135. Cambridge: Polity Press.

1988b. Description in the Social Sciences I: Talk-in-Interaction. *Papers in Pragmatics* 2(1/2):1–24.

1989. Reflections on Language, Development and the Interactional Character of Talk-in-Interaction, in *Interaction in Human Development*, ed. Marc Bornstein and Jerome S. Bruner, pp. 139–53. New York: Lawrence Erlbaum Associates.

1990. On the Organization of Sequences as a Source of 'Coherence' in Talk in Interaction, in *Conversational Coherence and its Development*, ed. Bruce Dorval. Norwood, NJ: Ablex.

1991. Reflections on Talk and Social Structure, in *Talk and Social Structure*, ed. Deirdre Boden and Don Zimmerman. Cambridge: Polity Press.

Schegloff, Emanuel A., and Harvey Sacks. 1973. Opening Up Closings. *Semiotica* 7:289–327. Reprinted in *Readings in Sociolinguistics*, ed. John Baugh and Joel Sherzer, pp. 69–99. Englewood Cliffs, NJ: Prentice-Hall.

8   Contextualization and understanding

JOHN J. GUMPERZ

Editors' introduction

John Gumperz is Professor of Anthropology at the University of California, Berkeley, where he has taught since 1956, first in Near Eastern Languages and Linguistics, and then in Anthropology since 1966. From his earlier work in the 1950s on dialect differences and social stratification in Washtenaw County, Michigan, and in a north Indian village community, Gumperz has been constantly dealing with the issue of language contact and linguistic diversity. His more recent interest in issues of bilingualism and interethnic communication is but an extension of his earlier research. Over the last three decades, Gumperz has been concerned with providing both the empirical evidence and the analytical framework for investigating the varied but systematic ways in which language shift both reflects and defines social and cultural boundaries.

In the chapter for this volume, Gumperz starts from the assumption that participants in a communicative event must be able to guide each other's interpretations of what is being said through the seemingly vast if not infinite range of potentially relevant factors and dimensions. The logical notion of "inference" has been extended by students of language use such as Gumperz to refer to those mental processes that allow conversationalists to evoke the cultural background and social expectations necessary to interpret speech. The notion of "contextualization cue" covers any verbal or nonverbal sign that helps speakers hint at, or clarify, and listeners to make such inferences. As discussed in this chapter, contextualization cues include prosodic features such as stress and intonation, paralinguistic features such as tempo and laughter, choice of code and particular lexical expressions. For example, through the way in which a particular word is stressed and hence foregrounded, speakers can convey to the hearers what their expectations are with respect to what is being accomplished through communication.

To illustrate these processes, Gumperz has chosen a case of blatant misunderstanding between a native (British) English speaker and a non-native, albeit fluent, speaker of English from India. As often done in the social sciences (cf. for instance the seminar work by Harold Garfinkel, the founder of ethnomethodology), a failure to apply the appropriate inferential processes is used as an avenue to explore the nature of tools typically employed in successful cases. Like William Labov's work on Black English Vernacular, Gumperz' work is unique for his ability to merge intellectual, social, and moral considerations within his analytical apparatus. Through a combination of textual and cultural analysis, we are shown how powerful certain aspects of speech are in perpetrating rather than resolving misunderstanding. Here issues of semantic coherence merge with questions about personal, social, and racial identity. The ability speakers and hearers have to evoke the contextually appropriate presuppositions (e.g. I am powerless, you are powerful, I am pleading, you are not accepting your role, etc.) is not just a matter of rational choices. The maintenance of cooperation around a common task or activity (e.g. having a conversation about what happened last week) implies an ability to maintain a social as well as moral involvement with our interactional partners. Thus the ability to linguistically define what the context is, or "what's going on'" in the words of Goffman, constitutes a major tool in one's social and economic success in life.

Contextualization and understanding

I use the term "contextualization" to refer to speakers' and listeners' use of verbal and nonverbal signs to relate what is said at any one time and in any one place to knowledge acquired through past experience, in order to retrieve the presuppositions they must rely on to maintain conversational involvement and assess what is intended. The notion of contextualization must be understood with reference to a theory of interpretation which rests on the following basic assumptions:

1. Situated interpretation of any utterance is always a matter of inferences made within the context of an interactive exchange, the nature of which is constrained both by what is said and by how it is interpreted.
2. Inferencing, as Sperber and Wilson (1986), Levinson (1983) and others have noted, is presupposition-based and therefore suggestive, not assertive. It involves hypothesis-like tentative assessments of communicative intent, that is, the listener's interpretation of what the speaker seeks to convey, in roughly illocutionary terms. These assessments can be validated only in relation to other background assumptions, and not in terms of absolute truth value.
3. Although such background assumptions build on extralinguistic "knowledge of the world," in any one conversation this knowledge is reinterpreted as part of the process of conversing so that it is interactively, thus ultimately socially, constructed. Interpretations, in other words, are ecologically constrained by considerations of sequencing, conversational management, and negotiation of meaning, and, since sequencing is by its very nature an interactive process, they are cooperatively made and validated.

These matters are, of course, relatively well known from the recent literature on interaction, discourse (Goffman 1974, Brown and Yule 1983, Levinson 1983), and conversational analysis (Atkinson and Heritage

1984). But, to the extent that discourse and conversational processes have been systematically investigated, analyses tend to rely on separate and often conflicting theoretical premises and methodological procedures. What I want to suggest in this chapter is that by treating verbal exchanges as involving contextualization-based, on-line, discourse-level inferencing rather than just concentrating on regularities of sequential organization across speech exchanges, we can integrate what is best in such divergent approaches into a more general theory of conversational inference. Such a theory should enable us to show how grammatical knowledge and knowledge of language usage and rhetorical conventions enter into the conduct of verbal encounters and to develop an approach to conversational analysis that accounts for the interactive processes that underlie the perception of communicative signs and thus significantly affect understanding and persuasion in everyday conversation.

I will try to document this argument on the basis of an in-depth examination of extracts from a single counseling session. Before turning to the data, let me present a few more details about how the speech signals relevant to contextualization work and how they enter into the communication process.

Contextualization relies on cues which operate primarily at the following levels of speech production:

1. **Prosody**, which I take to include intonation, stress or accenting and pitch register shifts.
2. **Paralinguistic signs** of tempo, pausing and hesitation, conversational synchrony, including latching or overlapping of speaking turns, and other "tone of voice" expressive cues. Although prosodic and paralinguistic signs have received extensive treatment in the recent literature, analysis has for the most part concentrated on clause-level phenomena and has dealt with meaning primarily at the level of expression, that is, the communication of emotion and generalized attitudes. What I want to argue here is that these signs also play an important role in affecting participants' perception of discourse-level coherence, thus influencing interpretation as such.
3. **Code choice** from among the options within a linguistic repertoire (Gumperz 1972), as for example in code or style switching or selection among phonetic, phonological or morphosyntactic options.
4. **Choice of lexical forms** or **formulaic expressions**, as for example opening or closing routines or metaphoric expressions, such as are now being studied in the area of lexical semantics, again primarily at the clause level and at the level of referential semantics. In the sociolinguistic literature, these optional phenomena tend to be studied by means of quantitative methods primarily as social variables at the supra-individual or group level. Yet, when viewed from the perspective of contextualization, they can be seen to provide a significant input to inferential processes.

How do contextualization cues work communicatively? They serve to highlight, foreground or make salient certain phonological or lexical strings *vis-à-vis* other similar units, that is, they function relationally and cannot be assigned context-independent, stable, core lexical meanings. Foregrounding processes, moreover, do not rest on any one single cue. Rather, assessments depend on cooccurrence judgments (Ervin-Tripp 1972, Gumperz 1971) that simultaneously evaluate a variety of different cues. When interpreted with reference to lexical and grammatical knowledge, structural position within a clause and sequential location within a stretch of discourse, foregrounding becomes an input to implicatures, yielding situated interpretations. Situated interpretations are intrinsically context-bound and cannot be analyzed apart from the verbal sequences in which they are embedded. Moreover, inferences are subconsciously made so that, as Silverstein (1977) points out, they are not readily accessible to recall. It is therefore difficult to elicit information about the grounds upon which particular inferences are made through direct questioning. The relevant interpretive processes are best studied through in-depth, turn-by-turn analysis of form and content.

Contextualization cues enter into the inferential process at several degrees of generality. Minimally, it is necessary to recognize three distinct levels. First, there is the perceptual plane at which communicative signals, both auditory and visual, are received and categorized. This involves more than the mere mapping of sounds into strings of phonemes and morphemes. What is perceived must be chunked into information units or phrases before it can be interpreted. The nature of the transitions between phrases and the type of relationship of one phrase to another must be determined. Other phenomena such as what students of prosody call "accenting," as well as shifts in pitch register and tempo and the like also belong here. Inferences at this perceptual level are first of all relevant to what conversation analysts call "conversational management." As such they serve to provide information on such matters as possible turn construction units (whether or not a speaker is about to complete a turn or needs more time to talk), foregrounding or backgrounding of items of information, separating shared or known items from new information, distinguishing between main points and qualifying information or side sequences. It is necessary to speak of inferencing in discussing these matters because previous analyses have shown that perception of the relevant signs and of their signaling value varies even among speakers of the same language (Gumperz, Aulakh, and Kaltman 1982: 32ff).

The second level is that of local assessments of what conversational analysts call "sequencing" and what from a pragmaticist's perspective one might refer to as "speech act level implicatures." Inferences at this level yield situated interpretations (Cook–Gumperz 1977) of what I have called "communicative intent" (Gumperz, Aulakh, and Kaltman 1982, Gumperz,

Kaltman, and O'Connor 1984). Both direct inferences and indirect or metaphoric inferences that go beyond what is overtly expressed through lexical content are included here.

Third, there is the more global level of framing, which, to use Goffman's terms, signals what is expected in the interaction at any one stage. I use the term "activity" here to account for the fact that contextualization may raise expectations about what is to come at some point beyond the immediate sequence to yield predictions about possible outcomes of an exchange, about suitable topics, and about the quality of interpersonal relations. The assumption is that such global predictions or expectations provide the grounds against which possible ambiguities at the perceptual or sequential levels can be resolved. It goes without saying that this separation into three levels is primarily an analytical strategy which serves to call attention to some of the complexity of the inferential processes; in everyday interaction, these levels merge. Participants themselves are concerned with their situated interpretations of what they hear.

I will illustrate these issues on the basis of my analysis of the data itself. But first some ethnographic background. The conversation discussed here takes the form of a heated and at times highly argumentative discussion recorded in fall 1976 while I was associated with an adult education center in Britain as a sociolinguistic consultant. The participants are "Lee," an ESL (English as a Second Language) instructor in her early thirties who also serves as curriculum planner and student advisor, and "Don," a student in his mid-forties. Don was applying for admission to a newly organized course on interethnic communication which was to be offered at the nearby E Community College. Lee is one of a group of ESL specialists who had jointly planned the course and she is scheduled to give guest lectures when it is offered at E College. In addition, she has also taken on the job of distributing information about the course at her home institution, the adult education center. Although Don holds a degree in political science from a university in India, he has, since his arrival in Britain in the early 1960s, worked as a manual laborer. He had applied for several white-collar positions but so far without success. In order to gain the background he feels he needs, he is now enrolled as a student both at the adult education center and at E College. At the time of the discussion, he is taking an advanced adult center course on communication skills for non-native speakers of English employed in industry. This is referred to in the conversation as the "Twilight course." After his Twilight instructor announced the new E College course in class, Don had telephoned Lee to ask for application forms. She agreed to send him the forms when they became available but went on to tell him that she did not think that Don was a suitable applicant for the new course. Sometimes later, while visiting the E College campus, Don discovered that the forms were already available there. He obtained a form and submitted his application. He then called Lee again and asked her why she had not sent him the forms as she had said she would. An appointment was made to clarify the matter in a face-to-face meeting in Lee's office. It is the tape-recording of this meeting made by one of the two participants which is examined here.

In my analysis of the transcript, I will adopt the strategy of examining the same data successively from several distinct perspectives. I will begin with a brief discussion of the transcription symbols used to create analyzable written texts from the raw tapes. Following Ochs (1979), I assume that all transcription is selective and motivated by analytical goals. My goal here is to set down on paper all those signs which, on the basis of my analysis of the interaction as a whole, I can assume participants rely on in their on-line processing of information – signs, that is, that demonstrably enter into participants' perceptions of interpretive frames (a subset of the total list given in Appendix A at the end of the chapter). I use the term "contextualization cue" to refer to these signs (Gumperz 1982). The assumption is that conversationalists' responses are ultimately based on empirically detectable signs, but that such raw perceptions enter into inference via cooccurrence judgments based on simultaneous cognitive processing of information at multiple signaling levels. In identifying such cues, I initially build on experience gained through previous systematic analyses of what speakers respond to in making contextualization judgments. The initial hypotheses of what the relevant cues are are then validated or disconfirmed on the basis of how well they explain our analysis of the interaction's interpretive outcomes.

The basic assumption that guides my transcription is that participants process speech not in terms of individual words or syntactically defined phrases, clauses or sentences as such but in terms of what phoneticians interested in speech perception have called breath or intonation groups, and what discourse analysts refer to as idea units (Chafe 1980) or information units. For the purposes of this discussion, I will use the term "informational phrase." Prototypically the best way to characterize such an informational phrase is on the basis of prosody as a rhythmically bounded chunk consisting of a lexical string that falls under a single intonation contour which is set off from other such units by a slight pause and constitutes a semantically interpretable syntactic unit. I want to argue that speakers chunk the stream of speech into processing units on the basis of cooccurrence judgments that build on prosody and rhythm, as well as on syntactic and semantic knowledge. As is true of prototype phenomena in general, not all these features need to be present at the same time. In marginal cases, determination of the phrase boundaries depends on what phrase divisions make sense in terms of the organization of the surrounding discourse.

Here is a list of the most important contextualization cues that enter into the present analysis. A complete list is given in Appendix A.

Phrase-final cues. Information units are bounded intonationally by phrase-final tune. In this transcript, I distinguish between (1) slight fall ("/"), which, although it indicates a separate unit, suggests that there is more to come, (2) final fall ("//"), which marks relative completion, (3) slight rise (","), as occurs in listing a number of separate items that form part of a larger whole, (4) final rise ("?"), as in questioning, and (5) truncated unit ("–"), strings that are interrupted before completion and are prosodically marked through various cues suggesting incompleteness. In some cases though not in the case of the present materials, it becomes necessary to distinguish one additional type of phrase-final tune, a holding intonation in which the tone neither falls nor rises.

Interphrasal transitions. In most conversations, transitions between phrases or turns are characterized by small breaks that are fairly constant in duration. When this is the case, no special symbol is used. It should be noted however that pausing is not essential for separating out informational phrases. In many instances, particularly in a single turn of speaking, the rhythmic and accentual features of phrasing alone enable us to recognize an informational phrase. (See, for example, the discussion about line (1L) of the transcript below.) Pauses of one second or more are transcribed by indicating the approximate number of seconds elapsed in angle brackets, e.g. "⟨2⟩." Pauses of up to 0.5 seconds are indicated by two dots and pauses of between 0.5 and 1 second are indicated by three dots. Latched turns, that is, those that follow immediately upon the previous turn with less than the expected break, are indicated by "==" at the beginning of the latching turn. Overlap, that is, the simultaneous production of speech by more than one participant, is marked by a single "=" before and after the overlapping stretches of talk.

Intraphrasal cues. Studies of English intonation have shown that within each phrase at least one syllable is set off from others by instrumentally difficult to segment but interactionally relevant combinations of loudness, pitch obtrusion, or change in amplitude. Following established practice, I will refer to this phenomenon as "accent." The present transcripts mark only those accents which are not readily predictable from English syntax by placing a "*" before the relevant syllable. For extra prominence, upper-case type is used. Other frequently used significant cues include shifts in pitch register, tempo, and loudness, which can occur either inter- or intraphrasally. They are marked in the transcript by special symbols, such as "hi," "lo," "ac" (accelerated) and "dc" (decelerated), and "f" (loudness), in square brackets, with curly brackets bounding the lexical string over which these features occur. No attempt is made to render phonetic detail in this transcript, although where such phenomena as vowel or consonant lengthening, marked intonational contouring, falsetto and staccato speech are found to have signalling import, these should be represented. Parentheses are used to mark unintelligible speech.

The transcript is presented as series of numbered two-part exchanges, with Lee's turn marked with "L" and Don's with "D." A line in the transcript includes one or more phrases which always terminate in one of the above phrase-final markers.

Let me now turn to the initial portion of the transcript to illustrate the way in which the cues enter into the inferential process. The full text is reproduced at the end of the chapter in Appendix B. Italics indicate increased loudness (see below).

```
1D:  this is not a–
1L:  == of *course/ {[ac] it is not a secret//}
2D:         =that it is a secret//=
2L:  (1)  =I haven't "said= it's a secret//
     (2)  {[ac] I didn't say it was a secret//}
     (3)  what I *said was/
     (4)  ..that it was *not a suitable course/ ..for you to *apply for//
     (5)  because it is (  )//
     (6)  .. {[lo] now if you *want to apply for it/}
     (7)  .. {[hi] of *course/} you can do what you *want//
     (8)  but/ {[hi] if you are *doing the twilight course at the *moment/}
     (9)  .. {[lo] it was *not something which–}
     (10) .. Mrs N and Mr G *thought/ *originally/
     (11) that it was a course to carry *on/ *with the *twilight course/
     (12) {[hi] but this is NOT the case//}
```

The recording starts a minute or so into the discussion. Evidently, Don has either directly or indirectly accused Lee of not wanting to send him the information about the E College course and seems to be claiming that she is trying to keep him from registering because she does not think he is qualified. The conversation gives the impression of a heated argument marked by overlap and latching and voices raised with respect to both pitch and volume. The two participants are intent on following their own lines of argumentation, often without attending to the other's contributions. The details of the contextualization processes revealed in the transcript illustrate what it is about the interaction that conveys this impression.

I begin with Lee's response in turn (1L). The initial "of course" is accented and treated as a separate informational phrase. When analyzed solely in terms of syntax, it might appear that "of course" syntactically and semantically qualifies what follows and that only one informational phrase need be recognized. Yet the phrasing and the shift in tempo suggests a division into two units. On this interpretation, (1L) becomes similar to line (7) of turn (2L), "of course, you can do what you want" (with the sole exception that in the latter case, a shift in pitch register is used to separate the two units rather than a shift in tempo). The interpretive consequence in this case is to link the "of course" with the preceding "now if you want to apply for it" rather than with what follows so that the utterance can be paraphrased as, "of course you can, you can do what you want." Applying the same argument to (1L), we can assume that Lee's initial "of course" is intended to refer to one of Don's previous utterances. This makes interpretive sense because the content indicates that Don is accusing Lee of treating the information as a secret as far as he, Don, is concerned, not of claiming that information about the course itself is a secret. So that Lee would not have been likely to respond to Don's "this is not a secret" with a literal "of course, it's not a secret." In (2L) in fact she says explicitly, "I didn't say it was a secret," stressing "say" with a strong accent. This illustrates the methodological point that phrase boundaries are not just "there" empirically, they are constructed and construed to serve rhetorical ends. By contextualizing (1L) as two phrases and accenting "of course," Lee seems to be suggesting that she is either responding to something that has just been said before the recording commences or to something that can readily be inferred from what had been said earlier.

Lee's next speaking turn in lines (2L1–12) reveals the basic features of her contextualization strategies. Note for example that in a number of phrases (e.g. lines 2, 4, 7) double-bar rather than single-bar final contours are used. This along with the strategic deployment of pauses lends the passage a certain air of definiteness. Turning now to (2L1), we note that the first part of Lee's utterance overlaps Don's (2D). She is apparently anticipating what he is about to say. Then having gained the floor, she repeats herself in accelerated tempo. Line (2L3) is followed by a brief, seemingly rhetorical pause which introduces Lee's exposition of her own perspective. Thus the accelerated repetition of "it is not a secret" can be taken as a floor-holding first part of a two-part lead in to the explanation that follows. Although lines (1L)–(2L2) contain four instances of "it is not a secret," each one has a different interpretation, depending on sequential position and how it is contextualized.

Lee begins her explanation in lines (2L3–5) by referring to what she had originally intended to tell Don in the first phone call. Note the positioning of accents. The contrastive accent on "said" in (2L3) mirrors the accent in (2L1) to suggest the paraphrase "what I actually said was." Accent placement on "not" and "apply" in the following line suggests the inference that at the time she had indirectly advised Don against applying. Lee's continued placement of contrastive accents on verbs and predicate qualifiers serves to maintain the tone set in the opening lines throughout the remainder of her speaking turn.

Beginning with line (2L6) the perspective shifts from what Lee had said to the present and to what Don might want to do. This part of Lee's explanation is additionally marked by frequent pitch register shifts. Line (2L6) "now if you want to apply for it," which refers to what Don might do, carries low register. Line (2L7) shifts to high register. (2L8) begins with the connective "but" in neutral register, which is then again followed by another change to high register. The speaker is alternately speaking in her own and in her interlocutor's voice and is using pitch register shifts to signal the contrast. There follows a brief pause and then an aside in (2L9–11) in low register. The explanation concludes in (2L12) with Lee's return to her own main argument, again in high register. The argumentativeness of her talk at this point in the interaction is here further underscored by the extra strong emphasis of "NOT" and by the "DO" later on in (3L). Her speech almost verges on shouting, a clear sign of how annoyed and frustrated she is by her inability to get through to Don.

To sum up, Lee relies on contextualization strategies of contouring and pausing, accenting, and pitch register and tempo shifts among others both to convey information and to give her argument rhetorical force. The relevant contextualization cues affect the signaling process by virtue of the fact that they (1) single out or group together certain sets of items, (2) set them off from the surrounding discourse, and (3) indicate how they are to be interpreted in relationship either to preceding or following units or to background knowledge in such a way as to construct a coherent argument. It is this perceptually based information that, when processed with reference to grammatical and lexical knowledge and sequential positioning, yields situated interpretations.

Now turn to Don's contribution.

 3D: (1) no// what you– you take *one thing at a time*//
    (2) this case// that whatever {[f] *they know*//}
    (3) I get that even .. hmm// for a D .. *me*//
    (4) {[lo] and I am *student in E *College*//}
    (5) and Mr W *knows me*// he// .. I am student in the *same school*//
    (6) {[f] he knows *my qualifications*/} and what– whether I'm suitable *or not*//
    (7) =but=
 3L: =this= has nothing to =DO with qualifications//

Comparison of Don's speech with Lee's preceding turn immediately reveals some systematic differences both in the nature of the contextualization cues employed and in the discourse-level relationships they signal. Note, for example, that Don's phrases for the most part end in double slash boundaries ("//"). He almost never employs (/) and (,) boundaries throughout the entire interaction. That is, his use of phrase-final signaling is less differentiated than Lee's and most probably differs in signaling import. Don's accent, moreover, does not ordinarily fall on a single syllable and, what is more, its phonetic realization is different: either a part of a phrase or an entire phrase is set off from what precedes or follows by a combination of slow tempo, staccato enunciation, and, sometimes, increased loudness. I have used italics to mark the relevant contrasts. Other differences in the use of pitch register shifts will be discussed later.

Clearly Don's contextualization system differs significantly from Lee's. Don's practices, moreover, are not idiosyncratic. In the examples below I have reproduced just a few of the many instances of similar phenomena that we have found in other tapes of Indian–English conversations to suggest that what is at issue here are culturally based differences in contextualization conventions.

Manager of a small firm interviewing a recently hired engineer:

A: how do you like your job//
B: I may tell you that *since joining the firm/* I have been *so happy//*

From an adult education class in which an Indian–English-speaking instructor is talking with a group of Indian–English-speaking students:

A: houses are as we say of three types//
.. detached/ .. a house *which is all by itself/* only *one door//*
and then you have two// semi//
and ah .. all in a row as you say// ... *terrace .. or town houses//*
now which one *would you think//* .. which would be *the cheapest to buy//*
any idea? *terrace house/* semi/ or detached//
B: I think miss// this *terrace house//*
in *England/* the more windows *you have in the house* the more *rates you pay//*
because you get more *sunshine in the house//*

(Gumperz 1982b)

A close analysis of Don's contextualization conventions is beyond the scope of this chapter, since it would require detailed comparisons with the grammar and rhetorical system of his native language. (See Gumperz 1982, Gumperz, Aulakh, and Kaltman 1982 for some preliminary discussions.) For our purposes here, it will be sufficient to concentrate on some of the interpretive consequences of the contrast between Don's and Lee's contextualization practices.

Interpreting communicative intent

Consider the content of Don's response in (3D and 4D).

3D: (1) no// what you– you take *one thing at a time//*
(2) this case// that whatever {[f] *they know//*}
(3) I get that even .. hmm/ for a D .. *me//*
(4) {[lo] and I am *student in E *College//*}
(5) and Mr W *knows me//* he// .. I am student in the *same school//*
(6) {[f] he knows *my qualifications/*} and what–
(7) whether I'm suitable *or not//* =but=
3L: =this= has nothing to =DO with qualifications//=

4D: (1)   ={[f] but you can't know/}=
    (2)   and can't {[f] *tell a person/*} .. just who is to come into *this*
    course//
    (3)   if .. suppose I came to *this course* from uh//
    (4)   .. *(had) you taken this impression//* .. {[lo] that I am *not suitable//*
    (5)   because I took this {[f] *course//*}

Since contextualization conventions are automatically applied without conscious awareness, British-English speakers, relying on their own native-language-based interpretive conventions, are likely to encounter problems in determining how Don's argument coheres. In lines of (3D-1-3) Don corrects himself several times and his remarks are therefore not easy to understand. On close examination, I arrived at the following interpretation, which Don confirmed later when I played him the tape. He begins by saying that he knows as much as "they", thus implying that his background is as good as that of others who will be admitted to the new course. Given this interpretation, a native speaker of English would expect the "I" in line (3D3) to be given more prominence than the "they know" in line (3D2), but in Don's speech the reverse seems to be the case. In line (3D4), Don goes on to introduce new information to the effect that he is already enrolled as a student at E College and that Mr. W. (a lecturer at E College who is also involved in the course) already knows him. Yet, "student in E College" is foregrounded while "I" is spoken in low pitch. On this interpretation, we would have expected the whole phrase to be given prominence. Similarly, in line (3D5) the name of the person who knows Don is backgrounded.

In turn (3L) Lee interrupts without giving Don a chance to finish. He responds by raising his voice and overlapping Lee's turn. When he has regained the floor, he goes on with his previous argument as if nothing had happened. What he is trying to say in this turn is that perhaps she mistakenly believes that because he is currently enrolled in the Twilight course he is not qualified for the new course. Don's way of referring to the two courses illustrates another interesting difference between the two contextualization systems. In lines (4D2–3), "this course" is foregrounded to refer to the Twilight course. In line (4D5) at the end of the turn, only "course" is foregrounded but the reference here is to the new course. In other words, the distinction between the two courses is conveyed only through pitch register and loudness shifts. As native speakers of English, we would expect differentiated syllable accents and additional qualifiers such as "other course" or "new course" to avoid problems of co-referentiality. It seems reasonable to assume that, although Don's sentences are on the whole grammatical, the differences in prosodic conventions may create processing difficulties for listeners relying on the native English contextualization conventions.

The text contains a number of instances that suggest that processing difficulties such as the above lead to serious misinterpretations of Don's intent on Lee's part. For example, when Lee interrupts Don in turn (3L), she focuses on his use of the word "qualifications," which is the last of several items that he foregrounds but clearly not his main point. Don then in turn interrupts and continues his argument where he had left off, whereupon Lee responds by giving more details about who the course was designed for as if course description were what is at issue rather than Don's argument that he as an individual could profit from the course.

4L: (1) but it is a question of the *job you're doing/
  (2) the course is for people/ who are/ {[ac] I'll *tell you/
  (3) it *says on the information//
  (4) {[hi] it's for youth *employment officers,
  (5) it's for members of the *police, it's for uh *teachers,
  (6) it's for people with *management positions,
  (7) {[ac] *those are the people {[hi] who are going to be on the (course//}}
5D: (1) {[hi] it-] {[lo] that's- that *your plan*//}
  (2) uh and ( ) who would benefit and *who would not*/ ah
    =you know/=
5L: (1)   =but {[ac] Mr D/=
  (2) {[hi] it's a TRAINING COURSE for people who are going to do those *jobs//}}
6D: (1) ==and/it lasts *until you say*// {[lo] *also for the people*]
  (2) *who are interested* in this sort oh uh::-
6L: yes//
7D: ==educa =tion//=
7L: =with re=ference to their work//it would be/
8D: ==yes/
8L: ==with reference to their *work//
9D: (1){[lo] (professional) *people*} ( ) them/
  (2) {[hi] or *the people* who are *personally interested*//
9L: why are you so/ {[lo] (unin-)/} you've APPLIED//
10D: yes//

In turn (6D), Don responds to Lee's list of types of suitable candidates by suggesting that the course is also for people who are "interested in this sort of education." That is, he is interpreting Lee's "people who are going to do those jobs" as referring to those who are interested in preparing to go into the relevant professions. Lee then takes advantage of Don's hesitation in turn (6D) to interject "yes" but when he then goes on with a latched "education," Lee once more overlaps, qualifying Don's word "interested" by "with reference to their work," placing extra strong emphasis on "work/" The two are evidently arguing about what is meant by "interested" but if Lee's turn (7L) is a rejection of Don's point, it is at best an indirect one and it is doubtful whether Don understands her. Don then responds with a latched "yes" in turn (8D), whereupon Lee repeats her qualification with less emphasis. She seems to assume that he is confirming her interpretation and that they are now agreed on this point. Don continues in turn (9D) by repeating "professional people" in low pitch register but then he raises his pitch to reiterate his earlier point, "the people who are personally interested," whereupon Lee now becomes very annoyed as if Don had gone back on his agreement, and in turn (10L) she accuses him of acting as if she had insulted him.

> 10L: (1) it doesn't MATTER anymore//
> (2) .. I don't understand/ why you are so INSULTED {[lo] with me//}

Don then denies that he had intended to "insult her," using the phrase "feeling sorry for myself."

> 12D: hmm I'm not *insulting you*// I just hm = feeling *sorry for myself*//=
> 12L: (1)   =no I didn't say you were//=
> (2) but exactly/ why are you feeling so sorry for YOURSELF//

Note that what Don accents here are the last three words of the second phrase. But in her own subsequent question, Lee asks "why are you feeling so sorry for yourself" as if Don had accented "myself." In other words, she is reading his utterance as if the accent had been on a single syllable, which it wasn't. This reinforces her impression that Don is personally offended. The discussion continues in this vein marked alternately by mutual irritation, attempts at repair and serious frustration, ending in Lee's shouted exclamation in (19L).

Although on the surface it would seem that both speakers are talking about the same general issues, they clearly approach these issues from different perspectives. Lee acts as if her own actions were the main issue and insists on explaining her role in the admissions process, while Don, according to his comments in the later follow-up interview, seeks in vain to turn the discussion around to his own professional situation. In spite of several attempts, they are unable to undo what both seem to sense are, in part, misunderstandings and to negotiate a shared perspective. In other words, we are not simply dealing with misunderstandings here but with the failure of the very repair strategies that participants must rely upon to resolve misunderstandings. I hope to have shown that the differences in contextualization conventions play a significant role in this mutual failure.

But there are important aspects of the conversation that need further explanation. If we look at the content of Don's responses, they seem – on the surface at least and from a native English speaking perspective – strangely inconsistent. In (5D) and (6D) he seems to claim that, in spite of Lee's denials, he nevertheless believes that she is actively involved in the admission process, thus overtly contradicting what she has said about her own role. In the latter part of the interaction, he goes on to suggest that he thinks that she has decided that he and other students in the Twilight course are not qualified and to argue that she is not likely to favor his admission. The more Lee attempts to set the record straight, the more he holds to this position. Yet on the other hand, Don denies that he is offended (11D, 16D) and, on the contrary, it seems from the way he talks, for example in (19D), as if he were trying to enlist her help and that he is upset that she has the impression that he is not suitable. For someone who is asking for assistance, his behavior certainly seems strangely inconsistent.

The apparent contradictions in Don's reasoning literally jump out at us when we look at the second section of the transcript.

```
20L:  I was *one of the members of the com*mittee/
20D:  ==yes//
21L:  (1) who de*signed the course at E College//
      (2) but I have nothing to do with the appli*cations or anything/
      (3) because I'm *here// it's a *college course/
      (4) not a *center course/ =and ok center=
21D:                          =no it's center-=
22L:  Mr D I know MORE about this course/ than *you do// I DESIGNED =it//=
22D:                                                              =yes=
23L:  (1) at E *College// but I am TELLING you/
      (2) I'm not involved in the appli*cations// I'm =telling you//=
23D:                                                 =but you have=
24L:  Mr D I KNOW whether or not/
24D:  you have an equal say even
25L:  I DON'T have an equal say actually/it's
25D:  .. yes//
26L:  I'm telling you/ .. I KNOW//
26D:  if if .. if if you feel somebody/ who is not suitable// you can say no
      (   )//
27L:  I'm NOT GOING to say/ANYTHING to ANYBODY//
27D:  if you feel somebody::/
28L:  (1) {[ac] it's got nothing to do with me//} if::/
      (2) {[ac] you have applied to E *College/}
      (3) *that– as far as I am concerned/ that's *that//
      (4) {[ac] it's up to .. *them//} it's got nothing to do with me/ at *all//
28D:  yes// still you have a say// you have opinion//
29L:  (1) {[hi] Mr D} stop *telling me/ {[hi] what I'm DOING/}
      (2) what I'm NOT doing// {[hi] I .. KNOW what I am doing//}
29D:  (1) no/ I'm not telling you/ what you do/
      (2) or what you .. not to do/ but I know .. the fact/
      (3) what you're/ .. and what you did/ what your opinion will be//

Several turns later:

30L:  but nobody is going to/ *ask me for my opinion//
30D:  (   ) I think so for the admission//
```

31L: (1) {[hi] Mr D] *stop telling me/ that I am .. a *liar// {[hi] I'm telling
you the *truth//}
    (2) oh *yes you are/ =you're-=

31D: =I'm not- telling you//

Beginning in turn (20L) Lee once more explains in detail her role in the admission process. In (21D) Don reacts to her last phrase with an overlapped "no it's center" which Lee takes as a denial of what she has just said, even though she did not give him an opportunity to elaborate his point. Lee's utterance evokes a "yes" on Don's part (22D). This could count as a mere backchannel signal acknowledgement that he has understood her, yet she again responds as if he were contradicting her. Once more, in (23D), Don's attempt to respond with an overlapped "but you have" is similarly interpreted. This pattern of Lee's interpreting Don's attempts to reply as contradiction goes on through much of the remaining portion of the exchange, particularly in turns (25L), (26L), (27L), (29L), (31L), until finally Lee comes out in (37L) with an exasperated

37L: (1) .. I don't know WHAT to say to you// you you- / you don't BELIEVE me/
    (2) what I tell you/ you don't .. ACCEPT what I say to you as true/
    (3) and I don't know * what to say to you anymore//

Yet on several occasions Don clearly denies that he is intentionally trying to contradict her or to tell her what to do.

29D: (1) no/I'm not *telling you/* what *you do/* or what you .. *not to do/*
    (2) but *I know* .. the fact/ what you're/ .. and *what you did/* what your *opinion will be//*
37D: (1) uh I .. I accepted most of *your word/*
    (2) and uh what what *I think/* that's my *personal opinion/*
    (3) *and that's why* I am saying that/
    (4) you are *saying this for/* and uh *that's your–* part of your job//
    (5) and I'm not uh ( )/
39D: (1) uh if *if I don't* get admission/ I am *not blaming* .. you for that//
    (2) if uh:: *forget about that/* I'm not saying/ to you anything/ and-

In other words, he repeatedly claims that he is not annoyed at her and, towards the end of the conversation, he asserts that he will not blame her even if he does not get admitted.

How can we explain this apparent breakdown of what Agar (1983) would call "coherence" in our ability to account for Don's actions? A likely solution for this emerged only after I had the opportunity to look in detail at these seeming contradictions together with two Indian–English speaking research assistants. Although all of us had spent quite a bit of time with the tape, we had at first not noticed this point. It was only when we began to try to guess at what Don could have been intending to say on the many occasions where he was interrupted that the two native speakers remarked that an Indian–English speaker might interpret Don's action not as contradicting Lee but as an instance of a kind of pleading. This type of discursive practice is typical of situations where a member of the lay public makes a request of a representative of a public institution. In India such situations are often treated as hierarchical situations marked by a sharp status distinction between the public official who is addressed as a superior and the client who acts as the dependent. Two kinds of discursive strategies are commonly involved in this type of pleading. On the one hand, lay persons, in arguing their case, represent themselves as innocent victims of circumstances.

We have a number of instances of similar phenomena in our tape-recorded materials. For example, in a roleplay enactment a customer complaining about a faulty sweater that he purchased said, "I bought this sweater some time ago and when I came home it was torn and I spoiled my money." In a second example, an unemployed clerk who has come to see a social worker at a neighborhood center to ask for help with tracking his unemployment check introduces his story with, "I'm in terrible trouble." In both situations the client frames his talk as if it were some personal mishap rather than talking about the issue in neutral institutional terms. Don's attempt to explain himself to Lee in (12D), "I didn't need it for myself. Because I came to this course. And that's why it happened. I'm not insulting you. I am just feeling sorry for myself," can perhaps be explained as a similar troubles talk strategy. What Don is arguing is not that he is sorry for himself but that he is sorry that he enrolled in the Twilight course because it is this that might have led Lee to misjudge him. While downgrading their own status, lay persons, on the other hand, as part of this same complex of strategies, depict the official as being all-powerful and in control, thus able to assist in finding a solution to the problem. Thus, superiors are often addressed with words to the effect that "you are important," "you are powerful," "you can help." When this leads to denial on the superior's part, clients tend to repeat their praise strategy and so on. If we interpret Don's behavior towards Lee in this way, his actions do seem to make sense. In other words, he is not claiming that she can change or actually bypass the rules of the course. He is simply trying to enlist what Erickson, in his analysis of similar counseling situations (Erickson and Schultz, 1982), has called "co-membership." He is asking her to take his, Don's, perspective and support him in making a good case for admission to the course.

Some of Don's replies can indeed be interpreted in this way. Consider (6D), "And it lasts until you say, also for the people who are interested in this sort of uh–." Perhaps what he intends to convey here is, "Maybe you can suggest that the admission criteria be interpreted so as to include people like me who would like to go into such professions." Similarly, in reply to Lee's (12L), "Why are you feeling so sorry for yourself?," Don replies, "Because I didn't have to come to this course," and then one turn later, "But you think that nobody in this class who is taking the course (is qualified)." Don did not have an opportunity to complete his utterance, but in view of his statements in (23D, 24d), "but you have an equal say," and (26D), "if you feel somebody is not suitable, you can say no," he evidently believes that the fact that he enrolled in the Twilight course has prejudiced her against him. If he assumes that as a result she is less likely to help him, he has reason to be disappointed.

Finally, let us look at Don's response in the sequence from (31L) to (35D), which begins with Lee's, "Stop telling me that I'm a liar." Don replies, "I'm not telling you you're a liar, that's your profession," and then when she persists in her argument, he repeats, "Your profession, I'm not telling, I never say liar." When Lee then accuses him by paraphrasing his words as follows, "You said, 'yes, you can do this, you can do that'," Don replies, "No, that's not lying" and in the next turn goes on with, "People don't admit the fact sometimes, and that's part of their job you know." He is evidently interpreting Lee's denials as typical of and expected of officials who have power and are reluctant to use it on the client's behalf.

To repeat, contrary to what Lee thinks, Don is not necessarily deeply insulted nor sorry for himself nor is he intentionally contradicting her, although perhaps he does show annoyance at the end. He is simply employing the discursive practices and acting out the interpersonal relationships that he associates with situations of official pleading. Furthermore, both Lee's perception of what he is doing as well as our own initial impressions are in large part interactively generated by the fact that more often than not Don is interrupted before he has had a chance to make his point and he is rarely ever allowed to complete what he wants to say. Our evidence seems to show that the differences in contextualization strategies, which, as we argued, led to Lee's initial perception that Don felt sorry for himself and was acting insulted, also stood in the way of both participants' efforts to repair the situation. We conclude that Don's seeming denials and his references to himself must be understood as formulaic contextualization cues, which suggests how he defines the verbal activity at hand.

Although the two conversationalists would clearly agree on what the overall speech event is in which they are involved, they differ significantly in their notions of what types of activities constitute this event, how these activities are reflected in contextualization conventions, and what can and cannot be said. Such differences are not rare and not confined to interethnic situations. But what makes this kind of situation special is that the differences in the contextualization conventions, the inferences made at the first and sequential levels, and the resulting misunderstandings keep each conversationalist from recognizing the other's perspective at the third level of activity. As a result, attempts at repair misfire and miscommunication is compounded rather than resolved by further talk. The long-term social consequences of miscommunications that occur under these circumstances have been discussed elsewhere (Gumperz, Aulakh, and Kaltman 1982). The present chapter can best be understood as a further step in the development of what Jenny Cook-Gumperz and I (1978) have referred to as "the process of arriving at a socially active notion of context." A notion of context, in other words, that deals with the cognitive processes through which cultural and other types of background knowledge are brought into the interpretive processes.

Appendix A

Symbol	Significance
//	Final fall
/	Slight fall indicating "more is to come"
?	Final rise
,	Slight rise as in listing intonation
–	Truncation (e.g. what ti– what time is it/)
..	Pauses of less than 0.5 seconds
...	Pauses greater than 0.5 seconds (unless precisely timed)
<2>	Precise units of time (= 2-second pause)
=	To indicate overlap and latching of speakers' utterances, e.g.

    R: so you understand =the requirements=
    B: =yeah, i under=stand them/

    R: so you understand the requirements?
    B: ==yeah, i understand them/
    R: ==and the schedule?
    B: yeah/

with spacing and single "=" before and after the appropriate portions of the text indicating overlap, and turn-initial double "==" indicating latching of the utterance to the preceding one

Symbol	Significance
::	Lengthened segments (e.g. wha::t)
˜	Fluctuating intonation over one word
*	Accent; normal prominence
CAPS	Extra prominence
{[ ]}	Nonlexical phenomena, both vocal and nonvocal, which overlays the lexical stretch, (e.g. {[lo] text//])

[ ]	Nonlexical phenomena, both vocal and nonvocal, which interrupt the lexical stretch (e.g. text [laugh] text//)
( )	Unintelligible speech
di(d)	A good guess at an unclear segment
(did)	A good guess at an unclear word
(xxx)	Unclear word for which a good guess can be made as to how many syllables were uttered, with "x" = one syllable
(" ")	Regularization (e.g. i'm gonna ("going to") come soon/)

Appendix B

1D: this is not a–
1L: ==of *course/ {[ac] it is not a secret//]
2D: =that it *is a secret//=
2L: (1) =I haven't *said= it's a secret//
    (2) {[ac] I didn't say it was a secret//}
    (3) what I *said was/
    (4) .. that it was *not a suitable course/ .. for you to *apply for//
    (5) because it is ( )//
    (6) .. {[lo] now if you *want to apply for it/}
    (7) .. {[hi] of *course/) you can do what you *want//
    (8) but/ {[hi] if you are *doing the twilight course at the *moment/}
    (9) .. {[lo] it was *not something which-}
    (10) .. Mrs N and Mr G *thought/ *originally/
    (11) that it was a course to carry *on/ *with the *twilight course/
    (12) but this is NOT the case//
3D: (1) no// what you– you take *one thing at a time//*
    (2) this case// that whatever {[f] *they know//*}
    (3) I get that even .. hmm// for a D ..*me//*
    (4) {[lo] and I am *student in E* *College//*}
    (5) and Mr W *knows me// he// ..I am* student in the *same school//*
    (6) {[f] he knows *my qualifications/*} and what– whether I'm suitable *or not//*
    (7) =but=
3L: =this= has nothing to = DO with qualifications//=
4D: (1)   ={[f] but you can't know/}=
    (2) and can't {[f] *tell a person/*} .. just who is to come into *this course//*
    (3) if .. suppose I came to *this course* from uh//
    (4) .. *(had) you taken this impression//* .. {[lo] that I am *not suitable//*}
    (5) because I took this {[f] *course//*}
4L: (1) but it is a question of the *job you're doing/
    (2) the course is for people/ who are/ {[ac] I'll *tell you/
    (3) it *says on the information//

(4) k{[hi] it's for youth *employment officers,
(5) it's for members of the *police, it's for uh *teachers,
(6) it's for people with *management positions,
(7) {[ac] *those are the people {[hi] who are going to be on the
    *course//}}

5D: (1) {[hi] it-} {[lo] that's- that's *your plan//*}
    (2) uh and ( ) who would would benefit and *who would not/*
      ah =you know/=

5L: (1)=but {[ac] Mr D/=
    (2) {[hi] it's a TRAINING course for people who are going to do those
    *jobs//}}

6D: (1) ==and/ it lasts *until you say//* {[lo] *also for the people*]
    (2) *who are interested* in this sort of uh::-

6L: yes//

7D: ==educa=tion//=

7L: =with re=ference to their WORK// it would be

8D: ==yes/

8L: ==with reference to their *work//

9D: (1) {[lo] (professional) *people/*} ( ) them/
    (2) {[hi] or *the people* who are *personally interested//*

9L: why are you so/ {[lo] (unin-)/} you've APPLIED//

10D: yes//

10L: (1) it doesn't MATTER any more//
    (2) .. I don't understand/ why you are so INSULTED {[lo] with me//}

11D: {[hi] hmm I am =*not insulting you//*==

11L: (1)   =I mean two *things/= {[lo] I said/ [ac] I said to you/
    (2) you can– you– I'll send you the things when they *come/ I've only
    just *received them//}
        (3) and *then I said to you/ that I *didn't think you were suitable/
        (4) ok/ *nothing =more//=

12D: (1)   =I didn't= need it for myself//
    (2) because I came to *this course//*
    uh heh heh/ and that eh– and that's *why it happened//*
    hmm I'm not *insulting you//* I just hm =feeling *sorry for myself//*=

12L: =no I didn't say you were//= but
    exactly/ why are you feeling so =sorry for YOURSELF//=

13D: =because I didn't= didn't ( ) have to
    come to this *course//*

13L: (1) yes/ well that's very good/
    (2) I don't understand why you're feeling so INSULTED//

14D: well but you think ( )// that uh *nobody in this class//* or who is *taking
the course at–*

14L: (1) no/ it isn't a question of *that//
    (2) Mrs/ well uh Mrs G *told me/
    (3) she had given the things out to the people in the *class/
    (4)because she thought it was something *suitable/
    (5) they would want to go on and *do/ when they had *finished this
    course/
    (6) that it was a *follow-up//

15D: yes//
15L: but it ISN'T a follow-up/ that's the point// it's something quite DIFFERENT//
16D: (1) but/ what this is uh/
    (2) I'm *crossing you* but I *already .. noticed about this course/*
16L: .. well that's ALRIGHT then/
17D: from there/ and I already *got this application form/*
17L: ⌐that's = ā lright/=
18D: =and I= *already applied//*
18L: that's OK//
19D: (1) and- ya- what- but the way you hmm (uh)/ on the *last day//*
    (2) when I found on *the last day/* then *I worked this out//*
    (3) {[ac] same thing uh thing//} now/ *this is confirmation of that/*
    (4) {[lo] uh you took *this impression/* that I am *not suitable/*}
    (5) and that's why you didn't *send me the application forms//*
19L: I RECEIVED THEM ONLY ON FRIDAY// [shouted]

Several turns later:

20L: I was *one of the members of the com*mittee/
20D: == yes//
21L: (1) who de*signed the course at E College//
    (2) but I have nothing to do with the appli*cations or anything/
       because I'm *here//
    (3) it's a *college course/ not a *center course/ =and ok center=
21D: =no *it's center*=
22L: Mr D I know MORE about this course/ than *you do// I DESIGNED =it//=
22D: =yes=
23L: (1) at E * College// but I am TELLING you/
    (2) I'm not involved in the appli*cations// I'm =telling you//=
23D: *but you have*=
24L: Mr D I KNOW whether or not/
24D: you have an *equal say even*
25L: I DON'T have an equal say actually/ it's
25D: .. yes//
26L: I'm telling you/ .. I KNOW//
26D: if if .. if if you *feel somebody/* who is not suitable// *you can say no*
    ( )//
27L: I'm NOT GOING to say/ ANYTHING to ANYBODY//
27D: if you *feel somebody::/*
28L: (1) {[ac] it's got nothing to do with me//] if::/
    (2) {[ac] you have applied to E * College/}
    (3) *that- as far as I am concerned/ that's *that//
    (4) {[ac] it's up to .. *them//} it's got nothing to do with me/ at *all//
28D: yes// still you have *a say//* you *have opinion//*
29L: {[hi] Mr D} stop *telling me/ {[hi] what I'm DOING/}
    what I'm NOT doing// {[hi] I .. KNOW what I am doing//}

29D: (1) no/ I'm not *telling you/* what *you do/* or what you .. *not to do/*
(2) but *I know* .. the fact/ what you're/ .. and *what you did/* what your *opinion will be//*

Several turns later:

30L: but nobody is going to/ *ask me for my opinion//
30D: ( ) *I think so* for the admission//
31L: (1) {[hi] Mr D] * stop telling me/ that I am .. a *liar// {[hi] I'm telling you the *truth//}
(2) oh *yes you are/ =you're–=
31D: =I'm not= telling you//
32L: ==*contracting me/ I *know my situation *better than you/ I know–/
32D: ==you're a liar/ that's *your profession–/*
33L: ==I know my situation *better than you//
33D: ==your profession I/ .. I'm *not telling/ I never *say liar//*
34L: (1) yes you .. DID/ you ( )- I SAID to you/ I have- it has *nothing to do with me.
(2) and *you .. said/ yes/ you .. can *do this/ you can do .. *that//
(3) I'm TELLING you/ I *can't/ and that's the *end of it// and I don't WANT to anyway//
34D: no that's *not lying//*
35L: I'm getting *tired of it//
35D: (1) people–people .. uh don't .. uh admit *the fact sometime/*
(2) and uh that's their- / part of *their job/* you know//
36L: {[hi] that's very *rude of you//}
36D: if you feel that way you can *say it/* .. that thing/
37L: (1) .. I don't know WHAT to say to you// you you– / you don't BELIEVE me/
(2) what I tell you/ you don't .. ACCEPT what I say to you as true/
(3) and I don't know *what to say to you anymore//
(4) I .. *told you/ what I've said I/ .. *told you//
37D: (1) uh I .. I accepted most of *your word/*
(2) and uh what what *I think/* that's my *personal opinion/*
(3) *and that's why* I am saying that/
(4) you are *saying this for/* and uh *that's your–* part of your job//
(5) and I'm not uh ( )/
38L: but I've TOLD you/ {[hi] it .. *isn't} part of my job/ part of my *job is to .. *teach//
38D: yes/
39L: I don't have *anything to do with *admission//
39D: (1) uh if *if I don't* get admission/ I am *not blaming* .. you for that//
(2) if uh?? *forget about that/* I'm not saying/ *to you anything/* and–
40L: *well// then what are you SAYING//
40D: I'm not saying *liar or anything/* =and I=
41L: =well/= then what are you .. saying// .. then// what do you WANT//

Acknowledgement

I am grateful to Norine Berenz for many helpful comments and to the staff of the National Centre for Industrial Language Training, Southall, UK, for allowing me to use the recording on which the analysis is based.

References

Agar, M. 1983. Political Talk: Thematic Analysis of a Policy Argument. *Policy Studies Review* 2: 601–14.
    1985. Institutional Discourse. *Text* 5(3): 147–8.
Atkinson, J. M., and J. Heritage. 1984. *Structures of Social Action*. Cambridge: Cambridge University Press.
Brown G., and G. Yule. 1983. *Discourse Analysis*. Cambridge: Cambridge University Press.
Chafe, W. 1980. The Deployment of Consciousness in the Production of a Narrative, in *Pear Stories*, ed. W. Chafe. Norwood: Ablex.
Cook–Gumperz, J. A. 1977. Situated Instructions: Language Socialization of School Age Children, in *Children's Discourse*, ed. S. Ervin-Tripp and C. Mitchell-Kernan. New York: Academic Press.
Cook-Gumperz, J. A. and J. J. Gumperz. 1978. Context in Children's Speech, in *The Development of Communication*, ed. N. Waterson and C. Snow. New York: Wiley.
Erickson, F., and J. Shultz. 1982. *The Counselor as Gatekeeper*. New York: Academic Press.
Ervin-Tripp, S. 1972. On Sociolinguistic rules: Alternation and Co-occurrence, in *Directions in Sociolinguistics*, ed. J. J. Gumperz and D. Hymes. New York: Holt, Rinehart and Winston.
Goffman, E. 1974. *Frame Analysis: An Essay on the Organization of Experience*. New York: Harper Colophon Books.
Gumperz, J. J. 1971. *Language in Social Groups*. Palo Alto, CA: Stanford University Press.
    1982. *Discourse Strategies*. Cambridge: Cambridge University Press.
Gumperz, J. J., G. Aulakh and H. Kaltman. 1982. Thematic Structure and Progression in Discourse, in *Language and Social Identity*, ed. J. J. Gumperz. New York: Cambridge University Press.
Gumperz, J. J., and J. Blom. 1972. Social Meaning in Linguistic Structures: Code-Switching in Norway, in *Directions in Sociolinguistics*, ed. J. J. Gumperz and D. Hymes. New York: Holt, Rinehart and Winston.
Gumpertz, J., H. Kaltman and M. C. O'Connor. Cohesion in Spoken and Written Discourse: Ethnic Style and the Transition to Literacy, in *Coherence in Spoken and Written Discourse*, ed. D. Tanner. Norwood, NJ: Ablex.
Levinson, S. 1983. *Pragmatics*. Cambridge: Cambridge University Press.
Ochs, E. 1979. Transcription as theory. In E. Ochs and B. B. Schieffelin (eds.), *Developmental Pragmatics*, pp. 43–72. New York: Academic Press.
Silverstein, M. 1981. The Limits of Awareness, in *Sociolinguistics Working Paper* 84, Austin, Texas.
Sperber, D., and D. Wilson, 1986. *Relevance*. Cambridge, Mass.: Harvard University Press.

9 Contextualization in Kalapalo narratives

ELLEN B. BASSO

Editors' introduction

Ellen Basso is Professor of Anthropology at the University of Arizona at Tucson. Trained in social anthropology, over the years she has become interested in the study of discourse as an opportunity for synthesizing her different interests in the constitution and representation of the self in non-Western cultures, the relationship between ideology and historical consciousness, the explanatory and didactic functions of narrative in non-literate societies, and biography as an historical genre. This chapter is a synthesis of some of these themes as revealed by the analysis of a particular Kalapalo narrative.

Linguists and anthropologists often differ as to what they take the "meaning" of a given text to be. More generally, the two groups typically diverge in their view and practice of the very process of interpretation. Linguists are typically concerned with the relationship between the referential aspects of meaning (i.e. the truth-value of a given proposition) and particular morphosyntactic forms (e.g. how to represent and explain the similarities or differences between two linguistic forms). Cultural anthropologists, on the other hand, have tended to be concerned with meaning as the relationship between the text and symbolic organization of ritual events and broader sociocultural dimensions, such as a people's ethos or sense of person (e.g. Turner 1974, Geertz 1973). Although both groups are interested in getting at some underlying "system" with which to explain the specific features of a text, their analytic strategies are quite opposite. Linguists tend to de- or under-contextualize the linguistic text, juxtaposing forms rather than speakers. Anthropologists tend to over-contextualize, bringing in background ethnographic knowledge that may not seem justified by or related to the available linguistic data. Until recently, these two traditions remained separate and did not mutually benefit each other. Recent developments within sociolinguistics, the ethnography of communication, and conversation analysis, however, have provided the analytical tools for bridging the gap between these two approaches. While an increasing number of empirically oriented grammarians are becoming interested in actual talk and are facing rather than avoiding the problem of a cultural niche for the collection of their texts (Du Bois 1980), anthropologists are paying more attention to the details of the linguistic constitution of social reality and social institutions. The work of John Gumperz (1977, 1982, this volume) on contextualization cues has been particularly useful for identifying specific grammatical strategies used to suggest or make present the sociocultural world implicit in speakers' utterances (Haviland 1986; Ochs, this volume; Sherzer 1987) or to build a narrative text as a performance (Bauman 1977, 1986; Silverstein 1985). The following chapter by Ellen Basso falls within the latter tradition. It looks at a particular genre of oral performance among the Kalapalo Indians of central Brazil as a narrative where the warrior–hero's identity and its transformations are constituted through subtle but recurring linguistic forms of the kind described by Gumperz as contextualization cues. We are thus told about such discourse strategies as repetition, use of inclusive and exclusive pronouns, agentive markers, code-switching, and so forth, as ways to weave a characterization of characters and events that become a central rather than a marginal feature of the message. The meaning of the story, Basso argues, is not just in the events we are being told about, or in the matching of those events with real or possible worlds in the Kalapalo universe; rather, the meaning – in the sense of the cultural significance of such stories for the performers and their audience – is in the ways that complex and culture-specific forms of knowledge are evoked and partly questioned through the use of subtle linguistic devices. The interpretation proposed by Basso is in fact quite consistent with Gumperz' current framework (see Chapter 8 above), where the presence of an "activity" level emphasizes the centrality of contextualization cues for a broad understanding of what is going on in the text and its suggested context.

References

Bauman, Richard. 1977. *Verbal Art as Performance*. Rowley, Mass.: Newbury House.
1986. *Story, Performance, and Event*. Cambridge: Cambridge University Press.
Du Bois, John W. 1980. Introduction – The Search for a Cultural Niche: Showing the Pear Film in a Mayan Community, in *The Pear Stories: Cognitive, Cultural, and Linguistic Aspects of Narrative Production*, ed. W. L. Chafe. Norwood, NJ: Ablex.
Geertz, Clifford. 1973. *The Interpretation of Cultures*. New York: Basic Books.
Gumperz, John. 1977. Sociocultural Knowledge in Conversational Influence, in *Georgetown University Round Table on Languages and Linguistics 1977*, ed. Muriel Saville–Troike. Washington DC: Georgetown University Press.
1982. *Discourse Strategies*. Cambridge: Cambridge University Press.
Haviland, John B. 1986. 'Con Buenos Chiles': Talk, Targets and Teasing in Zinacantan. *Text* 6(3): 249–82.
Sherzer, Joel. 1987. A Discourse-Centered Approach to Language and Culture. *American Anthropologist* 89: 295–309.
Silverstein, Michael. 1985. The Culture of Language in Chinookan Narrative Texts; or, On saying that . . . in Chinookan, in *Grammar Inside and Outside the Clause*, ed. J. Nichols and A. Woodbury. Cambridge: Cambridge University Press.
Turner, Victor. 1974. *Dramas, Fields and Metaphors: Symbolic Action in Human Society*. Ithaca, NY: Cornell University Press.

Contextualization in Kalapalo narratives

For John Gumperz, the phenomenon of "contextualization" plays a crucial role in understanding conversational interaction. Variation in form, how people channel interpretation of what they are saying, differences in communicative styles within a speech community, and instances of mis-communication and misunderstanding are all illuminated by a focus on contextualization. As I understand his model, Gumperz considers contex-tualization to be a dynamic process "that develops and changes as the participants interact" (in other words, it is inherent in and contingent upon the fact of dialogue itself). Using linguistic features that are marginal or semantically insignificant, speakers contextualize what they say in order to signal implicit meaning. Thus, while contextualization cues "carry informa-tion, meanings are conveyed as part of the interactive process," and cues are usually not used out of context.

Understanding the phenomenon called contextualization is therefore of great importance to our ethnographic understanding of the role of langu-age use in experiencing and representing human connection: to our understanding of explanations, interpretations, assessments, and evalua-tions; of creativity in verbal art; and of the dialogical, interactive, transactive "voicing" phenomena of speech-centered events.

Anthropologists therefore have a good chance now to move from a neglect of the explanatory functions of speech to a deeper concern with the logic of arguments in discourse and their psychological and social implica-tions. Insofar as we have tended to persist in empiricist, objectifying projects, we have given priority in our studies of language to the marking of types of **evidence** over the ways **conclusions** might be represented, to how an argument is **supported** (by evidence, for example), rather than to how it might be **received** and responded to. The logic of an argument, the specific concepts and categories manifested therein, have taken prece-dence over the actual place of explanations in discourse. The sociolinguist's position, however, is that the emotional quality of interpersonal contact is as important for communication as the substance of what is said. Consid-ering that evaluative conclusions or assessments have important implica-tions for the quality of a particular interpersonal activity, our current focus on discourse becomes especially important in studying explanations eth-nographically. John Gumperz' work on "contextualization" plays a critical role in this project.[1]

In this chapter, I discuss contextualization from the perspective of narrative speech (*akiña*) among the Carib-speaking Kalapalo, who live in the Upper Xingu Basin of central Brazil. Kalapalo narratives are dialo-gically constructed, with a listener–responder contributing in several important ways to the construction of the story. Although – with the exception of questions (which are encouraged) – these responses tend to be stereotyped, and in fact the narrator takes primary responsibility for the quality of the performance, it is up to the listener to make explicit note of the significant explanatory points of the story, putting the pieces together in a conclusive statement that makes explicit much of what was implied. Like all Native American storytelling, Kalapalo narratives are notably complex in their overlapping poetic, didactic, explanatory, and psychological functioning, for which descriptive linguistic, ethnopoetic, and interpretive–symbolic methods of analysis are all necessary. A focus upon contextualization in narrative discourse illuminates these functions in special ways, just as, I hope to show, contextualization itself is given a somewhat different perspective from that gained by examining conversations.

1   The distinctiveness of grammar in Kalapalo warrior biographies

In Kalapalo narratives, quoted speech is the most important means of developing individual characters and their interpersonal relations. Most activity is in fact speech-centered, suggesting how the Kalapalo associate interactive relations with speech. In many of these narratives, characters tend to validate each other, as they agree with one another's goals and plans, verify evidence, and sympathize with one another's feelings. These activities occur during conversations in trickster stories, but are framed as deceptions. But in one important genre, the warrior biography, speech-centered events are increasingly and variously conflictual, building up to incidents of resistance, reinterpretation, angry or disgusted disagreement, bitterness, and sarcasm. And it is precisely in those conversational segments that the contextualization I am concerned with in this chapter is important, contributing most strongly to a sense of the opposed, persistent, and irreconcilably different points of view that characterize a warrior and his more personal enemies.

In the story called "Wapagepundaka" (which serves as my example), the warrior (*tafaku oto*) –hero leads a group of men to a musical performance in a settlement of fierce people. These *angikogo* initially welcome their visitors, but, after sending them off at the conclusion of the ritual, they ambush and kill them for a cannibal feast. Wapagepundaka manages to escape with the help of a young maiden, whom he promises to return to marry. When Wapagepundaka (the sole survivor of the cannibal massacre) returns to take revenge with the rest of the community, he discovers that his own father has killed the woman who earlier saved his life. Furious at this betrayal, the warrior abandons his own people as they prepare to feast on the bodies of their victims. He seeks out a small community of foreigners among whom he hopes to marry. In order to be accepted among them he must persuade them that he has not come to kill them all. After a series of actions designed to make these people accept him, he finally is successful.

In this story, there is considerable creation of doubt in the listener about who is who, and the moral doubt accompanying this confusion about identity seems to be an ideological ploy. In the course of showing how easily the practices of warfare lead to fanatical forms of destruction, the storyteller disputes in plausible ways any glorification of the terrible image of the warrior, a man who destroyed the honor of his war victims through verbal insults, mutilation, and cannibalism. Offered in place of this image is a peaceful man, empathic rather than antipathic, tolerant rather than vindictive, constructive and productive rather than destructive. It is the warrior–hero Wapagepundaka himself who attempts to change from the first to the second. I write "attempts" because the warrior must learn to control his own seemingly fierce passions. Much of this thematic content is presented through the developmental patterns created through quoted conversations, especially between the warrior Wapagepundaka and other people.

2   Contextualization in Kalapalo narratives

Contextualization in Kalapalo has to do with interpersonal relations, with how the personal feelings of individuals are to be understood. Most important are feelings associated with the formulation of plans to achieve personal goals. For the Kalapalo, feelings are actions that initiate complex processes, which in turn result in permanent changes to the individual and society or even the world most generally. Feelings, as the basis for (reasons for) action, are thus of considerable interest to Kalapalo storytellers, who provide various cues to listeners regarding how different characters are feeling. By "feeling," I mean an emotional action, that is, a person's emotional response to someone else (or to the social environment in general); in Kalapalo, feelings are often made out to be the reasons underlying a person's goal-orientation. (Curiously enough, labels for emotions, which have their basis in certain "active" areas of the body such as genitals or stomach, are hardly ever heard in the course of storytelling; particular emotions are usually understood through what the character has been made to say.)

In Kalapalo narratives generally, contextualization of interpersonal relations is a fairly long process, developing in "biographical narratives" the substance of the story itself. It is hard to speak of any single occurrence of contextualization independently of others. Far more interesting is a pattern developed from various kinds of contributing cue elements. I outline them here along a continuum of speech-centeredness.

The first involves references to experiences of time, including sleeping (which introduces new action possibilities for a character) and travelling (associated with persistence, determination, and the goal of creating an "alternative self" characterized by experiences of creative, transformative power).

A second common cue is repetition. For the Kalapalo, the repeated expression of an idea (or any activity) "accumulates" until, as obsession, it begins to persuade, to transform. When a "motivated" number of instances is reached, reinforcement, intensification, completeness (in the case of things done four or eight times), and ultimate success and conclusiveness (when things are done five or nine times) are the results. An example occurs in the story of Wapagepundaka during the long section in which the hero gradually tells his companions five times (and in increasingly sharp detail) what happened to his friends during their visit to the fierce people (examples [f]–[j], presented later in the chapter). After the fourth account, Wapagepundaka's surviving companions agree to help him take revenge; the fifth account occurs as they all confront the evidence of capture on their way to the enemy settlement, as if their resolve to kill the enemy is made final only when they can see for themselves what happened. A second example of repeated action is found in the account of how Wapagepundaka persuades his new relatives-in-law that he has come to live among them in peace, that (contrary to their expectations) he has no intention of killing them all. That a certain action is **repeated**, or that a person – through activity – is himself a part of a pattern, is a significant matter in any Kalapalo (and perhaps all Native American) psychological description.

A third kind of contextualization cue involves how pronouns are used. There are two relevant types of usage. The first has to do with reference to focalized agency, which is important with respect to the patterning of a character's activity. For Kalapalo, a hero is a primarily persistently repetitive agent, a trickster is a non-repetitive, "scattered" agent with many arbitrary goals, and, if a warrior like Wapagepundaka, persistent **and** contrary to another character's point of view. Agency is marked in nouns and pronouns formed from the ergative suffix *feke*.[2] These agentives can also mark discourse focalization of a character when they are placed at the head of an utterance; normally an agentive appears after the verb. In a long story such as "Wapagepundaka," focalized characters are occasionally defocalized; refocalization of agents whose focality has been temporarily removed can be achieved by using the pronoun *ngele*. Focality of a character is crucial for understanding the relations of power between individuals in the story. Focalized characters are inevitably the most powerful, if only during the incidents in which they appear focalized. Thus, for example, in "Wapagepundaka," the hero is usually focalized, but at the moment immediately prior to his ambush the fierce people become focalized. They remain so throughout his people's captivity and execution, until Wapagepundaka managers to escape.

Another contextualization cue involving pronouns is a contrast set up by the way inclusive and exclusive "we" agentives are used. For example, at the very beginning of the story "Wapagepundaka" ((a), lines 12–26), a contrast is developed between Wapagepundaka and his "cousin" (*ifau*) Tufadyaga, through each man's use of these pronouns. The relevant material appears in boldface in Kalapalo and English. Indentations are used to indicate variations in intonational contours (see Basso 1986: 26–8).

(a) *Ah, kupiñanoko kupulundako witsa igei, nïgïfeke.*
EMPH 1pinc+brother+pl 1pinc+travel+CRM 1p+be this
place+C, say+PERF+ERG
"Why, I'm out here now so that all of us will travel with **our** older brothers," he answered.

> *Ah, kupiñanoko kupulundako witsa igei.*
> Why, I'm out here so that all of us will travel with **our** older brothers."

Eh he nïgï.   *Unama nïgifeke.*
agreement say+PERF   where+DE
"All right," he answered, "Where?," he asked.

15 *Ah, takwagï angunetigi etelïko   utetako   figey,*
     flutes   play+ADV go+PRM+pl 1p+go+CRM+pl CON+ID
"Now, I'm going somewhere to perform the *takwagï,*

> *takwagï angunetigi.*
> to perform the *takwagï.*"

Eh he ketepapa.
    IMP+go+CFT
"All right, **you** go if you wish."

Kigefa   nïgifeke, kigefa.
HORT+go+CON
"Let's go **together**," he said, "Let's go **together**."

Ah, afïtï utelula, afïtï utelïla.
   denial 1p+go+PRM+NEG
"Well, no. **I** won't go, **I** won't go.

20   *Wegefofo kupidyau igeta, wege.*
    2p+SUB   1pinc+brothers   take+CRM, 2p
    You can take our brothers this time, **you**.

> *Wegefa kupidyau igeta.*
> **You** take our brothers.

Ah, iotofekefa   afekidyïko   tuelïko   ake
    club+master+ERG+CON 2p+shoot+PRM+pl kill+PRM+pl with

opiñïko   witsani   nïgifeke.
revenge+DIR+pl 1p+be+PPM

Why, after the Club People shoot you through and through with arrows,
I'll be alive to avenge you all," he continued.

> *Iotofekefa tuelïko ake opiñïko witsani. wege kupiñano igeta.*
> "After the Club People kill you I'll be alive to avenge you all.
> **You** take our older brothers.

> **Wege.**
> **You.**"

25 **Tisuge** *teta   kupiñanoake,*
   1pexc go+CRM 1pinc+older brother + with
   "We'll go together without you, our older brothers and I,

> *tisuge.*
> **We,** without you".

The fourth type of contextualization cue, personal labeling, makes
reference to Kalapalo ideas of (and names for) social obligations and
identities. Social classification through personal labeling creates the possibility of a distinctive interpersonal ethos. In "Wapagepundaka," we see
this in several places. Where the enemies are called "the stinking people,"
there is apparently an allusion to treachery. Examples are found in (b),
lines 50–1, when they are escorting their guests around their settlement,
usually a friendly gesture; and (c), lines 100–1, when the visitors wait
outside the settlement for them to help carry the food, when in fact they
are about to be made prisoners. Ambiguity begins to set in, though, when
in (d), line 139, Wapagepundaka's people are said to stink too:

(b)   50 *Andengapa tïfitsengekiñe   etïfïgï   afudyatini*
            here+PE   R+stench+INST+N   arrive+PERF   together+ADV
            agetsi, agetsi
            one   one
            Here now probably a stinking person accompanied each of them.

> *Tïfitsengekiñïfa etïgï afudyati.*
> A stinking person accompanied each of them.

(c)   *Sinïngolefa,   ah takeingïakenga.*
          come+PERF+pl+M T   bending around
          Then while they passed through the open country,

          Ah itsetangapafa   itsugutu   tepïgï   atanilefa   ifekeni,
              3p+there+PE+C   seated+ADV   go+PERF   were+MT   3p+ERG+pl
          for some reason they sat down to wait for the others.

      100   *Eh, tufïtsengekiñïfeke.*
            Yes, for the stinking people to do something,

> tufïtsengekiñïfeke.
> the stinking people.

(d) 139 *Isituekitanifofo, isituekitanifofo*
   3p+stink+CRM+pl+SUB
   "Their stink will be gone by then, their stink will be gone by then."

Closely connected to labeling is the fifth cue, code-switching, which is relatively rare in Kalapalo stories. This cue seems to be used to represent failed or deliberately thwarted attempts to communicate with foreigners. In "Wapagepundaka," an example appears in (e), lines 161–2, when the narrator switches from Carib to Tupi in representing Wapagepundaka's response to a question about who he is. He tries to deny that he is really Wapagepundaka, pretending to be his own cousin, apparently a former member of the enemy group (here is one place where the listener begins to be unsure of who is who):

(e) *Um, ah Wapagepundaka.*
   "Well, so Wapagepundaka.

 160 *Wapagepundaka igenikafa wegei.*
         this+UE+C 2p+C
   You're Wapagepundaka, aren't you?"

   Anite nïgifeke. Anite.
   (denial)
   "Anite", he said, *"Anite.*

   Tufadya idye nïgifeke.
      (me)
   "Tufadya idye . . . I'm Tufadya," he answered.

   Ifatuwïko ngele, ifatuwïko.
   3p+cousin+pl AP
   Tufadya was their nephew, their nephew.

3 Kalapalo evidentials as contextualization cues

Most important, in some ways most mysterious, are the evidentials or "markers of reasoning" which appear in the speech of warriors to such an extent as to make it a very special speech style, different from that of any other character represented in traditional narratives.

Kalapalo evidential suffixes present several problems, not the least of which is what to call them. They constitute a complex set of particles, qualifying descriptions of action – that is, events – including most especially emotional events, for which there are reasons and which are under the control of agents. The sheer number of forms and combinations is formidable: 7 basic forms (belonging to a single form class), at least 15 forms obviously compounded from these basic forms, 13 other not-so-obviously compounded forms (of which 3 or 4 probably constitute two separate form classes), and an as yet unknown number of combinations involving each of these classes. Kalapalo evidentials mark both types of evidence and types of conclusiveness of statements. They interact in important ways with lexicalized evidentials and stereotypic responses used in agreement and disagreement.

Such a system must be highly involved in contextualization. The question of course is, "Contextualization of what?" Is it assessment or evaluation of the description of action in which the grammatical elements appear? Or (as appears more probable to me at this stage of my understanding) might it be the particular experience of contact between persons that is itself more generally contextualized by the discourse feature quoted speech? Such a question is a discourse-focused one, and thus needs to be answered by examining the discourse processes in which evidentials appear, and especially the manner in which interpersonal psychological processes are represented in narrative.

To discuss this in detail, I use as my example the section of "Wapagepun-daka" in which the hero, returning to his people as the lone survivor of the cannibalistic massacre, ties himself back to the group and describes what happened to his followers. This comes out only bit by bit, the terrible details being revealed only at the very end of the narrative segment, when the remaining faction is on its way to take revenge. The following sections in which evidentials appear are excerpted from the full text of this segment, though I have tried to preserve as much of the conversational activity as possible, since I am concerned as much with the responses to statements involving evidentials as with those grammatical features themselves.

The first instance (f) occurs when Wapagepundaka is met outside the settlement by his cousin Tufadyaga, to whom he has signaled (as was customary when men carrying food returned from a ceremony, so as not to be thought of as enemies). The evidentials are in boldface in the excerpts.

(f)   *Ah, ufau,   wege gele **aka** fegey.*
           1p+cousin   you   still+CE C+NDP
       "My cousin, I do see you're still very much alive."

       *Ah uge   gele **taka** upidyau ake.*
           I   still+CE 1p+brothers with
       "As you see, my brothers and I are still very much alive."

       *Undema kupidyau?   atiko**kagele**.*
       where+DE 2pinc+brothers   there+pl+CE+still
       "Where are our brothers?" "They're still back there."

       Ah   timbukufeke   itamitako   fegey
           manioc+ERG   3p+carry+CRM+pl   C+NDP
       "They are carrying some manioc starch back there now."

Eh he nïgifeke.
"Very well," he answered.

In the first three lines are evidentials *aka* and *taka* (in boldface in the text), referring to first-hand, especially visual evidence that the speaker confirms. This pair occurs most often in greetings and other routinized activities that open important events, often followed by discussions of plans or ongoing activities, which are then validated. An example of this kind of discussion and validation (by the expression *eh he*) is found in the last two lines. After Wapagepundaka arrives home, a similar greeting pattern follows, as in (g), but here doubt is indicated in the form *laka*, concerning first-hand evidence that is uncertain and weakening in the opinion of the speaker:

(g) *Ah wegegele **kafegey** nïgifeke.*
   you+still CE+C+NDP
  "I do see you're still very much alive", was said to him.

 *Ah tisuge**laka**gele.*
  1pex+EE+CONJ
 "Indeed, we still should be so."

 Undema fidyau?
 "Where are your brothers?"

 Atikogele. Atikogele.
 "They're still back there. They're still back there."

 Ah timbuku tafitako egele.
 "They are still carrying some manioc starch back there."

 eh he nïgifeke.
 "All right," they answered.

This doubt is reinforced even more as the people wait in vain for the arrival of the traveling party, (h), in which (in the third line) the evidential *male* indicates strong doubt (even rejection) of hearsay evidence.[3] At the end of this segment Wapagepundaka admits openly that the men are dead. The women are expressing more than doubt; they are separating themselves from the men, and from Wapagepundaka in particular:

(h) *Unago, unago, inde ingufokinïngo,*
  that one   here sink down+INST+PPM+pl
  When they saw the sun move, and move until it was way over here,
  low on the horizon,

  ah ifitsaukopetsï   tïfoni,   ifitsaukopetsïfa.
    3p+wives+pl+IP+AC PASS+cry+ADV
   well, the wives of the dead men began to weep. Those wives of
   theirs.

> *Undemale   fidyau   anïgï?*
> were+DE+DT   brothers   be+PERF
> "How can your brothers really be where you said they were?"

> *Ah afïtïfa   elimokola nïgifeke.*
> denial+C 2p+sons+pl+NEG
> "Your sons are not alive any longer!," he said to them.

[Note: In the last line of this example, the emphatic contradictory negative which is in boldface is a discontinuously constructed evidential, therefore operating syntactically in a way different from the others pointed out in the discussion.]

Later, Wapagepundaka tells the men who did not visit the fierce people that they must all return to take revenge. In order to do so he becomes very explicit about what happened to the victims, speaking of them as having been insulted in the worst way, by having been reduced to morsels of food:

(i)   *Inkefofo,   kupidyau   opidyïïña   kutelu.*
       look+SUB   2pinc−brothers   avenge+PRM+DIR   2pinc+go+PRM
       "Look, the next thing we must do is go back and avenge our brothers.

       *Kupidyaufeke   **wãke**,   tuiñambafo **wãke**.*
       2pinc+brothers+ERG   RPE   PASS+nibble+CRM+N
       I saw our brothers serving as morsels of food for them.

       Tiñambalefa kupidyau   enïgï   angikogofeke.
       eat+CRM+MT   do+PERF   fierce+pl+N+ERG
       The fierce people were feasting on our brothers."

> *Eh he kingi.*
> agreement say+PCM
> "Oh they were, were they?"

>> *Eh he kingi.*
>> "Oh they were, were they?"

Undema? Laa!
where+DE far away
"Where?"   "Far from here!

360 *Ah   tisifenïgï   **wãke**. Afïtïngo   itsopïgïlefa   ugelefa.*
   1pex+grab+PERF RPE not+PPM   murder+PERF+MT I+MT
   We were captured so quickly! And I was almost wiped out then and there."

> *Eh he kingi.*
> "Oh you were, were you?"

Eh he nïgifeke.
"Very well", he answered.

Kigeapa nïgifeke.
"Let's go as you say," his cousin continued.

As he describes what happens, Wapagepundaka uses the evidential form
wāke (together with the exclusive "we" and pseudopassive verb forms).
This evidential marks distant past, first-hand evidence, and a conclusion of
utter certainty. The tone is something like, "I bear witness"; its use is
unusual in that each verb phrase in the sentence is marked by this form, not
just a single verb phrase, as is more usual with Kalapalo evidentials. The
implication is that there is no other possible interpretation; either the
speaker stands out as an isolated voice against any possible others, or is
made out to be the central, leading voice around which all others cluster in
agreement. The latter use of *wāke* is central to the public discourse of
hereditary leaders, who are the social centers of their communities. In the
present example, *wāke* suggests a necessary and unopposable fusion of
speaker and all listeners. His cousin replies by using the expression "*Eh he
kingi*," which is to be taken to mean that he believes Wapagepundaka but
cannot validate the actions of their enemies (lines 357–8, 361). Wapagepundaka hardly needs to convince his listeners of the truth of what
happened, since they can see with their own eyes the remains of food that
were thrown about when the men were captured:

(j) *Lepene,   tifetufugukoiña.*
     then   PASS+grab+be+PERF+p1+DIR
     Then, they came to where they had been captured.

   Inkefa,   inkefa,   ufisï,   nïgifeke.
   look+C   look+C   lp+brother
   "Look, look, my brothers," he said to them.

      Tisifetïgï   *akigei wāke.*
      1pex+grab+be+PERF   CE+ID+C
      "You can see for yourselves, this is where we were cap-
      tured.

         Tingipingope   akigei wāke.
         1pex+possess+N+IP
         Right here you can see for yourselves the remains of
         what we had with us.

            Tingipingotsïfa   akigei.
            1pex+possess+N+AC
            You can see right here just what we had
            with us.

   Inde   fegei   tisifeta   ifekeni,   inde
   right here C+NDP 1pex+grab 3p+ERG+pl right here
   Here is where they captured us. Right here.

      Inde fegei tisifeta ifekeni.
      They captured us right here."

Elsewhere (as in the fourth line of (k), taken from a later segment) the evidential *wāke* can also suggest the opposite, a situation of opposed and irreconcilable voices, as when Wapagepundaka discovers that his wife has been killed while his men take revenge in the enemy settlement:

(k)   *Ho ho   ailitalefa   ifekeni.*
       EX   cheer+CRM+MT   3p+ERG+pl
       "Ho ho!" now they were all celebrating what they had done.

              Undema   ufitsu nïgifekeni.
                        1p+wife
              "Where's my wife?" he asked them.

       Ngele felei.
       AP   C+RDP+C
       "That's on her body over there."

       Ele   ale wāke, wiñïgï   tikungui.
       RDP DT RPE   1p+be+PERF   PASS+help+N
       "She acted differently, I remember. Having saved my life."

       Utelaketsigei, ah   sinïgïmbelï.
       1p+go+CE+NEC come+PERF+AV+PRM
       "Watch me leave right now," and he went home then and there.

In the fourth line, the evidential *wāke* and the disjunctive taxis *ale* (having to do with action having a goal different from some previous occurrence) are used by Wapagepundaka to distinguish the woman's own bravery and sincerity from that of his treacherous father. Note that, while *wāke* marks first hand, visual evidence, the interpersonal tone can vary (as in examples (j) and (k)), and is in any case entirely different from that conveyed by the first-hand visual evidentials when used alone, as in (f) and (g).

In the story of Wapagepundaka, evidentials appear at moments of heightened tension between persons: in situations of doubt, of potential divisiveness, and of actual disputes. They occur when a shared meaning is sought (on the one hand), or where it is being thwarted (on the other): moments of initial contact between persons, of poor insight, negotiation, resistance to an interpretation, or of outright denial of shared experience. In this story, as elsewhere, Kalapalo evidentials occur prominently in greetings, in the ritual declamations of hereditary leaders, and in the stilted speech of affines (on the one hand), as well as in sequences of dialogue where persistent persuasion, irony, and sarcasm occur. Contextualization through evidentials in Kalapalo is thus a matter of creating psychological boundaries and locations somewhere along an axis falling between fully shared imaginative intimacy and self-isolating resistance. Evidentials are used as contextualization cues when speakers perceive the need to isolate themselves from others, to create new boundaries around groups (to which they choose, or do not choose, to belong), or to join themselves to people in newly significant ways. In some of these instances, evidentials are constitutive of independence, individuality, or open conflict. In others, they help to form the most intense kinds of solidarity of which the Kalapalo are capable. In all cases, claims are being made about shared interpretations of experience.

In using these evidentials, Kalapalo speakers convey impressions not only about how the making of inferences leads to particular conclusions, but how that particular aspect of reasoning contributes to different points of view or to shared interpretations of action. While it is true that one can use semantic features (linked to the logic of argument) to define the meaning of these forms, these features do not seem to account for where they appear in dialogues – in other words, why some incidents of speech are so marked and others not. To understand this one must look beyond the specific linguistic components of the utterances to broader discourse contextualization processes such as pronoun usage, social classification, code-switching, and repetition that contribute to the interactive formation of meaning.

4   Conclusion and implications

The Kalapalo evidence contradicts Gumperz' assertion that contextualization cues are "marginal or semantically insignificant." Rather, they **are** the story's emergent structure, as well as strategic, tactical, instrumental symbols, clarifying speech-centered, emotional activities. They are artfully used language resources that are important to the **story**, forming the style of the individual actors.

While much Kalapalo contextualization is grammatically constituted, contextualization operates most completely at the level of narrative discourse. Of course, this is the perspective on contextualization I take from Kalapalo biographies, in which character development is obviously the main matter the listener reflects upon. But this perspective is hardly incompatible with Gumperz' findings about contextualization in conversation. What serves instrumentally to channel meaning in a speech-centered event becomes (in more elaborate combinations) a higher-level and therefore more encompassing or dominant guide to meaning in narratives. In thus elaborating its own function, contextualization in narrative assists understanding and memory of the complex forms of knowledge that are best conveyed through that discourse process. These forms of knowledge seem less than adequately conveyed in casual conversation.

However, like conversation, Kalapalo narrative discourse is interactive and at least potentially dialogical, as are the embedded conversations in which characters themselves participate. Understanding and experiencing anew (both from the perspective of a person listening to the story, and from that of a character in the story) are far from solitary activities. The distinctive point of view of a warrior such as Wapagepundaka – his personal version of reality, and especially his uniquely tragic vision – emerges from an interactive field of metaphoric interpretation, planning and goal-orientation, and the comprehension of consequences, all speech-centered and dialogical, that is, rooted in conversations. It is only as these speech-centered activities unfold that we learn about the Kalapalo warrior's activities of comprehension, increasing alienation, and ultimate tragic understanding.

Conversational analysis might turn in this direction, combining the closely held focus on detail in texts that makes the study of discourse unique in anthropology, with a broader conception of meaning. So, for example, considering "context" as a progressive, emergent process, the relation between contextualization and ideology needs deeper exploration. The variety and explicitness of contextualization cues in Kalapalo warrior narratives may be related to the challenges those men made to an order that no longer worked, and which was in need of replacement through a renewal of the interpretive motive. This need to interpret anew naturally led to recontextualization, where cues were used to mark resistance to the old, and an opening up of new ways of understanding. This function was preserved in the speech of warriors, which is thus very much a commentary on contextualization itself.

Acknowledgments

My research among the Kalapalo was supported by a National Science Foundation Research Grant (BNS 78–00849), the University of Arizona, and the Wenner–Gren Foundation for Anthropological Research, Inc. I am also grateful to the official Brazilian agencies that assisted my research, the Conselho Nacional de Pesquisa and the Fundaçao Nacional do Indio. The Kalapalo text and a full translation of the story "Wapagepundaka" are being prepared for publication; they are available upon request.

Notes

1 In addition to John Gumperz' *Discourse Strategies*, an important publication on explanation that adopts this perspective is a paper by John W. Du Bois (1986), which addresses the problems of evidence, authority, and persuasion in ritual speech.
2 Kalapalo is an ergative language; see Franchetto (1986, 1990) for case marking and verb agreement in Kuikuro, a closely related language.
3 *Male* clearly has the status of evidential here and in other examples, but is phonologically very close to a series of taxis forms, some of which have implications for how action is conceived of by an actor: *gehale*, repeated action;

kifale, surprising action; *gele*, continuous action; *fale*, opposed action; *tale*, action whose goal is no longer sought. *Male* may be a combined form, from *ma* (contradictory) and *fale* (opposed action). It is also possible that there is a continuum of psychological meaning between the Kalapalo taxis and evidential forms.

Key

AC: anaphoric copula; ADV: adverbializer; AP: anaphoric pronoun; AV: anaphoric verb; C: copula; CE: confirmation of experience evidential; CFT: conformative taxis; CON: connective; CONJ: conjunctive taxis; CRM: continuous aspect, reportive mood; DE: doubt evidential; DIR: directive; DT: disjunctive taxis; EMPH: emphatic expletive; ERG: ergative; HORT: hortative; ID: inanimate pronoun; IMP: imperative mode; INST: instrumental; IP: inalienable possessive/ part of whole; MT: metonymic taxis; N: nominalizer; NDP: near deictic pronoun; NEC: necessitative; NEG: negative; PASS: passive; PCM: punctate aspect, customary mood; PE: probability evidential; PERF: perfective; PPM: punctate aspect, potential mood; PRM: punctate aspect, reportive mood; PT: preventative taxis; R: reflexive; RDP: remote deixis pronoun; RPE: remote past/customary knowledge evidential; SUB: subsequent action taxis; UE: uncertainty about hearsay evidential.

References

Basso, Ellen B. 1986. Quoted Dialogues in Kalapalo Narrative Discourse, in *Native South American Discourse*, ed. Joel Sherzer and Greg Urban, pp. 119–68. Berlin: Mouton de Gruyter.

Du Bois, John. 1986. Self-Evidence and Ritual Speech, in *Evidentiality: The Linguistic Coding of Epistemology*, ed. Wallace Chafe and Johanna Nichols, pp. 313–36. Norwood, NJ: Ablex.

Franchetto, Bruna. 1986. *Falar Kuikuro. Estudo etnolingüístico de um grupo karibe do Alto Xingu*. Doctoral dissertation, Departmento de Anthropologia, Museu Nacional. Universidade Federal de Rio de Janeiro.

1990. Ergativity and Nominativity in Kuikuro and other Carib Languages, in *Amazonian Linguistics*, ed. Doris L. Payne, pp. 407–27. Austin: University of Texas Press.

Gumperz, John. 1982. *Discourse Strategies*. Cambridge: Cambridge University Press.

10 Radio talk-show therapy and the pragmatics of possible worlds

FRANK GAIK

Editors' introduction

Frank Gaik received his Ph.D. in Rhetoric, Linguistics, and Literature from the University of Southern California. He has published articles on adult literacy and Irish poetry. For some time he has been interested in how to integrate the study of creative writing with an activity-centered approach to human communication. In his chapter for this volume, Gaik presents an analysis of therapy talk in radio talk-shows that draws from a number of concepts originally developed within linguistics and philosophy. In addition to employing such analytical notions as Levinson's (1979) "activity type" and Gumperz' (1982, this volume) "contextualization cue," Gaik also borrows from David Lewis the notion of "possible worlds" to show how a concept originated within logical semantics can become a powerful tool for the analysis of how speakers manage to switch activities and modes of discourse within the same event, in this case a five-minute radio therapy session. The new insight in this chapter, when compared with earlier work on possible worlds, is the negotiated nature of such changes of worlds within and across activities. The therapist may try to engage the caller in a different kind of activity, through the use of irrealis elements in his talk, but whether or not this strategy will work depends on the caller's willingness or ability to accept such a change. The use by therapists of such irrealis expressions as *could, might, may, perhaps,* etc., can switch or suggest a potential change from one realm of discourse to another, namely from the "counselling" to the "therapy" mode. We are reminded here of Duranti's discussion in Chapter 3 of respect vocabulary in Samoan. There too, the use of one or more words from a particular set (the respect vocabulary) has the power to activate a particular type of activity – one where the social, as opposed to the more personal, identities are evoked, and where participants are expected to assume a more controlled and dignified demeanor. In both cases, we are shown how linguistic features of everyday talk are constitutive of what Wittgenstein (1953) called "forms of life."

References

Gumperz, John J. 1982. *Discourse Strategies*. Cambridge: Cambridge University Press.

Levinson, Stephen. 1979. Activity Types and Language. *Linguistics* 17: 365–99.
Wittgenstein, Ludwig. 1953. *Philosophical Investigations*, trans. G. E. M. Anscombe. New York: Macmillan.

Radio talk-show therapy and the pragmatics of possible worlds

1   Introduction

Psychotherapeutic discourse – "The Talking Cure" as it has been aptly called – has attracted special attention from students of language because it provides strong evidence of the need to take context into account when explaining the relevance or appropriateness of speech acts (Brenneis 1986, Erickson and Shultz 1981, Lakoff 1980, Leavey 1980, Maranhao 1986, Shafer 1981). An amusing example of such data is supplied by Laffal (1965: 85):

Doctor: What is your name?
Patient: Well, let's say you might have thought you had something from
          before, but you haven't got it anymore.
Doctor: I'm going to call you Dean.

To understand what makes this conversation coherent, we must have reference to the doctor's inferences and, beyond that, to the whole activity in which the doctor is engaged – including the extralinguistic knowledge that validates the doctor's inferencing. Yet the interdependence between linguistic forms and context in therapeutic discourse is highly complex, stymying analysis or at least limiting generalizations. In the first place, the **ends** (Hymes 1962) of psychotherapeutic conversations are often multiple (involving both short- and long-term goals), and embedded. As Stephen Levinson has remarked, for example, one important contextual feature of therapy is the therapeutic theory that directs the doctor and provides the unstated premises to link conversation turns and make conversations relevant (Levinson 1979: 375–6). In addition, eclectic psychotherapists may use several theoretical frames at once.

Further obstacles to a comprehensive analysis of therapeutic discourse remain: First, relevant contextual features (such as a knowledge of the life history of the patient) may be unavailable to the linguist working from a transcript, although these features may have helped determine how both doctor and patient interpret a particular speech act (Labov and Fanshel 1977: 351). Second, the affective nature of most therapeutic conversations increases the need for analysis of intonation, body language, and facial expression (Labov and Fanshel 1977, Goodwin 1981). These contextual features make the mere "overhearing" of a therapy session a quixotic enterprise. Finally, we must consider that therapeutic discourse itself is highly marked and has the power to evoke or **key** (Goffman 1974: 43) the therapeutic activity in ordinary conversations (Lakoff 1980). This phenomenon is most noticeable when other participants resist such an attempt to recast discourse with such comments as:

(1) Stop playing pop shrink.
(2) Stop practicing therapy without a license.
(3) Whattya trying to psychoanalyze me?

Remarks like these, as well as pop-cultural artifacts (such as bumper stickers bearing such legends as "I'm OK, you're a jerk"), demonstrate that speakers and hearers recognize when a therapeutic purpose is being evoked. They also suggest that participants can resist therapeutic reframing and refuse to acquiesce to what Rieff (1968) has called the "Triumph of the Therapeutic."

These dynamics emerge forcefully in radio talk-show therapy, a branch of therapeutic practice that allows one to temporarily bracket some of the contextual problems that arise when studying face-to-face therapy, namely issues of eye-gaze, body language, and gesture. The data in this study come from fifteen talk-show therapy conversations transcribed from Los Angeles radio stations in October 1985. After describing the central features of talk-show therapy, I shall focus on the pragmatics of irrealis, non-factive modality, and references to possible worlds in these conversations, demonstrating how they orient patients and doctors to the goals of the phone call (see Appendix). I disagree with the conclusions reached by Labov and Fanshel (1977) that the function of irrealis in therapeutic conversations is to mitigate the force of speech acts and argue instead that irrealized discourse helps to bring about the "cathartic" effects of therapeutic discourse by allowing the participants to experience possible worlds.

2   Radio talk-show therapy

2.1   Talk-show therapy as practice and conversation

Is talk-show therapy really a form of psychotherapy at all? Though the question is disputed among talk-show doctors who assert the superiority of short-term, or even one-shot, therapeutic intervention over extended therapy (Fisch, Weakland, and Segal 1982), talk-show therapy is clearly a version of therapeutic discourse in the sense that talk is the tool used to improve the mental health of the client. The goal of talk-show therapy, like that of standard therapy, is generally to provide emotional support through discussion, introspection, and advice. Talk-show therapy tries to accomplish these ends in a highly attenuated form (usually within five minutes), but this time constraint, combined with the doctor's need to effect some change in the caller before hanging up, brings into focus the general persuasive strategies and conversation moves of therapeutic discourse in general.

2.1.1 *Audience*

In addition to its brevity, talk-show therapy also has an important public or "commercial" quality: because the conversation is part of a radio talk-show, it is never private, but instead enacted before an audience of listeners, some who are anonymous and some who might call in to comment upon a previous conversation. The doctor's reputation is on the line during every call; the therapist must seem competent, effective, and influential. It is therefore obligatory that the conversation achieve closure. This result is attained by a ritualized structure. Typically, after some greetings and introductions common to all call-in shows, the conversation turns therapeutic when the caller states a topic – the "need" or the "problem." The doctor first asks questions to elaborate on the problem and to elicit background information before a diagnosis is made. The questions are directed to provide more details and to dramatically flesh out the caller's character; they seem to be asked as much out of regard for the audience's interest as to elicit relevant information for therapy. When the story has emerged sufficiently, the doctor begins to analyze the caller's situation. During this segment the caller responds only with back-channel cues, and, as the music rises in the background, the doctor typically continues to speak while the caller's phone line is slowly faded out.

2.2   Radio therapy as commercial conversation[1]

What type of conversation is talk-show therapy? That question can be approached by noticing how technology negotiates problems typical to conversations – namely openings, establishing topic, and closings. Technology and studio direction are crucial to guarantee a smooth conversation and thus a satisfying piece of entertainment.

Establishing topic is a good example: callers to the talk-show must first describe their problems to a screener before they go on the air. The screener helps the caller to reformulate the question and sometimes to focus it. Some screeners may also prompt the caller along lines such as the following: "Tell the doctor that your problem is . . . " The screener then types the name of the caller and the topic onto a computer screen, which the doctor consults to determine which call to take next and to get a general idea of the topic before the caller begins talking. Although this procedure appears to serve a purpose similar to that of the intake interview that precedes extended face-to-face therapy or counseling, it also has the more immediate function of establishing a finite topic and facilitating conversation.

Of course problems arise. A caller may spend too much time on introductory remarks, to which the doctor responds by "pushing" with such lines as "How can I help you, today?" Or, the caller may state the problem imprecisely, a situation that is typically caused, as in the following example, by a caller's attempt to adopt the language of the screener without fully comprehending or **internalizing** it (Vygotsky 1962):

Caller: Umm - I'm at a point where I'm stuck and frustrated - creating a lot of stress for my ownself.

Closings – another difficult spot in conversations, as Schegloff and Sacks (1973) have demonstrated – are also handled neatly in radio talk-show therapy by technical devices. As the doctor begins to give advice or to recommend actions (moves that signal an extended turn on the doctor's part), there is always the problem of the caller breaking in to question the doctor's advice or to raise another (unscreened) topic while on the air. To prevent such a difficult or awkward closing, the caller's line is gradually faded out while music rises in its place.

Another "commercial" concern – preventing extended silences or "dead air" – places an additional constraint on the conversation, inasmuch as the silences that occur in face-to-face therapeutic interactions (often interpreted as significant, pregnant, or productive) would be intolerable on the radio ("dead air").

3   Talk-show therapy as event and activity

Talk-show therapy can be examined as what Levinson calls an "activity-type." Activity types are "goal-defined, socially constituted, bounded events with **constraints** on participants, settings, and so on, but above all on the kinds of allowable contributions" (Levinson 1979: 368). In goal-directed talk activities in which questions are frequently used, Levinson states that a particular role, a class of intentions is assigned to the questioner (382). Thus, he adds, "a very good idea of the kind of language usage likely to be found within a given activity can thus be predicted simply by knowing the main function of the activity as seen to be by the participants" (394).

Yet to understand the corresponding inference rules, and the ways that participants **negotiate** roles and the "main function of the activity," radio talk-show therapy must be analyzed for the activities that can be evoked within the larger **event** (Hymes 1972, Duranti 1985). For embedded within the main function of a talk-show therapy session, including its commercial goals, are two different purposes or modes of interaction that require their own roles and ways of speaking. Within any talk-show therapy conversation (the event), one activity or another tends to dominate, placing further constraints on the relevance or value of contributions (Gumperz 1982: 167). These are (1) the therapeutic activity and (2) the counseling activity.

3.1   Therapeutic and counseling activities

These activities, each of which has its own rules of interaction, represent two opposing poles in the ideology of psychotherapy. (And these ideologies are additional contextual features that constrain the inferential base from which the doctor interprets.) On the one hand, the doctor can evoke the classical psychoanalytic ideal of non-directiveness, and thus seek to avoid any prescriptive or directive role – in the interest of motivating the patient into further introspection, self-analysis, and eventual autonomy (Labov and Fanshel 1977: 32). When this procedure is evident in talk-show therapy, the **therapeutic activity** or **mode** is dominant. On the other hand, there exists a more directive mode of interaction, in which the patient seeks advice on a particular problem, and the doctor frankly offers advice or guidance. Traditionally, this sort of interaction has been assigned to **counseling** not therapy. Counseling has been described as a process designed to help a person answer the question "What shall I do?" (Tyler 1961). When the talk-show interactions move towards these purposes, they are working in the **counseling activity** or **mode**.

The differences between the therapeutic and counseling activities emerge in both topic and end (Hymes 1964). In the therapeutic, the topic is the caller's feelings, usually stated as such in the caller's first or second turn. Here are three instances:

(1) Caller: Umm - I'm at a point where I'm stuck and frustrated - creating a lot of stress for my ownself.

(2) Caller: Well the problem I'm having right now is I think because of things that happened during my childhood I'm holding on I keep - well - every once in a while during the year I go back to the past and it's really painful.

(3) Caller: And what I'd like to ask about is – O um ten years ago I had a relationship with a lady (. . .) I still see her on a very regular basis (. .) we belong to a club together (.) and uh I just don't know how to deal with my feelings cuz I uh (.)

Doctor: You're still in love with her.
Caller: I sure am.

What typically follows from such an opening is a therapeutic interaction, the purpose of which is to identify the possible sources of the caller's feelings – sources which can be from the past or from the caller's current situation.

In the counseling mode, by contrast, the topic is not a disabling anxiety but a problematic situation, usually involving a relationship with another person, which is seen as the immediate and only cause of trouble:

Caller: This is Betty - I'm sixty = and I have a son - Bill - who's twenty. My main worries are he's going to college and he simply will not support himself in any way.

The purpose of a counseling interaction is not, therefore, to identify the causes of feelings; it is, rather, to identify possible **solutions** for dealing with a problem or at least lessening its debilitating impact.

4   Irrealis and possible worlds

In this study I pay particular attention to the pragmatics of irrealis in talk-show therapy and how this feature **keys** the therapeutic over the counseling mode. Irrealis, as grammarians use the term, refers to such modal verbs as *could, would, might, can,* and *may* that point toward "possibility, epistemic necessity (tentative inference), prediction, and which do not typically involve human judgement about what is or is not likely to happen" (Quirk *et al.* 1972). Utterances in which irrealis appears (also called "irreal" or "irrealized utterances") are typically considered by grammarians to be non-factive; that is, they commit the speaker neither to the truth nor the falsity of the proposition (Lyons 1977: 795). In this standard sense, to "irrealize a proposition" is to mitigate its illocutionary force. The assertion "Jacques went to California" becomes irrealized when modal verbs or non-factive phrases are added to indicate the contingent or the hypothetical nature of the statement:

> Jacques **could** go to California.
> Jacques **may** have gone to California.
> **Perhaps** Jacques went to California.
> **It's possible that** Jacques went to California.
> **What would happen if** Jacques went to California?

As Talmy Givón describes it, the irrealized proposition is "weakly asserted as true; the speaker is offering the proposition as hypothesis, expecting strong challenge and having little evidentiary support" (1984: 121).

Though the grammatical understanding of irrealis is standard, it is the **pragmatic** function of irrealis – what we might call its subjective, phenomenological character – that must be also noticed. As Lyons cautions, when discussing modality, "Although there are methodological advantages in restricting one's attention to what we earlier referred to as microlinguistics . . . there are limits to the process of depragmatization, as far as modality is concerned" (Lyons 1977: 849). The subjective quality of irreal modality, according to logicians, is the ability of an irrealized utterance to evoke possible or alternative worlds. The difference lies between a **certain** utterance (true in all possible worlds) and a **possible** utterance (true in some possible world). Lewis (1973: 14) explains:

I believe that there are possible worlds other than the one we happen to inhabit. If an argument is wanted, it is this. It is incontrovertibly true that things might be otherwise than they are. I believe, and so do you, that things could have been different in countless ways. But what does this mean? Ordinary language permits the paraphrase: there are many ways things could have been besides the way they actually are.

Irrealis has a special function in radio talk-show therapy to prolong the therapeutic conversation by directing it toward subjective and speculative topics (to suggest that "things might be otherwise than they are") and away from simple counseling (which is based on the belief that "since things are as they actually are, what can be done?". An exchange from talk-show therapy illustrates the special role of irrealis. In the conversation from which this illustration is taken, the doctor and caller have concluded that the caller's anxiety stems from memories of her father's frequent departures (on business trips) when she was a child. As she recounts these experiences, the caller remembers them vividly and, indeed, begins to reexperience them. At one point, during this memory, the doctor continues to probe. She asks:

Doctor: How old were you when Daddy **goes** away?

Note the shift in tense. Out of context, the question is ungrammatical, but within the therapeutic conversation, it provides a crucial function by allowing the caller to have access to two worlds of inferencing simultaneously: the "adult" one, in which she analyzes the memory, and the "child" one, which she both remembers and, in a way, continues to experience. The past experience is embedded within the present moment of enunciation. And it is done in such a way that the past experience can be made present by the act of talking ("Daddy goes away"). The caller here experiences St. Augustine's "present of past things" in memory as well as a "present of present things" in direct perception (*Confessions* XI: 20; Lyons 1977: 811).Lyons formalizes these differences in the following way: "The intensional world (w_i) from which, as it were, we are asked to look at the extensional world (w_j), is the one that is defined as being identical, temporarily, with the speaker's world" (Lyons 1977: 821). Nevertheless, the pragmatics of irrealis in therapeutic discourse cannot be explained by semantics alone but must be examined within the higher purpose of psychotherapy, for ever since Aristotle, aestheticians have held that the "cathartic" effect of imagined or irreal experience requires this precise sort of double-perception or double-experience described by Augustine and Lyons (Jauss 1982: 92).

4.1   Irrealis as contextualization cue

The pragmatics of irrealis and the activities embedded in the event of talk-show therapy are mutually interdependent. In the therapeutic activity, irrealis is necessary to present the caller with alternative hypotheses about the sources of his or her anxiety and to motivate further reflection and self-inquiry. In the counseling activity, by contrast, one finds that irrealis is not instrumental but counterproductive; its use tends to interfere with the doctor's ability to give advice about the actual world. The counseling mode, which sets the stage for the doctor's advice, can only work if the caller realizes that certain events – or the actions of other people – are unchangeable and out of the caller's control. Instead of reference to a possible world, therefore, the caller must "deal with" the realities of a certain world or current reality. Once this is done, the caller can be advised accordingly. In the counseling mode, therefore, speculation must be discouraged.

On the one hand, then, the mode of interaction determines and constrains the appearance and appropriateness of irrealis; on the other hand, irrealis serves as a contextualization cue (Gumperz 1982) to signal which activity is to be dominant at any one moment or phone call.

This interdependence becomes most glaring in conversations in which caller and doctor have failed to agree on the purposes of the phone call. These are conversations of which it might be said that as far as the doctor is concerned the caller has misdiagnosed the proper mode of interaction for his or her situation, and the doctor must reframe the goals of the event. Such actions are rare and risky for the doctor, of course, who must be responsible for actually changing the topic of the phone call, a difficult maneuver inasmuch as the caller has already had the topic clarified and articulated by a screener. Schegloff and Sacks (1973) have demonstrated that callers usually set the topic of a phone call in the first topic slot, but in talk-show therapy the initial statement of topic on the part of the caller does not become operative without uptake (Austin 1962) on the part of the doctor, who must approve and confirm the caller's stated topic.

In one call, for example, the caller had begun by stating that her problem was her husband's manner of handling money, which caused her to feel insecure. The caller's purpose is to cope with her husband's manner of handling money, and thus she expects the conversation to take place as a counseling activity and expects the doctor to offer advice. In the exchange below, however, a reframing occurs. The doctor introduces a possible alternative world for the patient (line 29) and begins speaking in the irrealis mode to suggest other sources that may underlie her anxiety. The doctor moves the caller from a certain view of her problem to a more contingent one and shifts the mode of interaction from counseling – in which the doctor offers advice – to therapeutic, in which the doctor and caller together explore the caller's feelings.

```
21    D:   =:right. And he doesn't gamble–
22    C:                    [No = no = no = no - nop.
23    D:   =or get into grandiose deals=
24    C:                    [No.
25    D:   =and things of that sort. Okay.
26         So– the fears that you're having
27         are irrational fears
28         and not coming from the current reality at all,
29  →      but rather from something **perhaps** from your pa:st. (0.5)
30    C:   Probably.
31  → D:   And it **may** have nothing to do with money at all.
32    D:   It **may** have to do a lot with po:wer,
33         It **may** have to do with will you really take ca:re
34    D:   of me. Ca:n I really trust you.
35    C:   Yes.
36    D:   Uh - am I really safe. Will it really be enough
37         for me,
38    D:   Whe - are you from a large family?
```

The irrealis at line 29 (**perhaps**) not only mitigates the assertion but, more important, presents an alternative explanation for the caller's anxieties – specifically, the doctor moves the focus of attention from the problems of the present world ("current reality") to that of one (as it were) in the past. The doctor accomplishes this shift by line 38, which signifies that the relevant background knowledge for this conversation has now changed from the husband's behavior to the caller's own early history: "Whe–are you from a large family?" Only in this last line is a syntactic question spoken with an interrogatory intonation. The previous questions are stated as possibilities (e.g. "It may have to do with will you really take care of me. Can I really trust you."). Thus, irrealis is employed in this conversation to shift the focus of the conversation, to alter the topic, to introduce possible worlds of interpretation, and to change the main activity from counseling to therapy.

4.2   Conflicts in shifting topic

Not all transitions from the counseling activity to the therapeutic work so smoothly, however. In the next conversation, Betty, the caller, seeks specific advice about her son. She is interested in getting advice on how to change his behavior. But the doctor identifies the problem as lying elsewhere – not in the son's behavior but in Betty's need to control that behavior. His strategy, then, is to shift her attention from her son to her own motivations and desires. To this end, the doctor introduces a hypothetical (irrealized) question to provoke speculation and to suggest possible worlds of interpretation (line 3):

2   C: This is Betty – I'm sixty – and I have a son - Bill - who's twenty. My main worries are he's going to college and he simply will not support himself in any way. He gets very poor grades (.) He's going with a woman of thirty-seven (..) and I just don't know what to do with him (.) I've cut him way down on money – and I worry about him not having enough money to live on – but I wanted to pressure him to getting a part-time job and get better grades.

3 → D: Umm. How much control **do you think** you have over that?

4   C: hhh. I don't know because um he hasn't called me in three weeks – so I'm not sending him the money till he ca::lls me. So – ho–ho - you see?

The doctor's question, "How much control do you think you have over that?' " can be paraphrased as, "How much control **can** (or **should**) you have over that?" The doctor suggests that her reactions to her son are not inviolable but amenable to discussion and reconceptualization. But Betty fails to take the cues to enter into the therapeutic mode and to begin speculating aloud. The doctor's question is meant to be rhetorical or hypothetical, but Betty interprets it as empirical. Inasmuch as she called the doctor for **advice** about her son (line 2), she takes his question as an attempt to fine tune her techniques to gain control (to help find a "solution"), not to question (or subvert) her desire for control in the first place.

The doctor tries again to motivate Betty to speculate on some possible view of her situation, more directly, in lines 14–18:

8 C: If ya know he's just - I don't know what to do
9   with him. I thought that may be might be a solution
10   but I don't know (. .) My husband had no solution, so I
11   said and we had an argument about it – I said I'm not
12   going to argue about it - I'm gonna call Dr. David
13   Viscott and see what he says (small laugh).
14 D: Yahbut yaknow there's a whole thing
15   that you're doing here
16   that I'm not sure you're aware of (. . .)
17 →   **To what extent do you believe**
18 →   you're using money to control him?
19 C: That money will control him?
20 D: No, to what extent are you u::sing money to control him?
21 C: Oh - not that great much.
22 D: You don't think so huh?

As Betty makes clear, she is calling for a "solution" (lines 9–10), an answer to the counseling question "What shall I do?" (Tyler 1961). She does not see the doctor's question (lines 17–18) as an introduction to speculation. She does not pick up the cue to change the focus of the topic from her son to herself. She interprets the doctor's question as a practical warning ("That money will control him?" line 19), implying that if the doctor suggests money will not control him, something else might. The doctor's "No" in line 20 demonstrates that there is cross-talk (Gumperz 1982). The doctor goes so far as to explicitly disagree with the caller (line 22).

In the next section of this conversation, the doctor tries once more (lines 26–8) to shift Betty's attention away from the actual situation of her son. To get Betty to see the situation from another perspective, the doctor asks her a hypothetical question, asking her to put herself in a possible world (line 28): Note Betty's answer in line 29:

```
26   D:    Ok? (. .) and he's not going to change as long as
27         you're providing goods and services (. . .)
28         Would you?
           (1.5)
29   C:    I uh - hhh - I never acted that way.
30   D:    If someone was taking care of all your needs (.)
31   →     You see when you keep a kid dependent
32         they are also angry at you because when you keep them
33         dependent you also control them.
34   C:    Su:re.
35   D:    And he has to ask you for everything - and he hates it (. .)
36         He doesn't really want to go to school (.)
37         He's going to school because he gets supported . . .
```

The doctor is explicit, adopting the standard strategy to elicit hypothetical thinking – asking "Would you?" (line 28). But as Gumperz notes, "the signalling of frames by a single speaker is not enough" (1982: 163). Betty misses the cue; she refuses to speculate on her own motivations; instead she clearly distinguishes her own behavior from her son's (line 29). In the very next turn, however, the doctor makes his final attempt to get Betty to empathize with her son's situation by imagining herself in his place: "If someone was taking care of all your needs (.)." But note how he gives up this strategy in mid-sentence (line 31). It is obvious that Betty has not picked up on his cues to enter the therapeutic mode and to place herself up for evaluation; she will not change her topic from her son's behavior to her beliefs and desires. To bring the conversation to some satisfactory closure, the doctor shifts from the hypothetical mode to the present tense and begins to make general statements about her relationship to her son (line 31). This is the signal that therapy is being abandoned in place of counseling; the doctor's previous attempts to lead Betty to speculation will be supplanted by his decision to offer explicit advice after all. The present tense, as it functions here, is what Gerhardt and Savisir (1987) have called the "normative present tense," because its use closes off speculation and dialogue in order to assert the norms of the community or the stability of current reality. This conversation constitutes a tug-of-war: Betty is interested in getting advice – a specific solution to help her troubled son. But the doctor attempts to turn the tables, to make it appear to her that her son is unchangeable while Betty is the one whose attitudes and behavior are manipulable, even (or especially) by herself.

4.3 Counseling and the problem of irrealis

Another example demonstrates how irrealis gets dismissed as unproductive in counseling interactions. In this conversation, the caller, Savo, has opened without stating his topic clearly; after some probing by the doctor, the "problem" is finally stated:

```
8    D:   Yes (.) and what can I help you with because it sounds
9         as if you've got things kind of (.) leveled out for
10        yourself.
11   C:   Uh Uh yes. I have okay, the problem is that (.) he's
12        not uh he's obviously not approving the way I am
13        emotionally, you know what I'm saying? Uh he
14        doesn't like y'know that way I behave and uh it sounds
15        like y'know that I'm =
16   D:   //hhh ((great sigh))
17   C:   = not gonna love you and (.) uh the way you are,
18        you know, I - you gotta be perfect.
19   D:   hhh Savo. You have =
20        This is not exactly a great surprise to you.
21        You know that your da:d has been very critical,
22        very at some times cruel,
23 → a:nd maybe this is the way he thinks
24        that good parents are supposed to be
25        maybe it's the way he was taught,
26        maybe it's the way he was raised,
27        uhm I don't know if he wakes up every morning
28        and says how can I destroy my son today,
29 → but you know that you're not ever going to have
30        the loving warm, accepting, approving father, that
31        everybody yearns for,
32        That isn't in the cards for you (.)
```

Savo expects to engage the doctor in a therapeutic activity; that is, he wants to further pursue the source of his anxiety by exploring the dynamics of his father's disapproval (lines 11–15). The doctor indicates frustration with the randomness of the question (line 16) and, acknowledging that she knows something of Savo's history, indicates that he has not broached a new topic but merely rehashed an old one ("This is not exactly a great surprise to you"). She then repeats what is known about the current reality by asserting the normative present tense (line 21): "You know . . ."

By rejecting the validity of further speculation on Savo's part, the doctor signals a move into the counseling mode. Lines 23–8 comprise a list of ways that Savo could further consider the possible reasons for his father's cruelty. Yet the doctor introduces the list of reasons (each marked by irrealis: *maybe, I don't know if*) only to dismiss them as irrelevant to Savo's case. Although the doctor actually suggests a series of hypotheses that might be useful to explore in a therapeutic activity, that activity – and therefore its purposes – is rejected (beginning at line 29). According to the doctor, further speculation about Savo's father is now counterproductive. Savo, like Hamlet, has become melancholy in his imaginings; it is time to quit them and move on. This example points to the need to distinguish between the appearance of irrealis and its function in context; in this case, irrealis evokes an activity that is contra-indicated; it is mentioned but not used.

Just as the irrealis mode is mentioned but dismissed, so is the chance to engage in the therapeutic activity. The therapist shifts from a series of possible avenues of exploration to statements in the normative present tense, establishing the counseling mode of interaction, allowing her to give direct advice to Savo and close the conversation. Other devices for establishing and maintaining the counseling mode include figurative language, such as metaphor, analogy, and cliché. In line 32, the doctor tells Savo "That isn't in the cards for you," and later, in the same conversation, she tells him "your father is an empty well, and you should use that image for yourself." In addition, analogies are drawn between Savo and other callers and even to the doctor, which, I would suggest, is a means of establishing what Bernstein (1970) calls "we solidarity" between the caller and the doctor. Metaphors, clichés, and markers of "we solidarity" function pragmatically like the normative present tense; they assert the norms of the community and key the typical actions and values of its members. Talk-show conversations dominated by the therapeutic activity, by contrast, avoid metaphors, analogy, and markers of "we solidarity" because one goal of the therapeutic mode is for callers to discover or explore the unique reasons for their anxiety. The lack of "we solidarity" in therapeutic conversations can also be explained by the dominant role the doctor holds as the expert in this mode of exploration (Labov and Fanshel 1977: 32). In fact, the assertion of solidarity on the part of the doctor would so vitiate the therapeutic mode of interaction that markers of solidarity can be seen as keying a transition from the therapeutic to the counseling activity.

To summarize the pragmatics of irrealis: in the talk-show conversations whose mode is primarily therapeutic, irrealis serves a crucial and necessary function to help the caller and doctor search for possible unique sources of the caller's anxiety and to promote introspection. When introspection becomes counterproductive, however, the therapist can **deem** (Grice 1982: 242) irrealis to be irrelevant and can turn instead to making normative statements about what seems to be the unchanging nature of the social world. If the caller explicitly seeks advice, the doctor will show a preference for metaphors and clichés as a way of establishing "we solidarity" and asserting or calling into play the norms of the community.

5 Irrealis as speech act: reexamining Labov and Fanshel

The function of irrealis to evoke possible contexts of interpretation moves us beyond the scope of speech act level analysis.[2] Irrealis serves larger instrumental functions in psychotherapeutic discourse, as can be seen by reexamining data from the classic study by Labov and Fanshel (1977). Although Labov and Fanshel do not analyze irrealis as an isolated phenomenon, they do analyze one case of irrealis (the therapist's hypothetical question). They mention the following example:

(The topic is Rhoda's problems with the cleaning habits of her aunt.)

$\rightarrow$ Th.: Well, what would happen if you **said** something to her – too – since=
R.: Well, you know, she –
Th.: -we're in the, in the business=
R.: Yes.
Th.: =of **talking**, *yes*.   (1977: 194)

Labov and Fanshel read this hypothetical question as an indirect request for action, mitigated by the additional metacommentary about the talking profession. They explain that this mitigation is necessary because the therapist had, by suggesting an action or giving advice, violated one of the rules of therapeutic conversation, the rule of autonomy:

The therapist does not direct the patient's life.

(1977: 195)

As noted earlier, therapists who give advice are at risk of practicing counseling (answering the question "What shall I do?") instead of therapy. Thus, Labov and Fanshel take the doctor's question to be a way of mitigating the underlying illocutionary force of the request.

This analysis, though it recognizes the objective function of irrealis to mitigate the truth value of a sentence, does not account for the speculative function of irrealis in therapeutic discourse. If it is true that the hypothetic proposition is actually a veiled suggestion, then the request is for action (action outside the therapist's office), not for more information. In that case, there would be no need to answer the question in conversation. Yet the doctor seems to require a reply to complete the goals for the session, for in the data below, she judges Rhoda's answer to be unsatisfactory.

Rhoda is supposed to answer a question about "What would happen?" if she were to ask her aunt to clean; instead, Rhoda tells a story about "what did happen" the last time she tried. So the therapist returns to ask another question that is parallel to the first:

Th.: But what would happen if you – um – you know – tried to arrive at some working relationship with her – To say you work all day an' I go to school all day – Maybe when we . . . uhm . . get to the point where we have t'have some – uh – effort made about dinner and so on that it could be joint, you know, let's figure out what **you** should do an' what I should do.
R.:   Sso - like - las' night – like, on Wednesday night is my late – one o' my late nights –
T.:   Mm.

Once again, Labov and Fanshel interpret the therapist's hypothetical question as an indirect request for information, whose underlying illocutionary force (mitigated by the contour placed on "would") is actually a direct command: "Try to arrive at some working relationship with her!" (1977: 214). However, if it is true that the hypothetical question here is not really a question, why does the therapist repeat it? I would characterize the moves here as following this pattern:

(a) Question
(b) Answer insufficient to the purposes of the conversation
(a) Repeated question
(b) Answer that is more revealing

Rhoda's first response to the therapist's question did not serve the therapeutic goal. Thus she was asked again. It is true, as Labov and Fanshel mention, that Rhoda does refuse the therapist's request, but her refusal violates the expectations of the conversation first, only then can it be seen as a psychological defense mechanism. Rhoda denies the implicit request to speculate. She does not adopt the hypothetical orientation that the therapist frames, nor does she begin to sketch out possible scenarios of what would happen if she asked her aunt to help. Instead of answering the invitation to tell the story of what would or might happen, she follows with a story of what typically happens. Rhoda's refusal can also be seen as a miscue; she misses the invitation to enter a possible world and explore the consequences of talking to her aunt. Rhoda's refusal, then, resembles Betty's in the earlier example: in both cases, the patient refuses to engage in speculation that would make her own attitudes and strategies the topic for analysis. It seems likely that both patients demonstrate their reluctance (or inability) to join the class of patients who would find speculation, hypothetical reasoning, and engagement with possible worlds to be meaningful ends in themselves (Scollon and Scollon 1981: 61; Heath 1983: 250).

Rhoda's therapist is doing more than modeling the kind of behavior that Rhoda should follow or making a veiled (or mitigated) assertion. What seems more likely is that she wants Rhoda to answer the hypothetical question by further speculating, by answering her question **not** in factual but in counterfactual terms: "If I were to do that, here is what would probably happen." The use of the hypothetical question is a form of **request**, as Labov and Fanshel note, but it is not so much a request for behavior change as it is a chance to have Augustine's "present of future things" as well as his "present of past things" (*Confessions* XI: 20; Lyons 1977: 811). The patient can call the future into existence, experiencing it in expectation. Irrealis is an "invitation to speculate," a request to enter the hypothetical world that might be too threatening at this moment of the subject's real life.

6   Conclusion

Irrealis serves a cathartic function in therapeutic discourse that cannot be accounted for by discourse analysis that sees the individual turns in a therapeutic conversation as separate speech acts. Irrealis inspires the patient to consider alternative worlds, to call these worlds into existence, and to discourse within their parameters. Irrealis is more than just a means of mitigating truth value; it is, rather, an important strategy in the persuasive rhetoric of the therapeutic encounter.

Appendix: markers of irrealis as index to possible worlds in psychotherapeutic conversation

(1) and not coming from the current reality at all, but rather from something **perhaps** from your past.
(2) And it **may** have nothing to do with money at all.
    It **may** have to do a lot with po:wer,
    It **may** have to do with will you really take ca:re of me.
    Ca:n I really trust you.
(3) How much control **do you think** you have over that?
(4) **To what extent do you believe** you're using money to control him?
(5) **Would you?**
(6) **If** someone was taking care of all of your needs
(7) **a:nd maybe** this is the way he thinks that good parents are supposed to be
    maybe it's the way he was taught,
    maybe it's the way he was **raised**,
    uhm **I don't know if** he wakes up every morning
    and says how can I destroy my **son** today.

(8) **Well, what would happen if** you said something to her –
(9) **But what would happen if** you – um – you know – tried to arrive at some working relationship with her –

Acknowledgments

I wish to acknowledge my debt to my fellow graduate students in Linguistics 510, who transcribed nearly fifty pages of radio talk-show therapy, and without whose help this study could not have been done. I also wish to thank Professor Elinor Ochs and the following for helpful commentary on earlier drafts: Niko Besnier, Alessandro Duranti and Charles Goodwin, John J. Gumperz, and Linda J. Palumbo.

Notes

1. The technological features of talk-show therapy were observed at KABC radio studios in Los Angeles in December 1986.
2. Lyons (1977) closes his comprehensive discussion of mood and illocutionary force by observing that "modality, as it operates in a good deal of everyday language-behaviour, cannot be understood, or properly analyzed, otherwise than in terms of lexical and instrumental functions of language, to which its descriptive function is, at times if not always, subordinate" (1977: 849).

References

Austin, J. L. 1962. *How To Do Things With Words*. Oxford: Clarendon Press.
Bernstein, Basil. 1970. A Sociolinguistic Approach to Socialization, in *Language and Poverty: Perspectives on a Theme*, ed. F. Williams. Chicago: Markham.
Brenneis, Donald. 1986. The Fiji Panayat as Therapeutic Discourse. *IPrA Papers in Pragmatics* 1(1): 55–78.
Duranti, Alessandro. 1985. Sociocultural Dimensions of Discourse, in *Handbook of Discourse Analysis. Vol. 1: Disciplines of Discourse*, ed. Teun A. Van Dijk, pp. 193–230. New York: Academic Press.
Erickson, Frederick, and Jeffery Shultz. 1981. *The Counselor as Gatekeeper: Social Interaction in Interviews*. New York: Academic Press.
Fisch, Richard, J. H. Weakland, and L. Segal. 1982. *The Tactics of Change: Doing Therapy Briefly*. New York: Jossey-Bass.
Freud, Sigmund. 1924. *A General Introduction to Psychoanalysis*. New York: Washington Square Press.
Gerhardt, Julie (Gee), and Iskender Savasir. 1987. The Use of the Simple Present in the Speech of Three-Year Olds: Normativity Not Subjectivity. *Language in Society*, 15: 501–36.
Givón, Talmy. 1984. The Pragmatics of Referentiality, in *Meaning, Form, and Use in Context*, ed. Deborah Schiffrin. Georgetown: Georgetown University Press.

Goffman, Erving. 1974. *Frame Analysis*. New York: Harper and Row.
Goodwin, Charles. 1981. *Conversational Organization*. New York: Academic Press.
Grice, H. Paul. 1982. Meaning Revisited, in *Mutual Knowledge*, ed. N. V. Smith, pp. 223–45. London: Academic Press.
Gumperz, John J. 1982. *Discourse Strategies*. Cambridge: Cambridge University Press.
Heath, Shirley Brice. 1983. *Ways with Words*. Cambridge: Cambridge University Press.
Hymes, Dell. 1962. The Ethnography of Speaking, in *Anthropology and Human Behavior*, ed. T. Gladwin and W. C. Sturtevant, pp. 13–53. Washington: Anthropological Society of Washington.
  1964. Toward Ethnographies of Communicative Events, in *Language and Social Context*, ed. P. P. Giglioli. Harmondsworth: Penguin.
  1972. Models of Interaction of Language and Social Life, in *Directions in Sociolinguistics*, ed. John J. Gumperz and Dell Hymes, pp. 35–71. New York: Holt, Rinehart and Winston.
Jauss, Hans Robert. 1982. *Aesthetic Experience and Literary Hermeneutics*, Trans. Michael Shaw. Minneapolis: University of Minnesota Press.
Labov, William, and David Fanshel. 1977. *Therapeutic Discourse: Psychotherapy as Conversation*. New York: Academic Press.
Laffal, Julius. 1965. *Pathology and Normal Language*. New York: Atherton.
Lakoff, Robin. 1980. When Talk Is Not Cheap: The Language of Psychotherapy, in *The State of the Language*, ed. Leonard Michaels and Christopher Ricks, pp. 440–8. Berkeley: University of California Press.
Leavey, Stanley. 1980. *The Psychoanalytic Dialogue*. New Haven: Yale University Press.
Levinson, Stephen. 1979. Activity Types and Language. *Linguistics* 17: 365–99.
  (ed.). 1983. *Pragmatics*. Cambridge: Cambridge University Press.
Lewis, David. 1973. *Counterfactuals*. Oxford: Basil Blackwell.
Lyons, John. 1977. *Semantics: Vol. 2*. Cambridge: Cambridge University Press.
Maranhao, Tullio. 1986. *Therapeutic Discourse and Socratic Dialogue: A Cultural Critique*. Madison: University of Wisconsin Press.
Quirk, R., S. Greenbaum, G. Leech, and J. Svartik. 1972. *A Grammar of Contemporary English*. London: Longman.
Rieff, Philip. 1968. *The Triumph of the Therapeutic: Uses of Faith After Freud*. New York: Harper and Row.
Schegloff, Emanuel A. and Harvey Sacks. 1973. Opening Up Closings. *Semiotica* 8: 289–327.
Scollon, Ron, and Suzanne B. K. Scollon. 1981. *Narrative, Literacy and Face in Interethnic Communication*. Norwood, NJ: Ablex.
Scribner, Sylvia, and Michael Cole. 1981. *The Psychology of Literacy*. Cambridge, Mass.: Harvard University Press.
Shafer, Roy. 1981. Narration in the Psychoanalytic Dialogue, in *On Narrative*, ed. W. J. T.Mitchell, pp. 25–50. Chicago: University of Chicago Press.
Tyler, Leona. 1961. *The Work of a Counselor*. New York: Appleton-Century-Crofts.
Vygotsky, L. S. 1962. *Thought and Language*, ed. and trans. Eugenia Hanfmann and Gertrude Vaker. Cambridge, Mass: Harvard University Press.

11 The interpenetration of communicative contexts: examples from medical encounters

AARON V. CICOUREL

Editors' introduction

Aaron Cicourel is Professor of Cognitive Science and Sociology at the University of California, San Diego, where he is also employed by the Medical School. For over three decades, Cicourel has worked on the ways in which knowledge is accessed or manipulated in a variety of contexts, including courts (Cicourel 1968), educational settings (Cicourel and Kitsuse 1963), and medical settings (Cicourel 1980). His concern for the structuring of everyday experience through social interaction and his critique of hidden procedures within institutional settings puts his work close to two other contemporary influential figures in the analysis of everyday interaction, Erving Goffman and Harold Garfinkel. With the former, Cicourel shares the focus on situated interpretation – Goffman's famous leading question "What's going on here?" can be repeatedly heard through Cicourel's work – and with the latter he shares the concern for the participants' unconscious inferential processes or implicit principles that characterize everyday thinking. Cicourel's unique approach to sociology, which he termed "cognitive sociology" (Cicourel 1973), is an original blend of European scholarship on the mundane basis of scientific thinking – Husserl's thought as filtered through Schutz's work was particularly influential in Cicourel's early research – and contemporary development within cognitive science. His long-term association with the Center for Human Information Processing and his regular exchanges over the last several years with such scholars as David Rumelhard, George Mandler, Michael Cole, and Roy D'Andrade has further informed his concern for the integration of traditional micro-sociology with current thinking within psychology and anthropology on the origin of context-specific knowledge and memory.

In this chapter, Cicourel returns to one of the main concerns of his intellectual career, namely the question of the definition of context in the analysis of verbal interaction within institutional settings. Whereas formal grammarians and structuralist anthropologists are interested in the discovery of underlying, abstract, often unconscious structures and processes that give meaning to linguistic or ritual forms, Cicourel is interested in the hidden aspects of reasoning and information processing that characterize researchers as well as members of a given culture. "How do you know that?" is a question that Cicourel often asks his colleagues when they present the results of their research projects. The replies (or attempts to reply) he receives in these exchanges constitute for him the starting point for methodological and theoretical reflections on how knowledge is stored and retrieved and issues created or ignored out of a myriad of details which are often used but not talked about by analysts. Cicourel's ideal model of the relationship between language and context is one in which the participants, before the analysts, have simultaneous access to several levels of analysis, including the local organization of turn-taking and their internal syntactic structure, lexical choices and semantic networks, as well as the broader context of the institutional settings where the interaction takes place and within which talk acquires meaning for the participants *qua* social actors (see Corsaro 1985). He distinguishes between two senses of context, which he names "narrow" and "broad," and proposes their integration for the analysis of everyday talk. Methodology is one of Cicourel's main concerns. In particular, he stresses the importance of ethnographic fieldwork and the ways in which it can help situate a stretch of talk within its larger institutional context. In this chapter, his methodological concerns are integrated with a detailed analysis of particular verbal exchanges within a medical facility. By using a technique similar to what film critics call "slow disclosure" (Sharff 1982), Cicourel slowly uncovers further layers of information about the participants, their institutional roles, their previous exchanges, and their shared knowledge. In so doing, he is able to directly address the issue of how much contextual information should be made available in the study of spontaneous everyday interaction. In Cicourel's chapter, we are shown that even the use of initials in a transcript hides unspoken principles and selective strategies. Until we are told that IDA and MR stand for *Infectious Disease Attending* and *Medical Resident* respectively, we could take them to be conventional mnemonic devices void of social meaning. But labelling is important for participants (when they talk about each other) and researchers alike. What does it mean to give a transcript with names of speakers, with their occupational roles, or with initials? What do we evoke when we say that a certain conversation is between a doctor and a patient, or between A and B? On the other hand, how much information should be offered? Shouldn't we avoid the possibility of an infinite regress, whereby the encyclopedic knowledge available to members will never be matched by the analyst's knowledge? Conversation analysis has opted for a research strategy whereby only the information that the participants themselves make available in the talk should be evoked by the researcher. However, Cicourel points out some possible limitations of this program when applied without a critical attitude. The omission of apparent extratextual information can be problematic to the extent to which it obscures information that was at some point relevant to the researcher during the collection of analysis of the material under discussion. The ideal researcher in Cicourel's model of discourse analysis is thus one who does not hide his or her sources of information and research choices but makes them into a common resource to be shared with the readers in an attempt to unveil the hidden processes of the selection of information which guides participants and analysts alike in the course of their daily lives.

References

Cicourel, Aaron, V. 1968. *The Social Organization of Juvenile Justice*. New York: Wiley.

Cicourel, Aaron V. 1973. *Cognitive Sociology*. Harmondsworth: Penguin.

Cicourel, Aaron. 1980. Three Models of Discourse Analysis: The Role of Social Structure: *Discourse Processes* 3: 101–32.

Cicourel, Aaron V., and J. I. Kitsuse. 1963. *The Educational Decision Makers*. New York: Bobbs Merrill.

Corsaro, William A. 1985. Sociological Approaches to Discourse Analysis, in *Handbook of Discourse Analysis. Vol. 1: Disciplines of Discourse*, ed. Teun A. Van Dijk, pp. 167–92. New York: Academic Press.

Sharff, Stefan. 1982. *The Elements of Cinema: Toward a Theory of Cinesthetic Impact*. New York: Columbia University Press.

The interpenetration of communicative contexts: examples from medical encounters

1   Introduction

A researcher's decision to tape-record conversation or discourse creates a contextual frame that limits what is to be identified as relevant data, their organization, and the kinds of analysis and inferences to which these data will be subjected. Research on conversation and discourse varies considerably in the extent to which an investigator will describe the circumstances of taping a conversation and her or his involvement with those taped. Similar conditions exist in other types of research on social interaction. For example, in field research, a participant observer must be sensitive to the fact that elicitation procedures can force informants to become aware of issues or conditions about which they normally are not aware or may be aware of only in the local context of everyday settings. Silverstein (1981) notes that much if not most of what is of interest to researchers is beyond the informant's ability to articulate meanings in ways we would like or expect. The researcher's questions can create contextual frames that may not be consistent with informants' everyday practices. A similar problem exists in laboratory experiments of social interaction where status and role relations are foci of attention. The investigator's and subjects' conceptions of status and role relations are contingent on implicit and formally defined notions of "context" created for the experimental occasion. We seldom know the extent to which simulated social relations reflect or are contrary to the kinds of experiences subjects have in their everyday encounters.

While many researchers will agree that talk and some notion of "context" shape each other as part of an emergent process that changes through time and space, not all students of language use will concede that ethnographic material, participant attributes, and patterns of social organization that are constitutive of talk need to be included in studies of the structure of conversation or discourse. For example, conversation analysts (Sacks, Schegloff, and Jefferson 1974; Schegloff, in press) prefer to focus on such things as sequential organization, and how that organization creates local contextual elements in conversation. The researcher's use of social categories in any analysis must be linked to participants' recognition of the categories as integral to the events being studied. This research attitude can result in a very formal type of analysis. Linguistic approaches to discourse analysis (Brown and Yule 1983) also minimize the role of ethnographic and organizational conditions that can also result in a formal analysis of utterance sequences. What remains unclear is the extent to which the decision to tape or use particular materials includes or excludes explicit and tacit knowledge about reported and unreported ethnographic conditions, participant attributes, and patterns of social organization that can selectively shape subsequent analysis. The researcher can exercise considerable discretion in what the reader will be shown or told about "context."

The content of conversation or discourse material can be made to appear rather transparent when we use brief, formal or informal exchanges among people we do not know, who interact in settings described in a limited way, or when we use casual, mundane everyday conversations among friends during informal exchanges. When the research analyst is working in her or his own society, and the reader is expected to be from the same society, it is especially convenient to use brief, formal or informal mundane conversations. The investigator's ability to comprehend these exchanges is assumed to be self-evident and is seldom if ever an aspect of the analysis. But if a fuller analysis of participants' conversation and ethnographic understandings about activities, objects, and ideas is desired, and that understanding presupposes prior social experience, and/or technical, scientific, or professional training, then other strategies besides a completely local analysis must be employed.

Verbal interaction is related to the task at hand. Language and other social practices are interdependent. Knowing something about the ethnographic setting, the perception of and characteristics attributed to others, and broader and local social organizational conditions becomes imperative for an understanding of linguistic and non-linguistic aspects of communicative events.

In the present chapter, I discuss several settings within a larger organizational bureaucracy that contribute to two senses of "context" that are routine aspects of conversational interaction in all everyday environments. One use of the term "context" includes an institutionalized framing of activities. In traditional social science theorizing, it is customary to speak of group-derived prescriptive norms that pressure and/or channel people with designated titles, presumed competencies, duties or responsibilities into certain physical spaces at certain times in order to engage in a finite number of specifiable activities. Within this institutionalized context or framing of activities, emergent processes of talk appear that create a more narrow view of "context" in the sense of locally organized and negotiated interaction.

The extent to which the investigator knows about the institutionalized and everyday events that participants and analysts categorize by the use of specific terms varies. For example, the analyst of particular settings may or may not be present when speech events are recorded. Within this more narrow sense of "context," therefore, the analysis of a tape and transcript may or may not begin with the investigator's direct experience with the ethnographic setting in which the speech events were recorded.

When the investigator knows little or nothing about the speech event and the event is rather short-lived and apparently not viewed as part of or influenced by existing institutionalized or bureaucratic activities, what gets identified as context can be more easily located in the talk said to be attended by the participants. The investigator can begin her or his analysis by examining the way the conversation is initiated, the way intonation and stress are used, the content of lexical items and phrases, the occurrence of pauses or hesitations, turn-taking moves, and the way topics are introduced, sustained, and altered or changed. The focus of attention can become the sequential organization of conversation material that presupposes that participants, investigator, and reader all share a common knowledge base that is largely tacit or unstated but which becomes partially articulated by the way the investigator begins to make claims about the categories to which the participants are said to be attending. The investigator and reader presumably can each examine the same data and make claims and counter-claims about the clarity and substance of the analysis.

The methodological strategy of using local talk as the source of information in the narrow sense of context can be self-serving by the way the researcher not only ignores prior and current organizational or institutional experiences of participants, but by the kinds of data that are presented for analysis. For many students of language and social interaction, therefore, the notion of context need not include references to the participants' and researcher's personal, kin, and organizational relationships and other aspects of complex or institutionalized settings. Casual, fleeting speech events, however, are often constrained and guided by normative institutionalized features that we associate with encounters in public places described in general but vivid terms by Goffman (1959, 1963, 1971) among others. These brief exchanges can also carry considerable cultural and interpersonal "baggage" for participants because of long-term social relationships unknown to or unattended by the investigator. The investigator who examines a speech event can therefore be forced to attend to its several senses of context narrowly or broadly because of the kinds of data presented to the reader.

The present chapter is identified explicitly with the view that both a broad and local sense of context are needed for the study of language use. The focus on discourse in the pages that follow should not be construed as being relevant only to conversational material, but also applies to the study of single utterances. I examine a complex environmental setting in order to underscore the importance of context at different levels of analysis. The following pages begin with a conversation in which three people emerge as speakers. Subsequent sections provide the reader with a brief overview of the organizational settings and the ethnographic circumstances in which the data were obtained. After investigating additional speech events, I close the chapter by illustrating how both immediate and other aspects of context must be taken into account if we are to understand language and social interaction in everyday life. The focus of this chapter, therefore, differs from but also builds on conversation and discourse theorists concerned primarily with the structural features of conversation such as turn-taking, side sequences, topicalization, coherence, and related notions. It is important to locate the analysis of language and social interaction in a wide variety of social activities that are implicitly and explicitly known to the participants and investigator.

2   A routine conversation

The speech event presented in Example (1) can be viewed as a routine conversation between three unidentified people who will be identified below.

Example 1: A conversation between three physicians

```
 1   PA:    (?) (low voice level) Is this the same one (we?)
 2           (ya?) did yesterday?
 3   IDA:   No. This is the eye lady.
 4   PA:    (?)
 5   IDA:   Cellulitis
 6   PA:    Oh.
 7   IDA:   With group A strep..in shock
 8   PA:    In shock. (Slight rise in voice level) How about that.
 9   IDA:   I[t?] was gonna be more interesting |if she didn't
10   MR:                                        |I'm(?)
11   IDA:   have bacteremia but (laughing and voice level
12           increasing) now she's had |bacteremia so
13   MR:                                |There's a little, there's
14           little (voice level increases) problem with that
```

15		that I'll, will go into more as far
16	IDA:	Yeah.
17	MR:	how much shock she really |was in,
18	IDA:	|was in, right
19	MR:	compared to what [abrupt shift] she's a liver lady.
20		you know, an' I don't know what her blood pressure sits
21		at. |It may not be real high to |start with.
22	IDA:	|Right. |Right.
23	PA:	So she didn't have peripheral, evidence of shock
24		really? |Just a low blood pressure.
25	MR:	|No, she wasn't, she wasn't ever clamp, you
26		know
27	PA:	Uh huh
28	MR:	clamped down *or* flushed or anything
29	PA:	OK
30	MR:	I can..and, and she doesn't
31		[abrupt shift] one thing that argues
32		against a lot of neuropathy, you know, from diabetes, for
33		one, she's only had it for three years, but two, you know,
34		her neuro exam an' her an' her peripheral vascular exams,
35		is really normal, is normal sensory, good pulses distally,
36		and stuff, and I just have a hard time,
37	PA:	Yeah
38	MR:	there'd be a lot of sy-sympathetic, you know
39	PA:	Right
40	MR:	phone calls.
41	IDA:	Have they got sinus films on yer yet?

Each dot between words = one second. The solid vertical line indicates points of overlap in the exchange.

Telling the reader that three physicians are involved is an initial attempt at penetrating what is occurring in this encounter. Lines 1–12 strongly suggest that the participants are engaged in a discussion regarding the medical condition of some other party. The investigator's control over when and what material will be shown the reader can, therefore, vary considerably and can create different interpretive frames. Saying that three physicians (they also could be other health care providers) are talking implies that they are probably in a medical facility of some kind, but there is no indication of precisely what kind or part of a health care facility they are in. Nor can we be sure if the patient is nearby, is an inpatient or an outpatient. We know nothing about the physicians' gender or personal characteristics nor their specialities. Nor do we know if this information is relevant to the analysis.

The opening lines (1–8) of Example (1) do not mention the term "physicians" nor is there any indication in lines 1–3 that a "patient" is involved. Having identified the three participants as "physicians," we can also say that they are talking about a "patient" who has been dubbed the "eye lady," for some unstated reason, or a patient who is experiencing difficulty with her eye.

Although the content of lines 1–3 of Example (1) ("Is this the same one [we?] [ya?] did yesterday? No. This is the eye lady.") does not suggest a health care facility, physicians, and a patient with eye problems, the term "cellulitis" in line 5 might be recognizable enough to send us to a medical dictionary as we begin our analysis. Alternatively, we might seek help from informants or examine further sequences of conversation in the hope that other lexical items, phrases, prosodic features of the talk, or thus far unstated nonverbal perceptions might increase our understanding of this encounter. For example, notice the remark by IDA in line 7 ("group A strep..in shock"), which could refer to an infection. The comment or observation by PA in line 8 ("In shock. How about that.") could be interpreted as expressing interest in the categories supplied by IDA and perhaps mild surprise. The subsequent remarks by IDA in lines 9, 11 and 12 of Example (1) ("I[t?] was gonna be more interesting if she didn't have bacteremia but now she's had bacteremia so") suggest that PA and IDA are both familiar with the terms "cellulitis," "group A strep," "in shock," and "bacteremia."

The significance the analyst attributes to particular utterances or to their sequential order, and claims about the participants' perception and understanding of a speech event, are often the result of examining subsequent utterances (Sacks, Schegloff, and Jefferson 1974). If we do not invoke institutional and local sociocultural details with which to identify the participants of conversation, the analysis of meaning is nearly impossible.

I will now abruptly shift my mode of analysis by telling the reader something about the participants in Example (1) and about how the data were obtained. The setting is generally known to the reader and investigator alike because of a commonsense understanding of categories such as "patient," "health care facility," "medical center," "hospital," and "medical school." Stating that the talk is in a medical setting does not tell the reader that there is medical talk taking place nor who is doing the talking and with what credentials. But claiming the participants in a given speech event are physicians talking about a particular (technical sense of) "patient" orients us to categories we associate with particular members of a medical setting and a basis for making claims about the use of these categories in their talk. The term "patient," for example, is used in at least two ways in this chapter.

For the reader of this chapter, the term "patient" probably implies a commonsense notion of someone who is not feeling well or is "sick." For the health care expert, however, the term "patient" can activate thoughts about someone with neurophysiological, biochemical, and psychopathological symptoms and conditions that are part of an extensive technical compositional semantics and clinical as well as mundane experiences. For the most part, the term "patient" will be used in the second sense just noted. Thus, even mundane terms such as "eye lady" (line 3, Example 1) and "she's a liver lady" (line 19, Example 1) imply an activation of technical knowledge and experiences that are part of complex socially organized activities.

3   The research setting and types of participants

The case material I present in this chapter represents a small portion of data from field research in two teaching hospitals. The material is part of routine institutionalized bureaucratic activities that are typically associated with health care delivery in Western countries. My observations and tape-recording of activities mostly involved physician–patient, physician–physician, or physician–technician interaction, and also include extensive field notes about the settings and the participants.

The medical settings observed are typical of teaching hospitals but are not necessarily representative of other clinic or hospital settings in which there is an absence of House Staff (interns, residents, and training fellows). The inclusion of House Staff adds hierarchical relationships and hence additional bureaucratic conditions that differentiate teaching from non-teaching hospitals. Additional details about organizational conditions, the influence of status and role relationships, and the expertise or background knowledge associated with such designations will be provided as the chapter unfolds.

The range of speech events in these settings can be diverse and can include a quick exchange of greetings, brief exchanges of gossip or rumors about patients, or staff, and discussion about the local baseball or football team's fortunes. There also can be brief and lengthy exchanges between physician and patient, technical discussions among physicians and between physicians and nurses or technicians, and somber or emotionally charged exchanges between family members and health care personnel. The exchanges can occur in a variety of settings such as the patient's room, in a clinic examining room, a hall or corridor, an empty elevator, the cafeteria, at the x-ray facility, the nurse's station, or a laboratory.

Over a period of months, I observed and then began to tape-record various clinical exchanges. These exchanges included outpatient clinics where patients may be seen initially or as a follow-up from prior visits or inpatient service. I also accompanied the resident or attending physician on ward rounds, or visits to the x-ray facility, to daily laboratory rounds, and to weekly grand or teaching rounds where cases of unusual interest are presented before attendings (one or more physicians qualified to supervise residents) from the county and residents from several hospitals.

The ethnographic activities alluded to above obviously provided many opportunities to express my ignorance about medicine and to ask questions of different experts. The field research was facilitated by my official connection with a school of medicine. Knowing some of my informants independently of the research setting because of committee activities in the School of Medicine made participation in the research setting easier and enabled me to ask many "dumb" questions as a non-medical specialist. But familiarity with the settings can also create problems. For example, my colleagues sometimes forgot that I am not a physician and spoke to me as if I were fully capable of understanding technical matters that were discussed. I often pretended to seem informed in order to not disturb the speech event, but later would have to ask for help.

My ethnographic experiences, consultations with people called "physicians," and occasional uses of a medical dictionary enable me to take a number of liberties in describing the material in Example (1). I can tell the reader that there is a female inpatient located in a medical teaching hospital with an eye problem as well as additional difficulties associated with the technical terms "group A strep" (line 7), "shock" (line 7) and "bacteremia" (line 11). I rely on the reader's commonsense understanding and my use of expert informants to claim that the physicians are talking about someone with an infection and perhaps something more serious (as may be evident by the references to "shock" and "bacteremia"). Less transparent here is the remark by IDA (lines 9–12) that the case would have been more interesting if the patient did not have bacteremia.

4   Reexamining the conversation in Example (1)

The exchange in Example (1) does not state that the three participants are attached to a health care facility of some kind nor is there any mention of a patient. The conversation begins in line 1 with the introduction of a topic ("Is this the same one . . .") and a reference to some object or someone that had something done to it the day before.

In Section 2 above, I alluded to the possible content of lines 1–7 of Example (1). An analyst might choose to ignore further discussion of content at this point and instead could focus on who speaks first and how someone responds, identifying turns, the selection of next speaker, topicalization, side sequences, adjacency pairs, registers used, topic and comment, deictic, anaphoric, metaphoric, and metanymic expressions, to mention some familiar aspects of the study of language in social interaction.

The opening question by PA ("Is this the same one [we?] [ya?] did yesterday?") in line 1, Example (1), can be seen as topicalizing an unidentified but particular type of object that other participants presumably recognize as fitting into a specific subset of a general category. We can subsequently categorize this object as a "patient" in the technical sense by assuming the participants are health care providers of some kind. The response by IDA in line 3, Example (1), rejects a particular subset of the unidentified hypothesized category but does allude to another subset by stating "This is the eye lady." In lines 5, 7, and 12 of Example (1), IDA seems to clarify the hypothesis about the category "patient" by describing particulars such as "cellulitis," "group A strep," "in shock," and "bacteremia."

The opening question by PA in line 1, Example (1), might also be loosely interpreted as one part of an adjacency pair (e.g. question–answer sequence) in which the second part consists of the "No" of line 3 by IDA. Perhaps this type of analysis might be stretched even more if we ignore the "No" of line 3 and the "Oh" of line 6 and say that the second part of the adjacency pair consists of fragments from lines 3, 5, 7, and possibly 12 of Example (1). To paraphrase the exchange, PA's question in line 1, "Is this the same one (we?) (ya?) did yesterday?" is answered by IDA in lines 3, 5, 7, and possibly 12 ("No. This is the eye lady," "Cellulitis," "With group A strep...in shock," and "now she's had bacteremia"). If we go beyond this loose illustration of sequential analysis, we can ask how much local context is the analyst required to construct in order to convince herself or himself and the reader that the interpretations being claimed are adequate for some sequence of text?

5   What counts as relevant ethnographic details?

I observed the exchange in Example (1) as well as other exchanges involving this patient. Consequently, I can assert from my notes that PA turned directly to IDA when posing the question about the "same one" in line 1. The speech event can be further clarified by noting that PA refers to a Pathology Attendant who is the Chief of the Microbiology Laboratory, and IDA is the Infectious Disease Attending. MR is the infectious disease Medical Resident for the rotation period during which the event occurred.

The exchange reported in Example (1) occurred after MR and IDA had both interviewed the patient and had discussed the case. Their participation in the encounter reported in Example (1) had already been anticipated because of the expected earlier exchange. PA is the expert here and methodically examines a series of small slips of paper each morning at 11:00 a.m. in which new or additional information about a patient's cultures is noted. IDA is also an expert about microbiological aspects of each patient, particularly the clinical ramifications of the case. By addressing IDA, PA asks the responsible clinical expert about the case in order to contextualize the laboratory findings. There are other people in the corner of a large room (which is actually one part of the suite in which the microbiology labs are located). There often is a fourth-year medical student doing a month's rotation in infectious disease cases, a pathology resident who assists PA with laboratory details including the cultures for each patient, slides, and petrie dishes to be examined that morning, an infectious disease resident from pediatrics, and one or two teaching fellows.

In a teaching hospital, IDA may begin with a few comments on the case but normally turns it over to MR for the details. After this, PA first examines the slide or cultures and either directly describes the morphology of the organism(s) or invites the medical student or fellow or a resident to tell the group what organism(s) is/are involved. PA then invariably gives the group additional information about the nature of the organism, the kinds of disease and/or symptoms associated with the laboratory findings, and the patient's likely prognosis with different types of treatment.

The opening line of Example (1), therefore, assumes coherence by reference to a presumed activity done with thus far unidentified others the day before. As noted above, the unidentified others in the present case are the MR and IDA. The response by IDA in line 3 shifts the topic to someone called "the eye lady." The inaudible comment by PA in line 4 of Example (1) could have been a request for details about the case. IDA provides one detail ("cellulitis"). From my watching his facial expression and hearing the intonation of his voice ("Oh" in line 6), I infer that the term is of interest to PA. When IDA provides additional information about the patient, PA repeats the last phrase ("in shock") and with a slightly rising voice level seems to be expressing mild surprise ("How about that"). Then IDA, in lines 9, 11, and 12, refers to how much more interesting the case would have been if the patient had not had "bacteremia" ("I[t?] was gonna be more interesting if she didn't have bacteremia but now she's had bacteremia so"). MR, however, in lines 10 and 13–17 ("There's a little, there's little problem with that that I'll, will go into more as far how much shock she really was in") seems to be questioning the patient's "shock" and these doubts are related to the issue of bacteremia with or without shock.

The remark by IDA in line 18 of Example (1) repeats the last two terms used by MR and adds "right" as if to support MR's observation. Earlier, I was with IDA and MR when the two discussed the case and knew that there were doubts expressed (in two separate medical histories) by other physicians about the patient's "shock." MR's completion of his remark from line 17 (stated as "compared to what" in line 19) was followed by an abrupt shift in the topic. Presumably the patient's "shock" was to be contrasted with an unstated something else ("compared to what") when MR decided to abruptly shift the topic to the patient's liver ("she's a liver lady, you know"). So in addition to being "the eye lady" of line 3, the metaphor shifts to that of "liver lady." The reader's technical knowledge may be strained by the phrase "a liver lady." My participation in the setting tells me we have a patient with a current eye problem and a prior liver problem attributed to a history of alcohol abuse.

On the basis of previous conversations with informants, I can report that one clinical sign of shock is very low blood pressure. MR's remark in line 21 ("It may not be real high to start with") refers to the time of admission for the patient when her blood pressure was observed to be low but where no one (including the patient) was aware of her normal blood pressure. The inference of possible shock, therefore, can be problematic depending on the patient's normal blood pressure. IDA had contributed to MR's remarks through their previous conversations the day before, and the "Right" uttered twice by IDA in line 22 could signal agreement with the present observation by MR and/or IDA's prior contribution. After reading the transcript, however, IDA reported that the intent of saying "Right" twice was to hurry MR into expediting his delivery and remarks.

In lines 23–4, PA provides some clarification of the patient's alleged shock by his "declarative-interrogative" that the patient apparently "didn't have peripheral, evidence of shock really? Just a low blood pressure." Although appearing to be a question, PA's remarks are spoken authoritatively through the use of a somewhat "matter of fact" or "self-confident" intonation and the mildly assertive nature of the content. There is also the ethnographic element that he is the primary expert here and can be indirectly asserting this expertise by his remarks in lines 23–4.

MR's rambling remarks in lines 25–36 of Example (1) address several possible topics that presuppose background in clinical medicine. For an attending, MR's remarks can become the basis for an organizational assessment of the resident or novice in infectious diseases. As non-medical specialists, students of language use in social interaction, we can only superficially assess the import of the material in Example (1) unless we seek the help of informants and have access to the kind of ethnographic information provided thus far.

6   Expanding the ethnographic context

I have presented a partial description of the way the selection of different ethnographic or organizational settings and types of speech events or social interaction can affect the analyst's interpretation of the research materials presented to a reader. In this chapter, I have ignored several administrative, professional, and technical matters that affect how patients are admitted into a medical setting, are diagnosed, and treated by different health care delivery personnel.

The present case involves a 48-year-old white female whose chief complaint was recorded in her admission history and physical examination as "swelling of the left eye." Additional details can be found in Cicourel (1987). Of interest here is her primary diagnosis of "periorbital cellulitis" or what was described as a "right-upper-lid abscess with periorbital cellulitis." My informants helped me translate this last phrase into an infected, swollen-shut left eye, that seemed highly inflamed to me, with purplish coloring of the skin around the eye that was apparently caused by blood seeping into the skin. The patient's left side of her face was swollen as well as her eye and ear. There was pus oozing out of the area of the eyelids.

I accompanied MR when he first went to the medical ward to see the patient. Before interviewing the patient, MR went to the nurse's station to review the patient's chart. As is often the case with infectious disease patients, an attending physician other than IDA usually will see a patient admitted to the medical service. In the present case, two attendings had interviewed the patient and had ordered laboratory tests before asking for an infectious disease consultation. The results of these tests were reported in the chart. MR's infectious-disease-oriented interview of the patient, therefore, was in part influenced by his having had access to the patient's medical chart. MR's questions, therefore, reflect aspects of these prior experiences.

In addition, this interview is influenced by his prior medical school training. The medical student's knowledge of infectious diseases can be traced to one or two courses (depending on the quarter of semester basis of the medical school) in microbiology. I attended some of the lectures in microbiology and also interviewed the director of the course, who is also PA in the conversation of Example (1). With the help of informants, it is possible to trace aspects of the basic science concepts and clinical medicine experience medical students are exposed to before they enter an intern or residency program. Knowing something about the physician's prior experiences in medical school and as a House Officer can provide the analyst and reader with possible aspects of the background knowledge tacitly or explicitly assumed or employed during a speech event. I do not have time to present all of the content of my interview with PA in his role as the microbiology course director, but instead will provide the reader with a few highlights that can be linked to the conversation in Example (1).

Trying to trace the kinds of basic and clinical science concepts that medical students and House Staff are exposed to before they attain the status of "attendings" is not meant to imply that such codifiable knowledge is the primary source of background necessary for the diagnostic reasoning and treatment directed at patients. In my work on medical communication and diagnostic reasoning, I have stressed the importance of tacit clinical experience and the everyday understanding of mundane social interaction as aspects of a world presumed to be known in common but not necessarily examined reflexively by participants in the medical or any other area of life (Cicourel 1982, 1986, 1987). I call the reader's attention, however, to the necessity of incorporating systematically codified knowledge (textbooks, detailed lectures, laboratory practices, apprentice-like experiences) into our understanding of bureaucratic and non-bureaucratic language use and social interaction. Inasmuch as sociolinguistics tends to address various kinds of everyday events in which the analyst can "pass" as an expert because of her or his background in language use and social interaction, the analysis of content is often viewed as fairly straightforward. By calling the reader's attention to the role of multiple ethnographic and/or organizational settings and informants, I underscore the complexity of the term "context" or "local" and more abstract senses of culture or social organization for understanding language use and social interaction.

According to the microbiology course director during an interview obtained early in my research and noted above, students should remember the following:

Example 2

1 "...what are the important bacteria, and, in terms of human
2 disease, and what are their unique microbiologic
3 characteristics...The streptococci can be differentiated
4 into the hemolytic ones and the non-hemolytic ones and
5 green ones. Those that are alpha-hemolytic make green
6 colonies. And among the beta-hemolytic ones we have the
7 group A strep, which is really the only accepted cause of
8 bacterial pharyngitis...The streptococci are in chains,
9 the pseudomonas and the enterobacteriaceae are gram negative
10 rods, and they look a lot alike on the gram stain...
11 And if you look at the streptococci for a minute, the group
12 A strep, is able to cause sore throats primarily because of
13 the M protein...
14 ...what are the unique microbiologic characteristics that
15 permit me to recognize this organism, let's say right out
16 of the blood culture bottle like you've seen us do up
17 there?....Did this patient have cellulitis, or lymphangitis?
18 Yes. Well, then it's probably a group A strep...

The technical remarks by the pathologist made during the interview conducted before the completely independent laboratory conversation of Example (1) refer to the clinical consequences medical students are expected to remember from courses in microbiology. The references to "streptococci" (line 3), "beta-hemolytic ones" (line 6), and "group A strep" (line 7) in Example (2) are directly related to the "sore throats" of line 12 and are a significant aspect of the diagnostic reasoning employed in the present case. Notice the reference to "cellulitis" and its association with "group A strep" in lines 17–18. The pathologist's remarks provide clear evidence of prior training on the part of physicians that plays a role in job-related speech events. Such training may be important not only to participants, but also to the analyst's understanding of medical communication and semantic aspects of diagnostic reasoning in the case under review and in medical settings generally.

The concepts mentioned by the pathologist in Example (2) are not merely aspects of textbook knowledge associated with prior training, but are also part of a medical student's laboratory experiences with the microorganisms noted in Example (2). Without this background knowledge based on studying textbooks, listening to lectures, and working in a laboratory setting, it would be rather difficult for a participant to display her or his group membership in the conversation of Example (1). In the case of a medical resident, there will have been prior experiences as an intern in which aspects of the material in Example (1) will have been discussed.

Another source of background knowledge that can influence speech events in medical settings is the way that novice physicians are exposed to an initial lecture (also given to them as a written handout) when they begin their training. The following lines are from lecture notes developed by an infectious disease attending physician. I quote selectively from the written handout given to the House Staff.

Example 3

1 "I. Septicemia – microbial agents in the bloodstream...
2   B. One is led to the diagnosis of bloodstream
3   infection by a **sudden change** in clinical
4   state...
5   All sorts of organisms can cause hypotension, but,
6   **in the absence of hypoxia (pneumonia) or heart**
7   **failure**, gram-negative bacteremia with endotoxemia
8   is by far the most common cause of sustained
9   hypotension...
10   D. Other causes of infectious shock
11   3. Streptococcal shock (group A strep), often in
12   the absence of bacteremia, associated with soft
13   tissue infections (usually severe)..."

Of interest are references to "microbial agents in the bloodstream" (line 1), "the diagnosis of bloodstream infection by a **sudden change** in clinical state" (lines 2–4), and "organisms [that] can cause hypotension" such as "gram-negative bacteremia with endotoxemia" (lines 5–7). A sudden change in clinical state can be a drop in blood pressure (hypotension), which in turn can be linked to the release of bacteria or endotoxins in the bloodstream that can lead to shock. The most succinct remark can be found in lines 10–13 of Example (3) because it comes fairly close to the case described in Example (1). The patient was found to have group A strep and bacteremia as noted by IDA in Example (1). The case revealed bacteremia but MR claimed the patient may not have been in shock. The presence of shock was never confirmed. The remarks contained in Example (3) and given to House Staff at the two hospitals in which I conducted my research directly associate this background material to specific aspects of the exchange in Example (1).

I will close this section by quoting a brief excerpt from MR's original interview with the patient. The interview occurred prior to the speech event reported in Example (1).

Example 4

1   I wanna take (?) your blood. (?) blood pressure (?)
2   (.....) (mumbling) A lot of people get, bacteria
3   in their blood, and ya get uh shock. [Low monotone
4   intonation] When your blood pressure goes down
5   because it means (?) the bacteria releases certain
6   toxins, depending on (?) area (?) [raised intonation]
7   Has your, blood pressure always run kind of on the low
8   side, ma'am?

Before MR and I entered the ward to see the patient, MR had reviewed the patient's chart and was aware of the two prior medical histories therein and hence was also aware of the suspected diagnosis of bacteremic shock. MR was also aware of many other medical facts and hypotheses about the patient's condition. MR's explanation (only partly shown here) to the patient about her medical problems (linking a drop in blood pressure to a prior release of "certain toxins") can be linked directly to the prior medical histories that existed in the patient's chart, the infectious disease attending's written handout, and the pathologist's description of what medical students should remember of their course work in microbiology. In turn, all of these matters, plus MR's interview with the patient, had an effect on the remarks by PA, IDA, and MR in Example (1).

7   Concluding remarks

The chapter has presented a few of the large number of interpenetrating medical events that form the local context for language use and social interaction in any given encounter. I have sought to discuss the topic of local context in terms of those cultural and organizational constraints, normative expectations, and immediate conditions that surround local speech events as they unfold.

The notion of interpenetrating medical communicative contexts seeks to place the local mutual shaping of talk and context into a framework that incorporates structural and processual aspects of social organization and reasoning during social interaction. The medical setting I chose as the point of departure for the present chapter was the source of a conversation between three physicians. The material presented in Example (1) can be subjected to different types of interpretation, contingent on the analyst's orientation to language use and social interaction and the extent to which the notions of background and context are employed.

The local interaction in Example (1) is intended to call the reader's attention to outside organizational experiences or institutionally guided and constrained social interaction and/or speech events that are directly relevant to the way local exchanges are likely to occur. For example, the interaction described in Example (1) can be linked to the microbiological aspects of medical education (Example 2) and the lecture on Septicemia (Example 3) given to the House Staff at the beginning of the medical academic year. All social interaction and/or speech events presuppose and are informed by analogous prior forms of socially organized experiences.

The analyst's decision to describe the materials in Example (1) as an exchange between three health care delivery workers or professionals creates a cultural context for the analyst and reader and simultaneously calls attention to the use of social categories that hopefully can be attributed to participants' recognition of their relevance for the speech event being examined. The analyst's decision to focus on particular sociolinguistic notions (topicalization, turn-taking, speech act categories, coherence, types of deixis, frozen expressions, preferred sequences, etc.) rather than the interrelationship between discourse and culture or the interrelationship between discourse and linguistic theory can trigger different expectations on the part of the reader.

Telling the reader that the three participants in Example (1) are physicians, that the exchange took place in a hospital microbiology laboratory while they were discussing a patient with suspected bacteremic shock, and preparatory to examining the patient's blood cultures, creates a cultural context within which the analyst and reader can understand what transpires. Our understanding deepens when the physicians are identified as a pathology attending, an infectious disease attending, and an infectious disease medical resident. Not only are the expressive style and the content observed contingent on organizationally constrained status and role relationships that can influence who speaks first, whose views will be influential or will prevail *vis-à-vis* action to be taken, but the analyst's and reader's ability to comprehend the significance of broader and local sociocultural issues may require extensive consultation with medical experts.

The present case actually began with MR and the researcher going to the nurse's station of a university medical center medicine ward to examine the medical chart of a patient suspected of having bacteremic shock. MR was performing an organizational obligation of initiating a consultation requested of the Division of Infectious Diseases.

The material from the microbiology course presented above reflects information medical students are expected to know, and the excerpts from the lecture given to new House Staff reflect the kinds of training experiences a novice like an intern or resident physician is likely to possess when reading a patient's chart and then interviewing the patient.

By the time the case reached the microbiology laboratory rounds depicted in Example (1), the patient had also been interviewed by IDA: MR and IDA had discussed the case in some detail; IDA had interviewed the patient; and IDA had consulted the patient's chart, added to it, and had consulted two standard textbooks on microbiology.

The analysis of material in Example (1), the excerpts on the microbiology course (Example 2), the infectious disease attending's lecture notes for new House Staff (Example 3), and the fragment from MR's interview with the patient (Example 4) represent a small part of a complex set of interpenetrating contexts. In the present chapter, I have documented only minimally the way informants helped me understand organizational conditions, local speech events and social interaction, the meaning of complex concepts, and procedures from basic and clinical medical science and practical experiences. I have, however, employed several types of ethnographic and textual materials in order to underscore what I have characterized as unavoidable aspects of organizational and local constraints and processes that are integral to rethinking "context."

A nagging issue that undoubtedly remains for many readers is the familiar one that an infinite regress can occur whereby the observer presumably must describe "everything" about a context. Such a demand is of course impossible to satisfy because no one could claim to have specified all of the local and larger sociocultural aspects of a context. Observers or analysts, like participants of speech events, must continually face practical circumstances that are an integral part of all research or everyday living. As researchers, we obviously privilege some aspects of a context while minimizing or ignoring other conditions. The observer is obligated to justify what has been included and what has been excluded according to stated theoretical goals, methodological strategies employed, and the consistency and convincingness of an argument or analysis. Meaning and understanding in everyday life are contingent on cognitive and linguistic activities, i.e., a knowledge of how to use language structures that we call metonyms, metaphors, and other imaginative constructions associated with particular lexical items, phrases or utterances, and personal experiences. Therefore, some specification of the environmental conditions in which these language practices emerge, are embedded, and evolve should guide the researcher's depiction of context. I have tried to indicate some of the conditions that can be identified in a medical setting to illustrate the way different senses of the term "context" can be pursued conceptually and empirically.

Acknowledgments

Parts of this chapter were initially presented at the Invited Session "Rethinking 'Context': Language as an Interactive Phenomenon, Part I" (Society for Linguistic Anthropology and General Anthropology Division), American Anthropological Association annual meeting, Philadelphia, PA, December 1986. A version of the paper appeared in the *Social Psychology Quarterly*. The present version has been expanded slightly and further revised. I am grateful to Charles Davis and Elizabeth Ziegler for their invaluable support and advice, and to Sandro Duranti, Charles Goodwin, Douglas Maynard, Hugh Mehan, James Wertsch, and two anonymous referees for their helpful substantive suggestions on earlier drafts. Douglas Maynard also provided very useful editorial suggestions.

References

Brown, Gillian, and George Yule. 1983. *Discourse Analysis*. Cambridge: Cambridge University Press.

Cicourel, Aaron. 1982. Language and Belief in a Medical Setting, in *Contemporary Perceptions of Language: Interdisciplinary Dimensions*, ed. Heidie Burnes, pp. 48–78. Georgetown: Georgetown University Press.

1986. The Reproduction of Objective Knowledge: Common Sense Reasoning in Medical Decision Making, in *The Knowledge Society*, ed. Gernot Bohme and Nico Stehr, pp. 87–122. Dordrecht: Reidel Publishing Co.

1987. Cognitive and Organizational Aspects of Medical Diagnostic Reasoning. *Discourse Processes* 10: 346–67.

Goffman, Erving. 1959. *The Presentation of Self in Everyday Life*. Garden City, New York: Doubleday Anchor Books.

1963. *Behavior in Public Places*. New York: The Free Press.

1971. *Relations in Public*. New York: Basic Books.

Sacks, Harvey, Emanuel A. Schegloff, and Gail Jefferson. 1974. A Simplest Systematics for the Organization of Turn-Taking for Conversation. *Language* 50: 696–735.

Schegloff, Emanuel A. In press. Between Macro and Micro: Contexts and Other Connections, in *The Micro–Macro Link*, ed. J. Alexander, B. Giesen, R. Munch, and N. Smelser. Berkeley and Los Angeles: University of California Press.

Silverstein, Michael. 1981. The Limits of Awareness, in *Sociolinguistic Working Paper 84*, pp. 1–30. Austin, Texas.

12 The routinization of repair in courtroom discourse

SUSAN U. PHILIPS

Editors' introduction

Susan U. Philips is Professor of Anthropology at the University of Arizona. Her major research projects in the last two decades show influence from a variety of approaches, including the ethnography of communication (Gumperz and Hymes 1964, 1972), ethnomethodology (Garfinkel 1967), conversation analysis (Goodwin and Goodwin, this volume; Schegloff, this volume), and Cicourel's interest in the organization of discourse in bureaucratic settings (Cicourel, this volume). Since her earlier work among the Warm Spring Indians (Philips 1972, 1983), Philips has been concerned with combining traditional ethnographic methods with detailed analysis of communicative behavior within particular institutional settings, namely schools and courts. In this tradition, she has contributed to the development of the methodology characteristic of the ethnography of communication whereby the researcher systematically compares patterns of speech production within and across events in the same speech community (e.g. Warm Spring Indians) or speech system (e.g. judges' speech in the courtroom). As she explains in this chapter, this method differs from the one usually adopted by conversation analysts, who tend to collect and analyze isolated stretches of talk (e.g. a telephone conversation) for their formal and locally produced properties, without being concerned with maintaining identity of speakers or setting across different recordings. Philips' notion of "context" thus includes a system of speech events typically linked across time and space by identity of speaker, genre, or activity.

Philips' chapter in this volume originated from a research project aimed at examining judges' speech in court – in the Tucson, Arizona, state court of general jurisdiction – as an example of their interpretation of written law. Philips wanted to understand how different legal realities are created in the courtroom through variation in judges' speech patterns. Methodologically, this was realized by taping a number of judges doing the same procedures (namely, taking guilty pleas) over and over again, so that the linguistic practices used in these contexts could be compared within and across individuals. Within this general framework, Philips' chapter addresses two main issues: (1) the extent to which what we consider to be spontaneous or emergent properties of ongoing interaction are in fact at least in part routinized talk which only gives the "impression" of spontaneity; (2) the role played by methodology in favoring certain analytical distinctions and theoretical explanations. Philips' commitment to a truly comparative and ethnographically oriented approach to the study of the "spoken law" has taken her more recently to the Kingdom of Tonga, a Polynesian society in the South Pacific, where she has been collecting and analyzing the language of dispute management in court and other contexts.

References

Garfinkel, Harold. 1967. *Studies in Ethnomethodology*. Englewood Cliffs, N.J.: Prentice-Hall.
Gumperz, John J., and Dell Hymes (eds.). 1964. The Ethnography of Communication. *American Anthropologist* 66 (6) Pt. II.
    (eds.) 1972. *Directions in Sociolinguistics: The Ethnography of Communication*. New York: Holt, Rinehart and Winston.
Philips, Susan. 1972. Participant Structures and Communicative Competence: Warm Springs Children in Community and Classroom, in *Functions of Language in the Classroom*, ed. Courtney B. Cazden, Vera T. John, and Dell Hymes, pp. 370–94. New York: Teachers' College Press.
    1983. *The Invisible Culture: Communication in Classroom and Community on the Warm Springs Indian Reservation*. New York: Longman.

The routinization of repair in courtroom discourse

The purpose of this chapter is to suggest that there is more routinization in the interactional construction of social context and meaning than is presently recognized. I do this here by providing evidence that repair-like phenomena, which are often taken as evidence of a speaker's ongoing planning of speech and/or attention to and incorporation of the verbal and nonverbal contributions or co-interactants (Sacks, Schegloff, and Jefferson 1974, Jefferson 1974, Schegloff, in press), are routinized and displayed in exactly the same way in the same socio-functional and sentential environments repeatedly.

Contemporary linguists follow Chomsky (1955) in emphasizing the productivity of grammars, and their potential to allow speakers to produce an infinite variety of actual sentence structures and meanings. While conversation analysis in many ways offers a radically different approach to the creation of meaning from that of generative linguistics, here too there has been an emphasis on spontaneity and creativity in the construction of meaning. Influenced by Garfinkel's (1967) view that the social self is realized in the process of interaction, conversation analysts effectively convey the extent to which meaning is not inherent in sentences; rather, as each speaker takes a turn at talk, he or she builds on the contributions of the preceding speaker, and in so doing provides evidence of particular understandings of that prior talk (Sacks 1967). Through this process the meaning of a particular sentence is both jointly constructed by co-interactants, rather than being the property of a single speaker, and is emergent, or continually changing, through the sequential structure of talk. Sacks, Schegloff, and Jefferson (1974) have also emphasized the extent to which such emergent meaning is locally managed in conversation, so that each next speaker is typically most responsive to the immediately preceding and ongoing (C. Goodwin 1981) communicative contributions of co-interactants.

Conversation analysts use the term "repair" to refer to various kinds of false starts, mid-sentence lexical substitutions, and additions and fillers such as "uh." Like turns at talk themselves, these phenomena are conceptualized as abstract devices whose actual deployment displays very ongoing and immediate response to the speech and nonverbal behavior of co-interactants (Sacks, Schegloff, and Jefferson 1974, Jefferson 1974, Schegloff, Jefferson, and Sacks 1977; Schegloff, in press). Repairs, then, play an important role in the joint and emergent construction of social context and meaning.

Recently, however, there has been growing recognition that actual employment of grammars and turns at talk is not so open-ended, creative, and spontaneous. Fillmore, Kay, and O'Conner (1988), for example, have offered an alternative view to that of the generative linguists of linguistic competence as comprised in part of a number of "idioms" – packages of combined syntactic and semantic structures that can be used to produce a range of unique meanings, as in utterances with the phrase "let alone," e.g. "I can't sing, let alone dance," and "I don't eat peas, let alone other vegetables."

The concept of routine has also contributed to the growing recognition that creativity and productivity in language use are constrained. Hymes (1962) used the term "routine" to refer to culturally specific formulaic interactional exchanges such as greetings that are fixed in not only semantic and syntactic form, but also in the sequential order in which such forms will be exchanged by speakers. Students of language socialization (e.g. Watson–Gegeo and Boggs 1977, Schieffelin 1980) have argued that routines play an important role in children's learning how to use linguistic forms in a socially appropriate fashion. Fixed routines, such as nursery rhymes, allow children to control linguistically complex forms that are later used in more creative and open-ended constructions. They also provide simple models of dialogic exchange that can be elaborated and expanded into more complex forms of dialogue later on. Finally, children's (M. H. Goodwin 1980) and adults' (Coulmas 1981) interactions often reveal an underlying discourse format that is routinized, yet has the potential to convey a variety of unique messages – a conceptualization analogous to Fillmore *et al.*'s "idioms," but rendered as dialogic or interactional.

For the purposes of the discussion to follow, I have in mind a type of routinization that is related to these concepts, yet is slightly different. Here I want to suggest that it is common for speakers to produce stretches of speech in interaction that may be experienced by co-interactants as new and spontaneous, yet may be an exact or almost-exact repetition of some or all aspects of a prior speaker's language form, or a repetition of the speaker's own speech from a prior occasion. Further, some such unrecognized routinized pieces of speech may be used over and over only briefly or fleetingly and then discarded, while others may be used over and over for extended periods of time.

My attention was first drawn to such routinization when, for other purposes (Philips and Reynolds 1987), I was analyzing data from four Arizona state court Voire Dires. The Voire Dire is the legal procedure in which prospective jurors are questioned by the judge and opposing lawyers prior to actual jury selection. One optional segment of this inquiry presents prospective jurors with a list of pieces of information they are each asked to provide about themselves (name, occupation, etc.), which each then does in turn in a brief monologue. As in similar situations most of us have encountered, where you go around in a circle and tell a little about yourselves before getting on with a group discussion, the first one or two monologues tend to set a discourse format for the rest, so that a routine discourse format emerges spontaneously in the immediate context, yet in its specifics it may never be used again. What was striking about these routines was that in some cases they were copied from prior speakers down to the exact syntactic form in which the information was delivered. Thus information that was delivered in two clauses by adjacent speakers in one Voire Dire was delivered in a single clause with a prepositional phrase by adjacent speakers in the second Voire Dire, as in the following examples:

Voire Dire (1)   A: **I'm employed with the city of Tucson. Aah been there over 9 months**. I'm a police officer.
                 B: **I'm employed at Davis Monthan Air Force Base**, 'n I've **been there since 1966**. Uh I'm a traffic specialist.
Voire Dire (2)   A: **I'm presently employed with IBS for about 8 months**.
                 B: I'm an advertising copywriter **currently employed with Jack Trustman Advertising for about 8 months**.

                                                      (Philips and Reynolds 1987)

The particular data that will be drawn upon in focusing on repair comes from a study of nine Pima County Superior Court judges as they take guilty pleas from criminal defendants. There are several different ways in which repairs are routinized in the data considered here, data which is drawn from the speech of three judges who will be referred to as Judge A, Judge B, and Judge C.

First of all, some judges have individual styles of repair, so that the same judge will repair his speech in the same way over and over. Thus Judge A repeatedly repeats the initial sound of a word, but usually only once or twice, before getting the word out, as in examples (3) through (6), which the other 2 judges **don't** repeatedly do.

(3) Uh, one count of theft of a **m..motor** vehicle.

(Tape L, Side 1, p. 2)

(4) I could put'cha on probation **i..if** I treated those as misdemeanors...

(Tape L, Side 1, p. 6)

(5) **D..do** you understand that?

(Tape L, Side 1, p. 7)

(6) Uh, you could'a **y..y..you** might've kept it for several days.

(Tape L, Side 1, p. 16)

Judge B, however, repeats whole words three or four times, as in examples (7) through (10).

(7) And, nothin **'th'th'th'the** jury could not, uh, uh, take—any, uh, idea that you were guilty because of the fact that you h'hadn't testified.

(Tape F, Side 2, p. 56)

(8) In addition to that, uh (3 sec. pause) no comment could be made **by, by, by,** uhm Miss Gonzalez about the fact that you hadn't testified.

(Tape F, Side 2, p. 56)

(9) The only way you're gonna lose, that **th'th'that that that that**, uh, that right is by, uh (2 sec. pause) pleading guilty and convicting yourself or having a jury find you guilty.

(Tape F, Side 2, p. 57)

(10) But, **know'knowing that, knowing** what the charge is, uh, knowing what the po'uh'you possible sentence could be, do you still wanna accept this plea agreement?

(Tape F, Side 2, p. 58)

A **second** type of routinization in this data base is the repetition of the exact same repair in the exact same functional, lexical, and syntactic context. This does not mean these repairs always occur here, but rather that they are prone to. In examples (11) and (12), Judge B displays the same hitch or slight pause at exactly the same juncture in two instances of the guilty plea.[1]

(11) Alright. Let the record—show the Court accepts Mr. Larson's pleas of guilty. **Finds that—it is voluntarily and intelligently made**, and there's a factual basis for the plea.

(Tape D, Side 1, p. 38)

(12) Alright. This is your last chance, Charles, you want me to accept your, your, your plea of guilty to this charg'these charges. I mean which

charge can be f'alright, let the record show the Court accepts Mr. Thompson's plea of guilty, **finds that – it is voluntarily intelligently made**, and there is a factual basis for the plea.

(Tape F, Side 2, p. 60)

In examples (13) and (14), and (15) and (16), Judge C displays "uh" following "that" in *that*-clauses in two instances of two different parts of the procedure. These examples may also reflect Judge C's individual style of repair. But this is a common type of repair.

(13) You have the right to have the Court tell the jury—instruct the jury **that, uh, you** are to be presumed innocent.....

(Tape A, Side 2, p. 54)

(14) And the Court would instruct the jury **that, uh, you** are to be presumed innocent.....

(Tape A, Side 2, p. 39)

(15) I'll order **that, uh a** pre-sentence investigation and report be made by the Adult Probation Officer of this Court.

(Tape A, Side 2, p. 78)

(16) Alright. It's ordered **that, uh a** pre-sentence investigation and report be made by the Adult Probation Office of the Court.

(Tape A, Side 2, p. 62)

A **third** kind of routinized repair evident in my courtroom data is what I will call the routinized repair of routine trouble, and here we come closer to the type of repair documented in conversation analysis. I have in mind the situation where one speaker makes a move which sometimes fails to elicit an expected response from a co-interactant, and so goes back over it, doing the first move differently to try to elicit the desired response.

In the guilty pleas from which the data for this chapter is drawn, most of the judges regularly asked criminal defendants how many years of schooling they had had. This was part of their elicitation of individual background information they felt would help them determine whether the individual could understand the procedure and "knowingly" waive rights. For reasons not entirely clear, this commonly asked and seemingly straightforward question often initially met with either no answer, as in example (18) below, or with slightly vague and ambiguous answers, as in examples (17) and (18). For this reason many of the judges both alternated this question form, as in Judge B's (20) and (22), and repeated their alternated versions in a single asking, illustrated in Judge C's examples (17) and (18) and Judge B's example (21).

Judge C

(17) Judge: What education do you have? How far d'you go in school?

Defendant: Graduate.

(Tape A, Side 2, p. 32)

   (18) Judge: What education have you had? (4 sec. pause) 'S how
                             much edu-schooling have you had?
          Defendant: Uhm (2 sec. pause) Seven.

                                          (Tape A, Side 2, p. 47)

   (19) Judge: Uh, what kind of education have you had?
          Defendant: Up, up through twelfth.

                                          (Tape A, Side 2, p. 66)

Judge B

   (20) Judge: Uh, how much school have you had sir?
          Defendant: Uh, I've got a (GED).

                                        (Tape D, Side 1, p. 30)

   (21) Judge: OK. Uh, how far did you get in school, sir?
                             How much education do you have?
          Defendant: I completed high school.

                                        (Tape D, Side 1, p. 38)

   (22) Judge: OK. How far did you get in school?
          Defendant: Eighth.

                                        (Tape F, Side 2, p. 47)

These examples are presented for each judge in the order in which they were taped to show that routinized alternates may be the source of routinized repair. In other words, when forms which are sometimes alternated don't work alone, they may be used together.

My final example of a type of repair commonly found in my data base is not strictly speaking routinized repair, but rather shows the way in which departure from a routine is repaired to return to the routine because as the speaker is speaking he realizes there is something unworkable about his innovation.

Example (23) shows how Judge A typically first introduces the general information that the defendant has certain constitutional rights, then begins their enumeration with the right to a jury trial. In (24) he begins with the enumeration of the specific jury trial right, then repairs this to mention the general rights first.

The routine

   (23)   .....And, uh, (2 sec. pause) lemme, lemme ask—this, do **you under-
           stand that you have certain constitutional rights which you'll be giving
           up** by, uh, by the entry of the plea of guilty to this charge? **And these
           rights include: a right to a jury trial** on the charge contained in the
           indictment.

                                        (Tape E, Side 2, p. 32)

Repair to return to routine

   (24)   .....Do you know that you have **a right to go to um, you have certain
           rights** which you're giving up by entering a plea of guilty to uh, um,

this charge **an' that is you (would) have a right to go to trial** on the
charge contained in the indictment of molestation of a child.....

(Tape L, Side 1, p. 48)

Examples (25) and (26) show how Judge B usually indicates to the
defendant first that in a jury trial the State presents witnesses **then** that
these witnesses can be cross-examined.

In (27) he mentions cross-examination first, then pauses for two seconds
and awkwardly repairs by saying this happens "after the State has
presented."

(25)   .....After the jury is chosen, the State would have to bring their
witnesses into open court to confront you an'y'y'a-and your counsel,
and you'd have the right to cross-examine these State's witnesses in
front of the jury. After the State has presented whatever evidence they
want, you'd have the opportunity to present whatever evidence **you**
wanted to present.

(Tape F, Side 2, p. 42)

(26) Judge: After the jury is chosen, then the State who's represented
by that, uh, lady there would have to bring their wit-
nesses into court—and they would have to testify from
that stand in front of the jury and you have the right to
cross-examine the State's witnesses, ask them questions—in front of the jury. Do you understand that?
Defendant: Yes.

Judge: Now-after they've presented whatever evidence they've
got, you'd have the right to present whatever evidence
you have in your own behalf.....

(Tape F, Side 2, p. 56)

Attempted repair to return to routine
(27)   And-after the jury is chosen, the-you-and your counsel have the right
to cross-examine the State's witnesses in open court (2 sec. pause).
After the State has presented-and in front of the jury. After the State
has presented their case, you would have the right to call witnesses in
your own behalf.

(Tape D, Side 1, p. 35)

In the judge's speech the innovation involves a change in the sequential
order of pieces of information which is perceived not to work, so that a
repair to the typical order is sought.

Discussion

In some conversation analysis (e.g. Jefferson 1974, Schegloff, in press) it is
argued that repair displays an orientation of the current speaker to a prior

speaker, and also to other situated aspects of the interaction. For example, Jefferson (1974) views "a k-Negro woman," as a corrosion from "colored" to "Negro" and notes: "This can be proposing 'I am not a liberal but am talking by references to the fact that you are'" (Jefferson 1974: 193).

Here too it can be posited that the courtroom repairs presented above display an orientation to situated aspects of the interaction, although not without going outside the data itself. In this study, three of the nine judges had highly routinized discourse formats, so that each judge said exactly the same thing to each defendant exactly the same way each time he carried out the procedure, including formulating his questions to defendants in such a way that their answers would not and could not disturb his sequential structure and wording of the procedure. These judges took the position that this strategy was not only the best way to assure that defendants were treated equally, but also the best way to make sure that they always said everything they were supposed to say to the defendants to preserve their constitutional rights. The speech of these judges was what we call fluent, showing little or no repair in the form of mid-sentence pauses or changes in wording. This is in keeping with what we stereo-typically expect from formal, public, planned speech.

The other six judges, including the three whose speech is presented here, also had a routine discourse format for handling the procedure, in that they intended to cover the same substantive issues in basically the same order each time a defendant appeared before them. But these judges, in contrast to the first group, were all committed on some level to the idea that each defendant was different in background and criminal act. They believed the procedure should be accommodated or tailored to each defendant to assure his or her comprehension of the procedure. For these judges such tailoring meant slightly varying the wording of the procedure from instance to instance. Some of these judges reported that this variation was moti-vated by what they learned about the defendant's social background through questioning at the beginning of the procedure, and they said they try to simplify their speech for defendants with less education. A second major source of individual variation the judges said influenced their presentation was the defendant's demeanor. Thus if a defendant seemed by facial expression or by hesitation in responding not to understand, the judge might rephrase what he said or try to simplify the rest of the procedure.

While there is no doubt that these six judges varied their wording of the procedure more than the other three, it is far from clear that the variation was really in some sense tailored to the individual defendants. What these judges **do** manage to display in their repeated ongoing framing of the guilty plea is a quality of newness, spontaneity, or unrehearsedness, a quality which is apparently designed to convey to the defendant, "I am here for you now and involved in jointly constructing this act with you, not routinely bored and simply processing you like a machine on a factory line. You are not just a number; you matter." One aspect of the speech of some of these judges, though not all, which lends it such a spontaneous quality, is the kind of repairs presented above.[2] What I am arguing is not that the judges whose speech displays these features necessarily display them intentionally. Rather, they **allow** them to persist and increase the likelihood of their occurrence by trying to build spontaneity into their procedures where other judges try to eliminate them **because** these six judges value the impression created through them. Yet because these judges do the procedure over and over, so that routinization is inevitable in spite of their valuing of spontaneity, in a variety of ways their repairs become routinized.

It cannot be argued from this data, however, as conversation analysts argue, that these repairs are truly locally managed and display the speaker's immediate orientation to co-interactants. They may give that impression. I have just argued that they are allowed in because they give that impression. But these repairs are routinized.

This raises the possibility that repairs and other phenomena seen as locally managed and emergent in conversation may be similarly routinized some of the time, as for example when a speaker tells the same story or raises the same topic on different occasions with different co-interactants. That this possibility has not come up in conversation analysis is due in part to the methodology associated with this type of analysis. Sociologists who study conversation are committed to the view that the characterizations of the devices and structures they identify should hold true for any and all conversations. As I understand it, they don't like to consider social structure because, they argue, structural features such as class and gender cannot be claimed to motivate the organization of speech unless they are explicitly shown to be oriented to in the interaction.[3] Conversation corpora are thus always *ad hoc* in a sense. Researchers do not typically tape the same speaker talking about the same topics on different occasions to different co-interactants as ethnographers of communication do, so that we cannot determine the extent to which the forms and meaning they characterize as emergent are truly so, or partake of some of the same routinization as more formal public speech.

In sum, this chapter argues that there is more routinization and less spontaneous emergence of meaning in the interactional construction of socially contextualized meaning than is presently recognized. This tendency to routinize is an important aspect of our inherent human language capacity. To conceptualize human language capacity and its systematic deployment in human communication in a manner consistent with empirical evidence, there is a need to give considerably more attention to the relative degrees or amounts of routinization versus creativity, spontaneity, and emergence in the social construction of meaning than this distinction has been given until now.

Notes

1 Slight hitches of the sort presented here are not **necessarily** repairs, but **are** typically associated with ongoing planning and/or speaker's management of and response to the behavior of co-interactants, as in C. Goodwin (1981).
2 In other words, just as forms associated with spoken discourse are incorporated into written discourse to give it some of the flavor of the spoken (Tannen 1982), here repair associated in American speech with spontaneous speech oriented to the behavior of co-interactants is maintained in highly routinized speech to give it the spontaneous interactive quality the judges feel it **should** have (but doesn't).
3 For example, were a defendant to address the judge as "Your Honour," that would be evidence that he was orienting to their legal role relationship. See West and Zimmerman (1983) for a discussion of this issue in relation to claims of gender-differentiated interruption patterns in conversations. See also Schegloff, this volume.

Transcription devices

y..y..you	Two dots between sounds shows repetition of initial sound of word.
..... Do you	Five dots at beginning or end of speech indicates that words in the turn before or after that speech have been deleted.
Boldface	Focuses the reader's attention on the behavior being analyzed.
Finds that—it's	A long dash shows a slight pause or hitch in the flow of speech within an utterance.

References

Chomsky, N. 1955. *Syntactic Structures*. The Hague: Mouton.
Coulmas, F. (ed.) 1981. *Conversational Routine*. New York: Mouton Publishers.
Fillmore, C., P. Kay, and M. C. O'Conner. 1988. Regularity and Idiomaticity in Grammatical Constructions. *Language* 64(3): 501–38.
Garfinkel, H. 1967. *Studies in Ethnomethodology*. Englewood Cliffs, NJ: Prentice Hall.
Goodwin, C. 1981. *Conversational Organization: Interaction between Speakers and Hearers*. New York: Academic Press.

Goodwin, M. H. 1980. He-Said-She-Said: Formal Cultural Procedures for the Construction of a Gossip Dispute Activity. *American Ethnologist* 7: 674–95.

Hymes, D. 1962. The Ethnography of Speaking, in *Anthropology and Human Behavior*. Washington, DC: Anthropological Society of Washington.

Jefferson, G. 1974. Error Correction as an Interactional Resource. *Language in Society*, 3 (2): 181–200.

Philips, S., and A. Reynolds. 1987. The Interaction of Variable Syntax and Discourse Structure in Women's and Men's Speech, in *Language, Gender and Sex in Comparative Perspective*, ed. S. Philips, S. Steele, and C. Tanz, pp. 71–94. New York: Cambridge University Press.

Sacks, H. 1967. Lecture 3, Spring Quarter. April 10; Lecture 4, Spring Quarter, April 12. On Proving Hearership.

Sacks, H., E. Schegloff, and G. Jefferson. 1974. A Simplest Systematics for the Organization of Turn-Taking for Conversation. *Language*, 50(4): 696–735.

Schegloff, E. 1979. The Relevance of Repair to Syntax-for-conversation, in *Discourse and Syntax*, ed. T. Givón, pp. 261–88. New York: Academic Press.

In press. Discourse as an Interactional Achievement II: An Exercise in Conversation Analysis, in *Linguistics in Context: Connecting Observation and Understanding*, ed. D. Tannen. Norwood, Mass.: Albex Publishing Co.

Schegloff, E., G. Jefferson, and H. Sacks. 1977. The Preference for Self-Correction in the Organization of Repair in Conversation. *Language* 53(2): 351–82.

Schieffelin, B. 1980. How Kaluli Children Learn What to Say, What to Do and How to Feel. Ph.D. dissertation, Columbia University.

Tannen, D. 1982. Oral and Literate Strategies in Spoken and Written Narratives. *Language* 58: 1–21.

Watson-Gegeo, K. A., and S. T. Boggs. 1977. From Verbal Play to Talk Story: The Role of Routines in Speech Events among Hawaiian Children, in *Child Discourse*, ed. S. Ervin-Tripp and C. Mitchell-Kernan. New York: Academic Press.

West, C., and D. Zimmerman. 1983. Small Insults: A Study of Interruptions in Cross-Sex Conversations Between Unacquainted Persons, in *Language, Gender, and Society*, ed. B. Thorne, C. Kamarae, and N. Henley, pp. 103–18. Rowley, Mass.: Newbury House.

13 The negotiation of context in face-to-face interaction

ADAM KENDON

Editors' introduction

Adam Kendon studied as an undergraduate at Cambridge University and, in 1963, received his D.Phil. from Oxford University for a thesis on the temporal organization of spoken utterances in conversation. His first publication, however, was concerned with the functions of gaze direction in interaction (1967). In this article he showed the relevance of considering the relationship between gaze direction and speech in conversation for an understanding of how utterance exchanges are organized. After a year working with William Condon in Pittsburgh and a year teaching at Cornell University, in 1968 Kendon joined Albert Scheflen at Bronx State Hospital in New York City. He worked with Scheflen on a project devoted to the analysis of interaction in natural settings, with special reference to cultural differences in how families used household space. During this time, Kendon undertook investigations into the spatial organization of interaction and completed a detailed study of greeting encounters. The resulting publication (Kendon and Ferber 1973) has become a classic of its kind. Kendon left Scheflen's project in 1974 and since then has been associated with Australian National University, Connecticut College, Indiana University, and the University of Pennsylvania.

In addition to several other papers and an edited volume on the organization of interaction, Kendon has published extensively on gesture and its relationship to language, both spoken and signed (1980, 1983, 1985, 1986, 1988a). He has also completed a major study of the sign languages in use by the Aborigines of central Australia (1988b). His most recent work on the organization of face-to-face interaction includes not only the chapter included here but a recent essay on the work of Erving Goffman (1988c). In his work on interaction, Kendon has developed an analytic framework in which human beings engaged in talk are viewed not simply as speakers, but rather as embodied entities performing relevant social action in concrete situations. Kendon has developed very finely detailed analysis of how talk, body movement, context, and a range of other relevant phenomena are deployed to accomplish basic structures of human social interaction. In the present chapter Kendon argues that in order for behavior to be interpreted and understood in an appropriate way a frame must be placed around the actions and utterances of the participants. His notion of what constitutes a frame is drawn from the work of Erving Goffman. Other writers in this volume also employ (sometimes implicitly) the concept of a frame as a resource for the study of context, and frequently build from Goffman. Kendon's perspective on framing is however significantly different from many other approaches. In this chapter Kendon draws upon a collaborative, multi-party concept of framing that was developed most extensively in earlier work of Goffman (especially Goffman 1961, 1963, 1967, but also 1974). Rather than focusing analysis on framing operations performed by the speaker alone within the midst of a single utterance, he investigates how separate individuals use body posture and spatial orientation to collaboratively frame participation in larger strips of talk. Kendon notes that within concrete situations participants are faced with the task of organizing their perceptions by differentiating behavior that is officially part of the activity in progress from events that can be treated as irrelevant to it. However, some of these officially disattended events can in fact provide important structure for the organization of the activity that is the focus of explicit attention. For example, by mutually orienting toward each other participants display their involvement in the activity of the moment, and their continuing access to new events within it. Such postural configuration is not, however, treated as an explicit event within the activity in progress (for example, if a story is being told, the mutual orientation of speaker and recipient(s) is clearly not an incident within the story) but rather as background to the phenomena that explicitly occupy the attention of the participants. The distinction Kendon makes here has close affinities with ethnomethodological interest in the "seen but unnoticed" underpinnings of social action (Garfinkel 1967, Heritage 1984), and the arguments made by Hanks in this volume about how the figure–ground contrast is central to the organization of context.

In discussing how participants in interaction organize their attention, Kendon makes use of Goffman's notion of "attentional tracks." He follows Goffman in distinguishing: (1) a main-line, story-line track that is the official focus of attention; (2) a directional track that provides organization for the main-line track; and (3) a disattend track consisting of events that are officially treated as irrelevant to the activity in progress. A particular main-line track provides a framework for the appropriate interpretation of events occurring with it. The issue arises as to how participants can move from one main-line track to another (see also Duranti's analysis of how lexical choice can invoke alternative frameworks for the organization of the interaction of the moment), and thus change the framework within which the events of the moment are to track to perform actions that propose movement to a new organizational framework, but which do not themselves count as official moves in their own right (see Jefferson 1974, 1987 for further analysis of how a contrast between official and unofficial actions provides a resource for the organization of interaction). For example, a party who desires to close an encounter can move his or her body so that the current framework of mutual alignment is changed in a way that signals withdrawal from the encounter (see the discussion of contextualization cues by Gumperz in this volume), while still producing talk within it. Co-participant(s) can accept this proposal by producing talk or other body movement that starts an explicit move toward closure, or counter it. By using the disattend track in this fashion participants are able to communicate about an intended action before they actually perform it. More generally the accomplishment of joint, social action requires resources for projecting what is about to occur so that separate participants can synchronize their actions so as to bring it about (analysis of this process can also be found in the Goodwins chapter in this volume).

Kendon also demonstrates how the access that participants display toward each other is crucial for the organization of context, a theme developed by Hanks (this volume, 1990) as well in his analysis of deictic structure. Kendon's work provides an example of how context can be analyzed as a collaboratively sustained interpretive framework that participants are able to negotiate and change within the interaction itself.

References

Garfinkel, Harold. 1967. *Studies in Ethnomethodology*. Englewood Cliffs, N.J.: Prentice-Hall.
Goffman, Erving. 1961. *Encounters: Two Studies in the Sociology of Interaction*. Indianapolis: Bobbs-Merrill.
    1963. *Behavior in Public Places: Notes on the Social Organization of Gatherings*. New York: Free Press.
    1967. *Interaction Ritual: Essays in Face to Face Behavior*. Garden City, New York: Doubleday.
    1974. *Frame Analysis: An Essay on the Organization of Experience*. New York: Harper and Row.
Hanks, W. 1990. *Referential Practice: Language and Lived Space among the Maya*. Chicago: University of Chicago Press.
Heritage, John. 1984. *Garfinkel and Ethnomethodology*. Cambridge: Polity Press.
Jefferson, Gail. 1974. Error Correction as an Interactional Resource. *Language in Society* 2: 181–99.
    1987. Exposed and Embedded Corrections, in *Talk and Social Organization*, ed. Graham Button and John R. E. Lee, pp. 86–100. Clevedon, England: Multilingual Matters.
Kendon, Adam. 1967. Some Functions of Gaze-Direction in Social Interaction. *Acta Psychologica* 26: 22–63.
    1980. Gesture and Speech: Two Aspects of the Process of Utterance, in *Nonverbal Communication and Language*, ed. M. R. Key, pp. 207–77. The Hague: Mouton.
    1983. Gesture and Speech: How They Interact, in *Nonverbal Interaction (Sage Annual Reviews of Communication, Vol. 11)*, ed. John M. Wiemann and R. Harrison, pp. 13–46. Beverly Hills, Calif.: Sage Publications.
    1985. Some Uses of Gesture, in *Perspectives on Silence*, ed. Deborah Tannen and Muriel Saville–Troike, pp. 215–34. Norwood, NJ: Ablex.
    1986. Current Issues in the Study of Gesture, in *Biological Foundations of Gesture*, ed. J. L. Nespoulous, P. Perron, and A. R. Lecours, pp. 23–47. Hillsdale, NJ: Lawrence Erlbaum.
    1988a. How Gestures Can Become Like Words, in *Crosscultural Perspectives in Nonverbal Communication*, ed. F. Poyatos, pp. 131–41. Toronto: C. J. Hogrefe.
    1988b. *Sign Languages of Aboriginal Australia: Cultural, Semiotic and Communicative Perspectives*. Cambridge: Cambridge University Press.

1988c. Erving Goffman's Approach to the Study of Face-to-Face Interaction, in *Erving Goffman: Exploring the Interaction Order*, ed. Anthony Wooton and Paul Drew, pp. 14–40. Cambridge: Polity Press.

Kendon, Adam, and Andrew Ferber. 1973. A Description of Some Human Greetings, in *Comparative Ecology and Behaviour of Primates*, ed. Richard P. Michael and John H. Crook, pp. 591–668. London and New York: Academic Press.

The negotiation of context in face-to-face interaction

Erving Goffman (1963) distinguished as "focused interaction" those occasions when two or more individuals openly join together to sustain a single common focus of concern. This is done, most characteristically, perhaps, in occasions of talk, but a single focus of concern must likewise be openly entered into when people play games together, dance together or engage in some cooperative task activity such as moving a piano or performing a surgical operation (Goffman 1961b). Goffman pointed out that in any focused encounter a particular "definition of the situation" comes to be shared by the participants. This serves to define what will be considered, for the time being, as irrelevant, as well as what is relevant. A **frame** comes to be placed around the actions and utterances of the participants which provides for the sense in which they are to be taken (Goffman 1961a, 1974).

The ease with which people can adopt a common frame for the interpretation of events may be illustrated by considering games. When we observe game players, as Goffman pointed out, we may see how readily "participants are willing to forswear for the duration of the play any apparent interest in the esthetic, sentimental, or monetary value of the equipment employed, adhering to what might be called **rules of irrelevance.**" (Goffman 1961a: 19). For instance, as Goffman points out, it does not matter whether the game of checkers is played with bottle tops on a piece of squared linoleum, or with pennies and dimes on a chalked-out set of squares, gold figurines on inlaid marble, or with uniformed men standing on colored flagstones. Insofar as the two players have agreed to play checkers, these items will be treated in exactly the same way. If one of the players were to deal with the pennies or dimes as money, however, or to start a conversation with one of the men on the colored flagstones, he would be breaking the "frame" that had been agreed upon, and he would place in jeopardy the continuance of the game.

While Goffman showed us in a number of ways that such a common frame must be presupposed if the process of focused interaction is to be understood, he did not really discuss the question of **how** such framing is achieved, except in quite general terms. By what means, through what kinds of overt acts, do people come to be able to assume that their co-interactants share with them the same perspective in the situation as they do themselves?

A quick answer to this has been to point out that many interactions are so routine that anyone entering them will know sufficient of what to expect and can count on others to know what to expect also. Thus each can assume that others understand the situation and no negotiation of understanding is needed. Yet, in most situations of daily interaction, where everyone is as well versed in its rules as everyone else, there remains considerable room for uncertainty. For instance, consider the question of how occasions of focused interaction are brought to an end. In maintaining themselves as participants in a focused interaction, participants must have negotiated a common perspective of relevance for each other's actions. In a conversation, for instance, a "topic" comes to be established, together with a "tone" in terms of which it is to be approached (whether it is to be treated seriously or lightly, for example). At any given point within the frame of the topic, participants must organize their utterances so that they will be relevant to the topic in some way. If the topic is to be changed or the whole conversation to be brought to an end, if confusion is to be avoided, it is necessary for all participants to agree to the change or termination before it actually occurs (cf. Schegloff and Sacks 1973). If such an agreement is not reached, then any action of P's that, from his own perspective, belongs to a new frame of interpretation, will be interpreted by the other participants in terms of the currently prevailing frame and, accordingly, will be perceived as irrelevant, inconsistent, or in some other way disjunctive. If we are in the midst of a conversation about how to grow roses, for instance, and a comment is expected of me on some point regarding this, but I use my turn-slot to tell of the new car I have just bought, this is likely to produce disorientation in my co-participants. For new actions to be perceived and responded to as meaningful, the shared understanding concerning what we are talking about, i.e. the frame of interpretation all participants are applying in common to what each other says and does, must be changed first. Thus for changes of topic or terminations of conversations to be accomplished in a well-managed fashion, participants must be able to communicate with one another about their intentions to change or terminate before they actually do so (Kendon 1976). The question is, how is this accomplished?

The processes by which participants are able to negotiate the frame or working consensus of an interaction depend to an important degree upon the willingness of participants to allow that only certain aspects of behavior count as "action" (Kendon 1985). Evidently, participants treat only certain aspects of each other's behavior as if they are something fully intended and to be responded to directly. If I clear my throat in the midst of an utterance this is not treated as part of what I am "saying." If I uncross my legs, take a drag on my cigarette or sip my coffee while another is speaking, such actions are not attended to by the other participants as if they are contributions to the conversation. Overt acts of attention to activities of this sort are generally not made at all. Whereas spoken utterances and bodily movements, if perceived as gestures, are regarded as vehicles of explicitly intended messages, directly relevant to the business of the conversation, other aspects of behavior are not regarded in this light. As we shall see in a moment, these "non-relevant" aspects of each other's behavior nevertheless can play an important role in the process by which participants regulate one another's attention and provide information to one another about their level and focus of involvement in the interaction. However, it is the tacit agreement sustained by participants to maintain this distinction between "relevant" action and "non-relevant action" that makes it possible for people to embark upon lines of action in respect to one another, and to observe each other's modes of dealing with those lines of action without, as it were, officially doing so. By making this distinction, by regarding only some aspects of behavior as "explicit" or "official," whereas other aspects are regarded as "unofficial," participants make it possible for themselves to explore one another's interpretive perspectives. They thereby can negotiate some measure of agreement before either of them needs to address the other with any explicit action.

Goffman (1974) has drawn attention to this differentiation in the treatment participants in interaction accord various aspects of each other's behavior by his concept of **attentional tracks**. He suggests that in any social encounter there is always an aspect of the activity going forward that is treated as being within a **main-line** or **story-line track**. A domain of action is delineated as being relevant to the main business of the encounter, and it is oriented to as such and dealt with accordingly. Other aspects of activity are not included, but this does not mean that they have no part to play. Thus Goffman suggested we may also distinguish a **directional track**. Here, in Goffman's words, there is "a stream of signs which is itself excluded from the content of activity but which serves as a means of regulating it, bounding, articulating and qualifying its various components and phrases" (Goffman 1974: 210). One may speak, too, of a **disattend track**, to which are assigned a whole variety of actions that are not counted as being part of the interaction at all. Goffman mentioned here, in particular, various "creature comfort releases" – scratching, postural adjustments, smoking, and so forth – that are, so to speak, allowable deviations from the behavioral discipline to which all participants in a focused encounter are expected to conform. As Goffman himself made clear, and as a moment's reflection reminds us, it is not, of course, that the actions treated as being in the disattend track are not cognized and responded to by participants.

On the contrary, they often play an important part in the very process of negotiating common perspectives that, as we have seen, is an essential part of what makes focused interaction possible. What I wish to suggest here, however, is that unless this kind of differential–attentional treatment is engaged in, the process by which participants negotiate the working consensus of the interaction would not be possible.

To illustrate the way in which participants may make use of "unofficial" or non-"main-track" aspects of each other's behavior in frame negotiation, consider the spatial–orientational organization of focused encounters. Participants in focused encounters typically enter into and maintain a distinct spatial and orientational arrangement. By doing so, it seems, participants can provide one another with evidence that they are prepared to sustain a common orientational perspective. By arranging themselves into a particular spatial–orientational pattern, they thereby display each to the other that they are governed by the same set of general considerations. By cooperating with one another to sustain a given spatial–orientational arrangement, they can display a commonality of readiness (Kendon 1973, 1977).

To understand how this can be so, we must first consider how the spatial and orientational position of an individual provides information about his or her attention. In the first place, it may be noted that **any** kind of activity involves the use of space and an orientation to a particular segment of the environment. If I sit at a desk to write, I command a certain space on the desk for this purpose. If I sit and think, closing my eyes to do so, I withdraw from active use of space around me perhaps, yet at the same time, to do this, I am likely to seek out a space that is not in use by others. In either case I can be said to be making use of a segment of the environment, although, in each case, in a very different way.

The segment of space that a person takes up in virtue of the line of activity he or she is pursuing I have called his or her **transactional segment** (Kendon 1977: 181). When two or more persons join to do something together, they come to have a **joint** transactional segment. Persons jointly interacting, jointly sustain an orientation to a common space to which they have an access that is different from others. We may use the term **formation** for any instance where two or more persons sustain through time a spatial–orientational arrangement of some sort – persons standing on a line are participating in a formation, for example. We may distinguish as an **F-formation**, however, instances where two or more individuals position themselves in such a way as to maintain an overlapping or joint transactional segment. Thus whenever two or more individuals are placed close to each other, orienting their bodies in such a way that each of them has an easy, direct, and equal access to every other participant's transactional segment, and agree to maintain such an arrangement, they can be said to create an F-formation. The system of spatial and postural behaviors by which people create and sustain this joint transactional space is referred to as an F-formation **system** (Scheflen and Ashcraft 1976, Kendon 1977).

It is noted that by establishing such a system of spatial and orientational relations, individuals create for themselves a context within which preferential access to the other's actions is established. Furthermore, such a system of spatial and orientational relations provides for a visually perceivable arrangement by which participants in a given focused encounter are delineated from those who are outsiders. Indeed, it seems that the kind of arrangements that arise in the F-formation provide a means of clearly demarcating the "world" of the encounter from the rest of the "world" around. Entering into an F-formation, thus, is an excellent means by which interactional and therefore social and psychological "withness" may be established.

F-formations vary in the actual shapes that they have. A roughly circular shape is common in free-standing groups of three or more people where all are participating in the same conversation, but it is by no means the only kind of arrangement. How persons arrange themselves in relation to one another and the environment will have consequences for the kinds of access each has to the others. Hall (1966) pointed out that at different interpersonal distances different kinds of information about the other are available and that this has consequences for the kinds of actions that can be used in interaction. Close up, one may whisper, further off, louder voicings are needed, but at quite large distances the small feedback gestures upon which interactants rely as they organize turn-taking become difficult to detect. As a result, there is a shift in the way the turn-taking system is managed. Such changes in the conditions of interaction have consequences for the kinds of transactions that are possible. Thus to adopt a space of a certain sort can be a way of adopting a "frame" of a certain sort. In this way what is possible becomes delimited but, by the same token, expectations about what is possible can be set up.

From the few studies that have been carried out on this point, it is apparent that there is, as one might expect, a systematic relationship between spatial arrangement and mode of interaction (Batchelor and Goethals 1972, Kendon 1973). This means that people will not only tend to adopt particular arrangements for particular kinds of interaction but, by adopting a given spatial arrangement or by moving to a position and orientation that might suggest a spatial arrangement of a particular sort, a person can thereby propose an interactive relationship of a particular sort. Spatial positioning is thus available as an expressive resource for interactants. Yet spacing and orientation are generally treated as "background" and belong to the "not counted" part of the stream of action. Spatial and orientational positioning can thus serve well as a device by which expectation and intention can be conveyed and hence negotiated.

Within the course of an ongoing interactional episode, the arrangement adopted within an F-formation may change. Observations by several different investigators show that such changes can occur in conjunction with changes in other aspect of interaction, such as a change from salutation to topical conversation, or a change in conversational topic, suggesting that this is one way in which frame changes within an interaction may be marked in overt behavior (Scheflen 1964, Scheflen and Ashcraft 1976, Kendon and Ferber 1973, Ciolek and Kendon 1980, McDermott, Gospodinoff, and Aron 1978, Streeck 1984). This allows us to see how participants may employ spatial and orientational manoeuvres as a means of testing out each other's alignments to a given interpretive frame or as a means of finding out if the other is willing to change to a new one. A participant wishing to change to a new frame may precede any actual change by small manoeuvres in the direction of the new position that would, if completed, constitute a position suitable for a different kind of interaction. If the co-participants are willing to follow the participant's lead, they will make complementary moves, rather than moves that would compensate for them and so maintain the status quo. Such preframe change negotiations can be observed especially when the closing of an encounter is being negotiated. Thus one may observe how one or other of the participants in a standing conversational group may begin to step back, increasing the distance between him- or herself and others. Such a move may be taken as an announcement of a wish for closure. Step-backs by the other participants may follow, and these serve to acknowledge the closure bid, thus making it possible for all of the participants to move into the closing phase of the conversation together (cf. Lockard, Allen, Schiele, and Wiemer 1978).

By entering into and maintaining an F-formation, participants are able to keep each other continuously informed that they are attending to the current occasion. Furthermore, as we have just seen, by showing themselves responsive to each other's adjustments in spatial–orientational positioning, participants can show whether they are ready or not for alterations in the frame of the situation. However, spatial–orientational positioning, or postural arrangements, as may be observed in seated groups, does not itself constitute the action of interaction. It is for this reason that it can serve so well in the process of frame attunement.

The "action" of the interaction is accomplished through actions, such as utterances, either spoken or gestural, or manipulative actions directed at the other, that are regarded by the participants themselves as moves of some sort in the interactive process they are engaged in. However, except perhaps in two-person encounters, and I think even here, there remains the question as to how participants are to know for whom a given act is meant and hence who is the one from whom the next move is expected.

Interactionally explicit acts, as I shall call them, always have an address. Within the frame embodied in the F-formation, thus, sub-frames must be established within which given interchanges of explicit acts occur.

A number of studies have now been published which include detailed analyses of how utterance exchange systems are established and maintained (Kendon 1970, 1973, 1985; Goodwin 1981). It emerges from these analyses that participants in utterance exchange systems interrelate their behavior in a number of ways that are distinctive for them and different from the way their behavior is related to other participants in the gathering. Typically both speaker and direct recipient orient their bodies at least partially toward one another so that one might say of them that they have established a sub-segment of their transactional segments in mutual overlap. They repeatedly focus their eyes upon one another and, from time to time, their eyes meet. The orientation of the body, especially of the head, is toward one another, but it is the intermittent aiming of the eyes at another that is one of the principal ways by which the utterer in an utterance exchange system indicates to whom his or her actions are addressed; and the orienting of the eyes to the utterer is one of the principal ways in which a person can indicate that he or she is a recipient. Indeed, one of the ways in which a recipient of an utterance may redirect the speaker to another is by looking away from the speaker and towards another member of the gathering. If the utterer, then, can begin marking the address of an utterance by patterning his or her gaze in such a way that his or her eyes are aimed repeatedly at the addressee, the recipient must cooperate by maintaining an appropriate patterning on his or her part.

Recipients, furthermore, are commonly observed to display a heightened congruency of posture with that of the speaker, and they also tend to exhibit a particular set of gestures, such as headnods and changes in facial expression, that are patterned in a systematic relation with the organization of the speaker's speech. If the recipient ceases to display these actions and, in particular, if he or she alters the target of his or her eyes to that of another member of the gathering, the utterance exchange system will alter in who it includes or it will come to an end. Since only those within a current exchange system have rights as "next speaker" within that system, if it changes its membership midstream, this also has implications for who may follow as next speaker.

A further feature of the relationship between participants in an utterance exchange system is that the flow of action of speaker and recipient is often rhythmically coordinated and this also can become a means by which persons may attune their expectations to one another. (Pelose 1987 provides a recent comprehensive review.) This is demonstrated by studies of how participants become established as co-participants in an explicit interchange. Micro-analyses of film records of several different episodes of interaction have shown how an individual can announce his or her readiness to be a recipient for another's address by moving into synchrony with him or her. To initiate an explicit exchange with another is always somewhat risky, since there is the possibility that the other party may not wish to reciprocate. By picking up on the rhythm of another person's movements one can establish a "connection" with them which, at the same time, does not commit one to an explicit initiation. If, after having joined the rhythm of another, no reciprocal move is made, it is possible to continue as if no attempt has been made to initiate an "axis" (Kendon and Ferber 1973).

We may see, then, that there are various ways in which aspects of behavior that participants never report on and do not attend to as if they were officially "meant" are nevertheless relied upon for providing the kind of advance information that any one proposing to interact with another must have. I have suggested that, in a number of different ways, persons can make manifest their intentions, they can reveal how they are interpreting the situation without doing anything that would count as making a definite move in an interactional sequence. For this to be possible, there must be a tacit understanding that certain forms of behavior are not to be counted as "moves" even though all those present are fully able to control much of their own behavior that is treated in this way and are fully aware that the information it may make available can be deliberately provided. I believe that it is the willingness and ability of each of us to treat our own and others' behavior in this differential fashion that makes possible much of the process by which the "frame" or "working consensus" of an encounter can be established, maintained or changed in a coordinate fashion. Without this, orderly face-to-face interaction would not be possible.

References

Batchelor, J. P., and G. R. Goethals. 1972. Spatial Arrangements in Freely Formed Groups. *Sociometry* 35:270–9.

Ciolek, T. M., and Kendon, A. 1980. Environment and the Spatial Arrangement of Conversational Interaction. *Sociological Inquiry* 50: 237, 271.

Goffman, E. 1961a. Fun in Games, in his *Encounters*, pp. 17–81. Indianapolis: Bobbs–Merill.

1961b. Role Distance, in his *Encounters*, pp. 85–152. Indianapolis: Bobbs–Merrill.

1963. *Behavior in Public Places*. New York: The Free Press of Glencoe.

1974. *Frame Analysis*. Cambridge, Mass.: Harvard University Press.

Goodwin, C. 1981. *Conversational Organization: Interaction between Speakers and Hearers*. New York: Academic Press.

Hall, E. T. 1966. *The Hidden Dimension*. Garden City, New York: Doubleday.

Kendon, A. 1970. Movement Coordination in Social Interaction: Some Examples Described. *Acta Psychologica* 32: 1–25.

334   *Adam Kendon*

1973. The Role of Visible Behaviour in the Organization of Face-to-Face Interaction, in *Social Communication and Movement: Studies of Interaction and Expression in Man and Chimpanzee*, ed. M. von Cranach and I. Vine, pp. 29–74. London: Academic Press.

1976. Some Functions of the Face in a Kissing Round. *Semiotica* 15: 299–334.

1977. Spatial Organization in Social Encounters: The F-formation System, Ch. 5 in A. Kendon, *Studies in the Behavior of Social Interaction*. Lisse: Peter de Ridder Press.

1985. The Behavioural Foundations for the Process of Frame Attunement in Face-to-Face Interaction, in *Discovery Strategies in the Psychology of Action* ed. G. P. Ginsburg, M. Brenner, and M. von Cranach, pp. 229–53. London and New York: Academic Press.

Kendon, A., and A. Ferber. 1973. A Description of Some Human Greetings, in *Comparative Ecology and Behaviour of Primates*, ed. R. P. Michael and J. H. Cook. London: Academic Press.

Lockard, J., D. Allen, B. Schiele, and M. Wierner. 1978. Human Postural Signals: Stance, Weight Shifts and Social Distance as Intention Movements to Depart. *Animal Behaviour* 26: 219–24.

McDermott, R., K. Gospodinoff, and J. Aron. 1978. Criteria for an Ethnographically Adequate Description of Concerted Activities. *Semiotica* 24: 245–75.

Pelose, G. C. 1987. The Functions of Behavioral Synchrony and Speech Rhythm in Conversation. *Research on Language and Social Interaction* 20: 171–220.

Scheflen, A. E. 1964. The Significance of Posture in Communication Systems. *Psychiatry* 27: 315–31.

Scheflen, A. E., and N. Ashcraft. 1976. *Human Territories: How We Behave in Space–Time*. Englewood Cliffs, NJ: Prentice–Hall.

Schegloff, E. A., and H. Sacks. 1973. Opening Up Closings. *Semiotica* 8: 289–327.

Streeck, J. 1984. Embodied Contexts, Transcontextuals and the Timing of Speech Acts. *Journal of Pragmatics* 8: 113–37.

14 Indexing gender

ELINOR OCHS

Editors' introduction

One of the pioneers in the field of developmental pragmatics, Elinor Ochs (formerly Elinor Ochs Keenan) carried out one of the earliest longitudinal studies of children's conversational competence (Keenan 1974, 1977). Ochs, especially through her long-term collaboration with Bambi Schieffelin, was one of those most responsible for giving new impetus to the field of language socialization (Ochs and Schieffelin 1984, Schieffelin and Ochs 1986). Strongly grounded in ethnography as a research method, the study of language socialization focuses on the process of becoming a culturally competent member of society through language activity. Within this domain, Ochs has been stressing the importance of looking at the larger cultural context in which adults communicate with a child. This means that stylistic characteristics of language used to, by, and around the child should be understood vis-à-vis local theories and local practices of child rearing, including the social relationship between the child and her caretakers and the notion of task (Ochs 1982, 1988). The important discoveries of this line of research go beyond the empirical discovery that Baby Talk is not universal (Ochs 1982) to include theoretical hypotheses about how cultural accounts of this register are based on local epistemologies and theories of social order.

Another important insight in Ochs' work is the idea that a theory of language socialization rests on a theory of indexicality (see also Hanks, this volume). In the model presented in this chapter, indexicality is depicted as a property of speech through which cultural contexts such as social identities (e.g. gender) and social activities (e.g. a gossip session) are constituted by particular stances and acts. Linguistic features index more than one dimension of the sociocultural context; the indexing of certain dimensions is linked in a constitutive sense to the indexing of other dimensions (e.g. tag questions may index a stance of uncertainty as well as the act of requesting confirmation/clarification/feedback; these two contextual features in turn may index/help constitute female gender identity in certain communities). Hence children's acquisition of linguistic forms entails a developmental process of delineating and organizing contextual dimensions in culturally sensible ways.

Ochs' earlier work on developmental pragmatics and her more recent research on language socialization come together in her current analysis of indexicality. Across the world's speech communities, there are pragmatic universals in the linguistic indexing of stance and act. That is, children everywhere are developing similar pragmatic competences. This accounts for why we can communicate at some level across societies. On the other hand, each social group has specific ways of organizing the distribution of stance and indexical action across social identities, relationships, and activities, with different values associated with each set of indexicals. Cultural competence entails developing knowledge of these more complex indexical systems. This research has also implications for our understanding of miscommunication across groups: communication across social groups may flounder as one group assumes the other shares not just stance and act meanings but the whole indexical network (see Gumperz' article, this volume).

Elinor Ochs is Professor of Applied Linguistics at the University of California, Los Angeles.

References

Keenan, Elinor Ochs. 1974. Conversational Competence in Children. *Journal of Child Language* 1: 163–83.
   1977. Making it Last: Repetition in Children's Discourse, in *Child Discourse*, ed. Susan Ervin–Tripp and Claudia Mitchell–Kernan, pp. 125–38. New York: Academic Press.
Ochs, Elinor. 1982. Talking to Children in Western Samoa. Language in Society 11: 77–104.
   1988. *Culture and Language Development: Language Acquisition and Language Socialization in a Samoan Village*. Cambridge: Cambridge University Press.
Ochs, Elinor, and Bambi Schieffelin. 1984. Language Acquisition and Socialization: Three developmental Stories and their Implications, in *Culture Theory: Essays on Mind, Self, and Emotions*, ed. Richard Shweder and R. LeVine, pp. 276–322. Cambridge: Cambridge University Press.
Schieffelin, Bambi, and Elinor Ochs (eds.). 1986. *Language Socialization across Cultures*. Cambridge: Cambridge University Press.

Indexing gender

1   The micro-ethnography of gender hierarchy

Gender hierarchies display themselves in all domains of social behavior, not the least of which is talk. Gender ideologies are socialized, sustained, and transformed through talk, particularly through verbal practices that recur innumerable times in the lives of members of social groups. This view embodies Althusser's notion that "ideas of a human subject exist in his actions" and his rephrasing of Pascal's ideas in terms of the imperative "Kneel down, move your lips in prayer and you will believe" (1971: 168). Mundane, prosaic, and altogether unsensational though they may appear to be, conversational practices are primary resources for the realization of gender hierarchy.

In the course of the following discussion, I will argue that the relation between language and gender is not a simple straightforward mapping of linguistic form to social meaning of gender. Rather the relation of language to gender is constituted and mediated by the relation of language to stances, social acts, social activities, and other social constructs. As such, novices come to understand gender meanings through coming to understand certain pragmatic functions of language (such as expressing stance) and coming to understand local expectations *vis-à-vis* the distribution of these functions and their variable expression across social identities.

With respect to gender hierarchy, the following discussion argues that images of women are linked to images of mothering and that such images are socialized through communicative practices associated with caregiving. Although mothering is a universal kinship role of women and in this role women have universally positions of control and power, their communicative practices as mothers vary considerably across societies, revealing differences in social positions of mothers. Mothers vary in the extent to which their communication with children is child-centered (i.e. accommodating). Differences in caregiver communicative practices socialize infants and small children into different local images of women. These images may change over developmental time when these young novices see women using different communicative practices to realize different social roles (familial, economic, political, etc.). On the other hand, continuity in women's verbal practices associated with stance and social action in the enactment of diverse social roles may sustain images of women that emerge in the earliest moments of human life.

The discussion will compare communicative practices of mothers in mainstream American households (Anglo, white, middle class) and in traditional Western Samoan households. Insights concerning mainstream American mothers derive from numerous child language development studies, particularly earlier research carried out by Bambi Schieffelin and myself on language socialization in this community (Ochs and Schieffelin 1984; Schieffelin and Ochs 1986a, 1986b). Insights concerning mothering in Western Samoan households are based on a longitudinal language acquisition and language socialization study conducted in Falefaa, Western Samoa, during 1978–9 and in 1981 (Ochs 1982, 1986, 1987, 1988, 1990).

2   Social meanings and indexicality

Before turning to the communicative practices of mothers and their impact on socialization of gender, let us turn our attention to a more general consideration of language and gender, both how it has been examined and how it can be more fruitfully examined. These comments on language and gender should be taken as exemplary of a more general relation between language and social meaning.

Sociological and anthropological studies of language behavior are predicated on the assumptions that (1) language systematically varies across social contexts and (2) such variation is part of the meaning indexed by linguistic structures. Sociolinguistic studies tend to relate particular structures to particular situational conditions, or clusters of structures to such conditions. The meanings so indexed are referred to as social meanings, in contrast to purely referential or logical meanings expressed by linguistic structures. Hence two or more phonological variants of the same word may share the identical reference but convey different social meanings, e.g. differences in social class or ethnicity of speakers, differences in social distances between speaker and addressee, differences in affect. In every community, members have available to them linguistic resources for communicating such social meanings at the same time as they are providing other levels of information. This system of multifarious signalling is highly efficient. Competent members of every community have been socialized to interpret these meanings and can without conscious control orchestrate messages to convey social meanings. Sociological and anthropological research is dedicated to understanding these communicative skills, interpretive processes, and systems of meaning indexed through language.

Research on indexicality has been carried out within several major disciplinary frameworks. Current thinking about social meaning of language draws heavily on the theoretical perspectives of the Soviet literary critics and philosophers M. Bakhtin (1981) and V. N. Vološinov (1973). This approach stresses the inherently social construction of written and spoken language behavior. Part of the meaning of any utterance (spoken or written) is its social history, its social presence, and its social future. With respect to social history, Bakhtin and Vološinov make the point that utterances may have several "voices" – the speaker's or writer's voice, the voice of a someone referred to within the utterance, the voice of another for whom the message is conveyed, etc. The voices of speaker/writer and others may be blended in the course of the message and become part of the social meanings indexed within the message. This perspective is a potentially critical one for investigating the relation of language to gender, where gender may generate its own set of voices.

A second tradition examining social indexicality of language is sociological and anthropological research on speech events and speech activities. Here Bateson's (1972) and Goffman's (1974) work on keying and frames for events, as well as discussions by Gumperz (1982) on contextualization cues, Hymes (1974) on speech event keys, and Silverstein (1976) on shifters and indexes are all useful in analyzing the social potential of language behavior. Silverstein provides further specification of indexes in terms of whether social context is indexed referentially or non-referentially. That is, social conditions may be communicated through the referential content of a word, phrase, or clause or through some linguistic feature that has no reference. With respect to indexing of gender in English, referential indexes include such items as the third person pronouns "he" and "she," and the titles "Mr." and "Mrs.," "Sir" and "Madam," and the like. Referential indexes have been a major source of discussion among those concerned with the linguistic construction of gender ideology (see especially Silverstein 1985).

From a sociolinguistic point of view, however, referential indexes are far fewer than non-referential indexes of social meaning, including gender. Non-referential indexing of gender may be accomplished through a vast range of morphological, syntactic, and phonological devices available across the world's languages. For example, pitch range may be used in a number of speech communities to index gender of speaker. For example, research on pre-adolescent American male and female children indicates that young girls speak as if their vocal apparatus were smaller than young boys of the same age and same size vocal chords (Sachs 1975). Here it is evident that pitch has social meaning and that young children have come to understand these meanings and employ pitch appropriately to these ends. Other studies (see especially Andersen 1977) indicate that children as young as four years of age can use pitch to index male and female identities.

A concern with indexicality is also at the heart of linguistic and philosophical approaches to the field of pragmatics, the study of language in context (Levinson 1983). Here a major concern is broadening the notion of presupposition beyond logical presupposition to include pragmatic presupposition, i.e. context-sensitive presupposition. Thus an utterance such as "Give me that pen" logically presupposes that there exists a specific pen and pragmatically presupposes that (1) the pen is some distance from the speaker and (2) the speaker is performing the speech act of ordering. From this perspective, we can say that utterances may pragmatically presuppose genders of speakers, addressees, overhearers, and referents. For example, in Japanese, sentences that include such sentence-final morphological particles as *ze* pragmatically presuppose that the speaker is a male whereas sentences that include the sentence-final particle *wa* pragmatically presuppose that the speaker is a female.

3   The indexing of gender

The notion of gender centers on the premise that the notions of men and women / male and female are sociocultural transformations of biological categories and processes (cf., for example, Ortner and Whitehead 1981, Rosaldo and Lamphere 1974, McConnell-Ginet, Borker, and Furman 1980, Gilligan 1982, West and Zimmerman 1987). That is, social groups organize and conceptualize men and women in culturally specific and meaningful ways. Given that language is the major symbolic system of the human species, we would expect language to be a source and moving force of gender ideologies. In other words, we should expect language to be influenced by local organizations of gender roles, rights, and expectations and to actively perpetuate these organizations in spoken and written communication (Bourdieu 1977). In relating sociocultural constructions of gender to social meaning of language, an issue of importance emerges: **few features of language directly and exclusively index gender**.

In light of this, we must work towards a different conceptualization of the indexical relation between language and gender. In the following discussion, I suggest three characteristics of the language–gender relation. The relation of language to gender is (1) non-exclusive, (2) constitutive, (3) temporally transcendent.

3.1   Non-exclusive relation

In looking at different languages and different speech communities, the most striking generalization is the paucity of linguistic features that alone index local concepts of men and women or even more minimally the sex of a speaker/addressee/referent (Brown and Levinson 1979, Ochs 1987, Seki 1986, Silverstein 1985). Most linguistic features, particularly if we go beyond the lexicon (e.g. kin terms that index this information), do not share such a strict, i.e. presuppositional, relation to the semantic domain of gender.

Rather, overwhelmingly we find that the relation between particular features of language and gender is typically non-exclusive. By non-exclusive, I mean that often variable features of language may be used by/with/for both sexes. Hence, strictly speaking we cannot say that these features pragmatically presuppose male or female. What we find, rather, is that the features may be employed more by one than the other sex. Thus, for example, in British and American English, women tend to use prestige phonological variants more than men of the same social class and ethnicity. Indeed women more than men in these communities overuse the prestige variants, producing "hypercorrect" words (Labov 1966, Trudgill 1974). Women in New York City, for example, overuse the postvocalic /r/ to the extent that they sometimes insert an /r/ in a word that has no "r" in its written form, e.g. instead of saying "idea," they hypercorrect to "idear" (Labov 1966). In this and other examples, the relation between language and gender is distributional and probabilistic.

In addition, non-exclusivity is demonstrated by the fact that many linguistic forms associated with gender are associated as well with the marking of other social information, such as the marking of stance and social action. Thus, for example, tag questions in English are associated not only with female speakers (Andersen 1977), but with stances such as hesitancy, and social acts such as confirmation checks. Certain sentence-final particles in Japanese are associated not only with male and female speakers but with stances of coarse versus delicate intensity. This system of linguistic forms conveying multiple social meanings is highly efficient from the point of view of linguistic processing and acquisition (Slobin 1985). Further, the multiplicity of potential meanings allows speakers to exploit such inherent ambiguities for strategic ends, such as avoiding going "on-record" in communicating a particular social meaning (Brown and Levinson 1987, Tannen 1986).

A question raised by such facts is "Why this distribution?" How does the distribution of linguistic resources relate to rights, expectations, and other conceptions of men and women in society? These questions seem more in line with those asked by social scientists concerned with the position of men and women *vis-à-vis* access to and control over resources and activities.

3.2   Constitutive relation

By positing a constitutive relation between language and gender, I mean that one or more linguistic features may index social meanings (e.g. stances, social acts, social activities), which in turn helps to constitute gender meanings. The pursuit of such constitutive routes is a far more interesting activity than assessing either obligatory or probabilistic relations between language and sex of speaker/addressee/referent, for here we begin to understand pragmatic meanings of features and their complex relation to gender images.

Let me provide a few examples of constitutiveness. Many of the linguistic features that in the literature are associated primarily with either men or women have as their core social meaning a particular affective stance. As noted earlier, certain linguistic features associated with men's speech in Japanese coarsely intensify the force of an utterance, while those associated with women's speech typically convey an affect of gentle intensity (Uyeno 1971, Seki 1986). We can say that the former features directly index coarse intensity and the latter a soft or delicate intensity. The affective dispositions so indexed are part of the preferred images of men and women and motivate their differential use by men and women. When someone wishes to speak like a woman in Japanese, they may speak gently, using particles such as the sentence-final *wa*, or to speak like a man they may speak coarsely, using the sentence-final particle *ze*.

Similarly, we can find particular linguistic features directly indexing **social acts** or **social activities**, such as the imperative mode indexing the act of ordering in English or respect vocabulary terms in Samoan indexing the activity of oratory. These acts and activities in turn may be associated with speaking like a male or speaking like a female and may display different frequencies of use across the two social categories.

It is in this sense that the relation between language and gender is mediated and constituted through a web of socially organized pragmatic

Figure 14.1 *Indexing gender in Japanese*

Linguistic form	Direct index	Indirect index
ze	coarse intensity	male "voice"
wa	delicate intensity	female "voice"

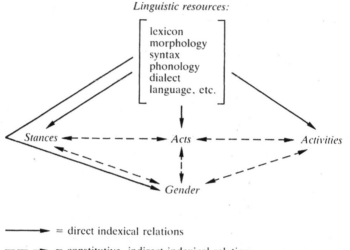

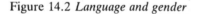

Figure 14.2 *Language and gender*

meanings. Knowledge of how language relates to gender is not a catalogue of correlations between particular linguistic forms and sex of speakers, referents, addressees and the like. Rather, such knowledge entails tacit understanding of (1) how particular linguistic forms can be used to perform particular pragmatic work (such as conveying stance and social action) and (2) norms, preferences, and expectations regarding the distribution of this work *vis-à-vis* particular social identities of speakers, referents, and addressees. To discuss the relation of language to gender in these terms is far more revealing than simply identifying features as directly marking men's or women's speech.

A more favorable model relates linguistic forms to gender either indirectly (through other social meanings indexed) or directly. This model displays different kinds of language–gender relations and begins to specify the kinds of meanings men and women are likely to index through language, the relation of these patterns to the position and images of men and women in society.

A model displaying how linguistic forms help to constitute gender meanings is presented in Figure 14.2. In this model, linguistic forms are resources for conveying a range of social meanings. Further, particular social meanings may be constituted through other social meanings. Although our discussion has focused on gender, the model can be taken as exemplary of how language conveys social identities more generally. Further, the model indicates that constitutive relations obtain between stances, acts, and activities as well as between each of these and gender meanings.

This model indicates two kinds of relations between language and gender. The first and less common is the direct indexical relation, as when a personal pronoun indexes gender of speaker or a kin term **indexes** gender of speaker and referent. This relation is represented by radiating lines from linguistic resources to social meanings. The second relates gender to language through some other social meaning indexed. In this second relation, certain social meanings are more central than others. These meanings however help to **constitute** other domains of social reality. That is, a domain such as stance helps to constitute the image of gender. This sort of constitutive relation is represented by two-headed arrows.

This model puts gender in its place, indicating that it enters into complex constitutive relations with other categories of social meaning. Indeed the model indicates that gender is not the only category of social meaning that may be impacted by a different social domain. For example, speech acts contribute to the establishment of speech activities and the other way around, the expression of stance contributes to the definition of speech acts, and so on.

A more complex representation of language and gender would specify which types of conversational acts, speech activities, affective and epistemological stances, participant roles in situations, and so on enter into the constitution or construction of gender within a particular community and across different communities. A more refined model would also introduce the notion of markedness. Certain acts, activities, stances, roles, etc. are frequently enacted by members of a particular sex, that is, they are unmarked behaviors for that sex. Others are less frequent behaviors, and yet others are highly unusual for that particular sex. These behaviors would be interpreted differently than unmarked behaviors. Where the behavior is highly marked, one sex may be seen as assuming the "voice" of another (Bakhtin 1981), or as acting like the other sex.

One of the major advances in language and gender research has been a move away from relating isolated linguistic forms to gender differences and toward specifying **clusters** of linguistic features that distinguish men's and women's speech in society. This shift represents a move toward defining men's and women's communicative styles, their access to different conversational acts, activities, and genres, and their strategies for performing similar acts, activities, and genres (Borker 1980, Gal 1989, Goodwin 1990). The starting point for this perspective is functional and strategic rather than formal. That is, researchers have focused primarily on what men and women do with words, to use Austin's phrase (Austin 1962) and have in this endeavor then isolated linguistic structures that men and women use to this end. Studies that start out by isolating particular linguistic forms associated with male or female speakers/addressees/referents tend not to reach this kind of functional or strategy-based account of men's and women's speech. Such studies do not initially focus on activities and situations and examine men's and women's speech *vis-à-vis* those social contexts. These studies, rather, describe a distributional pattern of linguistic forms across the two sexes. Once this pattern is isolated, some *ad hoc* accounting is inferred.

We now have access to a range of studies that are stylistic and strategic in orientation (cf., for example, Gal 1989, Schieffelin 1987, Philips and Reynolds 1987, Brown 1980, Zimmerman and West 1975, West and Zimmerman 1987) Several studies have noted the tendency for men to participate more in speech activities that involve formal interactions with outsiders and women to be restricted to activities within family and village contexts. In these cases, men and women display different competence in particular genres, including, of course, their grammatical and discourse structures (cf., for example, Gal 1989, Keenan [Ochs] 1974, Sherzer 1987, Shore 1982).

Other studies have emphasized ways in which men and women attend to the "face" of their addressees in performing conversational acts that may offend the other. Studies of women's speech in several societies (e.g. Tenejapa [Brown 1979, 1980], American [Lakoff 1973, Zimmerman and West 1975], Japanese [Uyeno 1971]) indicate that women tend to be more polite than men. Brown's study of tenejapa Maya society is by far the most compelling and detailed. Her research indicates that Tenejapa women talking with other women tend to be more polite than men talking with men. When women and men talk to one another, they are equally polite. Tenejapa women talking with other women tend to use different kinds of politeness features than do men with other. They use linguistic structures that show support, approval of another, what Brown and Levinson (1987) have called "positive politeness," whereas men tend to use linguistic forms that indicate a sensitivity to the other's need not to be intruded upon, what Brown and Levinson have called "negative politeness."

The association of women with greater politeness is not universal. My own research among the Malagasy (Keenan [Ochs] 1974) indicates that men are far more polite than are women. Women are seen as abrupt and direct, saying exactly what is on their mind, whereas men are seen as speaking with care and indirectness. Hence women are seen as inappropriate spokespersons in formal speech activities involving other families, where delicacy and indirectness are demanded. Women rather are selected for other activities. They are the ones to directly confront others, hence the primary performers of accusations, bargaining with Europeans, and gossip. Men control oratorical genres as well as a wide range of poetic and metaphoric forms highly prized in this society.

Similarly, in a more recent study of men's and women's speech in Western Samoan rural society, I have not found that Samoan women are more polite than men of the same social status, except in one particular context. As listeners to narrative tellings, women tend to use more positive politeness supportive feedback forms than do men of the same status. In other contexts, however, the expression of politeness differs more in terms of social rank of speaker (e.g. titled person or spouse of titled person, untitled person) than in terms of gender. With the exception of Brown's study, research on men's and women's attention to face and expression of politeness needs to be pursued more systematically, taking into account a range of situational parameters (the speech activity, the speaker–addressee–author–audience–overhearer–referent relationships, the genre, etc.). A wider data base is needed to understand differences in men's and women's communicative strategies and to resolve contradictory findings within the same society (cf. for example Connor–Linton 1986 on politeness among American middle class adolescents).

3.3   Temporally transcendent relation

Thus far we have considered how linguistic forms may help constitute local conceptions of male and female at the time a particular utterance is produced or is perceived. Japanese speakers index femaleness as they use the sentence-final particle *wa*, for example. Language in this sense has the power to constitute the present context. The constitutive power of language, however, **transcends** the time of utterance production/ perception, hence the property of temporal transcendence. Language can also constitute past and future contexts. I call the constitution of past contexts "recontextualization" and the constitution of future contexts "precontextualization" (Ochs 1990). Each of these functions can be carried out through a variety of verbal practices and forms. For example, the practice of speculation can recontextualize past events or precontextualize future events by changing "certain" events into "uncertain" events (Ochs 1982). Similarly, the practice of praising can recontextualize a past act as an accomplishment, and accusations can recontextualize past acts as wrongdoings and personal characters as irreputable. All conversational acts that function as first-pair parts of adjacency sequences (Sacks, Schegloff, and Jefferson 1974), e.g. questions, invitations, compliments, precontextualize the future in that they set up expectations for what the next conversational act is likely to be (e.g. answers, acceptances/declines).

The relevances of temporal transcendence to this discussion of language and gender is that societies establish norms, preferences and expectations *vis-à-vis* the extent to which and the manner in which men and women can verbally recontextualize the past and precontextualize the future. The roles and status of men and women are partly realized through the distribution of recontextualizing and precontextualizing acts, activities, stances, and topics.

The potential of language to recontextualize and precontextualize will be of import to our discussion of mothering. The status of women in mainstream American society and Western Samoan society is in part constituted through the particular ways women as mothers recast the past and precast the future in their interactions with infants and small children.

4   Communicative styles of mothers and other caregivers

4.1   Underrated mothers

One of the major concerns in gender research has been the social and cultural construction of gender in society. A logical locus to examine this process is interaction between young children and older members of society. By examining the kinds of activities and acts caregivers of both sexes engage in with children of both sexes and the manner in which these activities and acts are carried out, we can not only infer local expectations concerning gender but as well articulate how these expectations are socialized. One important tool of socialization is language. Not only the content of language but the manner in which language is used communicates a vast range of sociocultural knowledge to children and other novices. This use of language we call "language socialization" (Schieffelin and Ochs 1986a, 1986b; Ochs 1986, 1988, 1990). Language socialization includes both socialization through language and socialization to use language. In the following discussion, I will propose a relation between the position and image of women in society and language use in caregiver–child interaction.

Although mothering is a universal kinship role of women and in this role women have positions of control and power, their communicative styles as mothers vary considerably across societies. Such variation in the language of mothering reveals differences across societies in the social position of mothers *vis-à-vis* their young charges. The discussion here will contrast caregiving communicative styles among mainstream white middle class (WMC) Americans with Western Samoan caregiving styles. Based on research carried out with B. Schieffelin (Ochs and Schieffelin 1984; Schieffelin and Ochs 1986a, 1986b), I will argue that images of women in WMC American society are socialized through a communicative strategy

Figure 14.3 *Verbal strategies that constitute mothering*

	Mainstream American (child-centered)	Samoan (other-centered)
Production strategies	Extensive simplification	Little simplification
Intepretive strategies	Express guess and negotiate meaning	Display minimal grasp
Praising	Unidirectional	Bidirectional

of high accommodation to young children. A very different image of women is socialized in traditional Samoan households, where children are expected to be communicatively accommodating to caregivers.

In their ground-breaking volume on sexual meanings, Ortner and Whitehead (1981: 12) comment that "women's universal and highly visible kinship function, mothering, is surprisingly underrated, even ignored, in definitions of womanhood in a wide range of societies with differing kinship organizations." I will argue that the white middle class social scientists' dispreference for attending to the role of mothering is an outcome of the very language socialization practices I am about to describe.

In the analysis to follow I focus on cross-cultural differences in strategies associated with three pervasive verbal practices of mothers and other caregivers:

(1) verbal strategies for getting messages across to young children (**message production strategies**)
(2) verbal strategies for clarifying messages of young children (**interpretive strategies**)
(3) verbal strategies for evaluating accomplishments of children and others (**praising strategies**)

I will demonstrate that through each of these verbal strategies, mainstream American mothers, in contrast to traditional Samoan mothers, construct a low image of themselves. The strategies adopted by mainstream American mothers minimize their own importance by (1) lowering their status, (2) giving priority to the child's point of view, and (3) even denying their participation in accomplishing a task. The strategies to be discussed are represented in Figure 14.3.

4.2   Organization of caregiving

Before detailing these strategies, let us consider briefly the organization of caregiving in the two societies under consideration. In traditional Samoan households, caregiving is organized in a somewhat different manner from that characteristic of mainstream American households. First, caregiving is shared among a number of family members of **both genders**. Mothers are primary caregivers in the first few months of their infant's life, but they are always assisted, usually by siblings (both brothers and sisters) of the young infant. Once the infant is somewhat older, these sibling caregivers assume most of the basic caregiving tasks, although they are monitored at a distance by older family members. In the village in which I carried out research, siblings took turns staying home from school during the week to care for a younger child. This type of caregiving arrangement is character- istic of most of the world's societies (Weisner and Gallimore 1977).

As is widely documented, Samoan society is hierarchically organized (Mead 1930, Sahlins 1958, Shore 1982). Social stratification is evident in the political distinctions of *ali'i* "chief," *tulaafale* "orator," and *taule'ale'a* "untitled person"; in titles within the rank of *ali'i* and within the rank of *tulaafale*; and among untitled persons along the dimensions of relative age and generation. Hierarchical distinctions are evident in domestic as well as public interactions.

Of particular concern to the discussion at hand is the fact that caregiving is hierarchically organized. Untitled, older, higher generation caregivers assume a social status superior to younger untitled caregivers who are co-present in a household setting. Further, caregivers enjoy a higher status than the young charges under their care.

Among the demeanors Samoans associated with social rank, direction of accommodation is most salient. Lower ranking persons are expected to accommodate to higher ranking persons, as in other stratified societies. Lower ranking caregivers show respect by carrying out the tasks set for them by their elders. They provide the more active caregivers, while others stay seated and provide verbal directives. Samoan caregivers say that infants and young children are by nature wild and willful and that accommodation in the form of respect is the single most important demea- nor that young children must learn. A core feature of respect is attending to others and serving their needs. A great deal of care is taken to orient infants and young children to notice others. Infants, for example, are usually held outwards and even spoonfed facing the social group co- present.

4.3   Message production strategies

One of the outstanding observations of mainstream American mothers is that they use a special verbal style or register (Ferguson 1964, 1977). This register, often called "Baby Talk" or "Motherese" (Newport 1976), is a simplified register, and it shares many of the features of other simplified registers, such as Teacher Talk, Foreigner Talk and talk to the elderly, lovers, and to pets. Characteristics of this register include the following: restricted lexicon, Baby Talk words (child's own versions of words), shorter sentence length, phonological simplification (such as avoidance of consonant clusters in favor of consonant–vowel alternation, e.g. tummy versus stomach), morphosyntactic simplification (e.g. avoidance of complex sentences, copula), topical focus on here-and-now versus past/future, exaggerated intonation, slower pace, repetition, cooperative proposition-making with child (e.g. expanding the child's utterance into adult grammatical form, providing sentence frames for child to complete.)

Baby Talk register has been a major area of investigation over the last decade or so in the field of language acquisition. The existence of such a register was argued by many to indicate that language acquisition was facilitated by such input. More recently, cross-cultural observations of caregiver–child communication indicate that simplified registers are not characteristic of this communicative context in all societies (Heath 1982, Ochs 1982, Ochs and Schieffelin 1984, Schieffelin and Ochs 1986a, 1986b, Ward 1971). We now know that the process of language acquisition does not depend on this sociolinguistic environment. Western Samoan, Kaluli New Guinea and black working class American children are not surrounded by simplified speech of the sort described above and yet they become perfectly competent speakers in the course of normal development. Given that such simplification is not necessary for the process of language acquisition, we might ask why then do caregivers in certain societies choose to communicate in this fashion with their children whereas others do not.

In Ochs and Schieffelin (1984), we proposed that Baby Talk is part of a more pervasive cultural orientation to children among mainstream Americans. In particular, we proposed that mainstream American society is highly child-centered and that there is a very strong expectation that those in the presence of young children will **accommodate to children's perceived wants and needs**. Such accommodation is both non-verbal and verbal. It manifests itself in a vast range of child-oriented artifacts such as child-proof medicine bottles, safety catches on cabinets and electrical outlets, miniaturization of furniture and clothes, and so on. Adults in the presence of sleeping children will similarly accommodate to them by lowering their voices.

In the domain of verbal communication, accommodation takes many forms. Beyond the use of Baby Talk register, a widely observed behavior of mainstream American mothers is their participation in conversation-like interactions with tiny infants. Mothers have been observed engaging in greeting exchanges with infants as soon as twenty-four hours after birth (Stern 1977). To pull this off obviously requires quite a bit of communicative accommodation on the part of the mother. Indeed what is characteristic of these **proto-conversations** (Bates *et al.* 1977) is the mother's willingness to take on the conversational work of the infant as well as her own. Thus mothers "ventriloquate" through infants (Bakhtin 1981) and in this way sustain "conversations" for some time.

Throughout the course of their infancy, children are thus participants in exchanges which are strongly scaffolded (Bruner 1975) by their mothers. Mothers are able to enter into and sustain communication with small children by not only speaking for them but as well by taking into consideration what the child is holding, what the child is looking at, what event just took place, when the child last slept and ate, and a variety of other child-oriented conditions that may assist in the interpretation of children's gestures and vocalizations. In this way, mothers are able to respond to children in what they perceive to be communicatively appropriate ways.

This scaffolding is also manifest in non-verbal interactions between mothers and children, as when mothers assist young children in building play structures or to realize some intention associated with other tasks. In Vygotsky's terms (1978), mothers are providing a 'zone of proximal development' for their children, where a socially structured environment enhances the attainment of particular skills.

Such extensive verbal and non-verbal accommodation on the part of mothers and others in caregiving roles is expected as part of the main-stream American caregiving role. Being a "good mother" or "good teacher" is to empathize with and respond to the child's mind set. Once a caregiver believes that she or he understands this mind set, a good caregiver will either intervene or assist the child in carrying out her or his desired activity.

In the sociocultural world of traditional Samoan households, where children are socialized to accommodate to others, it is not surprising to learn that mothers and other caregivers do not use a simplified register in speaking to infants and young children. Such a register indexes a stance of accommodation by speaker to addressee. Samoan does have a simplified register, but this register is used towards foreigners, who historically have been missionaries, government representatives, and others who hold a high social position. In this context, a stance of accommodation is appropriate, just as host accommodates to guest.

In the case at hand, we see that linguistic forms in collocation convey particular stances – here simplified speech conveys accommodation to addressee – and these social meanings in turn help to constitute and index particular social identities. Of cross-cultural significance is the observation that societies differ in the social identities of speakers and addressees associated with this stance. Hence the same set of linguistic features that directly index one social meaning, i.e. accommodation, in two speech communities (mainstream American, traditional Western Samoan) indi-rectly index different social identities (i.e. caregivers and children, members to foreign dignitaries). Simplified registers display accommodation in that they respond to a perceived communicative desire or need of the addressee, e.g. the need or desire to decode a message. Accommodation is universally associated with demeanor of lower towards higher ranking parties. That mainstream American mothers use a simplified register pervasively has a constitutive impact on the image of women in that this practice socializes young children into an image of women as accommodating or addressee-centered in demeanor. In traditional Western Samoan households, mothers and other caregivers rarely simplify their speech to young children. This practice socializes young children to be accommodating, i.e. to attend carefully to the non-simplified speech and actions of others.

4.4   Interpretive strategies

A second manifestation of child- versus other-centeredness or accommodating versus non-accommodating verbal practices is located in cross-cultural differences in mothers' and other caregivers' responses to children's unintelligible utterances (see Figure 14.3).

As with simplified registers, Western Samoan and mainstream American speech communities generally display similar verbal practices in responding to unintelligible utterances. However, important differences lie in the social conditions under which particular practices are preferred and appropriate. In both communities, unintelligible utterances may be (1) ignored, (2) responded to by indicating unintelligibility (e.g. "What?," "I don't understand," "Huh?," etc.), or (3) responded to by verbally guessing at the meaning of the utterance (Ochs 1984). The two communities differ in their preferences for using these strategies when speaking to young children. Overwhelmingly, mainstream American mothers prefer to respond to young children's unintelligible speech by verbally guessing. Overwhelmingly, Western Samoan mothers and other caregivers prefer to ignore or point out the unintelligibility of the child's utterance.

These differences reinforce different images of mothers and other caregivers in the two societies, i.e. more/less child-centered and more/less accommodating. Verbal guesses are more child-centered and accommodating than simply indicating unintelligibility in two senses:

(1)   Expressed guesses entails greater perspective-taking, i.e. taking the child's point of view. Guessing involves attempting to formulate the child's intended message, which in turn may entail taking into consideration what the child is looking at, holding, what the child just said, and other cues. Pointing out that the child's utterance is not clear does not entail this kind of sociocentrism, and if the child wishes to get a message across, he or she must reformulate the message to better meet the recipients' communicative requirements. Otherwise the utterance will be ignored.

(2)   Expressed guesses are hypotheses or candidate interpretations presented
      to the child for confirmation, disconfirmation, or modification. Expressed
      guesses thus allow the child to participate in negotiations over the
      meanings of utterances produced by the child. Another way of looking at
      this phenomenon is to say that in verbally expressing a guess, mothers give
      the child the right to influence mothers' interpretations of the child's
      utterances. In contrast, displays of non-understanding do not engage the
      child in such negotiations.

Once again we can see that verbal practices and the linguistic forms that
realize them (e.g. yes–no interrogatives helping to constitute guessing,
particles such as "Huh?" expressing minimal understanding) participate in
the construction of local images of mothering.

Another way of analyzing message production practices and interpretive
practices is to say that Samoan and mainstream American mothers define
different goals in their interactions with young children and that these goals
in turn entail different linguistic practices. Mainstream American mothers
often set the goal of engaging infants and small children as conversational
partners, and they do so from within hours of their child's birth for lengthy
stretches of time (Ochs and Schieffelin 1984). Once they establish conversation as a goal, mothers are obliged to make enormous linguistic
accommodation for that goal to be accomplished. Children who are a few
hours old, for example, can hardly be expected to speak for themselves,
therefore the mainstream American mother who insists on such conversations takes on both conversational roles, speaking for the infant as well as
herself. The generalization of importance here is that mainstream American mothers systematically set goals that are impossible for a child to
achieve without dramatic scaffolding by the mother.

The Samoan way is different, for Samoan mothers and other caregivers
do not establish goals for the child that demand such extensive accommodation from others. They do not engage infants in proto-conversations,
which demand that the caregiver assume the perspective of the infant and
speak for the infant, as characteristic of American WMC interactions with
young babies. Samoan caregivers simply do not place infants in communicative contexts that demand this kind of verbal scaffolding. The Samoan
way is to delay such communicative exchanges until the child displays more
verbal and communicative competence.

4.5   Praising strategies

The final strategy relevant to the construction of gender meanings in society
concerns mothers' and other caregivers' evaluative comments on an
activity involving a child (see Figure 14.3). In this discussion, we attend to
the property of language introduced earlier as "temporal transcendence,"
i.e. the capacity of language to recontextualize the past and precontextual-

ize the future in addition to contextualizing the present. Among their many functions, evaluative comments reframe or recontextualize a past act or set of acts. Praising, for example, recontextualizes a past act/activity as an accomplishment. In this sense, praising has a backwards performative function. Through the uttering of a praise, the speaker turns any act or set of acts into an accomplishment. Of interest to this discussion is the fact that (1) mainstream American and Western Samoan mothers and other caregivers recontextualize past acts/activities as **different** kinds of accomplishments, and (2) these different contextualizations help to constitute weak and strong images of the mothers and others.

From the discussion so far, you are aware that mainstream American mothers provide extensive assistance in communicating with young children – simplifying, guessing, and even speaking for them. We have also noted the tendency for mothers to heavily assist children in carrying out certain activities, e.g. constructing a toy, drawing a picture, tying a shoelace. From a Vygotskian perspective, such activities may be seen as "joint activities" (Vygotsky 1978), accomplished by mother and child. In contrast, however, mainstream American mothers typically recontextualize such activities as solely the child's accomplishment (Ochs and Schieffelin 1984). This is accomplished by directing praises at the child such as "Good!" or "Look at the beautiful castle you made!," with no mention of the mother's role nor any expectation that the child should praise the mother for her part in accomplishing the task at hand. In other words, these mothers deny their own participation; through their own praising practices, they make themselves invisible. It is precisely this kind of verbal reframing that socializes infants and small children into images and expectations of mothers.

In Ochs and Schieffelin (1984), we noted that this kind of behavior defines the child as more competent than she or he may actually be. (The child could not do these activities without the caregiver's scaffolding.) This behavior as well lowers the position of the caregiver (usually the mother). We have claimed that these behaviors along with the widespread use of Baby Talk and other verbal behaviors serve to minimize the asymmetry in knowledge and power between caregiver and child. Indeed we have claimed that caregivers in mainstream American society are uncomfortable with such asymmetry and they mask differences in competence by acting as if the other were more competent and they less competent. Hence with respect to other societies, caregiver–child communication in current mainstream American society both reflects and creates (socializes) a more egalitarian relationship. This is not to say that these caregivers do not exercise power and control over their charges (cf., for example, Corsaro 1979), but rather that they do so less than in other societies. Mainstream caregivers do not claim "ownership" to products of joint activity, they speak like small children (simplified register), they take the perspective of the child and do not expect the child to assume their perspective until rather late in their development.

In contrast to American middle class households, in traditional Samoan communities, activities are often recognized as jointly accomplished. This recognition is realized linguistically through a praising practice distinct from that typical of mainstream American praising. Whereas in mainstream American interactions, praising is typically unidirectional, in Samoan interactions, praising is typically bidirectional. There is a strong expectation that the first one to be praised will in turn praise the praiser. Typically the praise consists of the expression *Maaloo!* "Well done!" Once the first *maaloo* is uttered, a second *maaloo* is to be directed to the producer of the original *maaloo*. In these *maaloo* exchanges, each *maaloo* recontextualizes the situation. Like mainstream American praising, the first *maaloo* recontextualizes an act/activity of the addressee as an accomplishment. The second *maaloo*, however, recontextualizes the act/activity as jointly accomplished. The second *maaloo* acknowledges the support of the first speaker as contributing to the successful achievement of the task at hand. In other words, the second *maaloo* recontextualizes the congratulator as someone to be congratulated as well. Children in Western Samoan households are socialized through such bidirectional praising practices to articulate the contribution of others, including mothers.

5   Gender hierarchies

In summary, I have suggested that mothering cannot be taken for granted in assessing gender identity across societies. While women's position in society has been reckoned in terms of their roles as sisters and wives, very little ethnography has been devoted to assessing their position as mothers. I have suggested here that mothering demeanor cannot be taken for granted. At least in the realm of verbal behavior, we can see significant cultural patterning. When I examine transcripts of children's interactions with others, I see a set of cultural meanings about the position of mother, hence about women, being conveyed to children hundreds of times in the course of their early lives through linguistic forms and the pragmatic practices these forms help to constitute. I do not pretend to have a handle on women's position in either current WMC American society or traditional Samoan society (cf. Mead 1928, Shore 1981, 1982). From a sociolinguistic standpoint, however, Samoan mothers enjoy a more prestigious position *vis-à-vis* their offspring than do mainstream American mothers (as currently observed in the developmental psycholinguistic literature.) On a communicative level, they are accommodated to more often by children and starting at a much earlier age than is characteristic of American households. Further, they socialize young children to recognize the contribution of caregivers and others to achieving a goal, in contrast to

American middle class mothers, who tend to socialize their children to ignore or minimize the role of the mother in reaching a goal. Finally, Samoan mothers have command over human labour in that they are typically the highest status caregivers present and have the right to delegate the more time-consuming and physically active caregiving tasks to younger, lower status caregivers at hand. Thus even among caregivers they are the least accommodating, and the linguistic record indexes this demeanor in numerous ways.

Samoan women enjoy their prestigious position in the hierarchy of caregiving and in caregiver–child relationships. Mainstream American mothers use certain indexes of power in their communicative demeanor, but not to the extent manifest in Samoan mothers' speech. American mothers enter into negotiations with their children over the meaning of children's unclear utterances; Samoan mothers (and other caregivers) do not. Mainstream American mothers treat even the tiniest of infants as conversational partners (Ochs and Schieffelin 1984); Samoan mothers do not. And the list of communicative manifestations of the relative statuses of mothers in these two societies goes on.

We are now in a better position to evaluate Ortner and Whitehead's remark that the role of mothering "is surprisingly underrated, even ignored, in definitions of womanhood" (1981: 12). This state of affairs is precisely what we would predict from the language socialization practices in mainstream American households in the United States and much of middle class Western Europe as well. "Mother" is underrated because she does not socialize children to acknowledge her participation in accomplishments. "Mother" is ignored because through her own language behavior, "mother" has become invisible.

References

Althusser, Louis. 1971. *Lenin and Philosophy and Other Essays*. New York: Monthly Review Press.

Andersen, Elaine. 1977. *Learning How to Speak with Style*. Unpublished Ph.D. dissertation, Stanford University.

Austin, J. L. 1962. *How to Do Things with Words*. Oxford: Oxford University Press.

Bakhtin, Mikhail. 1981. *The Dialogic Imagination*, ed. M. Holquist. Austin: University of Texas Press.

Bates, Elizabeth, Laura Benigni, Inge Bretherton, Luigia Camaioni and Virginia Volterra. 1977. From Gesture to First Word: On cognitive and Social Prerequisites, in *Origins of Behavior: Communication and Language*, ed. M. Lewis and L. Rosenblum. New York: Wiley.

Bateson, Gregory. 1972. *Steps to an Ecology of Mind*. New York: Ballantine Books.

Borker, Ruth. 1980. Anthropology: Social and Cultural Perspectives, in McConnell-Ginet, Borker, and Furman (1980), pp. 26–44.

Bourdieu, Pierre. 1977. *Outline of a Theory of Practice*. Cambridge: Cambridge University Press.

Brown, Penelope. 1979. Language, Interaction and Sex Roles in a Mayan Community: A Study of Politeness and the Position of Women. Ph.D. dissertation, University of California, Berkeley.

  1980. How and Why Women are More Polite: Some Evidence from a Mayan Community, in McConnell–Ginet, Borker, and Furman (1980), pp. 111–36.

Brown, Penelope, and Stephen Levinson. 1979. Social Structure, Groups, and Interaction, in *Social Markers of Speech*, ed. K. Scherer and H. Giles, pp. 292–341. Cambridge: Cambridge University Press.

  1987. *Politeness: Some Universals of Language Usage*, pp. 56–289. Cambridge: Cambridge University Press.

Bruner, Jerome. 1975. The Ontogenesis of Speech Acts. *Journal of Child Language* 2: 1–21.

Connor–Linton, Jeff. 1986. Gender Differences in Politeness: The Struggle for Power among Adolescents, in *Southern California Occasional Papers in Linguistics*. Vol. II: *Social and Cognitive Perspectives on Language*, ed. Jeff Connor–Linton, Christopher J. Hall, and Mary McGinnis, pp. 64–98. Los Angeles: University of Southern California.

Corsaro, William. 1979. Sociolinguistic Patterns in Adult–Child Interaction, in *Developmental Pragmatics*, ed. E. Ochs and B. Schieffelin, pp. 373–89. New York: Academic Press.

Duranti, Alessandro, and Elinor Ochs. 1986. Literacy Instruction in a Samoan Village, in *The Acquisition of Literacy: Ethnographic Perspectives*, ed. B. Schieffelin and P. Gilmore, pp. 213–32. Norwood, NJ: Ablex.

Ferguson, Charles. 1964. Baby Talk in Six Languages, in *The Ethnography of Communication*, ed. J. Gumperz and D. Hymes, pp. 103–14. *Special Issue of American Anthropologist* 66:6, Pt. 2.

  1977. Baby Talk as a Simplified Register, in *Talking to Children*, ed. C. Snow and C. Ferguson. Cambridge: Cambridge University Press.

Gal, Susan. 1989. Between Speech and Silence: The Problematics of Research on Language and Gender. *Papers in Pragmatics* 3(1): 1–38.

Gilligan, Carol. 1982. *In a Different Voice*. Cambridge, Mass.: Harvard University Press.

Goffman, Erving. 1974. *Frame Analysis*. New York: Harper and Row.

Goodwin, M. H. 1990. *He-Said-She-Said: Talk as Social Organization among Black Children*. Bloomington: Indiana University Press.

Gumperz, John. 1982. *Discourse Strategies*. Cambridge: Cambridge University Press.

Heath, Shirley. 1982. What No Bedtime Story Means: Narrative Skills at Home and School. *Language in Society* 11: 49–77.

Hymes, Dell. 1974. *Foundations in Sociolinguistics*. Cambridge: Cambridge University Press.

Keenan (Ochs), Elinor. 1974. Conversation and Oratory in Vakinankaratra, Madagascar. Ph.D. dissertation, University of Pennsylvania.

Labov, William. 1966. *The Social Stratification of English in New York City*. Washington, DC: Center for Applied Linguistics.

Lakoff, Robin. 1973. Language and Women's Place. *Language in Society* 2: 45–79.

Levinson, Stephen. 1983. *Pragmatics*. Cambridge: Cambridge University Press.

McConnell–Ginet, Sally, Ruth Borker, and N. Furman. 1980. *Women and Language in Literature and Society*. New York: Praeger.

Mead, Margaret. 1928. *Coming of Age in Samoa*. New York: Morrow.
  1930. *Social Organization of Manu'a*. Honolulu: B.P. Bishop Musuem Bulletin 76.
Newport, Elissa. 1976. Motherese: The Speech of Mothers to Young Children, in *Cognitive Theory, Vol. II*, ed. N. Castellan, D. Pisoni and G. Potts. Hillsdale, NJ: Lawrence Erlbaum Associates.
Ochs, Elinor. 1982. Talking to Children in Western Samoa. *Language in Society* 11: 77–104.
  1986. From Feelings to Grammar, in Schieffelin and Ochs (1986b).
  1987. The Impact of Stratification and Socialization on Men's and Women's Speech in Western Samoa, in *Language, Gender and Sex in Comparative Perspective*, ed. S. U. Philips, S. Steele, and C. Tanz. Cambridge: Cambridge University Press.
  1988. *Culture and language development: Language acquisition and language socialization in a Samoan village*. Cambridge: Cambridge University Press.
  1990. Indexicality and Socialization, in *Cultural Psychology: Essays on Comparative Human Development*, ed. G. Herdt, R. Shweder, and J. Stigler, pp. 287–308. Cambridge: Cambridge University Press.
Ochs, Elinor, and Bambi Schieffelin. 1984. Language Acquisition and Socialization: Three Developmental Stories, in *Culture Theory: Essays in Mind, Self and Emotion*, ed. R. Schweder and R. LeVine. Cambridge: Cambridge University Press.
Ortner, Sherry, and Harriet Whitehead. 1981. *Sexual Meanings: The Cultural Construction of Gender and Sex in Comparative Perspective*, ed. S. Philips, S. Steele, and C. Tanz. Cambridge: Cambridge University Press.
Rosaldo, Michelle, and Louise Lamphere. 1974. *Woman, Culture and Society*. Stanford: Stanford University Press.
Sachs, Jacqueline. 1975. Cues to the Identification of Sex in Children's Speech, in *Language and Sex: Difference and Dominance*, ed. B. Thorne and N. Henley. Rowley, Mass.: Newbury House.
Sacks, Harvey, Emanuel Schegloff, and Gail Jefferson. 1974. A Simplest Systematics for the Organization for Turn-Taking in Conversation. *Language* 50(4): 696–735.
Sahlins, Marshall. 1958. *Social Stratification in Polynesia*. Seattle: University of Washington Press.
Schieffelin, Bambi. 1987. Do Different Worlds Mean Different Words?: An Example from Papua New Guinea, in *Language, Gender and Sex in a Comparative Perspective*, ed. S. Philips, S. Steele, and C. Tanz. Cambridge: Cambridge University Press.
Schieffelin, Bambi, and Elinor Ochs. 1986a. Language Socialization, in *Annual Review of Anthropology*, Vol. 15, ed. B. Siegel, A. Beals and S. Tyler, pp.163–246. Palo Alto: Annual Reviews.
  (eds.) 1986b. *Language Socialization across Cultures*. Cambridge: Cambridge University Press.
Seki, Minako. 1986. Gender Particles and Linguistic/Non-Linguistic Context. MS, Department of Linguistics, University of Southern California.
Sherzer, Joel. 1987. A Diversity of Voices: Men's and Women's Speech in Ethnographic Perspective, in *Language, Gender and Sex in a Comparative Perspective*, ed. S. Philips, S. Steele, and C. Tanz. Cambridge: Cambridge University Press.
Shore, Bradd. 1981. Sexuality and Gender in Samoa: Conceptions and Missed Conceptions, in Ortner and Whitehead (1981), pp. 192–215.
  1982. *Sala'ilua: A Samoan Mystery*. New York: Columbia University Press.

Silverstein, Michael. 1976. Shifters, Linguistic Categories, and Cultural Description, in *Meaning in Anthropology*, ed. K. Basso and H. A. Selby, pp. 11–56. Albuque   University of New Mexico Press.
  1985. Langu   and the Culture of Gender: At the intersection of Structure, Usage and Ideology, in *Semiotic Mediation*, ed. Elizabeth Mertz and Richard Palmentiers, pp. 219–59. New York: Academic Press.
Slobin, Dan. 1985. Why Study Acquisition Crosslinguistically, in *The Crosslinguistic Study of Language Acquisition, Vol. 1*, pp. 3–24. Hillsdale, NJ: Lawrence Erlbaum Associates.
Stern, Daniel. 1977. *The First Relationship: Infant and Mother*. London: Fontana/Open Books.
Tannen, D. 1986. *That's Not What I Meant!: How Conversational Style Makes or Breaks Relationships*. New York: Ballantine Books.
Trudgill, Peter. 1974. *Sociolinguistics: An Introduction*. Harmondsworth, England: Penguin Books.
Uyeno, T. 1971. A Study of Japanese Modality: A Performative Analysis of Sentence Particles. Ph.D. dissertation, University of Michigan.
Vološinov, V. N. 1973. *Philosophy and the Philosophy of Language*, trans. L. Matejka and I. R. Titunik. New York: Seminar Press. Original publication in Russian, 1929.
Vygotsky, Lev. 1978. *Mind in Society*. Cambridge, Mass.: Harvard University Press.
Ward, M. C. 1971. *Them Children*. New York: Holt Rinehart and Winston.
Weisner, Thomas, and Ronald Gallimore. 1977. My Brother's Keeper: Child and Sibling Caretaking. *Current Anthropology* 18(2): 169–90.
West, C., and D. Zimmerman. 1987. Doing Gender. *Gender and Society* 1(2): 125–51.
Zimmerman, Donald, and Candace West. 1975. Sex Roles, Interruptions and Silences in Conversation, in *Language and Sex: Difference and Dominance*, ed. B. Thorne and N. Henley, pp. 10–129. Rowley, Mass.: Newbury House.

Index